Memoirs of Prince Metternich 1773-1835, Volume 4

MEMOIRS

OF

PRINCE METTERNICH

FOURTH VOLUME

LONDON: PRINTED BY
SPOTTISWOODE AND CO., NEW-STREET SQUARE
AND PARLIAMENT STREET

MEMOIRS

OF

PRINCE METTERNICH

1815–1829

EDITED BY

PRINCE RICHARD METTERNICH

THE PAPERS CLASSIFIED AND ARRANGED BY M. A. de KLINKOWSTRÖM

TRANSLATED BY MRS ALEXANDER NAPIER

VOL. IV.

LONDON

RICHARD BENTLEY & SON, NEW BURLINGTON STREET

Publishers in Ordinary to Her Majesty the Queen

1881

CONTENTS

OF

THE FOURTH VOLUME.

————————

SIXTH BOOK.

THE EASTERN QUESTION.

BOOK VI.

———◆◆◆———

THE EASTERN QUESTION.

1823—1829.

1823.

EVENTS OF THE DAY.

Extracts from Metternich's private Letters from January 6 to August 29, 1823.

637. *Vienna, January 6, 1823.*—I have spent two free days in Munich, which I devoted entirely to work; I set out at four this morning, and here I am once more with my Penates. It was indeed a terrible journey in the ever-increasing cold!

In Munich things fell out as I had foreseen. It was singular to see how my mere appearance there caused the greatest expectation * among all the different parties. This again shows what a miserable thing faction is. It is only needed to place four energetic men, who know what they want and are agreed in the manner of carrying out their wishes, in the four corners of Europe, let them raise their voices and their arms at the same moment, and the whole concern vanishes like so much

---

* Metternich's stay in Munich just after the Congress at Verona gave rise to all sorts of conjectures. Count Trauttmansdorff, the Austrian Ambassador there, wrote to Vienna on January 6:—'New adjustments of territory, the removal of the King of Wurtemberg to Poland and the extension of Bavaria on the west, contingents against the Turks, the marriage of the Princess Sophie of Bavaria with an Austrian Archduke, the alteration of the Bavarian Constitution—all these are talked of as being the objects of your Excellency's wishes. Among the cultivated classes, however, the preference is given to the constitutional questions between the Austrian and Bavarian Courts, and the diplomatic corps are of the opinion that your Excellency's demands are limited to a new press law and the abolition or the publicity of the proceedings at the Diets.' For the reason of the Chancellor's visit to Munich see No. 635, vol. iii. p. 665.—ED.

smoke. People are really very foolish. I can find no more power of judgment among them than among children, who if they see a great cloud they want to climb up and walk upon it, as if it were firm ground. When I speak of 'judgment' I take the word in its most positive signification and separate it entirely from mind or intellect, for this is generally possessed by the very men who suffer from want of judgment. I much fear that this is the case with Canning also.

638. *January* 30.—We have sustained an irreparable loss. Count Wrbna (Lord Chamberlain) is dead. All the necessary qualifications which were peculiar to him will not easily be found united in one man. He died after a severe illness contracted in Verona.

This morning I had an interview with the Emperor. He is in great perplexity, and so am I. He asked me whether I was inclined to take the place; ·a question which I answered very promptly in the negative, for, if I know myself at all, it is not possible for me to take on myself another burden, and most certainly not that of service at Court. Better die naturally than be killed by needle-pricks.

I am just reading Madame Campan's Memoirs of Marie Antoinette. I have hardly got to the middle of the first volume, but it is quite clear to me that the work will do more harm than good. It represents many things in a ludicrous light which now really appear so. The book will do no good, for the conclusion to which it leads is not much more than that Marie Antoinette was a very good, young, and beautiful woman; but what is called 'respect' suffers much thereby. No analysis ought to be attempted, especially of so high a personage, whose traditional claims and position are so important, because the analysis itself destroys that kind of feeling. The spirit of the age is satiated with works like these Memoirs; if as with a sponge on a water-colour drawing you wash away the colours you come to nothing but the bare ground.

This is indeed known well enough, and is no new discovery. The only question is whether the painting is worth the price, and above all whether it is of greater value than the materials out of which it is made.

639. *February* 2.—To-day I have news from Paris to the 28th ult. Some perplexities are preparing in London. I, for my part, am not sorry, for amid the positive evils of the affair I prefer an undecided attitude. What will come out of it all? Heaven alone knows!

The King of Wurtemberg has allowed himself to be carried away by a folly which he will find very serious.* From blind rage against me he now takes counsel only of his passions, which are of all counsellers the worst. If I had prescribed his course to him he could not have carried out more exactly what I have for a long time thought of him. Still it is extraordinary how the anger of senseless people in itself leads to mischief. This truth finds its application in public as well as private life. People of this stamp knock down the whole erection, and that too when it seems to be on the point of completion. The Emperor Alexander will not take the matter lightly; that I think I can answer for.

The news of the 28th will make a great sensation in London; but not much on me, for it is what I expected.†

640. *March* 1.—I have read Las Cases through. It interested me, because I was mixed up in the whole

---

* See Nos. 671, 672.—ED.

† Refers to the warlike speech of the King at the opening of the French Chambers.—ED.

affair. It is the work of a fanatical adherent, who quite
forgets that there is no more useless labour than to
point out that Bonaparte was an excellent man. I have
already often declared that, according to my opinion,
Bonaparte was in no wise wicked as this word is understood in common life. He had too much practical
understanding for that. He was a very strong man,
and in the different setting of another age he would
have become a very great man. Las Cases, moreover,
experienced from Bonaparte the usual treatment. He
made use of his pen to have the romance of his life
written. But history is not to be made romantic thus,
and the Napoleon of Las Cases bears the same resemblance to the true Napoleon that the Achilles of the
opera does to the immortal Achilles himself. I have,
moreover, stumbled upon more than one positive lie.

641. *March* 5.—I am busy about a very anxious
work. Paris now presents a most peculiar spectacle.
I know the ground in Paris very well, and my knowledge
of the city in the time of strength enables me to judge
of its position in its present time of weakness. In this
country everything is unexpected ; even what seems
reasonable is only so outwardly, not really : commotion
is here the consequence of excited passions, and of all
these not one springs from true feeling. Never since
there was such a thing as business in the world was an
affair handled as it is at this moment in France. It
really looks as if people in this country were trying to
refine upon suicide. They drive forward, but at the
same time bring the car so close to the precipice that it
must inevitably turn over.

642. *April* 4.—I send Brunetti to Paris, and if
possible to Spain, where he will fill the office of ambassador to the King, who is once more free. This is the

design of Heaven, and if the French do nothing stupid the King will shortly rule once more.

Affairs are now of a very delicate nature, not because they are extremely difficult in themselves, but because it is to the French Government that the conduct of them naturally falls, and that is weak and is itself breaking up. Happily the other great Powers will act with decision. It borders on the miraculous that I have succeeded in bringing about such a harmony of procedure between the Emperor Alexander and ourselves. When it is considered from what opposite points the two Empires have started to arrive at this harmony, it seems like a dream.

The old Fürstenbergs celebrated their golden wedding yesterday. It was a touching occasion on account of the number of the present descendants; the third and fourth generations had to be omitted, as no place could be found for them at table. Prince John Liechtenstein gave the banquet.

For the rest there is nothing new, no one dying and no one dead. Melanie is better, but she must (according to my opinion, which is shared by her physician) still take the greatest care. She is the same young girl who some years ago so much resembled my Clementine; she has, however, much altered. She is now tall and very pretty, but in quite another style from Clementine. Laurence has immortalised my Clementine; he painted her just as she took her flight from this world.

The Opera is excellent. They are playing 'Othello,' the 'Barber,' and 'Zelmira.' The Italian company at the Vienna Opera is the best I know. It contains no mediocrities, and the first singers are the best Italians. The Opera affords me great delight, for my life is so monotonous that the sound of something quite different from what I am daily condemned to hear thrills through my whole being.

643. *April* 30.—Here everyone is occupied only with Spain and the Italian Opera. If the war goes on as well as the Opera, Europe is saved. I do not know whether Victor heard Lablache sing in Milan. He seems to me like the 'Stephansthurm' that tried to sing with its great bell, but he also brings out tones that would do honour to a nightingale.

All Vienna is in spirit on the Ebro. The progress of the French war operations makes the same impression here as if it were a victorious Austrian army.

644. *May* 1.—This day's date has a pleasant sound, but the weather does not correspond with the time of year. This day is generally an epoch in Vienna life. All walk to the public promenade and surrender themselves to the pleasure of the first signs of spring. Unhappily it has hardly begun to grow green, and the first shoots are still in bud. My poor garden is much more like the age of infirmity than that of youthful freshness. If it goes on in this way I shall lose the trees which I saved in 1822. It is literally true that it has not rained since April in last year.

What must touch most painfully the feelings of great speakers like the British Ministers is, that while reading the Parliamentary debates Europe shrugs its shoulders ! In all the dreary wastes of the daily journals I have not found a word, not one single word, in their praise. It is just the Radical papers that have the sharpest and most vigorous criticisms. What, then, does Canning want? Whose part will he take? What is he about? For, after all, a man must have some object or end in view.* I really begin to lose the very

---

* This refers to Canning's great speech, April 14, 1823.—ED.

small portion of respect I had (not without difficulty, God forgive me) attained for the man. Canning keeping step with the Minister President of His Most Christian Majesty! A fine century for this sort of men—for fools who pass for intellectual but are empty; for moral weaklings, who are always ready to threaten with their fists from a distance when the opportunity is good. When obliged to contemplate all this, as I am, to hear everything and read everything that I must hear and read—this really requires a kind of endurance which almost amounts to virtue. But how fruitless is this virtue and how toilsome its exercise! What a pity it is that Wellington is so timid; a man with so upright a heart and so noble a countenance!

645. *May* 15.—The anniversary of my birth is dear to me, for but for that event I could neither have loved nor hated. I am busy preparing for the reception of my family; my sad, solitary life comes to an end, and my heart once more awakes. I am not made for loneliness and I need life about me. The absolute stillness around is to me a symbol of death. I like too to see the delight in social life in other men. I do not trust anchorites: they are mostly tiresome or tired out, and, what is worse, they are often wicked men.

646. *May* 17.—My family arrived this day, I having gone some miles to meet them. They are all in good health; my wife and children look extremely well, and the latter—whom I have not seen for three years—are much grown. I should have known Leontine, but the little one (Princess Hermine) has entirely altered. She is very like my mother, possesses therefore some of my charms. Victor is very well. The children cried with joy to see me again. What comforts me is that long absence has weakened the deep sorrow of my wife on re-entering the house where, as a mother, she suffered so much. I have quite altered the place, and put out of sight everything that would remind her of that sad time. Providence has given to the lapse of time great power over human feeling, and this is not the least of its blessings.

647. *May* 22.—Spanish affairs go on as they must go now that they have been taken in hand. What a miserable Power is that which is founded on error, is only supported by lies, and has no strength but the weakness of its opponents. This is a portrait of Liberalism. No sooner are its pretensions examined than they are seen to be without foundation; and when its resources are investigated nothing is forthcoming. And yet there are people who claim to be intelligent who hold by Liberal theories and glory in their results.

That which hinders so many persons from obeying truth, from giving themselves up to it entirely, is the utter want of all tinsel peculiar to it. It is the destiny of truth to be developed with ever-increasing power; we grasp it in its early immaturity, and when the day comes that it shines forth in all its innate splendour it makes its way without our help, and all merit seems to belong to it alone. Those who have nourished it in its early beginning, and have watched over its progress to perfection, are quickly wiped out of the memory of men. This is not a result flattering to vanity, and they are few who devote themselves to that which confers so little on their love of self. This is my confession of faith and my judgment on myself.

648. *May* 27.—I once more live in domestic happiness, as if I had never been without it, and enjoy it with true delight. Victor is much liked here; he is thought extremely well bred, which is a great satisfaction to me. Certainly his good carriage and pleasant manners strike one in comparing him with the other young men here. My wife's health is apparently much improved, and I put aside my fears for the future. Although I only see my family at breakfast and dinner it is the greatest comfort to me. Man is not intended to be alone, and those who assert the contrary are unhealthy either in mind or heart.

649. *July* 2.—I have been in bed for ten days in consequence of taking cold. Four days ago I thought myself well enough to be up all day, which had the evil result of sending me to bed again for three days. To-day I feel the return of health, but I shall not be quite restored till the twenty-one days are over. I know by experience that so much time is needed when once fever attacks me.

650. *July* 18.—What a pity it is that the Queen of the Sea and the sometime ruler of the world should lose her salutary influence. What has become of the great and noble British Empire? What has become of its men and its orators, its feeling for right and duty, and its ideas of justice? This is not the work of a single individual, of one weak and feeble man; Canning is but the personification of the symptoms of the terrible malady which runs through every vein of the fatherland—a malady which has destroyed its strength and threatens the weakened body with dissolution.

651. *July* 20.—A letter from Palmella* informs me that his King is adored by his faithful people, and

* Count Palmella-Sousa, Portuguese Minister of Foreign Affairs, was expecting with impatience the moment when King John VI., who had returned from Brazil, should bestow the promised constitution on Portugal.—ED.

that he will reward them with a *charte à la française*.
That which Palmella thinks of doing to-morrow, or
perhaps even began yesterday, he has already attempted
in Brazil. What he desires and is now doing consists
simply in making use of the so-called remedies which
our clever generation has discovered. His prescription
runs thus: You see death before you, take poison;
but our fathers said, You are poisoned, take an anti-
dote. This kind of cure seems too simple in our day—
that is, to a generation so flooded with light. There are,
however, some very practical men, who know very well
what our fathers knew—that poison is deadly; but
this is the very reason why others recommend it to free
from death. And who are these wise men who boldly
place themselves on the standpoint of truth? The
Radicals! I will do them full justice. I thoroughly
understand them, and I much prefer people whom I
understand to those who are not to be understood
chiefly because they are themselves groping about in
darkness.

652. *August* 9.—In the last few days I have
sent off despatches in every direction. Everywhere
there is confusion of ideas, weakness in carrying them
out, and disgust for those who desire only the good,
and for that very reason strive for nothing but the
triumph of sound common sense.

The Emperors Francis and Alexander will meet at
the beginning of October. The Russian monarch has
invited the Austrian, who has accepted the invitation
with the greatest pleasure. The Emperor Alexander
desired that it should be kept secret for his sake, and
for the sake of the cause which both monarchs look
upon as their own. Great and extraordinary interests
are bound up in this meeting. It will make much

noise, like a gunshot, but only as a signal, not as a war cry.

My views regarding Turkey are different from those generally entertained. Turkey does not make me anxious, but France and Spain. Pozzo di Borgo will certainly not rejoice over the meeting. We shall at the most be eight days together, which is time enough for those who understand how to make use of it. It is not yet decided whether the journey to Italy will take place at the beginning or the end of the winter.

653. *August* 15.—Vienna is empty. Six rational people are not to be brought together. I say rational, not pleasant, people; for six pleasant persons is a number difficult to bring together in any country and at any time whatever.

For some years this day was, to me, always signalised by an effusion of Napoleonic temper: the blows of the great exile of St. Helena either fell on me or were dealt to some one in my presence. Years have passed away since those now famous days, but the power of the date is still so fresh that on each return of it past impressions return so forcibly that I feel as if I were placed once more where I was then so much against my will.

The Bonaparte family are having an answer written to Las Cases. Several of its members accuse him of lying and calumny. The fact is that with regard to the family it was not Las Cases, but Napoleon who lied, or at least said what his brothers and sisters did not like to hear.

654. *August* 21.—The meeting of the two monarchs is fixed for October 6. Of course I shall be there. The thing in itself, apart from the importance of what it includes, will have an effect like the firing of a gun of the first calibre. I am far from being a friend of noise, but if it cannot be avoided I endeavour to use it for positive and salutary ends. This is, too, under the given circumstances, part of my plan. My head is at work, and my blood boils. God grant that something may come of it, and that that something may be good.

655. *August* 29.—The mistaken steps taken by Villèle since Verona are quite explained by what he has done to-day. The measure is now full, and he will only add to the awkwardness of his position without attaining his object. The French, who are gifted with much imagination, think they can understand the Revolution because they have endured it. This is just as if a woman who has had several children should say she perfectly understands confinements. Both forget that there are two entirely different things—the fact of enduring and the art of assisting. There was but one single man in France who understood how to master the Revolution, and that man was Bonaparte. The King's Government inherited from him, not the Revolution, but the counter-Revolution, and they have not known how to make use of this inheritance. I judge of the Revolution more truly than most men who have been in the midst of it. It is with me as with those who watch a battle from very high ground. It is only from thence that everything is seen; in the midst of the fray the eye cannot reach beyond a given circle, and that circle is always small. From the mistakes which the French Government have already made in Spain, no one can say what the end will be : if it turns out well (which is possible), then it will be the good bursting forth and triumphing of itself over everything in spite of both friends and foes. This is my view, and

experience will confirm it. France is to-day like a vessel on a stormy sea guided by inexperienced pilots.

I expect to leave Vienna on September 16, stay four or five days at my house in the country, go to Czerno-witz on October 3, and return to Vienna about October 25 or 26.

THE JOURNEY TO CZERNOWITZ.

Metternich to his Wife.

656. *Rzeszow, September 25, 1823.*—I have arrived here a few minutes before the post leaves, and I cannot deny myself the pleasure of sending you news of myself and my proceedings. And good news too ; I accomplished the journey most happily and quickly. The same day that I started I arrived at Teschen at eleven in the evening. Yesterday at nine I reached Bochnia, and here I am at Rzeszow at five o'clock. I shall leave to-morrow at daybreak, so as to be at Lemberg by eight or nine in the evening.

The country is quite different from what I had imagined. It is very beautiful and highly cultivated. The entrance into Galicia is mountainous, and is like Upper Austria ; then comes the plain, enclosed and wooded and very pretty. What spoils the country is that Jews are met at every step ; no one is to be seen but Jews : they swarm here. I travel with M. de Tatistscheff ; I have taken him into my carriage, which he naturally prefers to his *calèche*. I hope you have all returned happily to Vienna, and that the cause which deprived me of the pleasure of having Victor with me has disappeared.

657. *Lemberg, September* 28.—I arrived here a little after midnight, after a very rapid journey. I stopped an hour at Lançut, which I saw thoroughly; then I took luncheon at Przeworsk. Lançut is a very fine country house in the style of Louis XV. Przeworsk is simple but very pretty; it is not a *château*, but an English house, neat and pretty. Here I awoke with one of those rheumatic feverish attacks which keep me in bed for two or three days without rhyme or reason. The doctor does not think my pulse bad, but I am in a continual perspiration. To-day I am better—that is to say, I perspire less. I shall, however, remain in bed for three days, to prevent a return of the malady. I can tell you nothing of Lemberg, for I have seen nothing. My house is very fine and well arranged.

658. *September* 29.—Yesterday I wrote to you from my bed; my indisposition (it has never been anything more) is passing away. The doctor has not once found me with fever, but merely a slight irritation which disappeared in the evening of the first day. I remain in bed, however, for two days; first to make sure of my recovery, and then to avoid being overdone with audiences, presentations, and fêtes of every kind. Potocka made a point of my passing the Rubicon. I only just escaped having to get up from my bed to be present at the ball, by means of the most vigorous protestations. For the rest, say nothing about it, for the poor people here are excellently disposed, but they are so thoroughly miserable that it would be difficult to know how to preserve them from ruin. This country is exceedingly productive, but it lacks all means of exportation, so that proprietors are literally almost dying of misery although up to the neck in superfluities. There are many parts of Galicia where a pound of beef costs one kreutzer; here it costs three. Two measures of oats cost a florin, Vienna value. One must not laugh at people so unhappy.

659. *October 2.*—I have not written to you for the last two days, for I have nothing to say but to complain of annoyances here. My health is a little deranged in the same way that has given me so much trouble sometimes in Vienna. Since the departure of the Emperor's physician I have seen the best doctor here. As my illness is more catarrhal than rheumatic, and as my eyes are also much inflamed, I have sent for a physician, a pupil of Beer and a friend of Jäger, who has done all that was necessary for me. My maladies, too, are all decreasing; you know I must always go through the *neuvaine.* My doctors declare that, so far as doctors are infallible, there ought to be nothing to prevent my starting on my travels again next Monday. You can understand how this accident annoys me. My illness is nothing, and I must take it patiently, for it seems to be part of my nature periodically to pass through these crises. I only suffer from annoyance, for I have not even any fever; but business weighs upon me, body and mind. No one else can do what has to be done, and this thought is in itself enough to cause fever.

660. *October 10.*—I am now quite well, my dear, after having passed thirteen days in all kinds of illness. I now feel convalescent, and indeed I feel it so strongly that I must have been really ill. I was fortunate enough to fall into the hands of a straightforward, practical physician. I feel that he at once seized on the peculiarities of my nature, and especially on the singularities and anomalies caused by so trying a life. My illness was partly from cold and partly the consequence of the anxieties of the Congress. Now, to cure the first of these maladies is very possible, but I defy any physician in the world to cure the second; so that my nervous system fell into a state of febrile agitation. God has preserved me and raised me from my bed of suffering, and the interview at Czernowitz has terminated, or will terminate, just as I desired. The Emperor will return here on the 12th. Nesselrode will come to conclude the work with me here. It will be the work of twenty-four hours.

661. *October* 13.—Jäger arrived here this evening; he will give you an account of the state in which he found me. My health begins to recover from the shock it has sustained, and my recovery will be confirmed by the excellent state of affairs. I shall have some months without severe labour. Nesselrode arrived here last night; he was with me this morning for two hours. The Emperor Alexander sent him to me to obtain my 'placet' to all the despatches. Far from refusing it, I was able to approve with all my heart. All this business, which I may date from my bed at Lemberg, will do honour to the two Emperors.*

All that Jäger told me of the family pleased me exceedingly; I assure you that good news will improve my health more than medicine. My malady was complicated by moral anxieties; consequently, moral remedies are the most efficacious, and none are so much so as news of your health.

* See Nos. 683–685.

C 2

662. *October* 17.—I am most thankful for the oranges you had the happy inspiration to send me; I had tried every possible way to procure them here, but in vain. *Hier blühen die Citronen nicht!* Jäger found me already getting better. I was delighted to see him, because he knows me so thoroughly, and his approbation of all that had been done by the doctor here reassured me. I am quite myself again now. **My** illness was one of those tiresome affections, catarrhal or rheumatic, which always send me to bed for ten days or a fortnight. In the usual state of things the inconvenience (for it is not a real illness) would have passed off as on former occasions. But just imagine my situation. Alone—the only man knowing anything of the business in bed at Lemberg, and the two Emperors *tête à tête* at Czernowitz. Two results only possible, immediate war between Russia and the Porte or immediate peace; and I, holding peace in my hands, and alone knowing the means of securing peace, ill in bed! I swear to you that no common strength of mind and will was needed to keep me from giving way. I did not succumb morally, but my *physique* received a terrible shock. I was fifteen nights without sleeping, and I was on the brink of a nervous fever. Now I have told you everything. I am still weak, but as my appetite is returning I shall soon regain my strength. Heaven has protected me in the midst of these troubles and anxieties. I had so far advanced matters before the meeting took place that the force of things of itself brought them to a termination without me. Peace is secured; everything is arranged in a marvellous manner, and the triumph is complete. This is a blessing for all Europe, and particularly for me; it gives me some chance of the repose after which I sigh like a bird after the open air, and which has fled from me during twenty years of uninterrupted labour.

663. *October* 19.—The Emperor left yesterday. I am here with Nesselrode and Tatistscheff, busy with the numerous despatches that we have to send off to all parts of the world, and also with the nomination of a Russian agent at Constantinople. I hope, however, to be able to leave either this week or next. We learned yesterday the deliverance of the King of Spain; I await the particulars with curiosity. If this deliverance is complete—that is to say, if there is no defect in the armour—peace is given to Europe for some time; and the coincidence of peace in the East and in the West is not the least singular of these facts. I beg you, my dear, to arrange everything so that on arriving at Vienna I can at once go to my rooms. If God grant me six months of quiet, and I can pass them in a good climate, away from business, or at any rate not in its very midst, I think I should recover ten years of life and health.

664. *October* 21.—I seize a few moments before the departure of a courier I am sending to Vienna to tell you, my dear, that I am going on well. My strength begins to return, my appetite is good, and I try to accustom myself to the air by taking a short drive every morning. This is the least I can do when I remember the nice little journey of 200 leagues which I must take as soon as possible. To-morrow I shall fix the day for my departure: it will probably be Saturday. I have finished my business with Nesselrode, who has gone this morning to rejoin his master. Tatist-scheff leaves to-morrow for St. Petersburg, and I should like to rest two or three days longer. I was greatly tempted to leave on Friday, but I have relinquished the idea from respect to human nature. They want me to see the neighbourhood of Lemberg. I have never seen people so in love with their native town as they are here. The road to the right is said to give a view like that of Naples; that to the left is like the Brühl near Vienna. A nearer view shews a town in a hole, and this hole wants both water and trees. The town is half fine and half ugly. There are many houses in it better constructed than those in Vienna, for there is some architectural style about them; then intervals either empty or crowded with barracks. The Eastern aspect begins to make its appearance.

P.S.—I cannot tell you, my dear, how happy I am to leave this place; I am dreadfully weary of it. All my life I shall remember the month of October 1823.

665. *Tarnow, October* 27.—I left Lemberg the day before yesterday. I slept the first night at Przemysl, the same place where a month ago to a day I had the ill luck to fall ill. Yesterday I slept at Rzeszow. To-morrow I shall make a very short stay. I shall sleep at Bochnia, the day after at Bielitz, a place on the frontier of Galicia. In all this I follow the Emperor's directions, for he wishes me everywhere to lodge where he has been. Consequently I am everywhere excellently well accommodated. I have the houses of the captains of the Circles. The courier who precedes me regulates the temperature of the rooms, so that I am everywhere as if at home. In Poland politeness requires that a room should be made excessively hot when prepared for a guest. The temperature was, however, moderated for me, to the great astonishment of the proprietors of the houses, who had been preparing to receive me, as an invalid, with a temperature two or three degrees in excess of what mere politeness required.

For the rest I cannot sufficiently praise the anxious kindness of the Emperor. He did not pass a single day without coming to see me at Lemberg ; he sat for hours by the side of my bed, or, after his return to Czernowitz, in my sitting-room, not to talk business, but to amuse me and chat about trifles. It was he who chose my physician at Lemberg, telling me he would have left me his own, but that he was convinced Dr. Massow was the better man. All along the road I found it was the Emperor who had arranged for my accommodation and given the most exact orders that I should be treated exactly as himself. Well as I had long known the true friendship of the Emperor, I confess that I should not have believed him capable of such delicate attentions. In the midst of all this some very odd things necessarily occurred, which I will tell you, and they will make you laugh.

When it was decided that I could not accompany his Majesty to Czernowitz, and I had chosen Mercy to take my place, I sent the latter to inform the Emperor. The Emperor, with his usual *bonhomie*, then said to Mercy, 'We should make a fine embassy of that. I know but little of the affair; you knew nothing till yesterday. Between us we should make a miserable figure. If we cannot get on I will send the Emperor Alexander to Prince Metternich. He will do more with him in half an hour than you and I in eight days.' Mercy could not help laughing, and the Emperor joined in the chorus. However, everything was arranged, and well arranged too. The Emperor of Russia, when he sent Nesselrode (who remained with me eight days to manage everything), wrote me a letter which was not that of a monarch, but of a friend disappointed of the meeting to which he had looked forward. I beg you

to ask an audience of the Emperor, in order to thank
him for yourself and for me for all the kindness and
attention I have told you he has shown me. You will not
mention the story of Mercy.   According to my reckon-
ing I shall be at Vienna on November 2 by dinner
time.

666. *Neutitschein, October 30.*—Here I am in Moravia, my dear—that is to say, in a civilised country, and
so near to Vienna that the courier will be there in thirty
hours.   I have never seen anything more striking than
the change from Galicia to Moravia.   The country is
the same, and is as fine on one side as the other; but
the first village on this side is the first which gives the
idea of being inhabited by men.   No rags; the houses
neat and the inhabitants well clothed; no Jews; no
squalor, misery, and death.   Two days ago, in a very
low temperature, I saw peasants working in the fields
with no garments but a shirt, and their children from
two to four years old sitting naked in the field their
parents were tilling.   I was inclined to cry out like the
French soldier, ' *Ah ! les malheureux appellent cela une
patrie !* '   The first little Silesian I saw had a nice
cap and frock, and was carried by his mother, dressed
in a good pelisse with thick red worsted stockings and
good shoes.   I could have wept over the one and
embraced the others.

RETURN FROM LEMBERG.

Extracts from Metternich's private Letters from November 8 to December 20, 1823.

667. *Vienna, November 8.*—I was very ill; certain external conditions so increased my malady that I should soon have arrived at that bourne from whence no one returns. A merciful God and the Emperor Alexander saved me, and everything went so well that my presence in Czernowitz, anxious as I was to be there, was not necessary. Everything is concluded and peace maintained; for which honour is due to the Russian Emperor, who kept his word to the Austrian minister. He was, moreover, endlessly good to me; he gave me proofs of his sympathy, not of the commonplace kind customary to monarchs, but as from one man bound to another by the same noble aims. For eight days Nesselrode was with me at Lemberg; he could not in everything take the place of his Imperial master, but he strove to carry out his intentions with that hearty loyalty we know in him. I am still weak and thin. My own physician, who has watched me since my return, tells me that the severe attack I have had is a proof that my nature is stronger than I supposed, but advises me to avoid all great efforts of the brain. The counsel is more easily given than followed. Happily the situation in general is such as to assist me.

668. *November 18.*—I have reassumed my usual

habits, but I must still be somewhat careful. It is a real piece of good fortune for me that my convalescence and that of Europe advance with equal steps. I have not had so little work to do for a long time, the whole social body is inclined to improve. Many parts are already healthy; others are becoming so : those that are unhealthy share the fate of withered branches—they break off. The French Radical papers take the greatest pains to avoid the confession that they have been entirely mistaken : they are now trying lies and calumnies and prophecies.

669. *November* 25.—My lungs are still very much affected, and if they were not sound it might go badly with me. I still need five or six weeks to make a thorough recovery. I should not require as many days if I could but fly over the Alps. My numerous ties, however, will not allow this, and it is a part of my torture to see the snowy mountain-tops and not to be able to get over them. The only news that reaches me is from London, and it is always the same. English diplomacy at present is careful to spoil whatever lies within its reach. People in London see so wrongly that they will go wrong there again as they have so often gone wrong before. But Canning's nature is still a very remarkable one. In spite of all his lack of discernment the genius which he undoubtedly has, and which I have never questioned, is never clouded. He is certainly a very awkward opponent; but I have had opponents more dangerous, and it is not he who chiefly compels me to think of him. This says everything. On July 18 Canning thought that the French expedition would miscarry. It has, however, succeeded ; and then forthwith he represented the question, which had become a European one, as purely English, and, indeed, as an English triumph. At any rate he should not have allowed his despatch of July 18 to go forth.

670. *December* 20.—I daily ask myself wherefore Providence has sent me into the world too soon or too late. It is a sad lot for a statesman to have to fight his way among perpetual storms. The world enjoys a few moments of peace all the more from being exposed to continual storms, and I should have been happy in a time when I could have had an equal amount of both. Had destiny willed it, I could have fulfilled my part as a statesman, and with little trouble made for myself a name; but the course of my life has been amid gales and storms, and such adverse influences bend the body more than the soul. If I had been fifty years old fifty years ago I should have been a more imposing figure than I am now.

THE WURTEMBERG CABINET AND THE RESULTS OF THE CONFERENCES AT VERONA.

Metternich to Baron Oechsner, January 29, 1823.

671. You are not, perhaps, sir, aware of the existence of a circular despatch which the Cabinet of Wurtemberg has addressed to its diplomatic agents *à propos* of that which the ambassadors of the three monarchs have received after the conferences at Verona. This document has only come to our knowledge through a copy sent to us from Frankfurt, since which its existence has been confirmed by the envoy of Wurtemberg at Berlin. Every courier brings us from different directions extracts from this despatch, and it will very likely appear immediately in some French or English journal, while the Imperial Court itself has never been officially informed of a matter in which it has so direct an interest. The despatch in question (No. 672) contains a serious attack against the three monarchs who signed the despatch of December 14 (No. 632), with a criticism of their transactions and their words ; lastly, it contains a formal protest against the consequences which the political procedure of the three allied Courts might have on the independence of those of the second order. It seems to the Emperor that a manifesto so unexpected and so unprovoked cannot be approached except in the system and forms of that solidarity which, happily for the interests of Europe, is established between his Imperial Majesty and his august friends and allies. We shall, then, reserve our reply till we are able to act in concert with the Emperor of all the Russias and his Prussian Majesty.

Meanwhile the Emperor our master cannot hesitate a moment, for his part, to deny any portion 'of the heritage of influence in Europe arrogated to himself by Napoleon.' Nothing is further from the Emperor's thoughts than the claim to exercise any interference whatever with the independent States. Neither the conduct of his Cabinet at Verona nor the terms of the declaration furnish the slightest pretext for such an accusation. All Europe has been a witness of the cares and efforts with which his Imperial Majesty has constantly met the torrent of general disorganisation advancing so rapidly over peoples and empires. The Emperor's voice has not always been listened to, his advice has not always been followed ; but his Majesty never expected that any Cabinet could find in his noble and pure intentions a project for interfering with public rights by disquieting innovations. Firm in principle and conscience, the Emperor is not accessible to injustice. A very different sentiment fills his mind ; it is that of the most sincere and profound regret at seeing the finest of causes misunderstood by those whose lasting interest it ought to be to defend it.

You will communicate this despatch to Count Wintzingerode.

CIRCULAR DESPATCH OF THE WURTEMBERG CABINET.

(Extract.)

672. *Stuttgart, January* 2, 1823.—You are aware no doubt that the Courts which did not take part in the Congress of Verona have just received official information of its existence, its objects, and its results.

It is important that your Excellency should be acquainted with the point of view from which your Court regards this interesting document.

Whatever may be the confidence claimed by the enlightenment and disinterestedness of the Powers who have inherited the influence Napoleon had arrogated to himself in Europe, it is difficult not to fear for the independence of the lesser States if this protection (*tutelle*) should be exercised by sovereignty less enlightened or less generous.

Certainly nothing could be more foreign to our thoughts than to dispute with the sovereigns who make so many and painful sacrifices to the maintenance of the monarchical principle (that palladium of civilised people) the right of watching over the welfare of Europe; but the means by which this *surveillance* acts seems to us to introduce principles more or less disquieting. Treaties concluded, congresses assembled in the interest of the whole European family, without the States of the second order being permitted to assert their views and make known their particular interests, the forms even with which they are admitted to the treaties and made acquainted with the decisions of the preponderating Courts, and the expectation of meeting with no difference of opinion in any of their allies—these different innovations in diplomacy certainly justify an express reserve of the inalienable rights of each independent State.

The causes of independence and the monarchical principle are both blended with the causes of Italy and Spain; the causes of humanity and religion with the cause of the Greeks; while the cause of general peace, common to all, does not allow us to consider the objects of the last Congresses, especially that of Verona, as foreign to Powers of the second class: and all these justify our regret that we were excluded, and that the German Confederation was not summoned there, although two of its members were at Verona and the whole can hardly be subordinate to the parts. . . .

Comments on the Circular by Metternich.

1. No act, no word, of the three monarchs has authorised the Wurtemberg Cabinet to ascribe to them any intention of treating independent States as minors. Far from claiming to exercise any kind of guardianship whatever, these monarchs, even on occasions when their help was implored, have always respected, to the point of scrupulosity, the authority, independence, and rights of the legitimate sovereigns to whom they have granted their aid.

2. The monarchs have most certainly the right of watching over their own States, and inviting other States to follow their example; but this is a very different thing from a claim to the right of general *surveillance*—a chimera gratuitously imagined by men who make it their business to calumniate the monarchs.

As little have the monarchs introduced disquieting principles. They have introduced nothing, made no innovations; the only object of their efforts is to maintain public rights and individual rights as they at present exist.

3. The allied monarchs are reproached with 'concluding treaties, assembling congresses, without States of the second class being permitted to make known their views and particular interests,' &c.

If we go back to 1814, 1815, and 1818, there have doubtless been treaties concluded, accepted, and signed, sometimes directly, sometimes by adhesion, by all the European States. At these epochs the sovereigns, founders of the Great Alliance, were considered by the unanimous desire of the Governments as the interpreters of their common interests, and consequently fully authorised to deliberate and treat in the name of the Governments. It would then be very extraordinary if after their having so many times testified the liveliest gratitude for the manner in which they acquitted themselves of this honourable task, they should be five years afterwards taxed with having done wrong in the services they rendered to Europe. Since the Congress of Aix-la-Chapelle no general treaty has been either concluded or proposed. . . .

4. By what title, under what pretext, can the Wurtemberg Court claim to be admitted to the conferences at Verona? The affairs of Italy only concern the Powers which have treated with the Courts of Naples and Piedmont concerning the military occupation of part of their territory. France and England, though having plenipotentiaries at Verona, have themselves acknowledged that it was the part of those Cabinets who signed the conventions of 1821 to arrange with the Courts of Naples and Turin the measures which their own safety and the general state of Italy would allow them to adopt for the relief of the country occupied by the auxiliary troops. The questions relating to Spain which were discussed at Verona were entirely within the province of the Powers, who believed it to be for their own dignity and interest, as well as that of social order, to occupy themselves with it. Russia, Austria, and Prussia were obliged to consult other Governments to know whether they ought to break off their diplomatic relations with

a country convulsed by factions, or to determine what sort of engagements they were under towards France when France was menaced with war with that same country. What the Cabinet of Stuttgart calls *la cause des Grecs* was in the eyes of the monarchs who met at Verona reduced to an examination of the most suitable means for preserving peace in the East, a question which requires an exact knowledge, not only of the state of things in those countries, but also of the antecedent negotiations, and in which the ministers of the German States would have probably found considerable difficulty in giving their advice.

The Cabinet of Stuttgart expresses its regret that the Germanic Confederation had not been summoned to the Congress of Verona, 'two of its members being there, and the whole can hardly be subordinate to the parts.' It is evident that there was no more reason for the intervention of the *Corps Germanique* in deliberations on the affairs of Italy, Spain, and the East, than the States of which it is composed. If the monarchs assembled had intended to occupy themselves with the affairs of Germany, they would not have excluded from their councils the princes called by their position to vote in such questions. But this was not the case, and the circular of December 14 makes no allusion to the affairs of Germany.

5. The Cabinet of Stuttgart seems to have entirely forgotten the bases of the Federal pact of Germany; it seems to have forgotten that Austria and Prussia only entered the Confederation under the express clause of the preservation of their character of European Powers. The duties and dangers attaching to this last quality may dictate a course for which they alone are responsible, and in which, according to the Federal laws, they could claim neither the assistance nor the support of the *Corps Germanique*. In the case of a war with the Turks a great part of the Austrian territory might be invaded, without Austria having the right to regard the expense and the chances of war as common to the Federation. If Austria and Prussia had attempted to fetter the *Corps Germanique* by any stipulations, or to compromise the safety of its members by transactions to which they remained strangers, the Cabinet of Stuttgart would have the right to say that 'the whole could

not be subordinate to the parts.' No such thing has taken
place at Laybach or at Verona, and the spirit in which the
allied monarchs have discussed European questions ought to
ensure for them the suffrages of Germany, as it will sooner or
later those of all Europe.

Metternich to Vincent in Paris.

673. *Vienna, April* 19, 1823.—You know of the
manifesto which the Wurtemberg Government has addressed to several of its embassies against the declaration
of the sovereigns at Verona. This manifesto would doubtless have authorised the most rigorous steps, and if the
principles of moderation from which we never depart, and
our relations with the King of Wurtemberg as a member
of the Germanic Confederation, had not deterred us, we
should perhaps have at once followed the course prescribed by the general situation and by the sacredness
of our cause. But whilst we were deliberating with
our allies on the common measures most convenient to
be taken in a case so unexpected, the King of Wurtemberg, less struck, as I believe, with our displeasure than
with the indiscreet applause of the 'Constitutionnel' and
other French journals of the same stamp, and dreading
to be confounded with the avowed partisans of the
revolutionary system, caused to be inserted in the
'Stuttgart Gazette' a sort of retractation of his manifesto, declaring his entire adhesion to the principles
proclaimed in the circular of Verona. This retrograde
movement suggested to us the idea of a last attempt to
recall, if it were possible, that sovereign from his unhappy errors. His Cabinet was told in the most conciliatory terms that the Emperor gladly accepted the
declaration contained in the article of Stuttgart, but
that, as a pledge of the sincerity of that profession, he

demanded of the Court of Wurtemberg some slight but useful modifications of the course it had taken in Federal affairs, to the great detriment of the common interests of Germany. Not one of our propositions was admitted. After this last fruitless effort we have, conjointly with the Court of Berlin, decided on confining our future relations with the Wurtemberg Government to those subjects which we are to treat of at the Diet of Frankfurt, suspending all political correspondence, recalling our embassies from Stuttgart, and leaving there only subordinate officers for the expedition of current affairs. Knowing that his Majesty the Emperor of Russia sees and judges as we do of the reasons which have led us to this resolution, we are persuaded that this monarch will not be long in placing himself in a similar position to ours with the King of Wurtemberg.

ON THE FRENCH INTERVENTION IN SPAIN.

Metternich to Esterhazy, Vienna, March 20, 1823.

674. Sir Robert Gordon has, within the last few days, received a courier, by whom he has been charged to make me acquainted with a despatch from the principal Secretary of State, containing questions on which the British Cabinet desires to obtain some light. Anxious to give this communication all the attention which the gravity of the subject demands, I have begged the English Minister to entrust me with Mr. Canning's despatch. In my reply I shall follow the order of that Minister's questions, and our explanations shall be frank and precise; they will thus be worthy of two Courts long intimately connected in relations as happy as they are fruitful in beneficial results to the whole of Europe.

The first question which the British Cabinet addresses to us touches on a declaration of neutrality on our part, which that Cabinet deduces from an article inserted in the Austrian 'Observer' of February 5. Mr. Canning has, in consequence of this version, confidentially communicated to us many portions of his diplomatic correspondence relating to the great interest of the moment. He has taken occasion to express the hope 'that the King's Government may be able to find in Austria a support for the efforts he is making to prevent an event (war between France and Spain) the consequences of which seem to strike the Imperial Government most forcibly.'

The article in the 'Observer' is clear and precise, and its object was only to destroy the game of a faction who, to bring about a fall in the funds, and especially in our own, had been endeavouring to make the public look upon a general war as the necessary consequence of any enterprise directed by France against the Spanish revolution. The Emperor's political sentiments are too notorious for him to enter into explanations in a newspaper article intended for our public. He has considered it sufficient to give the lie to the faction without entering into the dispute between the principles of preservation and destruction.

The idea of neutrality in this struggle is incompatible with our political system. Fighting for the same cause for more than thirty years, forced sometimes, by events too powerful for him, to suspend his action, but resuming it as often as more favourable circumstances allowed him, the Emperor could not declare himself neutral if a principle were in question on which the existence of his empire and the well-being of his people depended, a principle which we have never ceased to regard as the fundamental basis of the Alliance, and which, after a quarter of a century of storms and revolutions, has at last given peace to Europe, a peace which the Powers have maintained with a constancy and scrupulosity unexampled in history, and which has been troubled only by the odious attempts of the habitual disturbers of the peace of nations.

The documents which the British Cabinet have much wished to communicate to us were, according to the confession of the writer, conceived ' with the object

of producing a friendly arrangement between France
and Spain.' By taking this object into mature consideration we shall easily arrive at the point which it
must be most important to the British Government to
see determined between us.

Every action of France on Spain can only flow from
two sources. It may be founded on the principle
which we profess, opposed, as it will always be, to
those of revolution; or it may spring from an exclusively French policy. France, in the first of these
cases, would act in conformity with the principle of
the Alliance; in the second she would deviate from it.
In the first of these hypotheses, she would have every
right to the support of the allies; in the second, Austria
and the other Courts professing the same principles as
ourselves would regard France as isolating herself,
and by that very fact without a right to their support.
The application of this reasoning appears to us simple,
just, and agreeable to the honour and good faith of the
monarchs.

In bringing forward the truths we have referred to,
we by no means pretend to announce anything new to
the British Government. We are too just and, I
must allow myself to add, too enlightened not to
have felt and appreciated on every occasion the force
of local influences, and we must recognise the power
which such influences may exercise on a Government:
the history of Austria in the Alliance has furnished
many proofs of our feelings in this respect. It was
after careful calculations of all these influences that we
acted in 1821. It was by respecting these necessities,
without, however, arresting their action, that the three
monarchs have saved Europe from the irretrievable
ruin which the Neapolitan revolution, the immediate

and natural result of the Spanish revolution, had prepared for it.

As we were in 1821 so we are in 1823. We admit·
that the Spanish revolution may present itself in a
different light to Great Britain and the Continental
Powers. England may long remain in the enjoyment·
of peace and prosperity when the Continental Powers are
given up to most real dangers. There are internal commotions, which act differently on States near the centre
of revolution and those at a distance. Such is the case
with the deplorable event which now occupies us.
England sees in the Spanish revolution nothing but an
ordinary revolution ; the instrument which has produced this revolution cannot alarm a Government
which, like that of Great Britain, is essentially more
civil than military. The Continental Powers, on the
contrary, see, and must see, in the Spanish revolution
the means used to bring it about. As an army—unless
they renounced the first conditions of their existence—
was absolutely necessary to them, the disorder which
has overthrown Spain is of the kind which poisons the
sources and attacks the principle of life. The Spanish
revolution makes much the same impression on the
Powers as an event of the same nature might on
England if it were headed by a few sailors attempting
to give the armed forces at sea the right of imposing
laws on the metropolis.

If, from this point of view, the two positions differ
essentially, the question of 1823 presents another and
not less sensible difference from that of the year 1821.
We find traces of it in one of the English despatches.
' Spain presents an aspect of peculiar interest to England.' Setting aside the political point of view, we are
as far from recognising this reality as we should be

disposed to deny that, in the natural order of things, the interests and the fate of Italy and Germany touch the interests of Austria more nearly than those of the Western Peninsula. Neither should we have interfered in Spain if Spain herself had not forced us to do so for our own self-preservation. We are not ignorant that the ill-disposed in that kingdom pretend that they have nothing to do with the affairs of any other nation. But if the most startling testimony had not risen in all parts to contradict this assertion, it only proves that the evil which devours Spain is of a character so contagious as to cause of itself, and without any positive action, the unhappy effects it has undoubtedly produced in more than one country of Europe.

Acting as this does with such a positive force upon us, can we mistake its action on the most direct interests of France—a country immediately contiguous with the evil itself?

Does England consider the action of France as an isolated case of intermeddling on the part of that Power in the national affairs of Spain? Mr. Canning, in his despatch to Sir Robert Gordon, says, 'The causes which now induce France to make war are of a nature altogether different to those which had been anticipated and provided for in the defensive stipulations of the proceedings at Verona. It appears to us that it is necessary first of all to determine the meaning to be given to this observation. If it only refers to the distinction between a defensive and an aggressive war, which is always vague, and sometimes difficult to determine, it may be easily answered by France. But there is more than one direction in which France may depart from the ground of the Alliance, and from the moment she did so Austria would no longer place any value on a principle of moral solidarity which ceases to find its application.

The question is thus reduced to one point. Is France to act according to the Alliance, and consequently according to the arrangements at Verona, or is she to take an entirely different line ?

In the first case, the allies are bound to come to her assistance ; in the second, they would not feel themselves called' upon to do so. In the first case, the Powers should certainly arrange that those of the allies who, in a given position, cannot act with a liberty equal to the others, should have the power of taking the course they may have already followed on a former occasion, without being exposed to any real inconvenience. In the second hypothesis, all the allies of France would be called upon not to allow her to reckon on a support which she would have no right whatever to claim.

The greatest of all dangers which could threaten the social body is undoubtedly any political war in Europe. Happily, we see no chance of such a thing unless from insufficiently explained positions. We are far from fearing that Great Britain will leave these questions in uncertainty ; but if they are not yet distinctly stated, the effort should be at once made to determine them with the care which their extreme importance requires.

Austria flatters herself that she has contributed to this end by the present despatch. While she believes it unnecessary to enter into new explanations as to her principles, she will never fail to express herself with sincerity and frankness on the application of those principles to objects directly connected with the common welfare of Europe.

Metternich to Vincent, in Paris, Vienna, March 23, 1823.

675. . . . Above all I must beg M. de Chateaubriand to believe, when seeking to know the opinion of our Cabinet in the grave affair of the moment, that the opinion which he heard me announce at Verona, the words and wishes which he heard me utter there, are those which we feel and profess to-day. Nothing is altered in our judgment on the Spanish revolution and the consequences, direct or indirect, which ensue from it both for the whole of Europe and France in particular. What we saw and said last November we see and we say to-day. If the Cabinet of the Tuileries has supposed the contrary for a single instant, or if it should still suppose it, it is, or has been, very much mistaken. The position of affairs is so grave that I should exceedingly regret such an error.

In expressing my feelings with so much frankness, I must at the same time beg M. de Chateaubriand to believe that we know the position of men and things, particularly in France, too well to wish or expect results incompatible with realities. This observation may be applied to the numberless embarrassments to which the French Government is exposed in the conduct of this most important and difficult affair. We understand these difficulties; we judge of them truly, and we deplore them greatly. The cause of France is that of Europe, even as the cause of Europe is that of France. This principle, which is our own, should be that of the French Government. M. de Chateaubriand is too enlightened not to recognise the force of this, and has declared it to the public and to us. The same principle does not seem to have been always equally apparent to his colleagues—a divergence which has been already the cause of much evil, and may lead to still further ill results. If I have expressed some uneasiness to you, and if I have not concealed that feeling from the French Ambassador at Vienna, it is because I am so thoroughly convinced that the welfare of all is connected with the carrying out of the undertaking against the Spanish revolution. It is not in my nature to keep silence when the first interests of the social body are in jeopardy.

I will not return to any of the subjects which I treated in my two last despatches. Great mistakes have been made; they have shared the fate of all mistakes. Some have been made since; they reached their height in the events of Madrid at the end of February and the beginning of March. It is not a question of recriminations; these never yet led to any good end, and I believe that M. de Chateaubriand is quite above them. The point is to come to some understanding on the necessities of the moment, and especially to provide for the future. It is to this end that the Cabinets should unite their efforts. I suppose the Cabinet of the Tuileries has been informed that the British Government has made an advance towards the Courts of Vienna, St. Petersburg, and Berlin, in order to assure itself of the feeling of the three monarchs. . . .

You will find enclosed our reply to England (No. 674). Mr. Canning has grounded his action at Vienna on a newspaper article, and the choice is not happy. I am still ignorant of the bases on which he may have founded his proceedings at Berlin and St. Petersburg.

I flatter myself that M. de Chateaubriand will believe that our reply is both precise and correct. The affair has reached its third stage, that of execution. The passions are excited, for the attack has reached the evil,

and its defenders are numerous.   On the other hand,
the more indecision there is in the policy, the more uncertainty about the parts to be taken and efforts for or
against such and such definite results, the more the
embarrassments will increase.   In such a situation safety
can only be found in the most open maintenance of
perfectly correct principles.   It seems to me superfluous
to assure you that, whatever happens, we shall not
deviate from our course.

Metternich to Vincent, Vienna, March 23, 1823.

676. The preceding despatch is for the eye of M.
de Chateaubriand. You will therefore allow him to
read it together with the enclosures.

It seems to me difficult for M. de Chateaubriand to
find any objection to our explanation to the British
Cabinet. What we say is what we think, and agrees
with what we mean to do.   Always ready to maintain
the principles of the Alliance by all the means in our
power, we shall never support what is diametrically
opposed to it, or what by an erroneous tendency could
in any way lead to its invalidation. . . .

The whole of your despatch of March 11 proves to
me that the new attempt to make a compromise, not
only with the principles of the Spanish revolution, but
with a faction which encourages that disorder, is entirely unknown to your Excellency.   After having
begged M. de Chateaubriand to judge of the conduct
of his Government simply according to the discourse
from the Throne and that of the Minister of Foreign
Affairs, and desiring to throw no doubt on the loyalty
of that Minister, I go so far as to admit that the attempt
of which I speak must have been the work of M. de

Villèle, and that M. de Chateaubriand is ignorant of it.
But what dependence can be placed on a Government
whose actions can only be judged of leniently when they
are to be attributed to the Prime Minister? . . .

The course of the French Ministry is difficult; we
allow that, and have never doubted it. The difficulties
with which it has to contend arise from two sources—
one being in the unfortunate form of government, which
favours evil impulses as much as it repels and makes
difficult the employment of the remedies of this *régime*
implanted in France, but foreign to the manners and
spirit of the people of that great State; the second source
of the evil can only be sought in the daily faults committed by the Ministers, and the mistakes into which they
are led by personal considerations, by the activity of
parties, and by their own inexperience. If the first of
these influences is insurmountable, it should not be so
with the second. What is to be done in the midst of such
confusion? The three Courts must stand firm by their
principles, and never lose sight of them for a single
instant. It is clear to me that if they make the least
mistake Europe may be lost. It is necessary to speak
clearly to France, and this is what we have done, in
terms of friendship and truth, in the despatch which
you are charged to read to M. de Chateaubriand.

The fate of the plan arranged at Verona will be
decided immediately. In the interest of the cause it
should be so already, and by a resolute advance many
embarrassments would be spared the French Government. . . .

The line which I have taken care to draw in my
despatch to Prince Esterhazy between the two principles
of action possible to France should serve us constantly
for a guide. This is what justice and the most ordinary

prudence require. To change the character of the plan made at Verona, by turning it into a means of consolidating and extending the influence of the Spanish revolution, instead of attacking it, would be too great an error to be encouraged by those Cabinets which are free from the intrigues and embarrassments in which the French Ministry are placed.

I send you the answer which M. de Chateaubriand has addressed to Prince de Ruffo. You will see that it does not at all agree with what that Minister said to you. This explanation does not even in the least correspond with the spirit of the proposition of his Sicilian Majesty.* The French Cabinet is not happy in its interpretations.

It is not a mediation between France and Spain which the King of Naples proposes; yet it is as a proposal of mediation that the generous offer made by his Sicilian Majesty is treated in a despatch from M. de Chateaubriand to M. de Caraman. The intention of this Sovereign is simply to throw in the weight of his undoubted legitimate power with the legitimacy which we defend, and which France certainly has a positive interest in defending. The King can wish nothing else; the offer, then, ought to be unreservedly accepted by France, for it is in every way beneficial.

M. de Chateaubriand, in speaking to you, appeared to see the question in this the only true light. In his official reply he makes an affair of what does not contain the first elements of one. This does not surprise me; it is quite in accordance with the course fol-

---

* The King of Naples had written to the Emperors of Austria and Russia, and to the Kings of France and Prussia, an autograph letter, 'by which, without yielding any of his rights, he offered to throw his weight into the balance in aid of the cause which his august allies were defending with as much frankness as firmness.'—ED.

lowed by the French Government. It dreads control, and consequently sees it in every proposal, however right in principle and however favourable for the success of an enterprise which has already too many difficulties. Into errors of this kind feeble administrations constantly fall.

The fear of the Ministry at the idea of the Ministerial conference is derived from the same source. No progress can ever be made, however, in affairs without this means. I do not doubt that the Russian Ambassador will receive orders from his Court to insist on a measure so necessary and so salutary. The means of arriving at the end in view can only be found in the most scrupulous care to remove from what we call a 'centre of information and decision' all that might make it a mere useless formality. Let the French Cabinet inform the representatives of the Powers of its belief, its desires, and its wishes. This can be effected by other means than that of an ostentatious assembly.

The Ambassadors can consult and agree upon the language they are to hold without the help of the round table. M. de Chateaubriand knows this, but as he does not wish for the thing, he rejects it under pretext of its form.

I beg you, sir, to be most careful in supporting the great interests with which you are entrusted. You will find the most perfect harmony with your colleagues to be the best means of doing so.

THE REGENCY IN SPAIN.

Memoir on the legitimate right of the King of Naples to the Regency in Spain.

(Supplement to No. 678.)

677. The most recent overtures from the French Cabinet bear on the following subjects :—

It has announced to the three allied Courts its intention of proceeding, after the entrance of the French army into the capital of Spain, to the formation of an authority charged with the provisional government of the kingdom.

It has declared its intention of accrediting to this authority a diplomatic representative of his Most Christian Majesty, invested with the character of Ambassador

It has expressed to them its desire that the three Courts will, on their side, accredit diplomatic agents to this same authority. It proposes that they shall also be invested with the character of Ambassadors.

M. de Chateaubriand has taken the initiative in the regulation of this service. He is of opinion that the representatives of the Courts to the Spanish Provisional Government at Madrid should be placed under the immediate direction of the ministerial conference at Paris.

The same overtures have been made to the embassy of his Sicilian Majesty at Paris.

The enterprise against the Spanish revolution, like all enterprises of this nature, has its three periods—of departure, of action, and of conclusion. In each of these it may either be promoted by the faithful and constant application of the principle which should direct it, or compromised and finally lost by the abandonment of that principle.

The first of these periods is passed; the second is now going on under the most favourable auspices : it is therefore the third with which it is the duty of the Powers to occupy themselves.

The monarchs, who in the whole course of their glorious alliance have never approached any great affair whatever without being able to state clearly the final result at which they aimed, and have never supported any measure which was not directed towards an object clearly and positively determined beforehand, can only regret that questions of such importance as those which the French Government have just raised should be first proposed at a moment when they ought to have been already decided on and arranged.

In taking these questions into consideration one soon feels the necessity of reducing them to their first elements. Spain, or at least those parts of the kingdom freed from the yoke of the revolutionists, must be governed. It ought to be governed by national authorities, and a central Government should be charged with this function. These principles are simple and just. The French proclamations have sanctioned them ; the overtures of the Cabinet seem to confirm them. Nothing, however, having been yet settled in carrying out these principles, it is necessary to ascertain the views of France on the following points :—Whether the central authority to be established at Madrid should take the character and bear the title of a regency of the kingdom, or whether its functions should be limited

to those of a simple administrative authority. In the
first as in the second of these cases the powers of the
Provisional Government could never leave the administrative and extend to the constituent line. According
to the different accounts which have reached us lately
from Paris, it appears that the French Cabinet are not
agreed among themselves either as to the composition
of the Spanish provisional authority or the forms in
which it should be established. We have a right to be
surprised at this state of things. Should not the
French Cabinet have made arrangements concerning
subjects of the greatest importance and most directly
connected with the work it has undertaken? Can the
success of the expedition have surpassed its expectations? We must be allowed to think so, considering
the indecision which continues to reign in its councils.

Some indications seem to prove that if France has
the formation of a regency in view, she aims at drawing
it from the provisional administrative authority itself.
How can such a plan be executed without a loss of
principle, and, in fact, of the indefeasible rights of legitimacy? The monarch being captive, the nearest successor to the throne contains in his person, without any
doubt, every right to the regency. In the present case
the two princes, brothers of the King, share the fate of
the monarch. The eventual successor at liberty and
the nearest to the throne is the present King of Naples.
Could any arrangement concerning a regency be made
without the direct concurrence of the regent by birth?

Our principles, and all sound theories of legitimacy,
refuse to admit this.

The same principle seems to us to apply to the
creation of a central provisional administrative Government, however it is composed. We cannot conceive that

any authority for governing Spain during the captivity of his Catholic Majesty could be legally constituted without the authorisation and direct concurrence of his Sicilian Majesty. According to our opinion, even the simple recognition of that authority by his Sicilian Majesty would not be sufficient to give it all legal rights. We know, too, that the King of Naples would not be disposed to agree to such a measure. This fact decides the question. The principles we have laid down are those of all the monarchies; they are especially those of the reigning House in France.

After the death of Louis XVI. the present King, then Monsieur, was declared Regent of the kingdom of France. In 1814 Louis XVIII. refused to recognise the validity of the constitutive acts of the only authority having an appearance of legality in France. What the King of France declared in 1793, and did in 1814, he must necessarily admit as right and just under similar circumstances. How is it that his Cabinet does not decide at once on those questions for which there are precedents, both French and Bourbon? How is it that he leaves to the Powers to whom he addresses these questions the trouble of deciding them?

There is a very simple explanation of this fact, an explanation which, perhaps, we should not give if particular circumstances had not authorised us, and, so to speak, forced us to recur to it. May not the French Government have tried up to this time to avoid placing itself on an entirely correct line, or may it not yet have renounced all possibility of making a compromise with the Spanish revolution, and terminating the difference, by means of an arrangement with those who have dragged the King of Spain from his capital? A fatal project, and subversive of the principles of the

Alliance, but one that a Government which has been but too often in the position of making such sacrifices may consider to be merely what it is convenient to call the amalgamation of new interests with the old.

If the French Government could give itself up to such a plan, or if it simply aims at conducting itself according to the circumstances of the moment, it should be the duty of the allies to avoid errors equally dangerous for the maintenance of the principles of legitimacy in Europe and for that of the sacred rights of the reigning House in France itself; for the conclusion which the French revolutionists and those of other countries would arrive at from such a grave error would certainly be of a nature to shake to its very foundations the legitimacy of the royal authority in France. These observations, both political and moral, are now concerned with a question of fact. The King of Naples has just declared himself; it is not, therefore, a question merely of reasoning, but of regulating that which, in the interest of the general cause and of all private interests, should be regulated and arranged. The King of Naples, in declaring that, by the imprescriptible rights of his birth, he regards himself as called upon to interfere in a direct manner in the measures to be taken in Spain, declares at the same time that in taking this part he believes himself to be acting in the interests of all legitimacy; that his ideas are directed simply to a salutary end; that, in short, far from wishing to raise difficulties in an affair so delicate, his wishes are confined to seeking means for turning the generous undertaking with which his Most Christian Majesty has charged himself solely to the advantage of both thrones and peoples. In consequence of this wish, the King requires that his incontestable

rights should be thrown into the balance with the
acts of France and his other august allies, and in no
wise aims at dictating the course to be followed, but
simply at consulting the Courts with regard to it. On
these premises, therefore, all calculations should be
founded, and it is to their application that we must
look for the success of an enterprise which will ensure
the definite triumph of the good cause against the subversive plans of the enemies of order in Europe. We
have taken these data into most serious consideration,
and we have arrived at the following conclusions :—

1st. The decrees of Verona testify to the line which
the Cabinets have drawn between the positions of the
Powers. Thus a just and large part has been reserved
to the decisions of France, to the entire liberty of her
military action, and to the considerations of every kind
connected with the peculiar—internal and political—
position of her Government. The three allies, in
declaring their moral solidarity with that Power, and
in making engagements to unite in action, have one
only condition to their engagements—an indispensable
condition, and one which they could not renounce
without abandoning the fundamental principle of the
alliance.

To reduce this to the most simple terms, France
takes the burden of material action for the support of
a cause common to the Alliance ; the choice of means
proper to carry out this action has rightly been left to
her own discretion. But, that the cause may not be
essentially altered, it was necessary that France should
found every one of her steps on principles which the
allies can acknowledge as their own. The French
Government agreed to this ; it could not do otherwise
without ruin both to itself and the cause. That which

was right at the starting-point must be equally right at
the point of arrival. We are convinced, in fact, that
the latter period requires as much or more care than
the former.

2nd. The French Cabinet now demands that her
three allies and his Sicilian Majesty shall appoint representatives to the Government to be installed at Madrid
on the arrival of the Duke d'Angoulême in that city.
This demand is made without either the ground of the
formation of this Provisional Government, its legality,
the mode of its composition, or the extent of its
functions being arranged or defined.

M. de Chateaubriand, in the last demand he made
concerning the immediate sending of a representative
from the Emperor, expresses himself in the following
terms:—

'We expect that the Duke d'Angoulême will be at
Madrid from the 20th to the 25th of May. It is very
desirable that the diplomatic agents from the allied
Courts should arrive immediately afterwards, to recognise the Provisional Government and to treat in concert
the grave questions which must be discussed there.'

Now, to recognise a Government one must know
first of all what it is; and to enter into negotiations
with it one must have recognised it. It is, therefore,
necessary that we should know first of all what the
Government will be.

Whatever it may be, the immediate arrival of the
representatives from the Courts is no longer possible.
This is not the fault of the allies; it is entirely owing to
the French Government.

3rd. The authority created by the general-in-chief·
of the French army at the time of his entrance into
Madrid must consequently be regarded even by himself·

as a temporary authority, whose functions will be subordinate to the installation of a regularly constituted Government for the government of Spain during the captivity of the King.

The Conference at Paris ought, without loss of time, to take into consideration the formation of this second Government.

This Conference, which should take place without the slightest delay, should bring together in a legal act all the measures to be arranged and concerted for the formation of the Provisional Government in Spain. The Powers not being able to recognise this Government until they know on what bases it is to be established, and if those which France proposes are compatible with the principles from which they never deviate, they ought, with as little delay as possible, to be instructed as to the proposed measures.

Metternich to Vincent, in Paris, Vienna, May 28, 1823.

678. . . . I herewith enclose a paper (No. 677) which contains, sir, in the most concise terms the principles you will have to bring forward and maintain in the deliberations which must precede the despatch of representatives from the Courts to the administrative authority to be established at Madrid.

The wise and generous work of France will be found to be established on the principles which the Alliance has ever since its origin considered as its fundamental basis—principles which were victorious at the time of the restoration of the reigning House in France, which have triumphed over the Italian revolutions and have for ten years maintained the political peace of Europe. It is the application of these same principles

which alone can in 1823 effectually combat the revolution in the Western Peninsula. This truth once
recognised—and it is with real satisfaction that we feel
that it is so in France as with us—it only remains to
consider the best means of bringing the matter to a
happy conclusion ; and it will be quite easy to come to
an understanding as to the means.

His Sicilian Majesty raises his voice ; his right to
do so is incontestable, but to be profitable to the
common cause it should be guided by prudence and
kept within the limits of sound policy. That of the
King of Naples will be so if it preserves the character
of an intervention with the definite object of strengthening the action of France against the Spanish revolution.

Such is, we are convinced, the sole idea of his
Sicilian Majesty, and it is on this basis that the Emperor
feels it necessary to rest.

The King of Naples does not aim at creating difficulties ; he wishes to lend strength to what would
never otherwise acquire it. His Majesty puts himself
second and the interest of the common cause first. He
desires nothing for himself, but everything for the cause.
His conduct, therefore, is of the same character as all
the decisions taken by the monarchs in the course of
their alliance. . . .

I need not dwell here on the undoubted advantage
that the concurrence of his Sicilian Majesty assures to
France and to her allies in her efforts against the
Spanish revolution. This advantage is as clear as the
support of right and justice will always be, whatever
the cause. But there is more than one political advantage that we do not hesitate to regard as directly
connected with this position of things.

1st. The attitude of France, in her quality of an active Power, places her above the attacks to which she has hitherto been exposed. Unjust and—according to our conviction—criminal as these attacks have been, the French Government will only be able to withstand them by actions founded on universally admitted principles of public right. France can no longer be accused of acting merely in her own individual interest in recognising the rights of a sovereign undoubtedly called to exercise functions temporarily withdrawn by unhappy circumstances from the King and princes of Spain. She will prove to everyone that the re-establishment of legal order in that unhappy country is the sole object of her efforts. The responsibility of the acts which the present state of things may require will not weigh on France exclusively; it will be shared by the Power whose intervention consecrates all that can be legally done in Spain during the captivity of the King. The Provisional Government will be then established on clear and correct principles, and the proceedings of France, which might have been taxed with ambition, will have all the value of generosity.

2nd. The immediate consequences of such a situation would not fail immediately to react directly both on Spain and on the Power which at one of the gravest epochs of modern times seems to abandon itself to the recollections of an ancient rivalry and a selfish policy as narrow-minded as it is false. Whatever may be the rage of the factions and whatever the outrages they commit, Spain will have her King. If in other circumstances than those in which Spain finds herself such a demonstration might appear superfluous, it cannot be so when a faction has even overthrown the order of succession in the reigning House. This is the case in Spain.

According to the illegal constitution of 1812, the princesses succeed in preference to the more distant male relations; the succession to the throne passed, according to that constitution, to the Queen of Portugal, and the advantage gained by the factions in such a case as that no doubt guided their calculations at the time they imagined this alteration in the order of succession to the throne. It is, however, not in this aspect alone that they regard it. Two other causes have contributed to their determination: one was the desire of proving that the limits of the present royal power, as well as the right of succession to that power, must depend on the good-will of the people; the other motive for the new order of succession was to prevent the nation amalgamating her dearest interests with those of the reigning House. To attain this end, what means more sure, in truth, than limiting the rights of this House to the chances of each generation, and, by calling to the throne a new family, bringing the faction to what must appear to be the very height of success? In a word, they thus make the future subject to mere chance!

I do not know how far these considerations have influenced the personal feelings of the King of Naples; they are of such importance in our eyes that we place them first in our calculations when seeking for the most decisive blows to deal against the spirit of revolution which threatens to engulf Europe.

3rd. There is no doubt as to the reaction on the British Government. As long as Mr. Canning guides the political affairs of that Power we cannot expect it to take a steady course; it is not in his nature. It is by placing herself in the most correct attitude that France will find the surest means of baffling England and furnishing to her allies the best means of repelling the sophisms and false pretensions of the rival Power.

The Emperor wishes, sir, that you should explain with the most perfect frankness the arguments contained in the present despatch both to the French Cabinet and to the representatives of the Powers. I send M. de Brunetti his instructions and letters of credence for the Provisional Government of Madrid. He is authorised to make use of the latter as soon as the decisions taken by the Conference at Paris unite the Courts in one principle of action.

Metternich to Vincent, in Paris, Vienna, May 28, 1823.

679. . . . I think it useless to repeat to your Excellency in a secret despatch the arguments contained in the various despatches, the use of which I leave to your judgment. At present the question is less of arguments than of a fact. The King of Naples has taken a part. It is dictated to him by a right which no one will contest, and founded on an example set by Louis XVIII. himself. What the King declares cannot be invalidated ; the point is, therefore, to make the best use of it. . . .

The fact itself is partly good, for—

It places the rights of legitimacy in a grand and new light.

It overturns with one blow the revolutionary constitutional edifice, for it saps one of its foundations and makes any surrender to that system impossible. . . .

Be good enough to treat this subject with extreme nicety and particular care in arranging the parts to be taken by the Neapolitan Ambassador and yourself. It is he who should maintain the rights of his master ; it is he, again, who will assist you in bringing the French

Cabinet to see that what the King of Naples wishes
the King of France ought to wish, not only in the abstract, but because of the incalculable advantages which
will result from it for his own position. . . . It is very
important to show to Chateaubriand and Pozzo that
the King of Naples has declared what he wishes, and
that from that moment we have only to make the most
of the favourable opportunities offered by his declaration.*

* The declaration of the King of Naples in regard to the Spanish
Regency was not well taken in Paris; the Duke d'Angoulême appointed a
Regency under the presidentship of the Duke d'Infantado on the entry of
the French army into Spain on May 25.—ED.

THE ELECTION OF THE SUCCESSOR TO PIUS VII.

Metternich to Count Apponyi, in Rome, Vienna,
June 20, 1823. ·

680. Your Excellency will have been for some time
in possession of your letters of credence as Ambassador
of Austria to the Conclave which is opened for the
election of the successor to Pius VII.; and Cardinal
Albani having accepted the offer which has been made
to him in the name of the Emperor of entrusting him
on this occasion with the secret of our Court, it only
remains for me to furnish you with the instructions
necessary to guide you in this important commission.
This is the object of my present despatch, which I beg
Cardinal Albani to regard as meant for him as well as
your Excellency, and of which I beg you to send a
copy to him immediately after the decease of the present
Pope.*

The instruction which ·I am charged to transmit
to you may be divided into two parts—that which treats
of the forms and ceremonies, and that which embraces
the principal thing. The first requires little explanation, because it concerns subjects which for the most
part are regulated by custom, and on which the acts of
the Embassy relative to preceding Conclaves will furnish
you with the necessary knowledge. Two of these subjects, however, require particular mention. One is the
harangue which you must address to the Sacred College
on presenting your letters of credence. The nature of

* Pius VII. died August 20, 1823.

the place and the circumstances not allowing of a very long address, you must confine yourself to a short and precise statement of the object of your embassy and of the manner in which your Court regards the future election of the new Pope. When the Ambassador is charged (as is generally the case) to present at the same time as his letters of credence the reply of his Court to the letter of notification of the decease of the last Pope, the statement above mentioned is naturally accompanied by some words of condolence on the event and of praise of the Pontificate which has just ended. That of the present Pope having been such that the Courts in general and ours in particular must sincerely regret his loss, not only is there no reason for your Excellency not conforming to this custom, but it would be advisable to strengthen that part of your discourse. The personal qualities of Pius VII., the strong faith and unflinching courage which he has shown in the midst of adversity and persecutions, will furnish you with a text, all the more happily chosen as in recalling these sorrowful recollections you can take occasion to render public homage to the conservative principle which alone can prevent the return of those epochs of grief and calamity and preserve Europe from new convulsions.

As for the part of your harangue making known the object of your embassy and the manner in which our Court regards the election of a new Head of the Church, it will be sufficient for you to assure the cardinals in a few words that his Majesty, in using the prerogative that belongs to him of being represented at the Conclave by an Ambassador Extraordinary, has no other end in view than of giving public and striking witness of his filial respect to the Church and the Holy See, of protecting the liberty of the suffrages of the cardinal electors, and contributing by the counsel and exhortations which he has charged you to address to them on his behalf to fix their choice on the individual most worthy of the tiara; that this is the one desire that animates our Court on the occasion; and that whoever may be the cardinal called upon to govern the Church, we shall sincerely applaud his elevation, and we shall rejoice with the whole of Catholic Europe if he possesses the qualities necessary for worthily sustaining so heavy a burden in the grave and difficult times in which we live.

The second of the subjects which I have said deserves particular mention is the nomination of the ecclesiastic who must accompany Cardinal Albani to the Conclave.

Canon Emiliani, who has sometimes been mentioned in the reports from the Embassy, and who was usefully employed in the last Conclave, might perhaps do; but as this is a choice concerning which I must depend principally on your opinion and Cardinal Albani's, I beg you, Count, to consult with his Eminence, so as to allow me to propose as soon as possible either Canon Emiliani or any other individual whom you may judge proper to fulfil these important functions. I am anxious to submit this proposition for the Emperor's approval and to make known to you the determination of his Majesty. . . .

I now pass to that part of your instruction which treats of the essential part of the matter.

I would observe to your Excellency, in the first place, that the joining of our Court in the affairs of the Conclave, without any afterthought and entirely in the spirit of the European alliance, can have but one object, that of influencing the election of the new Pope in a way useful to religion and the general interest of

Europe. Free from private predilection for any one cardinal in particular, the Emperor simply desires to see a virtuous man ascend the Pontifical throne—one who joins to an enlightened piety a conciliatory spirit and moderate principles; who will, in short, be in every way equal to the grave and difficult circumstances in which he will find himself called to take the reins of the spiritual government of the Church and its States. Instead of the different parties which but too often have divided the Conclaves, his Imperial Majesty desires to see but one, whose views and conduct will simply tend to place the tiara on the head most worthy to wear it.

You see, Count, that the instruction which I am charged to give you is reduced to requiring you with all your power and by all honest and worthy means to bring about the exclusion from the Papacy of every cardinal not possessing the qualities above mentioned, and the nomination of the one who appears to you to unite those qualities in the most eminent degree.

But although a mission so honourable must strengthen the position of those who are charged with it, you cannot hide from yourself, Count, that, notwithstanding the advantages to yourself and Cardinal Albani, you will both need all your prudence and skill to enable you to attain the proposed end.

It would be judging very badly of the position of a negotiator instructed to influence the conduct and deliberations of a Conclave if one did not acknowledge that in the course of these deliberations, or rather of these manœuvres, where so many ambitions are roused, so much vanity has to be overcome, a thousand incidents may arise, a thousand aspects present themselves, which such a negotiator could not foresee. Now, if he has not the art of judging every day, every hour, of the true position of things, if he does not possess the talent of seizing opportunities and of penetrating the thoughts of those with whom he treats, he fulfils his mission but imperfectly.

If, however, there are for such a negotiator difficult situations, in which it is only of himself and the present moment that he can and should take counsel, there are also certain general rules of conduct, and some fixed landmarks, in the history of Conclaves, regarding which it may not be useless for me to say a few words.

Constant experience has proved that the formal and open exclusion which the Courts that have the privilege of sending ambassadors to the Conclave have the right to give to a cardinal decided upon is really inconvenient, and that almost always the above-named Courts, when they have made use of this right, have been injured by it. This consideration has determined his Majesty not to allow the employment of this means except as a last resource, and only then if in the course of the Conclave appearances of an election which it would be important for us to prevent at all risks should become so evident as to leave us no other expedient. In such a case your Excellency must not lose an instant in making us aware of it, and you must wait the further directions which it will be necessary for me to send you.

But I am persuaded that we need not fear things taking such an unfavourable turn, especially if the Crowns charge their respective plenipotentiaries to prevent, by indirect exclusion, the election of every candidate who, according to their common judgment, does not possess the qualities necessary for a Pope. . . .

A truth equally confirmed by experience is that the

Sacred College does not see with indifference, or without a sort of umbrage, the intervention of foreign Courts in the election of the Pope; hence it follows that the surest means for the plenipotentiaries of the above-named Courts to exercise some influence in the election is to avoid making their intentions too apparent. . . .

You will consequently have to assure the cardinals on every occasion, as your Excellency will have already done in your harangue to the Sacred College, that his Majesty has accredited both of you to the Conclave simply with the view of protecting the liberty of voting, and, by the counsels and exhortations which you are charged to address in his name to the cardinals, assisting to place the tiara on the head of a Pope such as the honour of the Holy See, the interests of religion, and the tranquillity of Italy and Europe demand. This is the most ardent wish of the Emperor, a wish which will be amply fulfilled if the choice of the future Pope falls on a cardinal whose moderate principles and conciliatory and impartial character secure the confidence of all the sovereigns, and give them the certainty that they will find in him a father and a common friend, having an equal affection for all, and induced as much by feeling as by a policy worthy of the Head of the Church to establish concord and peace among themselves, and to support and second them in the noble design of consolidating concord and peace in the whole of Europe.

THE DISPUTED POINTS BETWEEN RUSSIA AND THE PORTE.

Metternich's Remarks on Nesselrode's Letter to Lord Strang-
ford in Constantinople, St. Petersbury, May 7, 1823.

681. The letter from Count Nesselrode to Lord
Strangford * states the reasons which have determined
his Majesty the Emperor Alexander, notwithstanding
his sincere desire of re-establishing as soon as possible
his diplomatic relations with the Porte, to delay sending a
Minister, or even a Chargé d'Affaires, to Constantinople.
The grievances specified in the above letter give an opportunity for the following observations :—

1st. ' The arrangement by means of which the Hospodars of Wallachia and Moldavia recently nominated by
the Porte have been chosen from the nobility of these
provinces is a change in the system of administration,
a change which, as such, should, to make it legal, have
been notified to Russia and received her formal assent.'

The Porte will not admit without much difficulty
that the rights conferred on Russia relating to the administration of the Principalities could extend to a
question on which nothing had been decided in the
treaties. It will answer to the objection of the Russian
Cabinet that it has never been bound in the choice of

* Lord Strangford, the English Ambassador at Constantinople, represented Russia at Constantinople, as the diplomatic relations between Russia
and the Porte were broken off. We omit this letter, as its contents are
given in other documents.—ED.

Hospodars by any stipulations or rules whatever. But his Imperial Majesty having generously declared that he does not wish to insist on that objection, it would be useless to dwell longer upon it.

2nd. 'The pretension of the Porte to establish a relation between the questions of the moment and one of the matters of negotiation anterior to the events of 1821 is considered inadmissible by the Emperor, and will never be recognised.'

This pretension, in the present state of things, no doubt looks too much like an attempt to pick a quarrel, and it is much to be regretted that the efforts which the ministers of the allied Courts have made to prevent this have not been quite successful. Nevertheless, thanks to their perseverance, they have managed that the article concerning the places on the Black Sea, with which this pretension of the Turks is connected, was not inserted in the official letter from the Reis Effendi to Count Nesselrode. As, besides, there has hitherto been no announcement that the ministers of the Porte regard the definite conclusion of this article as a condition which must precede the re-establishment of diplomatic relations, but that, on the contrary, they seem only to have brought it forward lest their silence on this point should have the appearance of abandoning their rights, it is to be hoped that they will be induced to put off this discussion to a more opportune moment, although it will always be difficult and painful whenever it is brought forward.

3rd. 'The arrest of the Russian nobleman Villara at Bucharest.'

In reply to the steps that we caused to be taken at Constantinople against an act of authority which, as at first announced to us, undoubtedly justified our intervention, the Reis Effendi has declared to the Internuncio 'that this arrest did not take place on an arbitrary order from the Pacha of Silistria; that it was commanded by the Porte and justified by official reports from Bucharest; that Villara was not arrested for political offences, but for purely administrative offences, he having before the troubles in Wallachia filled the post of Grand Treasurer of the province and been guilty of fraud and embezzlement.'

We do not yet possess sufficient data to enable us to judge correctly of such contradictory versions, except that many circumstances induce us to think that the Reis Effendi's version is not entirely without foundation. Be that as it may, we do not believe that this isolated fact, which appears to have nothing in common with the political amnesty, can be sufficiently important to influence the ulterior resolutions of his Imperial Majesty of Russia, and we flatter ourselves that this monarch, always guided by the highest considerations, will share our opinion on this subject.

4th. 'The evacuation of the Principalities by the Turkish troops is not complete. They still remain in the provinces, although no extraordinary event or urgent need justifies the prolongation of their sojourn.'

We are persuaded that if the Russian Court now had agents in the Principalities, it would see as we see the necessity of the presence of the very small number of Turkish troops who are left in these provinces. Public tranquillity is not yet firmly re-established, and some time must elapse before it can be, after such violent storms. The countries are, moreover, infested by bands of brigands and thieves, the usual inheritance of revolutions in uncivilised countries. Without the assistance of an armed force, however small, people could not with any safety leave the cities, and the principal roads would be impracticable. The Hospodars are not in a state to replace the Turkish soldiers by a national troop ; their pecuniary means, very much weakened by late events, will not allow it. Also, far from complaining of the stay of the Ottoman troops, whose conduct, according to the unanimous reports which reach us, has been irreproachable up to this time, these princes themselves desire and claim the preservation of the last means which remains to them for the maintenance of order and peace. We shall communicate these observations to the Russian Cabinet, and we are sure that this enlightened Cabinet will feel their force.

5th. 'The firman of the Porte for the establishment of a Turkish mercantile marine is of a nature to cause the most complete stagnation in the commerce of the Black Sea, and very sensibly to affect the prosperity of the Russian provinces situated on that sea.'

The complaints of the Russian Cabinet against this unjust and absurd regulation are quite justified, and we thoroughly agree with them. Not that so chimerical a project—one for the execution of which the Porte lacks all means—can inspire us with serious alarm for the navigation and commerce of other nations, but it prepares the way for innumerable vexations, and many parts of the new regulation are incompatible with common rights and with the treaties and arrangements which secure the commerce of the Christian Powers in the Levant, and notably with the treaty of commerce between Russia and the Porte.

However, the very instructive and well-reasoned paper added to Count Nesselrode's letter has pointed out but two paragraphs of this firman which are absolutely inadmissible for Russia, and in truth equally inadmissible for the other European Powers interested in the commerce of the Levant. These paragraphs are : the fourth, which grants to Turkish ships in all the ports of the Ottoman Empire the privilege of unloading and re-loading before all other vessels, which must not begin to load until the former have completed their cargo ; and the ninth, which allows in future only the trans-ferring of merchandise from a Turkish vessel to a Frank vessel, or from a Frank vessel to a Turkish vessel, strictly prohibiting Frank vessels from trans-ferring merchandise to another Frank vessel.

These two articles, establishing an odious monopoly in favour of Turkish vessels, vexatious and absolutely contrary to all the treaties, cannot be passed over in silence by any of the Powers taking part in the com-merce of the Levant, and his Majesty the Emperor of Russia will never consent to them.

But as we are speaking of a regulation which has scarcely seen the light, which has not even been offi-cially communicated to the foreign embassies, and which rather bears the impress of an improvised measure than of a well-considered ordinance, it appears to us that it would neither be impossible nor even excessively diffi-cult to persuade the Ottoman ministers to sacrifice the two paragraphs in question, or to modify them in such a way as to satisfy the just dissatisfaction of Russia. These ministers, whatever may be the usual height of their pretensions, must do justice to the extreme care-fulness with which the Russian memoir expresses itself on an act the object of which cannot escape the Cabinet of St. Petersburg, and against which, neverthe-less, it has only raised objections which were dictated by justice and the evident interest of the internal prosperity of Russia. They can no longer deny that

in all these questions of navigation his Majesty the
Emperor Alexander has given proof of a moderation
and magnanimity very uncommon.   Instead of insisting
on the re-establishment of the advantages which Russia
had enjoyed uninterruptedly for forty years, the Emperor
contents himself with demanding that, by the admission
of the ships of other nations trading in the Black Sea,
or by some other arrangement leading to the same end,
the commerce of his provinces on that sea and all the
great interests connected with it shall be replaced in a
position analogous to that in which they were before
the commencement of the troubles.   This demand is
eminently just.   The allies of Russia feel bound to give
him all their support; and if the Porte sincerely desires
a complete reconciliation with Russia, it must be made
to comprehend the absolute necessity of yielding on an
article which Russia will always regard as an indispensable condition of that reconciliation.

6th. 'Russia cannot give up the alternative established
in the *procès-verbal* of Verona concerning the affairs of
Greece; she continues to regard it as an indisputable
preliminary to her reconciliation with the Porte.'

We have duly weighed and considered the difficulties belonging to this question.   Russia has declared
that, in order that she should be quite satisfied concerning the fate of the Greeks, it is necessary 'that the
Porte should prove by a series of facts that it respects
their religion, and that it seeks to re-establish the internal tranquillity of Greece on solid and durable bases.'
The Porte maintains, on its side, that this series of facts
is established; that in the whole course of the recent
campaigns not an act injurious to the Greek religion was
committed, either by its agents or by its troops; and
that it has never ceased to proclaim pardon and am-

nesty to those of the insurgents who submit to its laws.
It is certain that, even admitting this apology, one
cannot discover in it a promise of a final settlement of
that deplorable struggle which has for so long desolated such an interesting part of Europe, and which,
as long as it lasts, will threaten the neighbouring Powers
with complications, vexations, and dangers of every
kind.   Our numerous communications with the Russian
Cabinet and our actions at the Porte have sufficiently
proved that we second with our wishes, our suffrage,
our earnest co-operation, any arrangement likely to put
an end to this unhappy insurrection. We know that
the other Governments agree with us, and that Lord
Strangford would be particularly glad to be able to
bring about such a desirable result. But how is it to
be done?

The jealousy of the Porte in all that relates to the
internal administration of its empire is extreme. In
times even when it was most in dread of an approaching
war with Russia it has constantly declared that it
would not allow any intervention of foreign Powers in
the future regulation of its insurgent provinces, and it
is clear that the most threatening demonstrations will
not induce it to renounce this language. But the
ground of the difficulty is not only in these arrangements of the Porte. The insurgents, on their side,
present insurmountable obstacles to all pacification.
They absolutely disdain the amnesty which the Government offers them; their actions as well as their words
every day show that they are far from wishing to lay
down their arms until they have attained their liberty;
they have not taken a single step showing any intention
of submitting; they have replied to the amicable advances which have been made to them that they could

not agree to speak of peace unless their absolute independence was previously recognised.

In such a situation nothing remains to the Porte, even supposing its intentions to be most conciliatory, most favourable to the insurgents, but the sad resource of war. It is not without the most sinister presentiments that we see the opening of a new campaign, the issue of which (unless by a happy accident an unexpected reconciliation takes place), must necessarily bring new complications and new disasters; for if the insurgents are victorious the war will be prolonged, as the Porte will never consent to their independence without being driven to the last extremities. And if the successes of the Turks were decisive enough to subdue the insurgents, they would be (from the very nature of a war between peoples almost equally ferocious) accompanied by horrors and catastrophes which would make humanity shudder. The Greek insurrection is, so to speak, entirely beyond the domain of diplomacy; it has become a question of fact, a problem which Providence alone in the depth of its wisdom can resolve. We do not see how, in the present state of the question, the Powers can, even by using all their means and efforts, change the aspect of it; and we maintain that Lord Strangford cannot be held responsible for not having obtained what is beyond all political power. His Majesty the Emperor Alexander, from his intelligence, penetration, and greatness of mind, will see this as we do.

In summing up what has been said in the preceding observations, we find that of all the grievances mentioned in Count Nesselrode's letter there are only two which admit and require the active intervention of the ministers of the allied Courts, the redress of which must necessarily precede the re-establishment of political relations between Russia and the Porte.

One is the pretension of the Divan to amalgamate with the affairs of to-day the subjects of an anterior negotiation—a pretension which the Porte must entirely abandon, contenting itself with the reply of the Secretary of State to the Reis Effendi.

The other is the new firman concerning navigation, which contains regulations inadmissible by Russia—regulations which the Porte must renounce unless it resigns itself to an indefinite prolongation of the absence of a Russian embassy.

Metternich to Ottenfels, in Constantinople, Vienna,
June 21, 1823.

682. I herewith enclose a despatch which the Russian Cabinet has begged me to pass on to Lord Strangford. Count Nesselrode having been good enough to send me copies of his letter to that ambassador, together with his communication to the Reis Effendi, I am able to add to the Russian despatch some reflections suggested by desire for the success of an affair so important for the first interests of Europe, and the Austrian monarchy in particular, as is the state of tension existing between Russia and the Porte (No. 681).

It would be difficult for me not to deplore that particular circumstances have thrown doubt on the conduct of the Ottoman Government at a time when the Cabinet of St. Petersburg is called upon to make some response to the first attempt at a conciliatory step on the part of Turkey. The apprehension of Villara was not in reality accompanied by all the aggravating circumstances with which it was announced at Bucharest. But the fact is none the less to be regretted; and if it

were necessary for the Divan to give proofs of the
harm it does to its own cause by the daily errors it
commits, it would find them in the unfortunate coincidence of this particular affair with the very moment
when the Cabinets are eagerly seeking for means of
reconciliation between the two neighbouring Courts.
Add to this the constant intrigues of the ministers of
the Porte to impede commerce—of all things that which
affects most directly the interests of Russia—and we
may congratulate ourselves on the immovable principles
of the Emperor Alexander, which have again resisted
circumstances all the more deplorable because the evil
they do to the cause supported by the Powers falls
in the end on the Government which is blind enough
to create them.

Count Nesselrode replies to the Reis Effendi in terms
which, if they are properly understood, must satisfy the
Divan. The Porte will no doubt complain that the
arrival of the representative of his Imperial Majesty of All
the Russias at Constantinople does not take place. But
can it infer from this fact any change whatever in the
benevolent and generous intentions of his Imperial Majesty? This is a mistake, and it belongs to the representatives of the Courts friendly to both Russia and the
Porte to prevent its too probable fatal consequences.

Lord Strangford, whom the flattering confidence of
his Imperial Majesty of Russia has invested once more
with the task of pleading a cause which we do not
hesitate to regard as common to the whole of Europe
—for this cause is the preservation of peace—is accustomed to hear the opinions of our Cabinet without
reserve. He may well have some confidence in views
which we have for more than two years brought forward with equal frankness both at St. Petersburg and

at Constantinople. I therefore feel able to speak to him
with perfect freedom, and I hope that this time too he
will understand me. It is not views peculiar to Russia
that I undertake to develop and maintain; it is our
own which I dwell upon in the present despatch. If
he finds these views in harmony with those of the
Emperor Alexander, this only confirms the fact that his
Imperial Majesty, in his projects for an arrangement
with the Porte, follows only the course most likely to
lead to the pacification of two neighbouring empires,
and consequently to the general good.

We place the matter thus :—

1st. That the difference which at first may have
appeared at Constantinople to have been the result of
some occult plan of the Russian monarch must now,
even in a city so full of errors and false calculations,
have lost the colour in which it at first, perhaps naturally, appeared.

2nd. It may consequently be supposed that many of
these prejudices no longer exist at Constantinople.

The whole truth is contained in the following
facts :—

An insurrection of the Greek subjects of the Porte
has broken out. There are twenty reasons, either permanent or temporary, for this insurrection. Russia
could have taken advantage of this deplorable event if
the policy of her monarch had been directed towards
that end. But on the contrary, this same monarch has,
since the first day of the insurrection of the Greeks, given
proofs to the least penetrating of his entire disapprobation
of the whole thing. The Porte, whose interests are all
concentrated in the re-establishment of its authority in
the insurgent countries, has not succeeded in attaining
this end during the last two years. The whole of Greece

is still in a state of insurrection; she would doubtless already have consolidated her internal condition if her tribes had known how to govern themselves. The astuteness of the Greeks and the stupidity of the Turks have caused the failure of two maritime expeditions; and the want of provisions, the result of a total absence of order and foresight, has twice shut out the Ottoman armies from completing the conquests which they accomplished by the simple movement which carried them forward. New Ottoman expeditions by land and by sea are being organised. Will they succeed? It is for the future to decide. I cannot myself reckon on any decisive successes on their part.

What the Emperor of Russia desired at first he still desires. He offered to the Porte for himself and his allies to assume an attitude likely to influence the Greeks; the Porte not seeing in this offer what there really was, and seeking to find everything there was not, the Emperor has not carried out his proposals. What might have been attained by vigorous and united action he has left to be solved by the future. This future (and almost a year has elapsed since his Imperial Majesty was called upon to assist the Porte) has not even begun to produce any real effects on the insurrection.

Who has done more justice than we have to the Sultan's moderation towards his Greek subjects beyond the insurgent countries? Who has been employed more than we have in trying to calm Russia's natural irritation, and in combating a faction too often increased by the excesses committed or tolerated by the Ottoman Government? We therefore consider that we more than any other Power have the right to speak the whole truth to the Ottoman Government, and not to flatter its errors. The more ready we are to take into account the moderation of this Government, the more right we have to oppose its errors.

3rd. Notwithstanding the imminent dangers with which the Porte was threatened, and in spite of the advice of friends, it would not hear reason, and the Empire of Russia having admitted the principle of waiting, a very simple policy should have made the Divan take the most active and prompt measures towards the submission of Greece. Nothing in its conduct (and I should not even except its recent maritime armaments) proves to me that the Ottoman Government does not take much more into its calculations the examples of the past than the needs of the present. Events will soon show us whether the military operations against the Morea, just announced, are of a serious character, or whether the Divan does not rather hope to see the insurgents yield from weariness of war. My opinion on the plans of the Divan leans rather towards the last of these suppositions.

What does the Turkish Government do in the meantime?

It injures Russia in its most direct permanent interests—those of its commerce.

It enacts measures which also impede and injure the commerce of other Powers.

It confines its policy to the mere desire that Russia should re-establish her ordinary diplomatic relations, without at the same time proving by its measures any sincere disposition to contribute towards the accomplishment of this wish. This is an accurate account of the present position.

I see, Baron, that you and all your colleagues at Constantinople are agreed with Lord Strangford as to the good which must result from the immediate re-establishment of diplomatic relations between the two Powers. I feel that I run the risk of being thought wrong by authorities which have great weight with me; my conscience, however, is easy. I defend the cause of truth, and the truth is that, whatever may be said for or against it, the sending an ambassador from Russia to Constantinople is impossible. The Emperor of Russia will not do it.

The Cabinet of Russia refuses the ambassador because it sees more in the affair than the submission of the insurrection. It attaches to the re-establishment of its ordinary diplomatic relations the idea of duration; it dreads seeing them compromised by the arbitrary measures of the Ottoman Government. It is therefore the friend and not the enemy of the existence of that Empire.

The point of view of the two Governments is essentially different. The Divan, accustomed to see in the Greek insurrection nothing but an intrigue of Russia, desires to defeat it. This calculation might have been reasonable some years ago; it is so no longer when his Imperial Majesty regards the revolt of the Greeks as a deplorable event and a cause of anxiety for the peace of Europe. The Emperor desires nothing but peace throughout the Ottoman possessions, and he should not be regarded as the rival of an empire whose existence has no more active support than the wise conservative policy of this monarch.

In such a state of things what can be done by the Cabinets friendly to the two Powers at difference? They should not waste their powers in trying to attain the impossible, but direct them towards possible means of conciliation.

In examining the chances of the latter I am inclined,

for my part, to place the Greek insurrection in the second
rank of my calculations, and all my thoughts are concentrated on the most important interest of the moment,
and that interest appears to me to be that of the commerce of Russia. And it is just this interest which
Ottoman stupidity most directly attacks, and injures by
measures not only unjust, but without real profit for the
Porte.

The Ottoman Government appears to me to be following the line of conduct too often followed by private
individuals in a state of bankruptcy. Knowing no
longer how to retain possession of their fortune, they
take to speculations which even if they succeeded could
not save them from ruin. It is a calculation of this
kind which makes the Divan fix its hopes on the merchant navigation of the Turks, a navigation which in
the days of the empire's prosperity did not exist, and
which certainly cannot be created in a time of disaster.

Lord Strangford justly observes that the interests of
Russian commerce can only be properly supported by
Russian agents; the fact is indisputable, but cannot be
realised while the Divan daily takes measures to prevent
the arrival of these agents. They tell us all this will
cease: that the ideas of the Divan will be modified by
the presence of a representative of Russia; that affairs
will regulate themselves as soon as he arrives and
assumes his duties: but are these certain facts? That
they may be so the Divan must prove that it is not
deceiving itself as to its powers; that it ceases to raise
obstacles to the reconciliation; that it is not losing time
in useless regulations; that it will be just and humane
towards its erring subjects, firm and just towards in-
corrigible rebels; that it seeks for reconciliation where
it is really to be found. The Divan will reply that

there is bad feeling at St. Petersburg ; I retort the accusation, and with more justice. I do not assert that at Constantinople there is bad feeling, but so many mistakes are made there as to break in their very hands the weapons which the friends of the Porte were ready to use in its service. The Reis Effendi will say, ' Let the representative of Russia come ; '—he will come as soon as it is clear that he will not merely have the task of saving the administrative interests of his own country; he will come as soon as his duties can be regarded as the ordinary cares between two Powers at peace.

' Affairs will regulate themselves if the thing is tried ! ' I reply to this assertion, without even examining it, that the Emperor of Russia does not judge of things as they are judged at Constantinople, nor of the chances attached to the immediate appearance of his representative at the Porte, a thing he does not mean to begin as a mere experiment—an experiment which might so easily involve the risk that the recall of the Russian agent would very soon follow his appearance at Constantinople.

Count Nesselrode suggests to Lord Strangford the sending an Ottoman ambassador to Vienna. Lord Strangford and yourself declare that this idea is impossible to be realised ; you are on the spot, and can judge of the Turks better than I can. What I say on this subject, therefore, is solely to destroy any false ideas concerning the object of this proposition. The truth is that the Cabinet of Russia desires nothing better than to enter into direct contact with the Porte. I have just shown you that the Emperor Alexander does not believe that this contact can take place yet at Constantinople without grave risks. The Divan will be prevented from consenting to the mode proposed by puerile fears of combinations which only exist in the innate suspicion of the Turks. This idea occurred to his Imperial Majesty of All the Russias from his desire to come to an understanding as soon as possible with the Porte; it is thus that we constantly encounter difficulties where the interests of the Porte, properly understood, ought to aid us.

It does not become me to tell Lord Strangford what he should do to enlighten the Divan. I have the most perfect confidence in that ambassador, as he must have known for a long time. All that I can do I do. I tell him all I know, and thus furnish him with the only useful weapons for the good of the cause, and at the same time establish a fixed basis on which he can found his calculations concerning the intentions of St. Petersburg, and on this head I fear no contradiction.

RESULTS OF THE MEETING OF THE TWO EMPERORS IN CZERNOWITZ.

STATE OF THE NEGOTIATION IN CZERNOWITZ.

A Sketch for the use of the Emperor Francis.

683. The Court of Russia requires, as preliminary conditions to the re-establishment of her direct diplomatic relations with the Porte—

1st. A compensation equal to the injury caused to the Russian provinces situated on the Black Sea by the loss of the power which Russia has enjoyed for more than forty years of covering with her flag the ships of other nations.

2nd. The suppression or the modification of certain articles of the last firman on the navigation of Turkish vessels provided with a patent from the Government.

3rd. The cessation of the impediments and vexations lately exercised on Russian vessels in the port of Constantinople.

Besides these three points the Court of Russia particularly insists on the immediate and complete evacuation of the Principalities as a condition *sine qua non* of the re-establishment of her diplomatic relations. According to the last reports from Constantinople, these three points had been conceded by the Divan, and were being definitely arranged, in consequence of what had been settled in the conference which Lord Strangford held on August 30.

As for the evacuation of the Principalities, on which point Lord Strangford met with a stout resistance, it is to be hoped that the orders sent on September 13 to the Internuncio of Austria, insisting in the strongest terms on immediate evacuation, will have enabled that minister and the English Ambassador to force the Divan to make this last concession; and that the latter, informed by this time of the interview between the two Emperors at Czernowitz, will have had the sense to listen to our advice. The courier whom we expect in a few days from Constantinople will inform us on this point; but even supposing that the Turkish Government still wished to offer any resistance, the way to prevent it would be a decided declaration, which could be made in the name of Russia by the English Ambassador and the Internuncio to the Ottoman Government, that if within eight days the evacuation was not concluded, diplomatic relations between the two Governments would not be re-established. This declaration, dated from Czernowitz, would not fail to have effect.

We are therefore authorised to regard the conditions on which Russia makes her diplomatic relations with the Porte depend either as fulfilled or on the point of being so. While this favourable result is being obtained at Constantinople the Emperor Alexander agrees in principle at St. Petersburg to the proposition which we have made to him to divide the negotiations opened with the Ottoman Porte into two periods; to re-establish his diplomatic relations with it as soon as it shall have satisfied the just demands of Russia concerning the commerce and evacuation of the Principalities; and to wait a more favourable time for the discussion of the arrangements relating to the intervention of the allied

Powers in the re-establishment of the tranquillity of Greece. The Emperor reserved this proposition for more mature consideration after he had been informed of the result of the last steps taken by Lord Strangford. Now, this result being favourable, as we have just seen, it seems that nothing should now oppose the immediate re-establishment of diplomatic relations between Russia and the Porte, since Russia has obtained the concessions on which she had made it depend, and if she does not now show herself satisfied the suspicion will arise that she wishes for war; while, on the other hand, she will place us in a disadvantageous position at the Porte, since we shall not be able to claim any concessions beyond those which we have obtained, and which Russia herself had stipulated as the condition of the re-establishment of her diplomatic relations.

As for ourselves, we have in fact arrived at the end of the negotiation, and we have faithfully fulfilled all our engagements with Russia, offering her the means of terminating her differences with the Porte in a way suitable to her interests, her dignity, and the conditions which she herself stipulated. If, while pleading loyally the interests of Russia, we had failed in our efforts, we should have found ourselves in a very inconvenient position with regard to the Porte; but from the moment they are crowned with success our intervention must cease, and if it does not entirely satisfy Russia we cannot go further without injuring ourselves and departing from the strict line of duty.

*Count Mercy * to the Emperor Francis, Czernowitz,
October 7, 1823.*

684. According to what Count Nesselrode has told me, to whom, by your Majesty's orders, I have communicated the course recommended to him by Prince Metternich, your Majesty will be able to say to-morrow to the Emperor Alexander ' that from the moment he is satisfied with the result of the negotiation confided to Lord Strangford and the Internuncio, who have obtained from the Ottoman Government all the concessions which the Court of Russia demanded as conditions previous to the re-establishment of her diplomatic relations with that Government, it will be as honourable as glorious for the Emperor Alexander to terminate this important affair with your Majesty personally by authorising Count Nesselrode, his Minister, to write officially to Lord Strangford " that his Imperial Majesty of All the Russias is satisfied with the result of his negotiations with the Ottoman Porte, a result all the more desirable as it affords a possibility of an early re-establishment of his diplomatic relations with that Government." '

This spontaneous declaration of the Emperor Alexander would place that sovereign in the eyes of Europe in a position all the more honourable inasmuch as, considering the unfortunate illness of Prince Metternich, it would be attributed exclusively to the profound wisdom of his policy and the beneficent influence of your Majesty.

* Count Mercy acted for Prince Metternich in the negotiations at Czernowitz when he was detained by illness at Lemberg.--ED.

Metternich to Ottenfels, in Constantinople, Lemberg,
October 16, 1823.

685. The wise determination which the Porte
has at length taken, after Lord Strangford's urgent
appeals in the name of the loyal friendship and earnest
desire for the preservation of peace of all the allied
Courts, has met from the Emperor of Russia that reception which we expected from the high sentiments of
that monarch. . . .

Strong in the hopes which we have never ceased to
place in the equitable resolutions of the Cabinet of St.
Petersburg, and in the determinations of a sovereign
always superior to secondary considerations, we now have
the satisfaction of seeing that the more clear and precise
explanations on the part of the Divan have been quickly
acknowledged and kindly reciprocated by the Cabinet of
St. Petersburg. At this moment we feel that we are
fully recompensed. The triumph of the Emperor of
Russia's moderation is complete ; and this triumph is at
the same time ours.

The determinations at which the Emperor Alexander
has just arrived being all contained in the official letter
which, by order of his august master, Count Nesselrode
addressed under date of Czernowitz, October 10 (September 28), to his Excellency Viscount Strangford, I
am anxious, after having consulted with the Russian
minister, to furnish you with the enclosed copy * of this

---

* In reference to the important result of the negotiations at Constantinople, in which Lord Strangford represented Russia, information of which
reached the monarchs at Czernowitz, Nesselrode wrote to Strangford as
follows :—' My august master charges me to inform you of his gratitude.
He sees, with infinite pleasure, that in consequence of your efforts the essential matter of the commercial relations has been settled according to his
wishes—that the Porte renounces the claim to deny the passage of the

reply, as taking the form of a common instruction and
as being eventually destined to serve as a guide for the
co-operation of the representatives of the Courts of
France and Berlin, after they have received the official
communication from their Governments.

The official letter from the Cabinet of St. Petersburg
includes all the points of litigation which had caused
the interruption of diplomatic relations between Russia
and the Porte. This important document must therefore henceforth become the basis of your action and
form the only groundwork for every step you take. It
will suffice for all that your position requires, and your
task, like ours, will thus be much simplified.

In it you will observe, sir, that the article on the
commercial relations, on which his Imperial Majesty
has declared himself fully satisfied, is so definite and
fixed in principle on the part of the Porte that, being
accepted on the part of Russia, the cares of the representatives of the Courts may henceforth be confined
to observing that the declarations of the Divan are
exactly carried out, securing their uniform and regular
observance, guarding the rights acquired by European
flags, and preventing the rise of new grievances between Russia and the Porte on this score. You will

Bosphorus to the foreign ships which frequent the ports of our southern
provinces; that all European flags will be admitted to the enjoyment of
this indispensable privilege; that the transference of cargoes may be carried
on in a way which ensures liberty and good order—that, in short, in consequence of your representations, visits of suppression, useless disputes, and
mistimed and unjust rights being abolished, the passage of the Straits of
Constantinople will no longer be an object of anxiety and the cause of constant commercial losses. The Emperor is firmly convinced, my Lord, that
these fruits of your negotiations will be as durable as they are useful, and
that having been able to induce the Porte to give a proof of conciliatory
intentions, you will be able to exercise the same talent in preventing its
return to a policy which must have isolated from it all the Governments of
Europe and brought upon it the scourge of a general war.'—ED.

observe, on the other hand, that if, in spite of our urgent remonstrances, the Divan still fails completely to satisfy the Cabinet of St. Petersburg by concluding the evacuation of the Principalities of the Danube, the smoothing over of this last complication in the direct relations of the two Empires seems to us the less doubtful as the solution is not only in the hands of the Sultan, but is for his own interest. The great value which the Porte must attach to the formal re-establishment of its diplomatic relations with its powerful neighbour will not allow us to believe that after such striking proofs of good-will and regard as those which it is receiving at this moment from the Emperor Alexander, it can doubt as to the complete return to the *status quo* before these differences with Russia occurred, or hesitate to give up the last traces of distrust and doubt and become thoroughly reconciled with all the European States.

This acceleration of the measures for the evacuation of Wallachia and Moldavia is the subject to which, sir, you will have to devote your chief care, duty as well as justice calling upon you to do so more particularly than the representatives of other Courts since, the possessions of Austria being contiguous with the two Principalities, we more than any other Power feel the inconveniences and the danger of the prolongation of temporary measures, now as entirely without object as without utility. . . .

As to the question concerning the re-establishment of tranquillity in Greece, this discussion must be entrusted to the collective intervention of the allied Powers, and I ·reserve to myself, sir, the power of sending you a special instruction on this subject, after I have consulted with the Cabinet of Russia. In the meantime I may beg you, sir, with us, to place full confidence in all the reasons

for hope to be drawn from the generous determination
of the Emperor Alexander to re-establish diplomatic
relations with the Ottoman Court, from the moment
he is satisfied of the evacuation of the Principalities
in conformity with the treaties. Count Nesselrode has
been authorised, as you will see, to make known to
the Divan 'that his Imperial Majesty has resolved to
make choice of a minister to Constantinople as soon as
he has finished his journey.' The Emperor, wishing
just now to give the Porte a public example of the
moderation of his sentiments, has decided to send to
Constantinople the present Councillor of State, M. de
Minciaky, whose loyal and enlightened views we have
frequently had occasion to praise, as you know; and by
the present courier the ambassador of Great Britain
receives from the Russian Cabinet a request to take the
necessary steps at Constantinople to obtain the firman to
M. de Minciaky, so as to secure to his mission the reception and the success which the Porte, more than any
other Power, has urgent reasons to desire. Under such
happy auspices, sir, you will hardly know how to support with sufficient eagerness and zeal the steps taken
by M. de Minciaky, and you will also constantly unite
with the ambassador of Great Britain in your intentions
and conduct, as well as with the representatives of the
Courts of France and Berlin, so as to cause the Sublime
Porte to put a right value on a position so much in
favour of its present interests and future hopes. We
are desired to forward to Constantinople the despatches
from the Russian Cabinet, which I herewith send by the
present courier. You will carefully forward them without the least delay, and be good enough to acknowledge
their receipt.

CONFERENCES IN ST. PETERSBURG ON THE PACIFICATION OF GREECE.

Metternich to Count Zichy, in Berlin, Vienna, November 13, 1823.

686. I have just learnt by a letter from Count Nesselrode, dated from Odessa the 3rd of this month, that the whole of the despatches sent from Lemberg on October 16 to Constantinople have been placed before the Emperor Alexander; that his Imperial Majesty quite approved of the arrangements which I made with his ministers, and that he has again consented that the affair of the pacification of Greece shall be previously examined and discussed between the allied Courts. In consequence of this determination, the Russian minister invites the Cabinets to furnish their representatives at the Court of St. Petersburg with instructions necessary to take part in the deliberations to be opened on this subject. I do not doubt that Count Bernstorff will have received the same instructions and the same overtures. It will also be necessary to address to the Prussian minister at St. Petersburg instructions with regard to the conferences which are to be held on this grave question, and it seems to me not only useful but indispensable that your Excellency should arrange confidentially beforehand with Count Bernstorff on the line we are to take when our turn comes in these conferences.

In the first place, I consider it very convenient

in more than one respect that the first general deliberations on the affair of the Greeks should take place
at St. Petersburg. I have every reason to believe
that the Emperor Alexander will consider that a mark
of attention in the singularly delicate position in which
he finds himself concerning that affair. You know,
Count, how men's minds are excited in Russia on
this question, and how much firmness it has required
to enable the Emperor to triumph over the agitation to
which it has given rise. The more noble and elevated
his conduct has been on this occasion, the more we
ought to facilitate as far as possible the reconciliation
of the public opinion of his country with his generous
determinations. Now, it is certain that the choice of
St. Petersburg for the seat of the conferences will have
a very favourable effect in Russia. This arrangement,
moreover, has undoubted advantages. The pacification
of Greece is a subject so beset with difficulties that it
would be wrong for us to wish to take the initiative in
the discussions to be held. It appears to me equally
just and desirable that the Cabinet of Russia should
take the initiative. When this Cabinet makes its first
propositions to us, we shall be able to examine and
criticise them ; and when we see that what they contain
is useful and practicable, we shall be able to form our
opinion with much more maturity and weight than by
forming it independently beforehand. This will be the
object of our minister at St. Petersburg. He will be
authorised to make, in the conferences to be held, observations which he may draw either from his own convictions or his general knowledge of the principles and
intentions of his Court. But he cannot decide on the
whole affair, or give any positive opinion, till he has informed us of the overtures made by the Russian Cabinet.

I presume, Count, that the other allied Courts will follow the same course; but I am particularly anxious that it should be approved and adopted by the Berlin Cabinet. Count Bernstorff is too enlightened not to understand the serious inconvenience which any other method of treating the pacification of the Greeks would involve. The personal dispositions of the Emperor Alexander are such that we need not fear being thrown by this question into new embarrassments and complications. But the least proposition on our side, if untimely, would have disastrous consequences, embroiling the matter instead of clearing it, and preventing the results so necessary to be obtained from these conferences. Count Bernstorff will not, I am sure, consider exaggerated the precaution and reserve with which I think it right to proceed in this business. Austria undoubtedly has more direct interest in it than any other Power. The numerous points of contact which we have with both Turks and Greeks, the geographical situation of our States of Hungary, Italy, Dalmatia, &c., the prosperity of our commerce and navigation, necessarily make us regard the pacification of the Ottoman provinces, as well as the future fate of all parts of Greece, as subjects of the highest importance.

I therefore dare to flatter myself that the considerations which guide me in this affair will be duly appreciated by Count Bernstorff, and that he will be ready to second a step which I really believe is the only one practicable to clear up the confusion of the discussions which we expect, and to prevent new difficulties being added to those which are inseparable from it. I beg your Excellency to say to this minister that I request him, as a real proof of friendship and confidence, at first only to furnish his minister at St. Petersburg with general instructions, reserving to himself to approach the essential part of the question when we know the opinions of the Russian Cabinet. For my part, I shall not fail to render him a faithful account of mine, and to concert with the Court of Berlin on all the steps we shall have to take in order to bring to a happy end one of the most difficult problems which could occupy the attention of the allied Courts.

1824.

EVENTS OF THE DAY.

687. *Vienna, January 8, 1824.*—I have plenty of news from all sides. In St. Petersburg everything goes well, very well. Many honours have been conferred on the occasion of the Emperor's name day, among others Peter Wolkonsky received the Grand Cross of St. Andrew, and Nesselrode has been promoted to the dignity of Privy Councillor. I was therefore quite right, that the ill favour into which the former seemed to have fallen was only apparent. I am very much pleased with Nesselrode's advancement, for I think it quite right that those should be promoted who do not put themselves forward. Nesselrode will now have more influence.

In London the Americans have gradually become very uncomfortable. Since Canning has seen that the Presidents of the transatlantic Republics can, with impunity, go much further in their liberal expressions than a member of the Cabinet of George IV. can venture to do, he is somewhat more reserved in his invectives. It sometimes happens, and that, indeed, in a very awkward way, that he allows expressions to escape him which wonderfully resemble the monarchical principle. This is an important step on which we may now reckon. Perhaps in no very long time we may hear from England more rigid principles about monarchy than from the Courts of the Continent. England, alas! will then only appear the weaker with all its severity of principles. It is to this that Liberal ministers lead the countries which trust in them. The most sincere among the revolutionists are the Radicals, and if I became to-day a follower of the Revolution, I would to-morrow hold forth in Spitalfields.

688. *January* 11.—Never were there greater contrasts among individuals than in London. In London we find a movement and friction in intellectual life such as is found in few other great cities. In Paris one side chiefly is prominent, the more or less frivolous; there they take everything lightly as if nothing were of importance; the wind blows everything away. In England things and people are under another moral law, and matters which have no value and no importance in Paris, have it in London.

Italy possesses few men; there are, indeed, some literary men who are dull and heavy there, as everywhere else, in spite of the innate frivolity of their national character. In Germany everything tends to ideology, and a deep sleep lies on everything else.

What vexes me with the English is, that they are all slightly mad; this is an evil which must be patiently endured without noticing too much the ludicrous side of it.

What you tell me from Rome about Apponyi does

great credit to your faculty of observation. He has certainly not the appearance of an intellectual, but rather of a good man ; but he has more power than is supposed. Apponyi is an excellent envoy, who will never make a mistake, and who will fulfil the task committed to him with tact and discretion.

689. *January* 18.—A great error has been committed, in which I feel myself as white as snow, while all my colleagues are more or less besmirched. The mistake is this, that in spite of all my prayers, of all my entreaties, of all my exclamations, the whole time of the French operations in Spain has been suffered to pass away without summoning the Paris Conference. In Verona the Conference was resolved on, but there is a great gulf between a resolution and its execution. The French did not wish to be restrained, and Pozzo di Borgo, who is always consistent when it is a question of withdrawing from control, has from the first hindered the meeting of the Conference, probably with the idea that his words alone would suffice. From this has resulted a delay of eight or ten months, and at the present time all the Cabinets are occupied only with what should long ago have been settled and concluded, in order to be laid before the King after his recovered liberty.

I have the latest news from London. The most recent is that Canning means one thing and his colleagues another, and that altogether neither the one nor the other properly know what they mean. In Paris things are much as they were, and it appears to me as if the two Cabinets were playing a game with dice. My position in the midst of this game may be imagined. I, who hate the unexpected and the false, have to contend with these two hostile powers, and have come to this, to desire for myself an out-and-out bad antagonist.

690. *January* 23.—I have had to-day a conversation of three hours with Wellesley ; a straightforward man, to whom it now becomes difficult to defend his chief on all sides. Canning defends himself so badly that what custom still permits itself to call English policy no longer represents anything ; uncertainty and vacuity do not constitute a policy, and a policy is one of those things least of all influenced by the self-will of an individual.

691. *January* 30.—I hear that the Emperor Alexander has entirely withdrawn from politics ; it is well known how much he formerly interested himself in politics, and that if his influence was not always of a decided character it yet made itself felt. Wellesley regards him as an admirer of Canning. I do not believe this, and I find in the preceding fact a proof that I am not wrong.

692. *February* 2.—I deeply feel the death of poor Cardinal Consalvi ; I esteemed him very much, and he felt himself much drawn towards me. He had an uncommon understanding and a fine temper, such as we seldom meet with ; like an Italian, hot-blooded and vehement, he was yet full of deliberation, like a German.

693. *February* 5.—The journey to Milan is settled, although the Emperor will not give it out as quite certain. He sets out on March 20, and hence I shall not be in Milan before the first days of April. Up to that time I have to meet the German ministers somewhere in the neighbourhood of their Courts ; they expect me as a Messiah, and they have really extremely important questions to negotiate with me. There is such a concatenation of business in my life that it accompanies my every movement as chains do galley slaves.

694. *February* 10.—According to my last news from St. Petersburg the Emperor Alexander is ill. By a fall from his horse he has seriously injured his leg. From time to time erysipelas shows itself on the wound, to which now fever is superadded. God preserve him!

695. *February* 12.—The English are everywhere losing their credit, especially in Italy. Liberals there consider themselves deceived by the English, and travelling Englishmen are no longer regarded as men with Parliamentary influence. The other travellers who once did much mischief were the Russians. Three or four years ago Italy swarmed with them, and every individual of them openly preached revolt, though he gave it to be understood that he was no agent of his Government. Is it credible at the present moment that during the journey of the Grand Duke Michael, La Harpe, who accompanied him, was received in every city by a club of the Carbonari, to whom he promised the Emperor's support. When we consider the weakness and inexperience of Italian Governments, it is unintelligible how one stone has remained upon another in that unhappy country. If I may impute to myself any merit, it is that of having opened the eyes of the Emperor Alexander to the things and persons who surrounded him. I must now prevent him going too far in an opposite direction.

696. *February* 21.—We are now enduring an excess of kindness from some and self-appreciation from others. I have all my life had to preach to deaf ears; now people begin to listen because their eyes are opened. This is especially the case in St. Petersburg. Nesselrode rubs his eyes, pricks his ears, and shakes off a sleep which is not unlike tetanus. The Emperor Alexander now sees clearly—of that I have daily proof; unhappily, it is somewhat late. Couriers fly in every direction; it is a difficult piece of work, with the help of the pen only, to induce people to join in with equal steps when it would be so easy to remain behind. I am stuck up like a preacher in the pulpit of a church where two-thirds of the audience come in at the end of the discourse and then want to hear all, which would have been so easy if they had arrived earlier. They want, namely, to hear again what I have neither the strength nor the desire to repeat; and this it is which makes my task so difficult and tiresome. I wear myself out, but do not complain if my efforts gain some advantage for the cause; but if this conviction is wanting, then indeed it is otherwise.

697. *February* 29.—More perfect agreement can hardly be imagined than that which now exists between us and St. Petersburg. And the cause of this agreement not being more perceptible is simply the obstinacy of one man.

698. *March* 11.—The Italian journey is put off till the beginning of September. Important reasons have led to this decision. One of them is, that we are now on such a good understanding with St. Petersburg that it would be awkward to increase our correspondence by going to a distance.

699.—*April* 23.—I shall go to Johannisberg about June 5 or 8, and intend to spend a month there. Under the pretence of paying a visit to my vineyards, I shall advance the great affairs (Nos. 721–725) which will come off at Frankfurt.

FROM JOHANNISBERG.

Extracts from Metternich's private Letters to Gentz, Johannisberg, from June 7 to June 30, 1824.

700. You will have heard from Baron Stürmer that I left Tegernsee on the 2nd instant. On the 3rd I started on my journey from Munich to this place, and on the 5th I arrived in good time on the spot. . . .

In Tegernsee I found Wrede, Rechberg, and Zentner all together. You know that I came to Bavaria with very little hope. I found the feeling here better than I expected. The age goes on so rapidly towards improvement that I found Tegernsee also much advanced. With Zentner, the man to whom I betook myself, it happened as it has done once or twice before. After an hour's conversation he was quite of my opinion. I was not to be satisfied with words, and manœuvred so as to obtain a paper written by Zentner, which, in the form of a proposal from Bavaria, contained more than ever I proposed to carry out in Frankfurt. Now my appetite has increased, and my journey will, I trust, have some results which will annoy your friend De Pradt still more than the pleasant results of the conferences at Carlsbad. Truth is a peculiar thing. You remember that after Carlsbad Rechberg was nearly accused of heresy. Now Zentner says that without Carlsbad Germany would have been lost, and that the greatest masterpiece was the Presidential proposal of September 20,

1819. The discoveries in the political trials which are now going on, discoveries which daily grow in number and importance, have a very favourable effect upon the Bavarian minister. The Government there are now in the same anxiety that I was in, but am no longer. The following is a fine story. The day that I went to Munich Wrede came running up to me, quite out of breath, to tell me that he had just got news from Anspach that give an entirely new character to the incendiary acts in Erlangen, which by this time have passed out of your recollection. ' Just imagine,' said Wrede to me, ' the German Republic is history. The individuals of the 25th Regiment complicated in the business have just made their confession. The youths of Erlangen proposed to republicanise Germany with the help of the students in the regiment, and incendiarism was the beginning of the business.' The Constitution was prepared for Germany as a republic under an elective Emperor. The King and all the Bavarian ministers were to be deposed, Lerchenfeld alone and by name excepted. It may easily be conceived what a pleasant reputation this favour must give the German Republican minister! The young philanthropic incendiarists of Erlangen do us to-day a service for which we cannot sufficiently thank them.

I will now go to work with Münch and his party. What I settle here I will bring on my return to Ellingen, where the Bavarian ministers will again meet me, and where with their assistance I shall, it is to be hoped, conclude the league, so that we may be able to appear at the Diet in August. I will not to-day enlighten you with details; let so much suffice for you that the wonderful notion exists that I shall ground the present conferences on some of Zentner's ideas. The King commissions me to send his greetings to you. If he could have ventured to do so, he would have asked you not to be too liberal. The world is still in its infancy.

I have arrived here simultaneously with the rejection of Villèle's scheme of reduction. Simultaneously, too, Dorothea Dino * crossed the Rhine, and I have kept her by me for a leisure day. She knows Paris thoroughly, and was therefore very welcome. Her opinion is, that we cannot possibly determine beforehand what influence the rejection of the proposed motion will have upon Villèle's position. She judges the man exactly as I do, but knows much more of him than I do. That which will distress him most is that, in order to gain votes, he has spent millions. Dorothea says that we can form no notion of the profligate character of men in Paris in all questions concerning money. Everything prepares the way for a breach between Chateaubriand and Villèle. Chateaubriand has declared against the law, and the whole ministry reproach Villèle with knowing nothing about it till he introduced the draft of it into the Chamber. This is a pretty instance of joint responsibility. Between them it will be the end of Chateaubriand. From the account of Baron Vincent I see that Chateaubriand is falling into bad health, and then he begins to caress me. Such caresses do not go for much in this world.

My news from England is of late date. Things there are not quite so bad. Canning is, in fact, in open conflict with his colleagues. Wellington's answer to my last letter I have received, and its tone is quite different from the first. Canning calls the Spanish note an excellent piece of work. He asked Neumann whether he knew

* Wife of Talleyrand-Périgord, Duc de Dino, nephew of the famous Talleyrand.—Tr.

the man who drew it up. Neumann answered that he believes it was Ofalia. 'No,' said Canning; 'he is a foreigner.' 'Do you believe it to be Pozzo?' asked Neumann. 'No,' answered Canning; 'Pozzo does not think and write so.' When Neumann then declared that he could give no opinion about that, Canning said to him, 'Prince Metternich must have drawn up the note; * it is too good to have been done by anyone else; the King, too, at once recognised the style of the Prince!' You see that the infallibility of his Majesty is now quite demonstrated. You know that at Paris they have agreed to Canning's demand that the note should be simultaneously supported by the ambassadors of the four Courts. Just the opposite has been done in London. Polignac, without concert with his colleagues, has taken a quite isolated step, and received his isolated, almost coarse rebuff, and swallowed it. When the courier whom Pozzo had sent to Lieven arrived, the whole business was over. I am very curious to learn what impression this *coup de Jarnac* will have had upon Pozzo.

Canning meantime declared himself not only satisfied with the Spanish piece, but professed his readiness to agree to its good ideas. I shall now appear in London with confidence on a new basis, and I will enter into a discussion on these matters, utterly disregarding all forms.

* The Spanish note which is here mentioned is probably identical with that which the Spanish Minister of Foreign Affairs of that day, Count Ofalia, addressed to the Minister of Great Britain in Madrid. By this note the representative of England was said to have been persuaded to join a conference of the great Powers in Paris, for the regulation of the affairs of the Spanish colonies in America—Austria, Russia, France, and Prussia having already given their consent. The grounds which Ofalia developed were based upon principles which Prince Metternich had often enough defended against the policy of Canning; but the emphatic assertion of Conservative interests for Spain, for America, and for all Europe, in the mouth of a Spanish minister, may have led to the conjecture that the note in question was dictated by a foreign hand.—ED.

In the Lisbon business England has behaved very well. The last accounts from Constantinople and Bucharest are not very consoling to me. The rascals are really too stupid. By the next post I will send a despatch to Ottenfels. In this matter the Government at London is blameless. And now, having given you my account, and drawn it with a fresco-pencil, I take my leave.

701. *June* 12.—My business prospers well. The result will exceed my hopes and calculations. On the prospects in Bavaria I have written to you, and will to-day add nothing further, because I put this Court at once out of question. Münch will probably write to you that the works which I brought with me have both surprised and satisfied him. The King of Wurtemberg has just made an advance towards me. He sends me Herr von Maucler. I have taken a very strong position beforehand, and also in consequence of the proposal of the King to come to terms with me. If Maucler comes in consequence of my answer, the King must be very anxious about the settling of the matter. Dr. Linden is to be banished from Wurtemberg. People are now coming to me from all sides. Some are good, and ask for help; others are weak, and leave me strengthened; the third are bad, and wish to find out what is really at stake. The latter leave me as ignorant as they came.

I expect Berstett on the 14th instant. Hatzfeld has made a terrible clearance in Berlin. Münch calls him the moral Hercules. There the party has been violently handled. They have taken advantage of a temporary illness of Herr von Altenstein to alter his whole department. Bernstorff feels himself profoundly mortified, and Wittgenstein trembles whether it can

come to good. The King appears to me to have acted
like a man who only waited for an opportunity to lay
about him on all sides. I expect Hatzfeld in the course
of to-day. He has brought his family to Düsseldorf.
Tatistscheff is in Frankfurt, and will be here to-morrow.
Meantime Chateaubriand is breaking up, and this will
make a great sensation at St. Petersburg, but only there.
Who is to succeed him we do not yet know. Here I
get news from Paris in sixty hours. The cause of his
fall is on the one hand his complete nonentity, and on the
other the stand he has made against the *rente* business.
For the present I remain quite passive in Paris. In
England the note has given much satisfaction, although
they have answered to the conference ' *honni.*' What
Canning has said about it I have recently communicated
to you (No. 700); now I am going to attack Canning
for this, and I send to-day a courier to him, by whom
I ask him to explain how he can reject as evil what he
thought so good. I have received from Wellington a very
good answer to my last·letter. I thank him for it, but
say that nowadays words are so many nothings.

I cannot as yet judge of the impression which this
change of ministry at Paris will make in England.
At any rate, it may be rather good than bad. The
correspondance amicale between these two enlightened
chiefs of the Cabinet has come to an end, and so far
this is good. Here you have my budget of news for
the day. The weather at Johannisberg is gloriously
beautiful. It was broken for two days by severe storms;
the temperature, however, was constantly warm and
steady. And the news are all so fresh and pleasant, that
it is a true delight to the diplomatic soul.

702. *Johannisberg, June* 21.—I authorised Stürmer
to let you read a despatch to Constantinople *sub volanti*,

which I send to him. Ottenfels has on this occasion
not shown good tact. How can he separate himself
in the general impression from Strangford and Minciaky?
The more he might wish that Russia might escape any
lesion from such a relation, the more should he have
associated himself with Strangford * in such a form, as
that rights should 'be maintained. As soon as anyone
is placed in the position of having to choose between
apparent generosity or unsatisfied rights the choice becomes very easy ; and this so few men understand! I
am convinced that the Emperor Alexander will never
begin war for the sake of fifty or a hundred more or
less Turks in the Principalities. I am also just as certain that he will never allow the Turks the right to have
even one Turk more in the country than before.

P.S.—I have just received your letter of the 15th
instant. You remark justly about Strangford's not understanding.† You see in this a new example how hard
it is to guide the things of this world. Strangford is,
moreover, so able a diplomatist that he should understand more easily than others.

'Si vis pacem para bellum' everyone understands.
Why? Because the saying is old, and has a classical
value. This saying, and nothing else, have I applied
throughout the whole history of the Greek affair, but
only in the way of negotiation. This men do not
understand.

I have filled my diplomatic arsenal, completed and

---

* Strangford seemed as if he found the proposal of the Porte to
reduce the troops in Wallachia to 1,000 men unsatisfactory, and that he
must, in the name of Russia, insist upon the restoration of the *status quo ante
bellum*. It is probable that this difficulty was also removed.—GENTZ.

† This refers to Strangford's exceedingly harsh judgment on the answer
given by us to the Russian Memoir for the pacification of the Greeks.—
GENTZ.

trained my troops, not in order to come to war, but to prevent it.

The Emperor Alexander has said not a word to me of the march to Spain since I said to him, 'We are agreed; the idea is glorious; but—how?' There are many things in this world in which the great difficulty lies in the *quomodo*.

I do not quite take your view of the reduction of *rentes*. I find the proposal neither unjust nor hard. That it has not been carried through is a purely party matter, and many consequences will result from this for France and the money markets in foreign countries, on which the opposition have not calculated, and on which they have laid no stress. For in France everything is a *question de personnes*.

The immense majority of the small *rentiers*, even those to whom the law appeared hard, convinced that it will be carried through, have sold their *rente* at par, or even above it; that is, they have gained about 40 or 41 per cent. on their capital. All these *rentes* have been bought by speculators, and amount to more than 30,000,000 francs. It will be a long time before they are sold again, and meanwhile they occasion much fluctuation in the funds. Villèle will scarcely bring on the question of reduction for discussion in this session.

703. *June* 30.—I had fixed the 15th proximo for my departure from this place, but I have made it a few days later, in order to wait for the answers from Berlin to my negotiations here and at Tegernsee.

On the 20th or 21st I shall go to Ischl, where I shall remain till August 14 or 15. I shall now send Prince Esterhazy to England, and will see whether I cannot deal a blow which, at any rate, will clear the ground. The thing is not altogether so bad. The

Cabinet begins to rise against Canning tolerably well, and the South American affair is rather waning. The fashion has changed. I shall soon be able to tell you something very curious about this.

In Paris things are as I have just written to you.

Beyond the *salons* and the public journals there is no further question of Chateaubriand. In a fortnight, with the exception of the *Journal des Débats*, the journals will be silent.

In Spain and Portugal matters are in confusion. The convocation of the Cortes in Portugal is a very hazardous undertaking, and is, moreover, entirely the work of the Ministers, who wished to shut out the Queen from the Regency, because they are certain not to escape the gallows if ever she become Regent. Whole volumes of the richest anecdotes about this Queen, as well as of the whole *incartado*, might be told to anyone who cared for such stuff.

Say many pretty things to Wellesley from me, and that my hopes rise. That will please him. As the Parliament is now at an end, the affair will soon show itself. Have you ever seen such a masterpiece of many-worded nothings as Canning's answer to Macintosh's speech?

There is such a crowd of men about me that, if I do not soon go, I shall not know what to do with them. My table is generally laid for five-and-twenty, and I often have forty and fifty. In the evening there are a great many whist parties. The weather is extremely warm when it is cloudy, and very hot when the sun shines. With the wine, however, it is all over. Good-bye.

704. *June* 30.—To-day I will give you an account of the position of my negotiation in the German affairs, and at the same time claim your official assistance.

Enclosed you will find the paper which I took with me to Tegernsee, respecting the renewal of the decrees of Sept. 20, 1819.

It will be sufficient, instead of going into that negotiation here, to send you Zentner's paper (No. 722). You will see that I made use of the time, and brought out the good side of the Bavarian statesman. In my opinion Zentner's paper is far beyond what I expected. Impartially read and judged, we find in it admissions and words which are of a kind that we scarcely understand how the father of the Bavarian Constitution (the first defender in Germany of the representative system) —in a word, how Zentner could write as he has done. The key to this lies in the reciprocal action of the distress of the financial system of the Bavarian Government, and of the moral bankruptcy which the representative system has suffered in popular opinion. The ministry finds itself in the sad condition of confessing to the Assembly of the States which is to meet at the beginning of 1825, that it has exceeded the budget which it received with approbation six years ago by many millions, and besides has to deal with a yearly deficit of three millions. It needs but this fact alone to explain the pliability of the Ministers. The demand for a *präsidial-proposition*, bound to maintain the principles laid down in the Bavarian paper, is quite Zentner's idea. At first I was recalcitrant, and then yielded. After this beneficent act received at my hands I have taken it upon me to appear as a negotiator against Prussia and Baden, and to assert the superiority of Bavaria. Here it was an easy thing for me to come to terms with Berstett and Nagler. Now I come to your business.

I have through Münch caused a *präsidial-proposition*

to be drawn up, and have specially bound him to retain, as far as possible, Zentner's words.

I pray you to revise this paper by Münch, and especially to make it pure in point of style.

This revised *präsidial-proposition* I require as soon as possible. If I could get it here it would be very advantageous. I have with this in view put off my departure from these parts till July 15 ; should you not be able to get it ready, the courier must be dispatched to me on the Regensburg road, by Anspach, Ellingen, and Würzburg. At Ellingen, where I shall meet the Bavarian minister on the 17th or 18th, I must have it without fail.

I have now got Darmstadt in hand. About Wurtemberg I do not at present concern myself. In all probability (and the opinions of Rechberg and Berstett on this matter are still more positive than my own), Stuttgart will say yes to everything.

My apostleship, then, will not have been without use. But I will not wear myself out in this, but let myself be carried on by the stream which brought me here.

EVENTS OF THE DAY.

705. *Vienna, July* 2.—In the midst of this chaos, I am like a man who, standing on an island with the tide rising around him, is excused from remaining. I remain firm in my place, I do not throw myself into the flood, but wait, to see if it comes nearer or retreats. I call out to some persons to keep close to me, others I urgently entreat not to throw themselves uselessly into the water. All hear me, but no one will understand me; sometimes they urge me to leave my position. I do not stir from it, but rather labour to put stone upon stone, if possible to make my footing higher and higher.

I shall remain here till the 15th, then I shall go to the baths in the Alps in Upper Austria. I shall stay there three weeks, and get back again to Vienna in the middle of August. The journey to Italy will probably take place in the beginning of October, and we shall pass the winter in Milan. If this plan is carried out, I shall send my wife back to Paris for the winter, and in any case I shall send my son there to work at the

I

Embassy. He has excellent manners, which is a great consolation to me in a life which has not many such joys.

706. *Ischl, July* 31.—I have been here since the 28th. The public journals, which do not generally pass me over, follow me step by step. If it were agreeable to the newspapers to know and say the truth, I would inform them that I have taken no step without a definite object or without a successful result. That any one of my successful movements would give the editors satisfaction or pleasure, I take leave strongly to doubt. My life has become a kind of apostolate. I have not sought it where so many who have no call practise their evil doings. Probably this is the reason why so many opinions are opposed to mine. Everywhere there is a flock of true disciples, who await their pastor, and I can no longer stifle my conscience and leave them without having offered them spiritual consolation. This sounds almost like a kind of exaggeration, but objectors should accompany me only once on my journey. Then they would see that in every place where I halt, at every spot which I hurry by, a crowd presses towards me, surrounds me, gazes on me, smiles on me, and offers to shake hands. It is not to be believed that this concourse of men is only a consequence of curiosity like that with which a mob runs after a dromedary or an ape. Against this actual facts protest, for the groups remain not dumb spectators, but make themselves heard.

707. *August* 13.—Yesterday I made a long and very picturesque excursion in a region of the rarest beauty. I went both above and below ground; they took me down a deep shaft to a vast underground hall capable of holding 5,000 or 6,000 persons. There I found my

name and arms brilliantly illuminated ; this reminded me of the transitoriness of human things.

Tatistscheff was with me ; he has little feeling for the beauties of nature, and prefers a political or professional complication, to any sight to be seen. There are more people of this kind than might be supposed.

My health is excellent. The baths suit me very well, and I foresee that I shall come back here. The weather unhappily is variable and rainy, but the country is equally beautiful with or without clouds. The mountains rise like spectres, their tops illuminated by the sun's most brilliant beams, while the vallies lie in the deepest shadow.

708. *August* 19.—I start on the 23rd, but I shall not reach Vienna till the 27th, because I am going to spend two days with the Emperor on one of his estates. In two days I shall have been nearly four months without any intercourse with my Imperial master, which has not happened to me before in all the fifteen years in which I have had the misfortune to fill this place. Fifteen years of work is much in this life, and I am *senior* among my fellows. Prince Kaunitz's was the longest ministry. He filled his place for forty years, and attained the age of eighty-four. At seventy-four I should leave as long a career behind me, but I shall not live to see it.

709. *Persenberg, August* 24.—I am with the Emperor in a real castle, which stands on high rocks in the Danube.

Nothing is more remarkable than the country residence of our Court. I am certain no one would believe that the Emperor can be satisfied with such homely arrangements, which are far beneath those of a wealthy landowner, not, indeed, sufficient for a well-to-do private

person. The household and living are those of a quite
poor gentleman. Everything in the slightest degree
bordering on luxury is banished, and one has hardly
the feeling of the enjoyments of homely comfort; indeed,
it is this very self-denial which pleases the Emperor, and
he thoroughly enjoys the little he has. He calls himself master of an insignificant *schloss*, with a few fields
round it, and that satisfies him. This might disconcert
the most Radical of Radicals.

710. *Vienna, Sept.* 1.—Summer seems to have come
back again, and here I am in town. The most glorious
sunshine lights up all the beautiful country I have left,
and is so kind as to shed its splendours on this place. It
seems that to pour out its stream of light costs it nothing.
Happily my garden is open to its full power. As we have
had so rainy a year the trees and grass are most beauti-
fully green. The autumn flowers are in full bloom, but I
do not care for them; they are like my age, and everything is uncongenial that reminds me of myself.

Yesterday an amusing incident occurred, which I
must not forget to mention. Tatistscheff got a picture
from Italy, which he thinks a Domenichino; whether
it is so or not is immaterial. The picture represents a
young John the Baptist; the saint is slightly draped
with a strip of red cloth, and much more resembles
an Amor than the Preacher in the Wilderness. Yesterday evening Tatistscheff received company. A tolerably
well-known Polish man of letters went up to the picture,
and looking at it very attentively, asked his neighbour,
'What is that?' '*C'est un Dominiquin*' (French for
Domenichino). 'What!' cried he, 'a Dominican never
looked like that.'

711. *Sept.* 6.—In a few days I shall go back to the
Emperor in the country. The fate of my winter will

there be decided. I shall advise him to put off the journey to Milan till next March, and I have important reasons for doing so.

Vienna is lonely and deserted. There is no one in
the city except the diplomatic corps. My only amusement is the Opera, which is all one can desire. Performances take place there which really charm the true
connoisseur. I, at least, am often enraptured. The intellect and the heart, as well as the senses, are fully satisfied, and in that satisfaction lies the highest enjoyment. I fear that few people are able to enjoy it so
much. It is more than mere pleasure, and would
amount to blessedness if it concerned purely moral
affairs.

712. *Sept.* 20.—I am very much pleased with Wellesley: he is an excellent man. He has a true eye for
affairs, and puts full trust and confidence in one; but he
is anxious, which seems to me very excusable. He would
not be so if he were satisfied that all was right at home,
which is not the case.

713. *Sept.* 23.—Louis XVIII. is dead, and there is
nothing more to be said in the matter. What some years
ago would have been a great event has now no signifi-
cance. The world is nowadays so far better, that Kings
can die undisturbed. The old King was a feeble ruler;
if he had been a private gentleman he would probably
have shared many of the errors of the age. Charles X. is
different. He has heart and feeling, and if he had more
firmness of character he would be a more than ordinary
monarch—for without being a regicide I may be permitted to assert that there are *ordinary* monarchs. At
any rate it is a happiness for Charles X. that he was not
in the position of Louis XVIII.; he would have been
ruined by the reaction of his return to France.

A certain Frenchman has made the remarkable assertion that one of Louis XVIII.'s services consisted in twice saving France from foreign invasion. So ridiculous a phrase shows extraordinary audacity. I expect that in some laudation of Ferdinand of Naples it will be said that he was a great ruler, because he twice saved the kingdom from Austrian invasion. Something of this sort might easily be said by conceited people, and long experience has convinced me that self-conceit is ever the cloak of insignificance.

714. *October* 14.—That miserable Eastern Question is again coming to the front. I am now engaged, as I have been for some time, in endeavouring to throw light upon the cause of the new complications, so as to bring them from the first into the right way. I talk to Wellesley with the greatest openness, and to Canning also, so far as it can help forward the cause.

The archducal marriage * was to have taken place on the 18th, the anniversary of the battle of Leipsic, but is delayed on account of the illness of the Queen of Bavaria. As this ceremony cannot take place on the 18th, we shall replace it by another; we shall open the new Gate in honour of the day.

715. *October* 20.—The report of my impending journey to Paris is untrue; I am certainly one of the most nimble of the diplomatists in the affair, but still I should find it rather beyond my powers to go to congratulate Charles X. on his accession to the throne. Yet I will not say that I may not make an excursion to Paris at the time of the Coronation. But I speak of possibilities merely, which depend on so many circumstances that I cannot reckon on them beforehand. Be-

* The Archduke Franz Carl with the Princess Sophie of Bavaria.—ED.

side this, the positions of the respective parties must be perfectly clear; in France there must be a great show of loyalty; I must not be entangled with the miserable Oriental complications, and England must renounce certain bad habits into which for some time she has fallen. I would come in an amiable mood to praise, and, if necessary, to encourage, but not to create anything new, or to reform everything. If matters prosper, if reason should again get the upper hand, I shall find means to make an excursion of a fortnight from Milan to Paris, in order to bring my wife thence to the Rhine. But will this come about?

716. *October* 23.—I feel wonderfully well. We have here an excellent physician, an Italian by birth, who met me the other day and said, ‘You look extremely well—that is, less like a scholar.’ This is really a very proper expression. In this year I have consumed much pure air, my nerves are quieted, and I look less like a scholar—a very good description, in which I find but one fault: namely, that it represents me as still looking heavy and dull, if not quite so much so as before.

717. *November* 3.—I am in the midst of the Court festivities and ceremonies. The little, or rather the big bride (for she is taller than I am) is beautiful, and, more than that, she is engaging. I shall be still some days in this commotion. The King of Bavaria is a very odd man, very pleasant, but talks of everything and says everything. He was like a father to me, and watched over a great part of my education. I was much with him, and he still treats me as a guardian does his ward, calls me by my Christian name, and awakens in me memories to which he looks back more sorrowfully than I do.

718. *November* 12.—Fain’s ‘Memoirs of the Year

1813 ' are worth reading. They contain my history as well as Napoleon's. Fain, Bonaparte's secretary, has done his duty, inasmuch as he has reproduced his master's views in the best light. I have added to the work a few notes, which contain only corrections of importance.

I was obliged to win back political independence for my country. To this end two ways were open to me— either to desert from a now hostile camp, or to go on honourably. In the first case, we must have followed the example of General Yorke; in the second, we must exchange the part of an ally for that of a mediator. This I have done, and the results show that I was right. In this sense one must read the 'Memoirs,' and specially the records quoted in them. Napoleon would gladly have seen us supporting his plans as allies; but what we refused to do at the time of his greatest strength, it would have been madness to grant in the time of his weakness.

The circumstances in which I found myself in the year 1813 were very difficult. The northern democrats, and, later, Alexander's liberal proclamations, did not make them easier. It was not necessary to appeal to popular excitement; calm and considerate statesmen would have completely succeeded in uniting patriotic feeling against a foreign tyranny which had become insupportable, without reference to the appeal of 1793 and 1796.

719. *December* 14.—On the occasion of the morganatic marriage in Berlin, which was celebrated with great secresy, several very comical incidents occurred. Amongst others, General Knesebeck was invited to dinner the day after the marriage. He met there the father of the new wife, and asked one of his comrades, ' Who is

this new member of the order?' 'Why, Count Harrach.'
'And who is the Count Harrach?' 'The father of the
Princess Liegnitz.' 'Who is the Princess Liegnitz?'
'The wife of the King.' This roused the indignation of
Knesebeck, who thought they were making fun of him,
and this indignation was not allayed when, a little later,
he learnt the truth.

720. *December* 30.—The way on which we are now
going is very direct, and the only possible one. This
privilege is owing to very uncomfortable circumstances.
I make no pretension except to know what we wish.
In St. Petersburg they would gladly do what they cannot do; in London they would gladly have that for
which the will is not sufficient; and in Paris they do
not rightly know what they wish. This is the true picture of the situation. For contemporaries this is not
flattering, and for me not fortunate, considering the
completeness of the *rôle* I had planned for myself.

Stratford Canning has behaved very well here; I
have brought him at every interview to see that I was
right. Under all circumstances one must suppose that
his cousin (Canning) must either unite himself with me
or modify his views so that I may act with him, for I
can never do what he does now, nor speak as he
speaks now. He or I, one of us, must be in the
wrong. Stratford is now on the point of starting for
St. Petersburg. The question is, Is it wise to send him
by Vienna? Do they want to convert us all on a sudden? We are too slow for that, and too well protected.
The situation appears to me almost like that of a general
to whom a command has been given, and who allows himself to be beaten before he has reached his headquarters.

RENEWAL OF THE CARLSBAD DECREES.

Metternich to the Emperor Francis, Ischl, July 18, 1824.

721. As I have concluded the affairs which have brought me to Johannisberg, I take the liberty of laying the following report of my proceedings before your Majesty.

In the year 1819 the revolutionary tendency of a faction in Germany (supported in an incomprehensible manner, even encouraged by many German Governments) brought upon itself by one act the universal attention of the world. The Russian councillor Von Kotzebue fell as the first sacrifice. Your Majesty will be pleased to remember that even before the journey to Italy the political horizon was so clouded that it became a serious question whether the absence of your Majesty from Germany would be prudent. My opinion was that by this journey more was to be gained than lost, and I grounded this opinion chiefly on the feeling that the absence of your Majesty would deprive the German Government of its first and strongest support, and the danger of the position in which error and an inexcusable lukewarmness had placed them would have the effect of arousing their attention. My view was soon justified. Scarcely had we been six weeks on the other side of the Alps when the first communication was made from the Court which had thrown itself in the most decided manner upon the revolutionary path. Convinced that a first step must be followed by

other and more decided ones, I answered the Bavarian
Minister with great calmness, and with the expression
of your Majesty's readiness to come to the help of your
allies with advice and action on every occasion. The
Kotzebue affair occurred in the meantime, and the votes
gained in strength and number. Wurtemberg, Baden,
Hesse, all turned to us, and I proposed to your Majesty
in the month of July my journey to Carlsbad and your
Highness's return to Vienna, instead of the projected
stay at Milan.

The Carlsbad Congress had the most happy results,
far surpassing all expectations. It led to the confirmed
conviction that the strength and value of the Government measures depended far more on the correctness of
their choice than on their number. Four decrees were
passed at Carlsbad, a number which, taken in the abstract, could scarcely, from any point of view, be looked
on as considerable.

The Diet was the supreme authority, but no arrangement was made for carrying out its resolutions.
We accordingly planned at Carlsbad a provisional execu-
tive administration.

The German Universities, hitherto entirely left to
themselves, had Government commissioners set over
them as presidents.

All the journals and periodicals were placed under
censorship.

A central court of inquiry into the intrigues of the
demagogues was established at Mayence.

These measures, concerted at Carlsbad among some
of the German Courts, obtained the sanction of the Diet
on September 20. I then felt convinced that the moment was come to give to the legislation of the Diet the
perfection and firmness which it still so much needed.

It naturally appeared to me that this moment, on account of the widespread terror in all the German Government, was most favourable for extending the great work. I saw plainly that this work could not be accomplished by the legal jurisdiction of the assembly of the Diet. I felt myself sufficiently courageous for the undertaking, and I therefore arranged the German ministerial conferences at Vienna. The result fulfilled my hopes, and even some scarcely formed wishes. At the end of a few months the Diet received seventy freshly organised laws, which were agreed to unanimously. I then unfolded to the assembled German ministers my opinion that the organised legislation of the Diet could now be considered as perfected. The experience of the four years just passed has confirmed my view. The advantage which has arisen from the confirmation of this truth, and which becomes more apparent every day, is, the general tranquillity of the German princes about their separate relations to the Diet, and the different effect of the Diet on each German State, a tranquillity which the free development of this salutary system could alone make possible.

The resolutions of the Diet of the year 1819 have not failed in their effect on Germany, and have acted more or less beneficially on the whole of Europe. If the alliance of the European Powers has shown how beneficially the principle of strength gained by the union of many for the general welfare acts in relation to politics, the example of Carlsbad shows the world that the union of Governments for salutary legislative ends is not less possible, and is equally productive of results. The party whose aim is to disunite States as well as individuals has evidently received its death-blow. The truth of this assertion must be apparent to every impartial observer, for the great impression which the Carlsbad decrees made on this party, as well as the happy results which they practically had, cannot really be ascribed to the mere excellence of the laws of September 20, 1819—an excellence which they cannot possibly have in the eyes of impartial judges. Since the year 1819 the governing powers, especially in South Germany, have had to endure many hard trials from the representative government which they had introduced with such inconceivable thoughtlessness. Each one of the State assemblies has given proof of the melancholy truth that all governments introduced by themselves have been shaken to their centres, and that the evil ensuing has been incalculable. On the other hand, to the people the truth was clear that the promised good was an empty dream, a vain design, or an inconsiderate scheme projected by some few individuals in their midst. In the same proportion as light and self-respect spread amongst the rulers, loyal feeling awoke in the people.

Your Majesty may be pleased to remember that, soon after the fortunate termination of the expedition to Spain (the third revolution which in the course of two years has been crushed to dust and ashes), the Baden Court turned to us, and expressed the wish to go further into the matter, and by the united strength of the Government to find means to carry out some necessary reforms in the interior of the States. I still continued to tread with measured steps the path pointed out to me by my already fulfilled wishes. Constant to the principle that with men and States alike dependence is to be placed on the exertion of their own strength rather than on borrowed help, I believed I ought not to press further than absolutely necessary. In time and what it brings forth lay much good, which I endeavoured to help forward, but by no means to anticipate.

I followed the advice which your Majesty had been pleased to give me of employing my attendance on his Highness the Grand Duke of Bavaria to obtain fresh information about the disposition of that Court. Your Highness knows that my hopes were not great of the Bavarian officials, but they far exceeded the reality. Without wearying your Majesty with the details of my negotiations in every place, I will hasten on to the results.

Your Majesty will find enclosed a work (No. 722) which I induced Freiherr von Zentner to give me at the Tegernsee as his proposal. This work being pure in design and powerful in expression, I took it as the basis of my future transactions. I wished to compromise Bavaria so deeply in the matter that it would be impossible for her to turn back.

Your Majesty will find in the larger paper Baden's feeling on the Bavarian question. . . .

On the day of my departure from Johannisberg the Grand Duke of Weimar came to visit me. I immediately secured him.

Your Majesty will also find enclosed the Presidential proposition which had been already prepared, and which needs no commentary. I have grounded it on the work of the Bavarian Court, and only developed it more thoroughly. It needs now only the Imperial sanction of your Majesty. The German princes will take it without opposition, and agree to it thankfully.

With reference to its effect on the separate German States, I can only add that in the beginning of the year 1825 the next State assemblies will take place in Bavaria and Baden. At these meetings the Governments will begin the reforms originated by the late decrees of the Diet. In the reformed regulations, publicity of the transactions will be forbidden; the daily disregard of this has been the cause of great evil latterly. By this means the possibility of the necessary reforms is increased, and they will be made either voluntarily or by compulsion.

I beg your Majesty to examine the Presidential proposition, and to return it to me either with or without your Highness's remarks. After having your Majesty's sanction, I shall immediately have it copied and sent to Freiherr von Münch. I should wish to accomplish this not later than August 9 or 10.

METTERNICH.

I send back the papers enclosed, and you can now despatch the sketch of the Presidential proposition. Your exertions to maintain peace and order in the world have not been in vain. May God crown them with success!

FRANCIS.

Persenberg, August 5, 1824.

722. [The paper by Freiherr von Zentner on the extension of the Carlsbad Decrees is omitted as being uninteresting and almost unintelligible to English readers.—TR.]

Metternich to Baron Münch, Ischl, August 8, 1824.

723. His Majesty the Emperor has been pleased to return the sketch of the Presidential proposition, not only without objection, but with expressions of the greatest satisfaction with the whole work. Your Excellency can now proceed to carry out the business, choosing the day which seems to you most suitable.

With regard to the publication of the Presidential report, I am more and more convinced of its necessity. However much I agree with the principle of reducing

as much as possible the number of publications at the
Diet, it does not appear to me that this applies to a
document of such great importance as the present. In
this statement truths are set forth which cannot be sufficiently spread abroad, and the clear and direct language
in which they are expressed will certainly not fail to
make an impression both on the well-disposed and on
the ill-disposed. Moreover, it is next to impossible to
keep such a document long secret, the communication
of which to all the German Governments, great and
small, makes many copies of it unavoidable, and which
is of such general interest that we run the risk of
seeing it sooner or later appear in some mutilated or
unintelligible translation in the French or English journals. For all these reasons I consider the publication
of the Presidential statement not only useful but unavoidable, and I beg your Excellency immediately to
take the necessary steps.

Metternich to Münch, Ischl, August 20, 1824.

724. From your Excellency's Report of the 16th
instant I see with no small satisfaction that the Presidential proposition has had the success desired, and that
its proposed measures have been accepted without opposition or alteration by the Diet.

Congratulating your Excellency and ourselves on
this result, in which your prudent guidance has again
been actively experienced, I hasten to place you in a
condition to express the gratitude of our monarch before the conclusion of its session in reference to the
expression of thanks to his Imperial Majesty which
stands in the protocol of the Bundestag.

At the end your Excellency will be pleased to lay

before the Diet, in the form you think most suitable, that—

From the resolutions passed at the sitting of the . . . his Majesty has derived once more the happy conviction that among the enlightened German Governments the most perfect and happy agreement prevails upon those principles by the maintenance of which not only the security, the inner peace, and true well-being of the several States of the Diet are incontestably conditioned, but also the continued existence of the body which embraces all the power and interest of Germany. This conviction alone, long cherished and now confirmed, could alone have inspired his Majesty with the courage and confidence with which he has hitherto invariably advanced in all the negotiations of the Diet. His Majesty would also, further, ever continue in the same disposition, and esteem himself fortunate to be able on every occasion to respond to the confidence of his august brethren in the Diet.

What I have further to remark in this business, so happily terminated, I put off till I receive your further accounts, and till I return to Vienna.

Metternich to Gentz, Persenberg, August 26, 1824.

725. The reception vouchsafed to me by the Emperor was of a nature to delight me, and that particularly because it showed me the great value which he attaches to the Johannisberg business. To value anything so highly its essence must be perceived, and that the Emperor does most thoroughly. He said a few words to me on the general position of things in Europe which hit like a sledge-hammer; the nail is driven in right up to its head, and that is why it is so firm. Unhappily, I had brought to me a few hours ago the printed Report of the sitting of the Diet, and a French translation of the Presidential proposition from Frankfurt. I send you both without loss of time, in order that the German version may appear in the ' Observer ' as soon as possible.

PRUSSIA'S AGREEMENT WITH AUSTRIA IN GERMAN POLICY.

Letter of King William III. of Prussia to Prince Metternich, Berlin, September 29, 1824.

726. The results of the labours which have occupied you at Johannisberg * have given me the greatest pleasure. I thank you above all for having succeeded so well in assuring and confirming the most perfect union in the views and interests of Prussia and Austria. The more value I attach to this union the more I appreciate the trouble that you have bestowed on the matter, and I find the great esteem I have so long entertained for you only the more justified. Assuring you again of my sentiments, I am, &c., &c.,

FREDERICK WILLIAM.

Answer of Prince Metternich (without date).

727. The letter which your Majesty has graciously condescended to send me overwhelms me with gratitude for the justice which you render to the principles which direct my labours.

My life, Sire, for some time, has had but one aim—that of assuring, by my feeble efforts, the noble cause which the monarchs, for the welfare of the world, have sought to maintain. Your Majesty knows that at the very moment when I was called to the helm of affairs

* See Nos. 721-25.—ED.

I based my policy on the most complete union between two States whose ever to be regretted errors had placed them in a rivalry which it seemed hardly possible for time to soften. My labours have been most happily crowned with the success which might be expected under the reigns of the Emperor and of your Majesty.

Allow me, Sire, whilst making this avowal, to entreat the continuance of that personal confidence without which I could do nothing.

Whilst asking this favour, your Majesty may rely on my remaining steadfast to the same line of action as that marked out by your Majesty and his Imperial Highness. As long as Prussia and Austria are united, and this union is clearly shown, every good thing will be possible to Europe. I am, &c.

ON THE PACIFICATION OF GREECE.

Metternich to Esterhazy, in London, Vienna, October 17, 1824.

728. The return of the Emperor Alexander to his capital will doubtless be marked by the consideration of the Greek affair between the Cabinet of Russia and the representatives of the four other Courts. I believe I should fail in a duty which the gravity and interest of the question imposes on me, if I did not employ the last moment which remains to us to establish a completely frank exchange of sentiments with the British Cabinet.

You know so well, Prince, our views and calculations during the unhappy complication in the Levant that it is unnecessary for me to enter into them at length. In your explanations with the English Ministers, however, you require to know our opinion relative to the position of affairs at the present moment, and I do not think I can explain these better than by the following sketch :—The foundation of our intervention in this question has been from the first that of entire confidence in the just and elevated views of his Majesty the Emperor of Russia as well on his own position as on the question itself. Our confidence has been found to be justified by the progress of affairs.

Having arrived at a point where it appears necessary to state the matter in clear and precise terms, we have proposed the separation of subjects which have hitherto been confused. Evidently these subjects were, on one side, the injury to the treaties between the Porte and Russia resulting from the enterprise of Prince Alexander Ypsilanti ; and, on the other, the insurrection itself. The Emperor of Russia, guided by his enlightened judgment, acknowledged our distinction to be correct. The other Cabinets accepted our point of view, and the renewal of diplomatic relations on the part of Russia was regarded as a pledge for the removal of the first of these difficulties.

The indefatigable labours of Lord Strangford, his character, and talents have enabled him to bring the affair to the first stage which we and our allies with us had regarded as most necessary. It would be superfluous to recount here the endless obstacles which the blindness, distrust, and jealousy of the Divan had thrown in the way of a work so beneficial for the Porte. Even now the complete evacuation of Moldavia is not accomplished.

I am anxious that the British Cabinet should be convinced, as we are, of the urgent necessity that the Cabinets should all agree on the following principles :—

1. With the resumption of diplomatic relations between Russia and the Porte, the political part of the affair is concluded.

I will speak afterwards of the contested points in Asia. They do not interfere with my calculations in the least. The form in which this first and principal part of the affair was treated placed Russia on one side and the Porte on the other. The allied Courts found themselves between the two Powers.

2. The part of the affair which remains to be arranged is the pacification of the insurgent countries.

Diplomatic relations being re-established, the former

attitude of the Powers is necessarily altered. Russia
finds herself face to face with the Porte on the same
line as her allies, and the allied Powers do not find
themselves placed between the Sultan and his insurgent subjects, but rather they face them both.

3. What do the Powers desire, and what ought
they to desire? They desire the return of internal
peace to the Ottoman Empire. This wish is not
grounded on an abstract idea of interference in the
internal affairs of a third Power, but in their own
interest, and for the maintenance of general tranquillity
in Europe. The Powers do not here place themselves in
opposition to the interests and rights of the Ottoman
Sovereign. They are, on the contrary, convinced that
they serve his interests and their own by a peaceful
policy.

By establishing these positions, by regulating according to them the starting-point in an affair of extreme delicacy and difficulty, the Cabinets are strong
with the strength of reason, and the weight of such a
strength cannot be calculated beforehand. It is, in fact,
on it that we rest our only hope.

There are still two very important questions to be
examined.

The first is whether the Cabinets may not regard
their intervention in the affairs of the Levant as terminated by the re-establishment of the ordinary diplomatic
relations between Russia and the Porte.

We do not hesitate to pronounce a most decided
negative. The insurrection of the Greeks in 1821 received its immediate impulse from the men of the hour.
Crushed in its first principles, it would have shared the
fate of the insurrections of Naples and Piedmont.

The whole of Europe, the public opinion of all

countries, takes part in an affair which has acquired a
general popularity. This popularity, we have no doubt,
is the fruit of profound ignorance ; but it has been
nourished and increased by parties to whom men are
nothing, and whose sole aim is confusion. It is still
increasing by the concurrence of benevolent minds,
always ready to yield to generous sentiments without
having duly examined either the facts or the inevitable
consequences of the illusions which carry them away.

If this disposition is more or less evident in the
different States of Europe, it should have been quite
otherwise in the Empire of Russia.

The merits of a sovereign who, placed in a position
like that of the Emperor Alexander, has constantly maintained principles as prudent as they are noble, are all the
more striking. To support the Emperor is a task imposed
on his allies by justice and sound policy. His Imperial
Majesty has given them pledges of his intentions worthy
of all gratitude. Honour and duty compel them to
serve the cause of the peace of Europe ; this cause is
that of the Emperor Alexander.

Austria, I need not say, does not run after business.
If that of which I treat were free to be left alone or to
be taken up, we should decide without hesitation to
leave it alone.

The second question to be examined is that of the
points in Asia which have been contested between
Russia and the Porte since 1812. This question is,
from its very nature, quite unconnected with the present affair. The labours of the Powers never have
affected, and never could be expected to affect, the
carrying out of all the treaties existing between the
two neighbouring Powers. By what right could the
Courts have given such an extension to the intervention

which they have exercised since 1821? Besides, far from raising any objection to the reservations made by the Russian Cabinet on this question in its diplomatic despatches, we have for our part constantly admitted and recognised them as just and useful. Affairs difficult in themselves gain nothing by being complicated by incidental questions. The Courts have never alluded to the stipulations of any treaties but those violated in consequence of the events of March 1821. They have not generalised the principle; they have, on the contrary, contracted it within well-known and easily defined limits. What they have not done hitherto they ought not to do in future. The idea of mixing up Asiatic questions with those which are foreign to them is Turkish. It is wrong in every way—

Because it tends to amalgamate matters of a different nature;

Because it is merely a weapon seized from panic;

Because, in short, the claim on which it rests is inadmissible. The Divan claims that the efforts of the Courts of Europe since 1821 in the interest of Russia shall now be turned in favour of the Porte. But if we are conscious that we have done much for the maintenance of political peace in Europe, we are no less certain that we have done no more for Russia than for ourselves, and much less than we have done for the Porte. The advantages of peace are not for the strong Power; it is the weak Power which particularly enjoys them; and if the Porte acknowledges that the maintenance of peace with its powerful neighbour may be partly due to the influence of the European Powers, it must also feel that without that salutary influence it would have found itself between the guns of Russia and those of the Greek insurgents. In the face of this, to call the maintenance of peace a service rendered to Russia would be both erroneous and ridiculous.

The conferences will be resumed after the return of the Emperor to St. Petersburg. Our most sincere wish is that the Cabinets may agree with us in regard to intervention. I have marked it out with precision and clearness. If we are deceiving ourselves as to principles, we shall be truly thankful to be enlightened. What is beyond doubt is the necessity for determining the course to be followed in this affair, and that can only be done by means of clear and precise instructions to the representatives of the Cabinets called upon to contribute them.

Metternich to Esterhazy, in London, Vienna, *October* 17, 1824.

729. I have in my preceding despatch, in an abridged form and official style, laid down the principles which we consider should serve as the basis of the next negotiation concerning the pacification of Greece. I have still to add some considerations which it would not be possible for me to do except in the most confidential form.

The British Cabinet will share our conviction that in the affair which awaits us there are two evident and incontestable truths. One is that good faith and the most perfect candour should preside over all the steps taken by the Powers; the other that, seeing the position of things and the character of the men who have to be gained over by reasonable and pacific words, this attempt, however well prepared and executed it may be, offers but slight chance of success.

The affair must, nevertheless, be attempted, because, if it is not, the Emperor of Russia cannot be delivered from the powerful and dangerous influences which, notwithstanding the wisdom and purity of his intentions, would cause a breach between Russia and the Porte. I much desire that the British Cabinet should attach the same value as we do to the classification of subjects made by us in our explanations with the Cabinet of St. Petersburg : namely, that whenever the first part of the long and complicated negotiation which has occupied us for three years—that part which we call political—is terminated by the fact of the re-establishment of diplomatic relations between the two neighbouring empires, Russia should regard herself as re-enrolled in the ranks of the allies, and placed on the same line with them. This formality—and it is much more than a purely logical distinction—connects Russia with the party ; it serves and strengthens the moral attitude of its monarch ; it offers and secures to him the power of moderating the natural impulse of the different classes of the Russian nation in favour of a rupture with the Porte.

We do not conceal from ourselves that it is more than doubtful whether the pacification of Greece will ever be brought to a satisfactory conclusion by means of a negotiation to the success of which the very elements are wanting.

The Porte, like the Greeks, will not yield to the proposals, however just and wise they may be. The Divan will refuse from habit, from indomitable pride, from its natural spirit of jealousy, which constantly prevents the very services the Powers· wish to render it from being regarded otherwise than as a pretension on their part to dictate as to its internal affairs, or a mask to cover some secret and ambitious views. The

Turks, in short, always see in an affair what is not there, and never see what is there in reality. The Greeks, on the other hand, will not listen to a proposal which does not rest on the principle of political independence, or—what comes to the same thing—which does not show that the Powers have determined to regard the Ottoman Empire as extinct in Europe. But even if a definite arrangement of the affairs of the East is prevented by insurmountable difficulties, it is still of the greatest importance to prevent new and unhappy complications in the future—complications which the united action of the allied Powers can alone prevent.

By a right and vigorous management of the negotiation the Emperor of Russia—who, as we firmly believe, aims neither at conquests nor at the thorough emancipation of the Greeks and the establishment of a new and revolutionary Power—will find means of justifying himself, by arguments founded on a sound policy, from what the popular voice in Russia will not fail to call indifference to Russian interests and desertion of his co-religionists. If the Emperor were not strongly supported by the counsels and language of his allies, this voice would end by defeating the firmest intentions of his Imperial Majesty. Any false attitude which the Courts might take, any appearance of indecision in the choice of that attitude, would offer dangerous facilities for the plans of the too numerous partisans of a war between Russia and the Porte.

I confess, Prince, that, with the feeling which I have of the extreme difficulty of the affair, it is only the conviction that the political peace of Europe would be at an end if it were not approached seriously that has decided me to direct to it the attention of our

Cabinet and that of our allies. Will war between Russia and the Porte be avoided by any diplomatic steps we may take? I cannot take upon myself to say; but what is clear to me is that, by a clear agreement between the Powers, the dangers will be diminished, the chances of the maintenance of peace augmented, those of war will become much less formidable, and in short, by a well-concerted plan, the Courts will preserve a liberty of decision and action which would be greatly curtailed if the only Power prepared to break with the Porte were obliged to consult merely her own interests and her own difficulties.

We have seen with satisfaction that the Cabinet of London is ready to enter into conference with that of Russia and with the three other Cabinets; we regret, on the other hand, that its first declarations on this subject have been accompanied by the assurance that, if the results should not justify the attempt, Russia will be regarded by England as mistress of her own movements, and that Great Britain will not interfere. An assurance of this kind does not serve the cause which the Emperor Alexander happily still regards as his own—that of the maintenance of political peace. Let us not deprive this monarch beforehand of the support which he may one day seek in the solidarity of a pacific policy between him and his allies. When that day comes, when war breaks out in the Levant, when the Ottoman Power is in danger of being driven back into Asia, and when a long series of convulsions will be the inevitable consequence of a change which will alter the present territorial boundaries and many political relations, both maritime and commercial—in that day will England be contented with the *rôle* of a benevolent spectator, quite uninterested in these vast changes? We not only believe that she does not wish this, but we are quite convinced that she could not do it. This is the crisis which we would prevent ; against this our cares and efforts have been for years and still continue to be directed, and this is the object in which we ask our allies to second us with all their might.

As to questions of detail and execution, we have given our ambassador at St. Petersburg directions which appeared necessary and sufficient for the opening and the earlier part of the conferences. We cannot, however, hide from ourselves that another work not less important and perhaps more difficult awaits us. It may be foreseen that as soon as the conferences are resumed the Russian Cabinet will ask for the opinion of the allied Courts on the plan of pacification which it communicated to them last February. The British Government, having announced the despatch of Mr. Stratford Canning with the express object of his assisting at the conferences, we must suppose that it has furnished him with instructions concerning this essential part of the deliberations ; and if such is the case, which we do not doubt, it would be of great interest for us to be previously informed, so as to judge how far these instructions agree with those which we ourselves addressed to that Minister, under the form of observations on the Memoir put forth by the Russian Cabinet.

I authorise you, sir, to allow Mr. Canning to read the present despatch, and to request secrecy as to its contents. You can understand the great value we must attach to a reply from him which would enable us accurately to judge of the feelings of the British Cabinet on a number of questions important for both Governments. We have explained ourselves to the Courts of Russia,

France, and Prussia on the terms of the preceding despatch. If I require from the Principal Secretary of State secrecy as to the confidential overtures contained in the present despatch, it would be superfluous to say that we bind ourselves to equal discretion on our part ; that is understood, and is customary with us.

METTERNICH'S AGREEMENT WITH PRUSSIA IN ORIENTAL POLITICS.

Metternich to Baron Werner, in Berlin, Vienna,
October 23, 1824.

730. I take advantage of the return of a Prussian courier to send you the present despatches. This is a moment of the gravest importance; a glance at the position in different parts of Europe makes it impossible to doubt this.

In France a new reign has just commenced. This event, which a few years ago would, no doubt, have borne a totally different character, now demands the consideration of the Powers.

England, which since the ministry of Mr. Canning has wandered in the paths of a false and dangerous Liberalism, gives us some hope of a return to sounder principles.

Spain is lost in the depths of moral and material disorder which, as it cannot be explained even by persons on the spot, can still less be judged of at a distance with any justice.

The Eastern Question has reached its first stage. Conferences relating to its second stage are already opened at St. Petersburg. The preservation of political peace will depend on the solution of the questions to be submitted to the Courts. Happily, Europe presents a concord between these same Courts which nothing has hitherto disturbed, and under the shadow of which the political and social reconstruction of the Continent will be attained. This concord has resisted the attacks which error, party spirit, and sometimes the views of a false policy have directed against it. The peace of Europe and the health of the social body will not be permanently disturbed as long as this concord exists. Convinced of this truth, our efforts should be to cement it; and, with this end in view, I beg of the Prussian Cabinet to take into mature consideration the confidential communications which you have to-day received orders to make. You will find enclosed a despatch which I have addressed to Prince Esterhazy and to Baron Vincent on the affairs of the Levant (No. 728). I beg the Prussian Cabinet to study this despatch carefully, for it shows our views with regard to the second stage of the affair, and is of such a nature that it can respond to it conscientiously. You can testify that this is the result of the extensive knowledge we possess of the position in Russia and elsewhere.

We may deceive ourselves; but it is at least in good faith, and we are not conscious of error. Every Cabinet, like every man similarly placed, must expect, must even desire, that those whom it wishes to share its opinions will point out to it how it is deceived, if it is so, when it believes it is keeping to the strict line of truth and right. If the Prussian Cabinet shares our views wholly or in part, it will direct its representative at St. Petersburg to express himself in accordance with this despatch, which will serve as a guide to our ambassador in Russia, whenever the conferences concerning the pacification of Greece are resumed.

You will find in the enclosure II. (No. 729) a secret despatch intended to be read only to Mr. Canning. It has been drawn up with the sole object of enlightening the British Cabinet, and of guarding it against any false interpretation of our policy. England is called upon to play so decisive a part in the affair that our efforts must be particularly directed to her. I beg from the Prussian Cabinet the most perfect secrecy as to the confidential communication I have made of this despatch. It is not always possible to speak the truth aloud; it is sometimes and in some places indispensable not to hide it.

It is not needful for me to inform the Berlin Cabinet of the position of things in Turkey. The reports of Baron de Miltitz keep it perfectly acquainted with all that is going on there.

The reports which I have received from Paris since the arrival of Count Zichy present a number of ideas which I have been able (No. 731) to compress into the short statement enclosed. I have no doubt it is perfectly correct. I beg you to show it to M. Ancillon. No action is called for on our part at a moment when prudence and confidence allow the Courts to take an expectant attitude only.

The protocol of the Conference of October 12 on the position of things in Spain will have been sent from Paris to Berlin as it reached us. We entirely approve the judgment and the decisions of the Conference.

Will you be good enough, sir, to ask the Prussian Cabinet to inform us, with as little delay as possible, of its opinion on the different affairs mentioned in the present despatch? It will be of great value to us by confirming the opinion we have formed already.

FRANCE UNDER CHARLES X.

A Memoir by Metternich, October 23, 1824 (enclosed with No. 730).

731. Never has an accession to the throne of France been accompanied with more perfect calmness than that of Charles X., and yet at the death of Louis XVIII. many people were afraid that this crisis would produce a shock which would shake foundations so new as those of the restored French monarchy. At the time of the King's decease some timorous Royalists talked of a proclamation, of the necessity of having out the troops, and receiving their oath. M. de Villèle opposed all these measures; and was wisely of opinion that the principle of the continuity of possession ought to be consecrated, and that the simplicity of a venerable custom would give to the new Power more real strength, than precautions which betrayed a want of confidence. The result has proved in favour of this calculation. Charles X. is peacefully seated on his brother's throne. This quiet change, which makes an historical episode of the revolution, undoubtedly proves that moral regeneration has made some progress in France. The firmness which Louis XVIII. displayed in his last moments has flattered the French self-love. The first appearance of the new King has been brilliant; it has satisfied everybody; it has produced a universal enthusiasm, which has been contagious even to the opposite party. And we may believe that the temporary suspension of the liberty of the press has not injured this success.

The fact is that Charles X., from the first moments of his reign, has evidently aimed at obtaining a popularity which he has really acquired, and which, in his position, is undoubtedly beneficial. It remains to be seen if he has not made too many concessions, and gone perhaps a little too far in his attitude—one might say his advances—towards the Left.

M. de Villèle felt this so strongly that, without waiting for a remark on this subject, he hastened to assure Count Zichy that this condescension of the King towards notorious Liberals was simply to facilitate their return, but that they must not suppose that his Majesty had any tendency towards their doctrines.

If this marked affability towards individuals who are only known by their perverse or erroneous opinions is merely to open a door for their repentance, conduct so moderate can only be praised, and the fruits of it are already felt, for the same men who so recently prophesied that the reign of Charles X. would be a reign of priests with a counter-revolution are suddenly metamorphosed into panegyrists of the new King. But many reflecting persons cannot see without fear as to the consequences so flattering a reception given to the coryphæi of Liberalism. Charles X. is frank, loyal, amiable, chivalrous, and religious; but at the same time he is weak, accessible to insinuations, self-willed and even violent in his prejudices. All this makes one dread a mobility in the conduct of the Government which is dangerous to authority, and a want of power to resist the Liberal influence which the Dauphin seems to exercise over his father.

The Liberalism of the Dauphin is a fact. It remains

to be proved whether the ideas of this prince have been
radically corrupted by the men who surrounded him
during his campaign in Spain, or whether it is a part
which he has adopted in the vain hope of forming an
intermediate party, in which he can unite and amalgamate all the Liberal and Royalist interests, both ancient
and modern. It appears, however, more likely that
this prince, loyal and brave, but commonplace, acts
from conviction. With a little sagacity he would soon
be convinced that his system of amalgamation is built
on the sand, and that a fusion of heterogeneous elements of that nature is impossible. It is, however, on
the opinions of the Dauphin that the Liberal party specu-
lates; and this blindness partly explains the eulogiums
which the Opposition showers on the King, and the attentions bestowed by the King on the Liberals.

The knot will be disentangled in a few weeks, for
the ministry will be obliged to act. Then the elements
which have been mixed, but possess no affinity, will
separate of themselves.

In the meantime all parties, both foolish and wise,
unite to overthrow the ministry—that is to say, M.
de Villèle. This minister, after several mistakes, appeared to have adopted the only line of conduct
suited to a statesman, and in spite of his awkwardness he is at this moment the only man whom those
who wish rightly can desire to see in power. He
seems to be tottering, however, and it is generally
believed that he will lose his post, either immediately
before, or immediately after the opening of the Chambers. In truth, the party opposed to him is too strong.
The Dauphin does not like him, and has shown his repugnance on more than one occasion. Although the
King sees in M. de Villèle the principal author of the

good understanding which has existed during the last
few years between him and Louis XVIII., and knows
that he owes to him the evident amelioration of public
feeling, this minister's loss of credit with his Majesty is
nevertheless perceptible ; and it is to be feared that the
influence of the Dauphin, who takes his seat in the
Council, will be able to overthrow him. The title of
Royal Highness accorded to the Orleans branch and the
abolition of the censorship of the press are two measures, of which the first has been adopted without the
knowledge, and the second against the advice, of the
ministers.

In the event—which is very probable—of the dismissal of the present ministry, the new ministry will
be formed either by the Dauphin or by the King. If
by the first, we may expect to see a semi-Liberal
semi-Royalist concoction ; if the King forms the ministry without his son, we can hardly foresee what
choice he will make, but no great things can be expected from many of his old Royalist friends. In the
meantime intrigue is in full force, and the party of
discontented Royalists includes M. de Bruges, Marshal
Soult, the Duke de Fitzjames, and M. de Vitrolles in
the ministry. That party which in France will most
need a thorough reform is the department of Foreign
Affairs. According to people who may be supposed to
know, the composition of this department is more than
mediocre ; and, unfortunately, there seems to be no one
capable of bringing it out of this state and following
a firm and substantial system. M. de Chateaubriand is
certainly not the proper person for this work—who sometimes runs to Mr. Canning, and sometimes imagines he
is acting according to the views of the Emperor of
Russia because he happens to agree with the opinions

of a Russian diplomatist. M. de Damas must have felt very much out of place as Minister for Foreign Affairs— a post for which the career of arms gives no preparation. In truth, his vague, reserved, and uncertain language denotes the embarrassment of his position, and already public opinion destines him to the command of the army of occupation in exchange for the portfolio.

Spain is at present the subject which occupies the meditations of the French Government most painfully. In a conversation which Count Zichy has had on this subject with M. de Villèle, that minister deplored the conduct of the King of Spain, open as he is to all counsel, the bad as well as the good. Being at length convinced of the enormous expense which the occupation is to France, the President of the Council hinted to M. Zichy the necessity of diminishing the army of occupation, limiting it to the holding of certain strong places, and massing the troops so as to be able to retreat. M. de Villèle proposed immediately to send M. de Talaru to Madrid, without, however, hoping much from the efforts of that ambassador.

For the rest Count Zichy found M. de Villèle very correct in his ideas concerning harmony in the political proceedings of the Courts.

THE ST. PETERSBURG CONFERENCES.

Metternich to Ottenfels, in Constantinople (confidential letter), Vienna, December 18, 1824.

732. I have nothing particular to add to my despatch of this day, except that the early arrival of Mr. Stratford Canning seems probable. After many tergiversations and all sorts of evasions, Mr. Canning seems to have at last decided to send this diplomatist ; or, rather, the Cabinet has forced the inclinations of the Principal Secretary of State.

The most recent news from St. Petersburg proves to me that the delay in the evacuation of the Principalities and the affair falsely represented by M. Pisani have not produced on the Emperor of Russia the effect which no doubt the Hetairists desired. The desire to end the thing predominates with his Imperial Majesty, and the day that by the renewal of her diplomatic relations Russia is replaced in the ranks of the allies will be a happy day for him. This is the true state of the case ; do not be misled by any appearance to the contrary. If you have an opportunity of explaining this to M. de Minciaky, it will do no harm. It is not for me to point out to him what he should do in circumstances which must be difficult for anyone in his position. But he should know that I understand the Emperor Alexander, and that we are determined to maintain his cause with justice and vigour. My words, therefore, cannot be misunderstood. You must, however, use a certain reserve in a thing of such a delicate nature. I leave all this to your good sense and knowledge of the world.

The affair at present is the division of subjects. It is important that the conferences at St. Petersburg should be opened promptly. Constantinople will sleep until a new impulse arrives from St. Petersburg. That this may be salutary it must be regulated and arranged as a whole and in detail, and to this end we must meet and debate. Here you have our policy complete ; every other is false in principle and wrong in calculation.

1825.

ILLNESS AND DEATH OF PRINCESS ELEONORE METTERNICH IN PARIS.

Extracts from Metternich's private Letters from January 12 to April 20, 1825.

733. Anxiety regarding Princess Eleonore. 734. Impending journey to Paris. 735. The Greek question. 736. Journey to Paris. 737. Melancholy feeling. 738. Death of Princess Eleonore. 739. Travelling plans. 740. Russian projects for coercive measures against Turkey. 741. Sad position in Paris. 742. Journey to Milan. 743. Departure of Metternich's daughters. 744. Despatches to St. Petersburg. 745. Villèle. 746. Departure for Milan.

733. *Vienna, January* 12, 1825.—I begin to have serious fears on account of my wife's health. I have known for some time that she had fallen very much out of health ; but her present state seems to me exceedingly critical, which touches me more deeply than all the events in the world. I can bear much without bemoaning myself, but I bear my cross more easily when I can impart my cares to a sympathetic heart. If the lungs are really attacked, nothing more can be done ; if the cause of the suffering lies elsewhere, she may be preserved to me. In so painful an uncertainty I know not where to turn my thoughts, and this anxiety is most painful. It requires the greatest devotion to my official duties, to the business which requires me here, not to leave everything and go immediately to Paris ; but I will not come to a decision till I can see more clearly.

Stratford Canning approaches his destination, and will not be well received in St. Petersburg. His cousin has taken a most hazardous step in sending him. Here I expect De la Ferronays. Things go better in Paris, worse in London. With the Englishman I have had my tussle; with the Frenchman I will fraternise. When Stratford Canning heard that De la Ferronays had come to Vienna, he said it must be supposed that the French Government had been induced to take this step in consequence of the resolutions come to in London. I answered that he might be quite easy on the subject, for I had myself invited the Count.

734. *January* 30.—My anxiety respecting the condition of my wife grows greater and greater. In consequence of the tender care practised in my family I have no direct information. The physician, Bourdois, was going to write to me, but he was prevented, lest it should make me anxious. I am sending a courier to him, with strict orders that he should tell me the truth. If I have to go to Paris, my journey will excite Canning's attention immensely; he will think the one sad cause of my journey only a pretext. That he is quite mistaken is immaterial to me, and on the whole will be no bad thing. Anxiety is often only a just punishment. According to Canning, Pozzo will rejoice the least at this. His reign is over in Paris, and will not return for a long time in St. Petersburg. As to the first circumstance, I have remarkable evidence. He will believe that I go to Paris to give him his deathblow, and God knows I have no such intention.

735. *February* 3.—The Greek question is clear and simple, if one is not afraid to look it in the face. I do not understand the part that Wellington plays; when not on the battle-field does he lose the energy he there displayed? There is military genius of a certain kind which depends on its artillery, and is nothing without it. Wellesley, who thinks as I do, wishes to retire at once; but I hold him back, because it is a bad plan to give pleasure to your opponents, and certainly in London they would not feel hurt by Wellesley's retirement.

736. *February* 8.—The news I have of my poor wife from the physicians determines me to go to Paris now, and then meet the Emperor at the end of March at Milan. I do not know quite certainly—I do not know, that is, whether the invalid's danger is immediate or remote.

737. *Paris, February* 14.—I am troubled to the very depths of my heart, and at the present moment good for nothing. Face to face with a catastrophe the prospect of which filled me with sorrow, I find myself, after thirty years of undisturbed married life, reduced to a frightful isolation. What shall I do with my daughters? To give them over to a governess is a very insufficient remedy, although I will never separate myself from my children. What sad blows has not my heart already endured from fate—everything has happened to me—to me, whom the world calls a fortunate man! What must it be to one who is called unfortunate!

The French journals busy themselves with my arrival, and put their own construction upon it. In London still more importance will be attributed to my sudden appearance in the rival capital. People are always uneasy when they are in the wrong; and if Parliament had not assembled, Canning would find an excuse to make his appearance here also. I am sorry that circumstances prevent his coming to meet me.

Seldom have two ministers taken more different stand-points in the same city than we should have done.

738. *March* 29.—I have sustained an irreparable loss; Providence has so ordained.* It is not for the survivors to give way to expressions of just lamentation when the best of mothers has parted from her children without a word of complaint. This mother died as she lived—her heart and her temper remained the same to the last moment. Her last days were occupied in giving pious counsels to her children for their guidance through life, in thanking me for what I have done or not done for her, in blessing and comforting all those for whom alone she had lived, as if the separation from her were not the cause of our most bitter sorrow. From her childhood deeply religious, she felt towards God as a child to a father. She went home to Him, not as before a judge, but in the calmest confidence in His fatherly goodness. It was the departure of a fair saint (*einer schönen Seele*) !

I shall send my daughters back to Vienna; my son will accompany me to Italy, and, as the Emperor's journey to Milan is postponed to May 4, I shall not leave Paris till April 16 or 18. My residence here will not be without good results.

I am writing to the King of England and to Wellington, who have invited me to London, to express my regret that it is impossible for me to go there.

739. *March* 30.—I shall probably remain in Italy till the middle of July, and then return to Vienna. From the middle of August to the beginning of September I will go through the course of waters at Ischl, and then establish myself again at the Chancellery.

* Princess Eleonore Metternich died in Paris, March 19, 1825. See No. 748.—Ed.

For some time past I have been trying to think of some plan for restraining the English policy within certain limits. Whether the means I have thought of are feasible remains to be seen; it will require great harmony among the Courts, for, if it is easy to agree on principles, it is often much more difficult to come to an understanding on details of a subordinate character.

I prepare many embarrassments for Lord Granville, telling him some truths to his face with the most good-humoured air, some truths which throw him into amazement, because he does not comprehend that certain things can be said which I am not able to be silent about. It was very confusing for him when he heard from me that I cannot comprehend and positively cannot make out certain emanations from the English policy, adding that it was probably my own helplessness and incapability of discovering it that made me feel as if I were thrust to the wall. This, of course, had the result of a change in the parts, and excuses and protestations were heaped upon me. His arguments led him into a hole, out of which he could not get till he had as good as acknowledged that the policy he had been defending was wrong. Having arrived at this point, he left off; but I took no notice, and continued.

I have lived to see most remarkable things in England. The present ministry begins to see more clearly, and will certainly bring about many beneficial things if it is not thrown out first. Of society I see only those who call upon me, and I see them separately. Men of all shades of politics meet in my anteroom, and certainly many of them have not met before for a long time. Thus the Archbishop of Paris and the Napoleon-ist De Montholon come to me, and the Legitimist De

Bonald, and a September man named Jullien. Contrasts can indeed go no further, for only extremes come to see me ; the red and white Doctrinaires shun me like the plague. Chateaubriand gives no sign of life.

740. *April* 2.—The postponement of the departure of the French courier who takes this letter to Vienna makes it possible for me to write to you. The courier takes instructions from the Cabinet here to the French ambassador in Constantinople, Guilleminot. I send mine to Ottenfels. They are very short. I did not know how to say more, and I doubt whether I shall find anything more to say when I know what the instructions were which were sent from St. Petersburg. I know everything that has taken place to March 16 inclusive. I imagine that you have already received reports from Lebzeltern. These cannot, however, teach me anything new. One's hair need not turn grey on account of the views, or rather the feebleness, of the Russian Cabinet as to coercive measures, for it is so unpractical that it can hardly take a rational form. When things are in such a position one need not take the trouble to point out that they are impossible ; it is better to leave the party that supports them to show that they are possible, and this I will do, according to time and opportunity. I propose to his Majesty to appoint Count du Montel to be commissioner to Greece. I know of no better man ; and then he is here, and can receive the necessary instructions from me. Moreover, if this commission prospers I shall be very greatly astonished. Canning seems to take pleasure in approaching the Eastern Question. My idea would be to leave him alone ; the more this is done the more closely will he draw in.

I am extremely satisfied with my present position.

The most thorough harmony prevails between the ministers and myself. I experience this in the most important questions, especially the Eastern Question. A reflection of these happy relations is seen in the proceedings of the French ambassador at St. Petersburg, and the same will be seen at Constantinople. My presence has been very beneficial to mark out and limit the standpoints clearly, and my expectations in this matter have not been disappointed.

741. The situation here is still very sad. If the good and evil peculiar to States like England and France can be said to be calculable in England, in France they are incalculable. A drama or a farce: nothing more; and yet the position in which France has been placed is the best that could have been done for the country. The only man whom I have discovered here among the crowd is Villèle. He has a firm will, and therefore all hope need not be given up. The Chambers are only there to make certain matters easy and others difficult: to make easy the laying on the people new taxes; difficult, the regulation of the people's well-understood interests. And here we have, they say, the highest social civilisation!

I have dined to-day in the Palais Royal, with the Duke of Orleans. The Duchess * I like very much. She is one of my oldest friends and a thoroughly excellent woman. We spent the evening together; and the Duke showed me his fine collection of modern pictures, among which there are many very pretty ones; the expression ' beautiful ' is not applicable to the present school.

742. *April* 7.—I shall remain here ten days' more, and then fill up the rest of my time with *détours* on my

* Marie Amalie, a Neapolitan princess, married to Louis Philippe in 1809.—ED.

way to Milan. My heavy baggage I shall send over
Mount Cenis; but I shall myself drive in my son's
calèche, by way of Marseilles, Nice, and the Corniche
to Italy. My son-in-law will take my daughters to-morrow to Vienna, and thus gives me a proof of his great
attachment. He is one of those people who are always
in a hurry; and for him to take ten days to get over a
distance which he could have managed in six is certainly
quite a hardship.

My life is portioned out as follows: I get up at seven
o'clock and write till ten, when the most remarkable
people come to me, many of them quite strangers to
one another—ministers, place-hunters, ultra-Legitimists,
Bonapartists, Jacobins, and Jesuits, a complete valley of
Jehoshaphat; at one o'clock I endeavour to get rid of
all my visitors, and go for a walk, to see how Paris has
altered in ten years. There is plenty of fine material.
At six o'clock I go to a not very agreeable dinner. At
nine I go home, or join some of the men whose company
is pleasant to me, like Bonald, Franchet, Rivière, Mathieu
de Montmorency, &c. There we analyse the perfection
of social institutions, or discuss the history of the time,
and these are my only happy hours.

743. *April* 9.—My daughters left us yesterday; the
parting with their brother was sad. For three years he
has filled the place of a father to them, and they love
and honour their brother as a real father; Victor is
a handsome and excellent young fellow. God preserve
him!

From morning to night I must unhappily be in the
world. People will give *soirées* in my honour, which
are worse than *soirées* in general. There are certain
persons whom I cannot refuse. Yesterday I was with
the Viscountess de Laval. Her house is the one where

for forty years Talleyrand held his court. The hostess, mother of the Duke de Montmorency, is infinitely *spirituelle*. We were eight men, Talleyrand being one of them.

(*To Gentz.*)

744. *April* 11.—To day I send despatches to St. Petersburg, and order Stürmer to let you see them. I think you will agree with all the views therein unfolded. If I were at St. Petersburg, I would conduct the contest quite differently; but, being at a distance, the direction of affairs must be entrusted to third parties, so that I must confine myself to principles. My principal object is to gain the strongest diplomatic position, and that is always the defensive. Besides, Lebzeltern puts all questions so clearly, and is so courageous, that I have no anxiety about the conduct of the affair.

I beg you to notice the English 'Courier' of the 6th inst. Canning must find that it is far easier, with his principles, to trifle with the Powers and with good men than with a revolutionary Republic. I am excogitating the working-up of a good article upon this happy state of things for a journal here; but how I come to do this is one of the signs of the times, and of my environment. I could write a volume about this; but, as I shall see you so soon, I will not give myself the trouble. Time for this, too, is wanting. Certainly, if I required more evidence than my inner feelings that I fill a quite peculiar, definite position in the world—a position shared by no one—my residence here would have served to inform me.

My relations with the ministry and with the King are assuredly without example. Things look so differently when one embraces only a period of time, or when one mixes in the common life which comes with a longer residence. People look upon me as a kind of lantern, which they approach to get light on a dark night. I cannot otherwise describe what I daily experience. Villèle and Damas are always running in and out to ask me questions which, God knows, are easy enough to answer. If I give a decision, they think it grand, when I should be ashamed of myself to do otherwise. It seems that the worthy men, instead of answers to their questions, are accustomed to hear the very convenient 'I don't understand.' I am not guilty of the crime of using such words, and so they discover that the lantern really gives light—of all the duties of a lantern surely the commonest.

So much is plain to me, that an ambassador from any Court whatever who is in the right—that is, who wishes what is good and knows how to speak it out plainly—must here play a great part. This part would have been excellently played by Pozzo if he had condescended to this fundamental condition ; but he is always in the wrong, and if an affair is intelligible to the bystanders, it is not from Pozzo's help. And it has now come to that with Pozzo, that if he *par hasard* speaks for once without personal views, nobody believes him. His money speculations have injured him more than anything, although he has become immensely rich. He is largely interested in the loan to the Cortes. Just imagine what must be their thoughts about his support of the Legitimists ! The increased intimacy which has grown up between the Purist party and myself has for me the greatest interest. This intimacy will have its results. The men who are at the head of that party force themselves upon me with the greatest confidence, and I now see through their actions, their plans, and their hopes as if I had been here for years. For the present moment let it suffice for them to be certain that here in the centre of all mischief, another disciple of the good cause has been made, and that his progress is as vigorous as it is practical. Action is characteristic of the French, and with empty words they are never content. I see a great deal of Bonald ; he interests me very much, and he is far more practical than I had believed. At the same time he is in many things of a crass ignorance that one only finds in France. He falls into a kind of stupid amazement at all that I know, and yet I may asseverate most solemnly that not a single case has arisen between us which to have been ignorant of would not have been perfect stupidity on my part. The reason why evil makes such rapid strides so easily is simply this, that it is only necessary to be an ignoramus to step out like a hero.

Bonald lately said something very fine, which is universally applicable. He says, *Le particulier des sots —et ils forment la majorité dans la société—c'est leur propension à découvrir les difficultés dans les bonnes choses, et les facilités dans les mauvaises.* (The peculiarity of fools—and they form the majority in society— is their propensity to discover difficulties in what is good, and facilities in what is bad.) This is a true saying ; it quite applies, for example, to the course of the English ministry. In the Alliance it finds everything difficult, and in its relations with the Liberals, on the contrary, everything easy.

A very practical man is Franchet. He is quite young, and a very pleasant, even light-hearted, man.

Yesterday I had the honour of dining with the King. Since the monarchy there have been only two examples of a private person dining with the King—the Duke of

Wellington in the year 1815, and subsequently Lord Moira as a personal friend of the family during their exile. The occurrence makes a noise here, too. I am certain the report will be renewed that the freedom of the press has fallen a victim to yesterday's dinner!

Peru has now gone the way of all flesh. I encourage them here to a step with respect to the Spanish Government, which is merely to inquire whether they are also ready to give up Cuba in the same way—that is, to do nothing to keep it?

745. *April* 12.—The present ministry is decidedly the best since the Restoration. It consists, however, of merely one man, and has a very difficult position. Amongst the ministers there are always some who, at a very critical moment, do their best to get into his place. The strength of Villèle consists in something he said to me lately. When I asked him, quite openly, 'Shall you remain, or will they turn you out?' he answered, 'I am determined to remain, and a determined man is not easily put on one side.'

746. *April* 20.—To-morrow I shall start, take the road I mentioned, and by May 8 meet the Emperor at Milan, the day of the Emperor's arrival at Monza. August I shall spend in Ischl. There is some talk of summoning the Hungarian Landtag in September. If that happens, I shall hardly have the necessary time to visit my estates in Bohemia.

RESIDENCE IN PARIS.

747. *Paris, March* 17, 1825.—I arrived here on the 14th inst. The state of my wife's health is, unhappily, what I had only too well foreseen. Her dissolution draws near with rapid strides, and if there be a respite it can but be of hours or days. The sad object of my journey, and the dangerous state of the invalid at the present moment, give me natural ground for declaring that I shall live in the closest retirement.

The good disposition in our favour has, under these circumstances, been very plainly shown. Immediately after my arrival I received the visits of the whole French ministry, and, at a diplomatic audience which took place on the day after my arrival, the King sent Vincent to me to say that he would not fix on any hour for me to visit him, but that he would leave it to me to choose the time according to my private engagements.

Yesterday I paid my respects to his Majesty. The King received me with extreme graciousness, spoke to me of the great confidence he has in your Majesty's firmness, and repeated at different times, as well as at the beginning of our conversation, ' his conviction that your Majesty is the grand support of Europe's salvation, and that duty and prudence must lead all the Powers to unite with confidence in Austria's policy, which, amid all the pressure of the times, has always shown itself true and sound.'

Hereupon the King took the Order *Saint Esprit* and presented it to me, saying that he had long desired to repay an old debt of recognition ; that he had intended to give me this Order at his coronation ; but he was too glad of the opportunity of bestowing it earlier and personally. Himself placing the Order around me, the King said, ' Take this as a sign of my gratitude and my friendship ; these you have earned from me personally, for I only bestow them where I believe them to be well employed, and I now offer them to you without reserve.'

I answered his Majesty as my own feelings prompted me, and added that I received the Order with the conviction that your Majesty would see in the manner of this gift a confirmation of the King's continuance in the right path.

After the audience, which lasted nearly two hours, and which I can best describe by assuring your Majesty that the King in every respect answers to my desires, I went to the Dauphin, the Dauphiness, and the Duchesse de Berry. I found the Dauphin very much embarrassed. His expressions were generally good, but guarded. The Dauphiness talked with me much and with affection of your Majesty, and their feelings of gratitude. The children, the Duke of Bordeaux and Mademoiselle, entered during our conversation. They are both small and delicate.

The Duchesse de Berry received me in the most friendly manner, and spoke heartily of your Majesty and the whole Imperial family.

With Villèle and Damas I have already had several conversations which have given me great satisfaction. Both receive me frequently and in the most confidential manner. I found the ideas confirmed which I had formed regarding them. Villèle is a man of large and penetrating understanding; Damas is simple and straightforward, not much known in his profession.

The whole attention of French policy is fastened on two things : the conclusion of the Greek affairs, and the course of English politics, especially with regard to the American colonies. The fate of the continent seemed to be decided ; the defeat of the Royal party in Peru left it no longer doubtful. Only Cuba and Porto Rico still remain under the dominion of Spain, and all information prepares me to expect the insurrection of the latter province. What an unhappy influence these events must have on the fate of civilisation is only too easy to calculate ; and how culpable is the man who now guides English policy and leads it utterly astray is no less certain. An insurrection in Cuba is, however, feared by Canning as much as anything can be feared, for its inevitable and speedy result would certainly be the same fate for the English colonies in the West Indies.

Grounded on these circumstances I have formed a scheme which I will take into consideration here on the very spot where only it can be carried out with speed and success. The first and most necessary thing is to provide Spain with money, but at the same time making sure that it is put to the right use. I do not doubt that I shall be able to accomplish something. It is with me just now as it has been at many periods of the greatest importance—that is, many desire the same, but none of them know how to manage it. So, God willing,

I will find out what is possible; man cannot do more. In respect to this business my arrival has also happened at a moment as important in itself as it is sad in my private position.   .

Meanwhile I am still only in the preliminaries, for I must myself feel my way. My quite free position makes many things easy, which would be difficult to others, for people come to me with confidence. Men here seem to be like sponges, which are greedy to suck in ideas. I will not neglect to give them what I can.

Prince Paul Esterhazy came here yesterday to stay a few days. He crossed, on the way, an intimation from me to remain where he was. He was sent directly from the King of England to request me to proceed to London. Enclosed your Majesty will find the letters of the King of England and the Duke of Wellington. Your Majesty will please to remember that I foresaw that this would certainly be done. Prince Paul explains to me the hopes which the King places on my appearance in London : his Majesty believes, that is, that it would be easy for me in two or three days to finish Canning's moral education. If he should not take it in good part, this would give ground and occasion for getting rid of him. How trifling, or, I might almost say, how senseless is this idea, need hardly be insisted on. I shall send back Prince Esterhazy in a day or two to express my regrets to the King and the Duke of Wellington that I cannot respond to their views, but I shall also point out to the former how far the evil must have gone to have made the appearance of an Austrian minister in England an impossibility. The invitation is very fortunate, for it necessitates a refusal; and, from the knowledge of things that I possess, I may say, without going too far, that this is a heavy blow for the English ministry, and it shall be my care to take advantage of it. In a few days I shall have the honour of giving your Majesty a further account of the general state of things.

METTERNICH.

I see with pleasure that you have made yourself acquainted with the state of things in France, and the manner in which the King has received you. God grant that we may be able to prevent or turn into good the evil arising from Canning's attitude and proceedings!

FRANCIS.

Vienna, March 27, 1825.

748. *Paris, March* 19.—The long foreseen calamity took place early this morning. The poor sufferer departed, as she had lived, peacefully, and with resignation to God's will. I had been for some time convinced that recovery was impossible, and my first glance told me that the hour of dissolution must be near. It was even delayed beyond what the physicians had thought possible. I have taken my children home with me, and shall keep them with me as long as possible; that is, as long as I stay here myself. My daughters I shall then send back to Vienna. My son I shall take with me to Italy. In what a sad position I find myself I certainly need not explain to your Majesty's fatherly feelings.

With great respect I beg that your Majesty will have me informed very exactly of the day of your Majesty's arrival in Milan. I will arrange my plans so as to meet your Majesty there.

METTERNICH.

As you know how great a share I take in all that concerns you, and have myself been placed in a similar position, you must be assured how great is my sympathy. Here religion, and the happy end of those who are dear to us, and whom we can no longer retain with us, are the only comfort. God keep your children in good health for your consolation!

I will let you know in good time before my arrival in Milan, which cannot, however, take place till the month of May.

FRANCIS.

Vienna, March 27, 1825.

749. *Paris, March* 28.—I send off the present courier, more with the intention of meeting your Majesty in Vienna than to make an exhaustive Report. This I shall not do till my arrival in Milan. I now limit myself to laying before your Majesty a general description of my present work.

From my Report of the 17th inst. (No. 747) your Majesty will have already seen that I was received here with great attention. Since my more intimate and repeated contact with the ministry, I find a strong confirmation of my original suspicions. I will divide my remarks into sections.

I. THE INTERNAL CONDITION OF FRANCE.

My feeling with regard to this your Majesty will see in the short statement in the despatch enclosed, which I sent yesterday to Count Lebzeltern at St. Petersburg.

In the descriptions it contains nothing is overdrawn. My feeling of the dreadful position of things is even stronger than I can express. I have known France under the Empire, and afterwards in the presence of the allied armies. After being ten years left to itself and the development of its constitutional relations, I enter it again, and I find things in a much worse state. . . .

It is only now that the consequences of the revolution can be correctly traced. All that is sacred has been loosened, and the system inaugurated at the Restoration, which unhappily was not suited to France, cannot restore anything of what has been lost. Thus society here loses itself in a conflict of passions, and under the influence of these passions the Government lacks all power to act beneficially in other ways.

This is a true picture; and when I admit it into a despatch to St. Petersburg, I do so with the intention that it should be a lesson for the Emperor. The will of the present ministers is good, but they have no resources at their command. They endeavour to procure them, but it will be a long time before they have any. It is difficult to form any idea of the demoralisation of the people. It will be sufficient to lay before your Majesty the following facts, which I got from the fountain head :—

The population of Paris may be roughly stated at 800,000. Of these 80,000 women and 10,000 men have no religion whatever.

More than a third of the population is unbaptised. The proper business for the religious at the present moment is to introduce religion. In the Quartier de St. Geneviève—where the lowest classes of the people live —it may be said that out of twenty households one consists of married people. At least half of them are not even to be found in any civil register. The only thing that can have any effect here is a religious mission like those sent among savages.

The system followed by the Government is decried and restrained by the Liberal faction.

In the course of the last ten years—consequently since the Restoration and since the freedom of the press, introduced at the same time—about 2,700,000 copies of atheistic, irreligious, immoral writings have been sold. That this trade is supported by the faction is shown by the fact that these works are sold at half-price to young people of both sexes, and they are often freely given away. In the higher classes the immorality at least is lessened by better education. But among these the greed of money and titles prevails. From the present Chamber of Deputies the Government has 220 petitions for the dignity of peer.

As a means of carrying out the laws the Government has made use of the coronation. The majority consists of individuals who hope to get their petitions granted on this occasion. The measures in themselves are generally considered bad ; but they are carried through, and the voters laugh loudly over the part they have played. That is to say, the whole work of the lower Chamber is a game, a kind of gambling, in which the so-called representatives of the common rights stake their wishes like the gold upon a faro table. The winners rejoice : the losers call names.

Meantime the present ministry is the first since the Restoration which acknowledges the evil to be an evil. The King himself thinks like the ministers. The Dauphin is the complete dupe of the faction.

II. Political Views of the Government.

These are clear and good. Not only have I heard nothing wrong, but much that is good and genuine. Villèle gives himself to politics in a way he could not do earlier : his expressed wish is the maintenance of political peace and the avoidance of possible frictions.

He knows that we see rightly, and he is therefore quite ready to go with us. . . .

Pozzo's influence is over. . . .

For the moment no one plays a political part except myself. In this respect I am rather embarrassed, for, in spite of my strict seclusion, the French ministry itself puts me forward.

III. MY NEGOTIATIONS.

These are limited to three matters—

1. General principles ;
2. The Eastern Question ;
3. The English-Spanish Question.

As to the first, I have not much to do but to strengthen the views on these subjects, and explain those principles which are not already known. Where this is really desired it is always an easy business. In the Eastern Question France goes entirely with us. Your Majesty knows that I have always considered this as a matter to be manipulated, and so it will be definitely solved. The third question is the most difficult and the most real, but I shall accomplish some good in it. My intention is to obtain some sort of division of the question of the maintenance of the Spanish islands still under the authority of the King from that of the colonies on the American continent. I have unfolded my plans to the present ministry, and they have entered into them with satisfaction. Pozzo follows me; he knows nothing to substitute for my proposals. Between this time and my departure the attempt will so far have afforded light that I shall be able to see whether anything new can be done with Madrid and London. I have more fear of Spain than England. On the affair itself I shall not be able to give your Majesty satisfactory explanations till my arrival at Milan.

METTERNICH.

750. *Paris, April* 1.—Through the courteous communication of the French ministry, I learn the first resolution of the Conference of St. Petersburg. Your Majesty will have received this information from Lebzeltern's Report, which he will send direct to Vienna.

The representatives of Austria, France, and Prussia have done their duty. In an intricate question the best has been attained, and no more was possible. All ideas turning on coercion are false and, rightly viewed, impossible. It is, therefore, hardly necessary to consider them. If they are brought forward again from the Russian side, there is one very simple rule to follow—the Cabinet which brings them forward must be left to show their possibility.

In the whole affair there is but one means and one end. The first has been adopted ; the second is our proposal of January 15. Everything intermediate is mere illusion, and on closer examination will always be proved so. . . .

I have not, so far, discovered any difference between the views of your Majesty on the Eastern Question and those of the Court here, and I am convinced of a thorough agreement of judgment and desire. The choice of a thoroughly suitable person for the mission to Greece is very difficult. I respectfully propose to your Majesty Lieutenant-Colonel du Montel. He possesses the necessary qualifications ; and then he is here, so that I can give him all the necessary instructions. I will, therefore, beg your Majesty graciously to confirm this choice. The whole mission will do nothing more than demonstrate that with the Greeks there is no possibility of negotiating, and this is the true solution of the affair.

The postponement of your Majesty's arrival in Milan places me in the very unusual position of having too much time before me. I cannot remain too long here, and I have no business in Milan before your Majesty arrives. I think, therefore, of leaving Paris on the 16th, and, instead of taking the direct road by Lyon and Chambéry, I intend to go by Marseilles, Nice, and Turin. In this way I can fill up the eighteen days between April 16 and May 4. The only inducement which might keep me here beyond April 16 would be some matter of business which at present I do not foresee. In any case I shall meet your Majesty on your arrival at Milan.

I send this Report to Vienna by a French courier, who is taking the French instructions to General Guilleminot. They are in spirit the same as ours, as well as everything that goes to St. Petersburg.

METTERNICH.

I approve the choice of Du Montel for the mission to Greece.

FRANCIS.

Vienna, April 14, 1825.

751. *Paris, April* 11.—I have every reason, so far, to be satisfied with my stay here. It will certainly have good results, for there is no single object of importance which I have not been able to clear up and set going.

The King is quite devoted to me, and he expresses this openly. Of this proofs are given which are not without importance in a country where courtier manners unite so easily with revolutionary feeling. Thus, for instance, the King invited me to dinner—a distinction

which, I believe, has, since the establishment of the
monarchy, only been extended to two private persons—
the Duke of Wellington after the battle of Waterloo,
and Lord Moira, as the personal friend of the late King
during his exile.   The dinner was quite *en famille*, in-
cluding only the King, the Dauphin, the Dauphiness,
and the Duchesse de Berry.   The Royalists exalt the
fact to the skies, and the Revolutionists believe that now
it is all up with the liberty of the press.

I will not attempt to give an account of my political transactions till I have the honour of meeting your
Majesty in Milan.   The ministry is in the best temper.
From Vienna your Majesty will receive the copy of a
despatch to St. Petersburg which I am sending there.
I have fixed on the 18th inst. for my departure.   I
take the road by Lyons, and instead of going over Mont
Cenis I make a *détour* by Nîmes, Marseilles, Toulon,
Nice, Savona, and Alessandria.   This will fill up the
time between April 18 and May 5, on which day I
shall meet your Majesty in Milan.   The road by Nice to
Turin is rather shorter, but at this time of year it is
often bad travelling over the Col di Tenda.   From
Savona to Alessandria there is no delay, and the *chaussée*
of the Corniche goes as far as Savona.   I am very glad
to see this neighbourhood, and it is an excellent time
of year.   For political reasons I must not stay here any
longer; people would attribute my long stay to some
motive which must remain without result, and I have
no reason to be in Milan before your Majesty.

I receive invitation after invitation from the King of
England.   He has gone so far as to propose to go to
Brighton, to allow me to avoid London.   But I have
been obliged to repeat my refusal.

MeTTERNICH.

752. Paris, April 17.—On the 15th I took my leave of the King and the Royal family. It would be difficult for me to show your Majesty all the good which has been effected by my residence here in every political respect. My position at Paris was no common one. If I wished for material proof on which to ground my conviction that the moral position of your Majesty in Europe is unequalled either in the past or in the present, I might here find it a hundred times over. Only to the minister of a Court equally trusted and honoured can people behave as they have done to me here. The King, the ministry, and all the well-disposed have come to me in a way which shows on what a high level Austria now stands. To estimate this high position rightly one must take into consideration the old prejudices, rooted in the feeling of the people here for centuries, against the predominance of the Austrian power. Of this feeling I have in the whole mass of people with whom I have come in contact found no trace, but I have found it everywhere exchanged for the most obliging confidence.

After my arrival in Milan I shall make it my duty to give your Majesty a detailed report of my stay here. I require for this purpose a leisure which I cannot find, and even if it were at my command, I would not commence the work till my residence here is concluded. In situations like mine the last hours are generally the most fruitful.

This much will suffice temporarily to assure your Majesty that the feelings and views of the Government, and of both parties in it, are plainly visible to me. I know the state of things now as if I had been here for years. In regard to the political standpoint of the Government little more remains for me to wish.

I will arrange my journey so as to arrive at Milan on May 8 or 9, which according to the last accounts from Vienna is the date appointed for your Majesty's arrival at Monza.

METTERNICH.

Noticed and approved. I hope to meet you at Milan after a prosperous journey.

FRANCIS.

Verona, April 29, 1825.

753. *Paris, April* 20.—I have put off my journey till to-morrow, because I could not find time for a conversation with M. de Villèle. There is now not one dark spot in diplomatic matters here.

On taking leave, the King gave me the enclosed letter for your Majesty. I send it on, for I am certain it is written with the best feeling.

Sir Charles Stewart has arrived in Portugal. The reception given to him was good, and his speech is no less so. The result remains to be seen. I have brought about the most thorough concord between the views of your Majesty and those of the Cabinet here on the Brazilian question. After I had settled this with them, I endeavoured to draw General Pozzo into it. If one may trust his words, he is gained over, and the progress of the affair will be thereby much improved. In any case the possible happy termination lies between Lisbon and Brazil.

It is a singular thing that one can with difficulty decide whether Bolivar's victory in Peru is true or not. Many things speak for it, many things against it. In a few days we shall see more clearly. I have done all that is possible here to bring about a reasonable course of proceeding in the Spanish affairs. Yesterday a conference about them was held, at which I was not present, because I do not wish to take any part in conferences.

On all these things it will be my duty to give your Majesty the fullest account. Nothing is altered in my travelling plans. I shall certainly keep to Lyons. At all events, I shall be at Milan either before your Majesty or at the same moment.

METTERNICH.

754. *May* 8.—I beg respectfully to inform your Majesty of my arrival in Milan yesterday. To-morrow I shall have the honour of paying my respects to your Majesty.

METTERNICH.

I expect you with pleasure.

FRANCIS.

Monza, May 9, 1825.

FROM MILAN AND ISCHL.

Extracts from Metternich's private Letters to Gentz, from June 16 to August 16, 1825.

755. *Milan, June* 16, 1825.—During my stay at Genoa the English frigate 'Naiad' came in; her captain (Spencer)—the same who made the last arrangement with Algiers—had just come from Greece. He told me as follows: In the middle of April he was with Ismaël (Ibrahim) Pacha before Navarino, and at the beginning of May with the Pacha who went against Missolonghi. Spencer assured me that the success of the two operations may be relied upon, for they are very well conducted, and, besides, the Greeks have no material of war, although none of them (and especially the garrison of Navarino) are in want for courage. Resources they have none, for everything out of the English loans of current money was divided among the Government officials. The regularity of the Turkish operations is alone to be ascribed to the European Liberals, who have all entered the Turkish service, although at home they act the Philhellenes. All the Frenchmen go to Ismaël Pacha. All Frenchmen join Ismaël Pacha; all the Carbonari join the Albanians. He (Spencer) expressed his surprise to many of them, but he always received for answer that they should go where money was to be got. They were well paid by the Pachas, and, besides, they sadly plundered the poor Greeks, so much so, indeed, that the Turks handled them in a far more Christian manner than the Philhellenes.

. . . As *petite pièce* Spencer told me that nothing pleased him more than the numerous bands of music which the Philhellenes had introduced among the Turks. In all the Mussulman camps they played nothing but Italian marches and airs. Captain Spencer had just as bad an idea of the Greek fleet as of the means of defence on land. He has now set sail again, and is to cruise in Greek waters and protect the trade which the Greek privateers have lessened day by day. In his opinion it is impossible for the Greeks to make a stand if the Turks continue to operate as they have done since the opening of the campaign. Every other word was always, ' The people have nothing, just nothing.'

The history of the Greek insurrection will be a very curious one. Spencer asserts that before his departure from Greece, in the middle of May, not a fight had taken place, either by sea or on land, except some unsuccessful sorties of the gallant garrison of Navarino.

I beg you to write these facts to the Internuncio ; they may be useful to him.

Our residence in Genoa will have good results. It would not be possible to earn a greater success than has the Emperor. The King is excellent, and the Prince de Carignan, who was in some fear of the Emperor—and of me, too, they say—has behaved very well. He said quite openly his *pater, peccavi,* and he seems quite determined to be a dupe no more. If ever the contrary happens I know not to which party his evil star will bring him—his late friends know him through and through.

I have passed many hours with him, and he has related to me stories of the *boutique libérale,* such as I had never heard. Among others he told me very important circumstances in the behaviour of the Duke d'Angoulême and his fine head-quarters. As to experience, he had made use of his residence with the French army and at Paris; and he speaks openly of the things, which gives him quite the appearance of a reformed character. If he is not so, he has at any rate no excuse on the Emperor's part, and still less on mine. '*J'étais la dupe,*' he said to me on taking leave, '*et je l'ai été en plein. Aujourd'hui je ne veux plus l'être et je ne le serai plus. J'ai appris à connaître le libéralisme et ses patrons, et j'en suis dégoûté.*'

His behaviour is in general quite true to these principles, and the King shares my feeling that he will not be caught again. God grant it! [See No. 789.] I have fixed my departure for the 1st prox.

756. *June* 30.—According to my last news from Paris, Villèle's system, which is so much attacked by the bankers, and especially by Rothschild, makes much progress. James Rothschild writes to me ' he can now assure me Villèle has gained his suit; the *rentes* will do very well, and Villèle will get the better of all his enemies because he is right.' In Paris Rothschild said to me, ' Villèle is wrong.' This is often the way with the world's judgment.

Nesselrode has lately written to Tatistscheff and given him the following account of Stratford Canning's last appearance at Warsaw. Stratford Canning wrote to Nesselrode from Moscow and told him that he had received communications and overtures of the greatest importance, and would therefore betake himself to Warsaw. After his arrival he explained that he had nothing to say, but to learn whether it might not be possible for Russia to come to an understanding with England on the means of making an end of the disorders in the Levant. Whereupon Nesselrode told him that the Emperor Alexander would never separate himself from his allies, and that it was open to England to join the common cause. The day following the Emperor begged Stratford Canning not to remain longer in Warsaw, as he had nothing to do there, and his presence could only give occasion to false impressions. Whereupon Stratford Canning departed.

The affair is doubly remarkable as showing both how mistaken Canning is, and that the Emperor's attitude is correct. But between a correct attitude and knowing what is wanted, and especially how what is wanted is to be carried out, there is a very wide difference!

757. *July* 3.—I write to you still a few words on the evening before my departure. I cannot take the Stilfser route, for in the last few days the Adda has overflowed, so that several bridges have been destroyed. I shall therefore cross the Splügen. Our whole diplomatic corps is dispersing. Hatzfeld is at Teplitz to preach to the King; from thence he will go to Carlsbad. Caraman goes by the Riviera to a family meeting at Zurich. Tatistscheff visits Carlsbad. The Wellesleys are at Genoa, and go from there through Tyrol to Weinhaus. Bernstorff also makes a sentimental journey along the Riviera. The newspapers will say now that the Congress is sending out its spies.

Postscript.—Cardinal Albani, who as Papal legate was sent here to compliment the Emperor, has also departed. I have for many years had the most friendly relations with the Cardinal, and he therefore visited me very often. When Albani, a little while ago, informed

me of his approaching return to Rome, he said to me
with a certain solemnity that he was commissioned by
the Holy Father to ask me a question. He then took
out of his pocket an autograph letter from his Holiness,
and begged me to make myself acquainted with its contents. In it were the few lines as follows : ' I have received with pleasure your confidential communication
respecting Prince Metternich's desire to be admitted
into the College of Cardinals. The Prince [here follows
a list of my meritorious actions] has so many claims to
this dignity, that I am ready to bestow it upon him.
But before I can nominate the Prince, be good enough
to ask him whether he really desires the Cardinalship,
in which case I will propose him in the next secret con-
sistory.'

You may imagine what an impression this overture
has made on me. I begged for an explanation from the
Cardinal, and he answered that he had inferred my
desire from some of my expressions—that is, from my
expressions concerning a red colour, which in talking to
the Cardinal I had mentioned as extremely pleasing to
me. The answer which I gave to the friendly interpreter of thoughts I had never had, you may well imagine.

758. *Mals, July 7.*—I left Milan on the 4th dined
at a charming villa of the Duchess Vincenti's on Lake
Como, and slept at Villa Trotti, at Bellagio. On the
5th I visited Villas Melzi, Pallavicini, Sommariva, and
some others, and went by Colico to Sondrio, where,
after a warm reception, with a great opera, illuminations, &c., I passed the night. At Bellagio I heard that
the road by Bormio is again passable : I therefore preferred it to the Splügen. At Colico good but distres-
sing Dr. Sacco waited for me and obliged me to go
through a part of the swamp with him. Happily, the

malaria did not seize me. At Sondrio, where we arrived
at ten o'clock I found the whole town in uproar. All
the preparations had been made for the reception of the
Emperor, and he had not come, so the inhabitants satisfied themselves with my humble self. Illuminations,
fireworks, operas, deputations—everything must I swallow.

After a bad night, we set out at five in the morning,
and arrived in the afternoon about four o'clock. I made
the journey without the least trouble in my great travelling coach and six, not wanting any extra horses.
We breakfasted at your former lodgings.*

Now listen to my opinion.

The Lake of Como is one of the most magnificent
works of nature and of art. I do not think you have
seen the villas, the most celebrated of which are Villa
Sommariva and Villa Melzi: the first is on the left bank
of the lake, opposite Bellagio, and has, besides other
advantages, a climate just of the kind I like. All southern plants grow here, and the difference between Bellagio and Tremezzina is exactly the same as between
Como and Naples. The Veltlin is a poor and even barren valley. I should not like either to live or die there.
The smallest valley in Tyrol is a paradise compared
with the Veltlin fifty miles long. But, on the other
hand, the people are so thoroughly Austrian in their
feelings that I cannot help loving them. The new road
is an imposing and splendid work; but it has two parts.
The Italian side is excellent; the northern I very much
fear will not remain as it is now. The nature of the
mountains is such as to render an alteration of the present road quite necessary; this can, however, be done
so easily that I cannot understand why it has been

* Gentz had formerly travelled by this road.—ED.

made as it is at present. By taking a new line twelve turnings would be avoided, and the ground would doubtless be much more firm. At the Cantoniera, where the engineer is living, and still higher up, the two roads would meet again. To-day the weather has been splendid, nevertheless we could not see the top of the Ortler, which was lost in a heavy mist. Some flakes of snow fell, but the road was perfectly dry. On both sides of it the snow forms walls as high as a man, which were pointed out to me by the engineer under the name of Gentz's snow. But you are also remembered in a quite different way. The engineers have been talking to me incessantly of ' Signor Consigliere,' and *ha fatto* or *ha detto questa o quella cosa* was always on their lips. I am very anxious that one of our papers should mention these great works, which are executed daily, and which are never allowed to be put clearly before the public in our dull atmosphere.* The air of Vienna is in some respects like that of the Alps.

All the pamphleteers of the world are telling us that we only know how to gain a thing, and not how to pro-fit by it. If you look closely at the course of human affairs you will make strange discoveries—for instance, that the Simplon Pass has contributed as surely to Na-poleon's immortality as the numerous works done in the reign of the Emperor Francis will fail to add to his. This fact irritates me, and helps to make me unhappy, like the ringing of bells at Milan. On the Stilfser I have discovered a rock on which, to take revenge for once, an inscription shall be engraved in letters twelve feet long. This rock shall tell posterity who

* At this time Metternich wrote an essay on the Stilfser road, in the *Beobachter* of August 4, 1825.—ED.

made this road, and when. As the letters shall be cut out two feet and a half deep, and twelve feet high, nobody will efface this inscription.

759. *Ischl, July* 13.—I received your letter to-day. I can only tell you my first impressions, but experience has taught me that my first impressions are generally also my last. What has been done in the affair? A refusal has been given which from the first was more probable than an acceptation.* The case in itself remains unaltered, like other things which cannot alter to him who truly and firmly stands up for truth. It is a very unpleasant truth that we stand so alone, although I do not want France.

I am sorry that you do not know the last instructions from Paris for La Ferronays. I have not a copy of them, or I would send it you; but trust my judgment, and believe that never was sounder work sent out. Damas says the same, but enters much more into details, and so energetically that nothing remains to be desired. Particularly ' *les mesures coërcitives* ' are declared by the French Cabinet to be thoroughly unsound. I am not in a hurry to send off anything to Lebzeltern which could be considered an instruction. What sort of one could I give? Everything is included in my two last despatches. What I said in the last of these, ' *La Conférence délibérera avec plus de facilité quand elle connaîtra la réponse de Constantinople— celle-ci fût-elle même mauvaise,*' will be proved right. The Conference has too much to do to take notice of empty words; it must turn its attention to facts. What is possible between the lines drawn by Russia herself? Not a war with the Porte, nor emancipation of the

* The Porte had rejected the principle of intervention recommended by the Powers at the Conference of St. Petersburg on April 7.—ED.

Greeks. The Emperor Alexander's idea is intervention on his side and the solidarity of the allies, as with the Austrians and French in Spain. This idea will surely find expression, and if I were a member of the Conference I would start it myself, because it goes against all common sense.

I predict that our fight will take place on this ground, although a mere chimerical one. My batteries are drawn up, and I am going to put the question in a practical way, as follows :—

Russia wishes for an active intervention. The Powers cannot act against their conscience. The question remains whether Russia will operate alone? If this is her intention the allies can only take a position outside, not against, these operations. These Powers will be Austria, France, and England. Prussia can be consulted only as to her moral support, as the Emperor Alexander cannot ask her for auxiliary troops !

The position I have imagined must be grounded on the following basis :—

1. A guarantee that Russia does not cherish any idea of conquest;

2. That she asks no indemnification for the expenses of war ;

3. That the commerce of the neutral Powers remains undisturbed ;

4. That the Porte, whatever the result of the intervention may be, shall be protected against any violation of her prerogatives.

Could you imagine such an agreement ? It is beyond my power. However, no other resource is left to the Emperor if he will act, and ' *les mesures coërcitives* ' are doubtless action. Of course I could never propose such a position, but it is a rock against which the waves will break themselves. The rock does not challenge the sea; the sea dashes against the rock. The consequence of this plan is that we cannot give up the affair. No! we have to wade through the mud as long as we can. My last despatches to Lebzeltern will prevent our losing the right direction. The whole affair is in every way bad, mean, and disgraceful. There has never been such a position in the world as that now adopted by the Conference at St. Petersburg. If one of the lesser Powers had raised such claims we could have smiled at it, and taught it to behave better; but this is not the case, and when a Colossus like Russia, not knowing what it wants, only follows the instinct for motion, policy drifts about as if in a whirlwind. It will be difficult to attain our end, but God will support me and give me power to guide the helm of State safely. I can assure you that the present affair is not more perplexing than if I had to write a very intricate melodrama; it will therefore have no bad influence on my use of the mineral waters, and a little salt will not spoil my despatches. These are my first words. In due time the next will follow. The separation from the Emperor will be useful. In St. Petersburg I will not put forward any vile Metternich ideas, but only the most noble and imperial; but in Paris I will take the lead.

Tatistscheff has news from Warsaw. Either he has received no answer to my communications or he has kept the answer back. If anything has been said, it must be idle words, for the Emperor was delighted with the course of affairs in the Landtag. The Diet of Hungary may be very useful to me in order to prove—if, indeed, we wanted such proof—that we cannot undertake any military operation. Here a purely Austrian consideration confronts the so-called Russian considerations; and wherever two equal powers meet, repose must be the result. I shall write to Constantinople, requesting as a favour to Austria the dismissal of the Beschli-Agas.[*] So much can be said in behalf of this measure that I shall find no difficulty in doing so. It is now with the Greeks as I have always told you it would be. There is no power of resistance in the majority of the nation, and the more separate parties a revolution has, the worse it will fare. Never has the Greek insurrection presented to my eyes the idea of a compact body; neither is the so-called Government a compact body any more than the Parliament at Naples, in spite of its big words, has been a Roman Senate. A great difficulty in the scheme of pacification proposed by the Powers is the nomination of Ibrahim Pacha to the Pachalic of the Morea. He is not likely to give up his reward so easily. In St. Petersburg, where ideas are easily confounded, this appointment will be considered as a union between the Morea and Egypt.

Nesselrode's idyllic journey to visit his farms near Odessa is a very good omen. At any rate, he is in no hurry: that is to say, the Emperor is not. September will be the critical month; if we get safely through September and October, we shall have gained the field. Do you remember that about the end of February I talked to you of a crisis we might expect in the autumn? I am not at all taken by surprise.

It is really a misfortune that I cannot return to Vienna by Johannisberg. I should meet on the Rhine the King of Prussia, Count Bernstorff, and the Grand Duke Constantine. This would have enlightened me

---

[*] The Beschli-Agas were the commanders of the Beschli, a troop of police-military organisation.

very much. I ought to be always *en ambulance*, like the hospitals in time of war. The politics of the day belong to such institutions. My journey to Paris has been invaluable in every point, and if it is still regarded in St. Petersburg with jealous eyes, this must be more from instinct than calculation.

760. *July* 24.—I hear from Lebzeltern that on July 5 the last news from Constantinople had not yet arrived, but I foresee that the news, when it does come, will produce but little effect. The Emperor will probably say, ' *Je vous l'avais prédit,*' and so saying, console himself. The power of events is too great, and can be as little resisted by the autocrats as by the ' Philistines.' Our merit in the whole affair is and has been the strengthening and perfecting of this power. If Bernstorff had been in Vienna, God knows how affairs would have stood with us to-day!

Senfft takes this letter with him to Vienna. He wrote some very good notes concerning Paris. All his views of the ministry and the political course of affairs are perfectly right. He only talks foolishly with respect to the Jesuits ; but everybody has his weak points, and it is far better that these should be connected with important than with foolish things. The King of Sweden has sold two ships of the line and three frigates to the Mexicans. The Spanish ambassador at Stockholm has objected very strongly to their putting to sea. The Swedish ministry has not yet answered them, and will hardly be able to do so. I do not dislike this affair, since it brings Charles Jean to maturity.

761. *August* 1.—Yesterday I received very sad private news and very good political news. The death of Prince Ruffo is a real misfortune for me. I lose in

him a true friend of twenty years' standing and a fellow-labourer in the Lord's vineyard, and, although he had been for some time morally enfeebled, he can never be replaced, if only because in his position another man may be hurtful to us instead of useful.

My political news are in the main as follows :—

1. My last despatch to Paris has met with entire approval. France is willing to follow in our footsteps, leaving to Russia to come forward with her proposals at the Conference, and to charge the ministry, which certainly knows not what it wants, with the burden of being forced to think.

2. The last instructions of Lebzeltern have been dis-cussed between him and Nesselrode. Nesselrode re-ceived them with a bad grace, and Lebzeltern inquired whether he (Nesselrode) flattered himself that, if the question of war were started, Austria would take it up. Upon this Nesselrode was silent, but sighed deeply.

Two days after my instructions from Milan those of the French Cabinet arrived. Nesselrode was quite wild about them, and as submissive about ours. He said to Lebzeltern, ' Prince Metternich has never changed his opinions nor his language; it is quite different with the French Cabinet : people there do not know what they want.' When Lebzeltern wished to know his opinion of what was going to happen, Nessel-rode answered again, with a deep sigh, ' *Je regarde l'affaire comme manquée.*'

This judgment is true without being profound! The definition of this ' affaire qui est manquée ' would be far more difficult. Hang me if I think Nesselrode could give half a reasonable one !

La Ferronays has been with the Emperor Alexander

before going to Carlsbad. The Emperor did not mention the Greek affair at all. Ferronays, who was determined to hear about it, asked at last if he should undertake his journey or whether he should remain in St. Petersburg to be present at the Conference. The Emperor told him to go, for the Conference was not to be thought of before September. (Here is a hint of a September as long ago as February and March.)

762. *August 5.*—The last news from the Levant is most interesting. Putting aside some incomprehensible mistakes the Porte has committed, I considered the affair there quite settled. Ibrahim Pacha is master of the Morea, and if the fleet of Kapudan Pacha had arrived with him before Nauplia all would have been lost. I think we shall very soon hear that Ibrahim has advanced again with a stronger force against this town, and if the fleet arrives at last, that will happen which has been so long brewing. The most probable result will be an agreement between Kolokotronis and the Pacha, and the year 1825 will only see a repetition of the same events as have occurred in all the former insurrections in Greece. This has always been my opinion, based upon the conviction that present events differ only outwardly from former events, and if there is any other difference it is this, that the strength and vigour of former times have given place to bombast. Hence it comes that events very quickly cover a vast space, but, like water, they lose in strength what they gain in extension. This feeling leads me logically to believe that, in spite of appearances to the contrary, the events of to-day can be far more easily overcome than of old. Why, then, are they not overcome? Because of the general weakness and shallowness of men, and because those who ought to lend a

helping hand are as miserable in their defence as their adversaries in their attacks. I consider myself, therefore, stronger than most of my contemporaries, because my nature leads me to an unconquerable hatred of empty words, and always prompts me to act. Think this over, and you will find that I am right, and that this is the cause of my moral calmness. This calm is only the continual feeling, which each day strengthens, of the misery of all affairs now in motion. Unhappily, I am too old to see their final solution, which will consist in a universal repose. But this repose will only be fatigue and the kind of disgust which follows upon long and resultless struggles. The only condition under which the course of events could take another turn would be the appearance of a truly great man in an elevated position. If nature can produce him, he will strangle the bugbear of this day as Napoleon crushed those of his and would have saved the world had he not been a very small man endued with great qualities and still greater faults. This is truly my confession of faith !

The day after to-morrow I will send Prince Esterhazy to London with his statement on taking leave. You will be satisfied with my despatch, and with my treatment of Canning, which is according to his merits. Nesselrode, however, is firmly convinced that I am his accomplice. If men who guide the helm, or at least are close to it, are clear sighted and well informed, their daily action cannot be incomprehensible. Equally luminous with his judgment on me are Nesselrode's views on Turkey, Greece, Spain, Portugal, America, and in the highest degree those with regard to his friend Pozzo, who perplexes him thoroughly; he perceives that he has entirely lost ground in Paris, but does not

know how to explain the phenomenon. Being very
sentimental, Nesselrode weeps over the boundless in-
gratitude of the French to their deliverer. A few days
before my departure from here I shall send a courier
to Lebzeltern ; and I shall doubtless hear from him first.
Fortunately, it is his left arm which he has broken : the
right he can flourish about in a free and easy way.

763. *August* 10.—You know, my dear Gentz, that
I have been occupied for a long time with the collection
of material for a history of the year 1809, the period of
my entering the ministry, to 1815. The material is
rich in itself, and I have the feeling that I alone possess
the clue to the greatest events of modern times, and
that posterity will be inundated by false views and
distorted facts unless I hand down to them that clue.
I have, therefore, made a rule to take up my pen whenever I have time and leisure. The sea is made of drops
and this is a truth I begin to realise. I have made so
many sketches that if I were to die to morrow all
important truths would be secure. You know how
little I think of my talent as a writer ; therefore I have
chosen the form of fragments, and I will leave it to an
abler pen to collect and arrange them as a whole.
These fragments are, of course, of a very varied
character. Some are particularly interesting to me,
and let me confess that I feel how much better you
would express what I wish to think and say than I
ever can. There I lay claim to your help for my
essays. Enclosed you will find the picture of Napoleon
as it stands before my eyes. I ask you to read and
polish it without changing the features of my Napoleon,
who would otherwise cease to be mine. This is not the
work of one day, and I am not going to hurry you.
Make use of your leisure time and your gift for writing,

but do not meddle with the man himself: he belongs to me. Take him as I give him to you, and apply to him my ideas, which you know so well. . . . Victor has copied this work from my first essay, and then I looked over it again. It is not copied a second time, because I suppose that you are going to do that while correcting, and because it is of moment to me that my undertaking should at first remain a secret. Many other pictures will follow which cannot be published till the originals have disappeared.

On finishing my work I see, as perhaps you will also, that I produce an entirely new picture of Napoleon. I have stripped the man of his garments, and shown him as he really was—without romance, without ornament, but also without the mire so often cast upon him. It might seem difficult to say anything new about the man, but I imagine that all I have said is more or less new, or rather that it has not been said before.

Do not weary of the work, and if we learn in the other world that my picture of Napoleon is the most successful, I will proclaim you as its author (see vol. i. p. 269).

764. *August* 16.— . . . 'Hurrah for good diplomacy!' you exclaimed the other day. I hope there is nothing bad in the diplomatic position I have chosen. Never has anything troubled me less than Nesselrode's ill humour. I know my man, and of all men living I fear him the least. In a private letter from Lebzeltern, which I will show you on my return to Vienna, the full truth concerning the Emperor is given, and it is, as I expected, good.

Your opinion of Pozzo was mine years ago. Something in my nature makes me follow a certain kind of man as hounds track game. As soon as I sniff them they double and make all approach impossible. Such men are more or less adventurers, as Pozzo, Capo d'Istria, Armfeldt, d'Antraigues, &c. Without knowing these people, my nature revolts against them. There is still another class of people with whom I cannot get on at all : Chateaubriand, Canning, Haugwitz, Stein, &c., belong to this class. Against them, too, my feelings instinctively rebel. I can almost guess their characters at first sight.

Pozzo will be overthrown in a miserable manner. Unhappily, the Russian Cabinet, not he himself, will have to suffer for it. Pozzo has prepared everything that he may fall softly. How can a great Power like Russia surrender herself chained hand and foot to a Corsican party-leader ? The Powers are like people who have the reputation of great inflexibility and who in treating their friends roughly only give back the affronts they have daily received from their valets and cooks.

The fall of Missolonghi is an important event. Please to send all the particulars by the next courier to Lebzeltern. Do not forget to mention the building of men of war for the Greeks at New York. From Vienna I will write to him about the proposals of the President of the United States ; but I wish first to talk over the affair with you. I have nothing more to say about St. Petersburg ; I look calmly forward to all events which can come from this quarter. Russia can only escape from her critical position by some sudden stroke. The most expensive one would be a war. A quiet explanation, in polite form, putting an end to the whole affair, would be a far less serious matter. I have given up my journey to Salzburg. I start from here on the 18th, sleep that day at Enns, and on the 19th reach Vienna.

FROM THE TIME OF THE DIET AT PRESSBURG.

765. *Ischl, August* 17, 1825.—I am really sorry to
leave Ischl. I shall regret this place with its calmness,
its charming neighbourhood, its pure air, and its pri-
vacy. I have been here surrounded by the children
nature has given me, but not by the crowd of menials
belonging to my position—these have disappeared in all
directions, and will turn up again on my return to
Vienna. In a few days I shall be at home again.

On September 11 the Diet of Hungary, one of the
most tiresome constitutional *divertissements* of the world,
will be opened. This Diet not only interferes with my
time, my customs, and daily life, but actually forces
me to change my language and my dress. I have to
speak Latin and dress like a hussar, and the refusal to
wear moustaches is the only liberty I take upon this
occasion. I shall not stay at Pressburg, but shall have
the pleasure of going backwards and forwards between
Pressburg and Vienna, which will make six hundred
German or twelve hundred French miles—the same
distance as between Vienna and St. Petersburg. If I
could begin life a second time I would be, as Heaven

pleased, a German, a Russian, an Englishman, or a
Frenchman—anything, in short, except a Turk—but I
would not leave my native place till the end of my
days. Where this place should be, I have not yet quite
decided, but I am sure I should not choose it on this
side the Alps, at least not above the 52° nor below the
32° of northern latitude. I leave to-morrow, and arrive
on the 19th at Vienna.

(To Gentz.)

766. *Pressburg, September* 28.—The Diet has been
opened and I cannot leave just at present, for I must
attend its sittings when it first begins, but I will profit
by the first leisure time to pay a visit to Vienna. By
that time the post from Constantinople will have arrived. Meanwhile affairs are going on well. A good
spirit prevails, but a great deal of inexperience is evident. The fatherly attitude adopted by the Emperor
in his address has taken the States by surprise, and, as
is usual in such cases, has inspired them with great
enthusiasm. In the sittings, a great deal of empty talk
goes on, which never rises to anything higher than
mere personal and local interest.

As a new but not uncommon example of how right,
as such, is acknowledged by the majority of the people,
I may mention the thorough confidence shown in me by
all parties. Certainly a democracy does not exist here ;
the struggle goes on between the pure Royalists and
the friends of constitution. Since the Emperor Joseph
II.'s accession to the throne the Government opposed
the Constitution. I caused the Emperor to take a
reserved position within the bounds of the Constitution ;
this perplexed most people and forces the Opposition
to fall in with my wishes while repeating Giroux's great

words, ' *C'est ce que je vous disais,*' or ' *J'allais vous le proposer.*' The first result of this frame of mind has been the enthusiastic manner in which the States have proclaimed my naturalisation. I know of no other instance of such a proceeding.

767. *October* 1.—At St. Petersburg they seem to be very much offended with me, which is quite natural. If the waves of the sea were endowed with human feelings their antipathy to the hard substance on which they dash themselves would be easily explained. According to the laws of nature such bodies must resist, they must remain unchanged, or their own turn to be destroyed will soon come. In the midst of the tempest the waves appear to be the strongest, but when the tempest passes away the rock is unhurt and the waves have disappeared. I am in the same position, and I trust that the tempest will soon be calmed. What have I to fear? The noise? What signifies noise in our day, when all kinds of voices may be heard in every direction? God will forgive these agitators, for they know not what they do.

The mischief must be sought where it is—that is, in the monstrous seething of crude ideas : it is enormous, but leaves no choice to those who guide the helm of State. He who can collect and arrange his thoughts ; to whom Heaven has granted a dispassionate nature ; who enters without hatred or love into the great questions of this world, with all rational beings on his side, must gain the victory or perish ; but dying thus, at least he dies in good company.

Thick mists lie on the Neva, but they will soon be dissipated, for they begin again to see there that the road which they have taken is not the right one, but as this view of things is disagreeable, they will for some time longer seek elsewhere what they can only find at home; and herein is, it appears to me, the true cause of the bad temper.

I am to-day going backwards and forwards between the two capitals, which happily are not farther from each other than two London suburbs; in the one I am a German, in the other a Hungarian. Strange fate!

768. *October 5.*—As time passes on and I with it, I have more and more the feeling that the only difficult businesses which occur are those which we have ill understood. Why should these matters be difficult, especially for great political bodies? Are not the Great Powers in a position to support each other by rendering assistance to each other? If this is not desired, then indeed difficulties begin; and they will not be desired as long as we do not form a distinct notion of what we really intend or should intend. Between the Power which needs advice and the Power which can give it there generally subsist petty jealousies, idle fears and suspicions, and paltry pretensions; and as long as this continues no progress is made. And thus it is with the famous Eastern Question in relation to the North. Since I have been connected with such matters I have had to do with no simpler. The question is so transparent. The Russian interest, the interest of the other Powers, then the Greek and the Turkish interest. Yet in St. Petersburg, instead of keeping this truth before them, they prefer to take in hand something opposed to their own special interest; in London jealousy of Paris, and in Paris jealousy of London, take the place of policy. In Nauplia, revolution takes the place of organisation according to circumstances; in Constantinople, they waste their strength in sophistries and quarrel over questions of etiquette. And then,

finally, come the Philhellenic Committees! General
Roche and Chateaubriand, Colonel Fabvier and the
Duke of Fitz James, Sir Frederic Adams and M. Hamilton, Mavrocordato and Theodoki, Capo d'Istria, and
the Pacha of Egypt—all these folks mingled together,
all speaking and acting in confusion, pushing and
driving—surely here, in such a mixture as this, sound
common-sense is not to be found.

(To Gentz.)

769. *October* 9.—Yesterday's French journals, and
especially the ' *Courier Français* ' of September 30, contain articles which prove that already the Liberal party
observes the tension between the Russian Court and
the three great Continental Powers. In fact, this is not
to be wondered at, for it is a line of demarcation between
Russian policy and Liberalism ; and the multitude of
agents and babblers in foreign countries all stand personally on Liberal soil. If their own wretched tendencies
did not draw them to that side, the confusion in ideas
which prevails in the Cabinet would be enough to effect
a union with Liberalism. All evils carry their own
punishment within them. The shrieks of hell will soon
reach the ears of the Emperor, and he will shudder.
The Liberals are our truest allies. I believe, however,
that we should at once give a solemn denial to the rumour of the formation of a *cordon sanitaire* on our
frontiers towards Dalmatia and on Siebenberg and Bes-
sarabia towards the two Principalities. . . .

I am reading now the ' *Portefeuille de* 1813 ' of
Norvins. The materials for this work have assuredly
been furnished by Maret, and it is as shallow, as stupid
and idealistic as this prosaic poet himself. The preface
is the best of what I have already read, and in it

there are some opinions which must seem very strange
to you and to me with regard to the portrait of Napoleon which has already reached your hands.

I select only the following :—

'If it was his nature [Napoleon's] to dominate the
world, if he had taken his own emblem for his flag,
he was also the man of monarchy, even of Catholic
monarchy, and not the man of republican liberty.

' Napoleon was not deceived, even when he thought
himself so necessary that they dare not overthrow
him. . . .

'He felt that he was the key-stone of the Continent, and he might believe that if he were violently
overthrown, it would be the revolution that while
applauding his fall would demand satisfaction from
Europe. . . .

'In his early years, the cry " *Vive la république!* "
was for him only a cry of pride, as was afterwards for
the army the cry " *Vive l'Empereur!* "

'It was not given to him to change or transform
himself, for he returned from the isle of Elba just as he
left Fontainebleau.'

I make notes to the book and therefore read it
slowly ; for it is worthy of marginal notes, being written
with honest enthusiasm. I shall get information about
it, and I am certain it will show that Norvins is the
editor and Maret the real author.

Here things are going on as usual. Seven or eight
miserable babblers have taken up the *Circular-Sitzung*.
They have quarrelled to such an extent that people
cannot but laugh at them. On Monday will be the first
sitting of the States (*Sitzung der Stände*), and then all
their fine work will be thrown overboard. This ' all '
only refers to the recruiting business. If the *Landtag*

goes on in this way, it will last eight or nine months; but perhaps means will be found to prevent this.

770. *October* 11.—Wellesley has read to me the despatch which came to him yesterday. It contains the confirmation of the conjecture which I before hazarded, that Canning will maintain his position and will oppose every attempt to make any change in it. And this is what is so peculiar; he says, ' I am neutral and will remain so,' and reserves to himself the interpretation of neutrality and its daily application. . . .

I shall hardly get to Vienna before next week. The work in the sittings (*Zirkeln*) has taken very long to mature into Reports. Yesterday was the first sitting of the lower board (*Tafel*); to-day there is a second, and the Reports have gone up to the Upper Chamber. Then a few days must elapse before the Government can be ready with its answer. It is here as it is in all meetings of the kind: seven or eight individuals shriek themselves hoarse, and the assembly thrashes empty straw.

771. *November* 7.—The Emperor is quite restored, and I believe that we shall certainly not have to remain over the 15th. Of the *Landtag* I will speak to you when we meet. Hungary is a real Bœotia, in which wiseacres, students raise themselves up as States of the Realm, and scholastic councillors (*Hofräthe*) represent the Government. Danger there is none, for ideas do not rise to that. As a specimen of an ebullition of the chief orator, the following words were uttered in yesterday's sitting (*Zirkel*):—' How is it that the intrinsic value of the Vienna banknotes is so far below that of the notes of the English bank? Only because we have no freedom of the press as the English have—that best security of the English bank '!!! The orator was much applauded. When, hereupon, the notorious Nagy Pál got up and moved for the representation of the peasantry, he was almost turned out of doors; and Vay, the chief demagogue in the assembly, declared that he would rather be hanged than take a single burden from the nobles, which was what this fourth class would very soon desire. I was glad indeed to get home as soon as possible.

772. *Vienna, Dec.* 22.—What a shocking event at Taganrog! (Nos. 786, 787.) How little worth are all human calculations. They have less weight than invisible, intangible atoms, which need but a breath of air to carry them to the end of the earth. In spite of my cold-bloodedness, this unexpected catastrophe has touched me most deeply.

At midnight of the 13-14th I received an express from our sub-consular agent at Warsaw. On the cover was written 'most urgent' three times repeated. I turned the letter over and over without being able to imagine what could be the cause of such urgency. When I opened it the first lines that met my eye told the news that the Emperor Alexander had died on Dec. 1. Could the truth of this be doubted? The letter had passed through the Warsaw post-office. Four whole days passed without the news being confirmed or corrected—on the fifth day certainty overpowered us.

773. *Dec.* 28.—We are still in the greatest uncertainty here how the conflict between the two Emperors will end. We live in an extraordinary century, that seems to be meant to go through the cycle of all experience. A throne which no one can mount is a *novum* in history, and this experience may be turned to the greatest triumph of philanthropy. But whatever may result from this, the blame lies with the Emperor Alex-

ander.   He had a peculiar and deplorable inclination to
go wrong as to the means of carrying out the good
intentions he had in his mind.   This defect in his nature
was also the ground of all the misunderstandings between him and me.   He often allowed me the honour
of looking into his inner thoughts.   I approved of
them, and we understood one another quickly enough
as to the starting-point and the end to be arrived at.
Then we both started on our way.   I went straight to
the end proposed : the Emperor went round about.   I
called to him ' Stop ! '   He cried in return, ' Do but
come with me.'   Now I cry at the top of my voice,
' Indeed you have taken the wrong road,' but he goes
on further astray, full of vexation at being left alone.
And this was especially the case in the Eastern
Question.

The contest which is now taking place between the
two brothers is a most serious event.   If it were
wished to try whether Russia could do without an
Emperor or Europe without a Russia, the two experiments certainly could not have been better introduced.
However this dead-lock may end, evil must arise from
it, and an evil which makes itself felt so widely may
easily become a calamity.   Constantine can no longer
refuse to accept the throne ; he must abdicate.   Will
he do so? ?   Or will two Emperors reign side by side in
Russia, to help or weaken one another ?

THE CONFERENCES AT ST. PETERSBURG WITHOUT ENGLAND.

Metternich to Ottenfels, in Constantinople, Vienna,
January 6, 1825.

774. Mr. Stratford Canning arrived here on Dec.
21. The object of his mission was solely to make us
understand the difficulties experienced by the British
Cabinet, or, to speak more correctly, the difficulties
which Mr. Canning finds in taking part in the Conferences at St. Petersburg. Mr. Canning, who manages
the Liberal faction, is afraid of committing himself by
entering into a measure which, in the eyes of that faction,
would undoubtedly partake of the nature of the Alliance.
He wishes on this occasion, as on every other, to be free
in his actions, and to be able to guide himself according
to circumstances. This is the secret of his political
course.

It seems to me unnecessary, Baron, to enter more
into details. It is sufficient that you should be warned
of a fact which doubtless will delay the overtures
which the Courts will make to the Divan. Our opinion
is that the conferences ought not to be delayed ; the
first point they will naturally take into consideration
will be the difference with England. I will take care
to keep you informed of the progress of an affair of
which you will be supposed to be entirely ignorant
till I am at liberty to give you instructions *ad hoc*.

Metternich to Lebzeltern, in St. Petersburg, Vienna, January 15, 1825.

775. . . . Greece is in insurrection against the Porte. The principal object of this movement is national and political independence.

Can the Powers support the cause of the independence of the Greeks on any principles of public right? This question is easily answered : the whole of Europe is at peace with the Sultan.

By what right, then, do the Powers interfere in an affair apparently only affecting the rights and interests of a third State ? In that of their own interest, inseparable from the maintenance of the public repose and political peace of Europe.

Insurrection and anarchy in European Turkey cannot be indifferent to the Powers—to those which are contiguous, for reasons which it would be superfluous to mention; to the generality, on account of the hindrance to their navigation and commerce; on account of the dangers arising from the dismembering of any State by civil wars ; on account of the efforts made by enemies of all rule and order to encourage a sanguinary struggle which would everywhere increase the spirit of insubordination and disorder; on account, in short, of the criminal hopes founded on the issue of the insurrection. The peculiar character of the struggle as between Christians and Mussulmans increases the embarrassment of the Governments ; and if this fact acts on the public mind everywhere, how much more does it increase the embarrassment of the sovereign of Russia !

Nevertheless, the desire to do away with the source

of the evil is too sound a policy not to animate the monarchs who for so many years have acted as bulwarks against these evils, although the application of their principles seems in this case to encounter peculiar difficulties.

The wish is legitimate ; it should therefore be supported by action, and this, to be just and useful, should be founded on reason.

Has the Porte the means necessary to bring the insurgent countries under its domination ? We believe it has; but the attempt can only lead to new complications, the effects of which it is difficult to estimate. The submission of the insurgent countries, brought about by the force of Ottoman arms, would be equivalent to the more or less complete destruction of the Greeks. The consequence of a partial defeat would only be to smother the insurrection, which would break out again upon the slightest cause. The difference, both moral and political, between our time and former times is so noticeable that an interval of repose such as that between the events of Greece from 1769 to 1779 and the insurrection of 1821, seems to us scarcely probable.

In all this we do not believe there is anything which has not been said or felt in the course of the last few years. What has not been expressed has yet served as a basis for what the Courts have done so far. They have at all times regarded as the common basis of their determinations :—

1st. Respect for the sovereignty of the Sultan ;

2nd. A capitulation which secures to the insurgents forgiveness for what is past and pledges of civil well-being compatible with the rights of sovereignty of the Porte.

What is the question to-day? To put in action what has been, and always will be, recognised by the Powers in spite of the unhappy division produced in their councils by the defection of England; for truth and justice remain eternally the same.

You, Count, are about to give the vote of Austria in the council of Continental Courts. You will draw from what I have now stated the basis which we recognise as that of our participation in these conferences and in their subsequent determinations.

This basis once fixed and established, the means and mode of proceeding must be determined. We do not hesitate to decide on that which gives us as many conditions of success as possible.

The Courts in making their united voices heard by the contending parties should be careful not to forget the difference of qualification in the two parties. Whatever may be the moral condition of the Porte, it has for the Courts the value of a regular Power. The revolution is of an entirely different character; the language and the tone of the Cabinets should mark this difference. The first overtures should therefore be directed towards the Porte. The Powers will have means of addressing declarations to the Greeks on the subjects which they think proper to make known to them; but there should be no negotiation with them, before they are connected with the Ottoman Government. Clear and precise language will greatly contribute to the success of the affair.

I do not believe that the Porte will absolutely reject the overtures which will be addressed to it by the Powers relative to the pacification of its provinces. And even if it should forget the respect which it owes to the first sovereigns of Europe, this would be no reason for

renouncing further explanations, for the Courts desire
nothing but what is reasonable. They are entirely
guided by an interest which they may justly consider
to be shared by the Porte itself. The proposal of a
cessation of hostilities between the parties at variance
seems to us a very convenient opportunity for sounding
the inclinations of the insurgents. I confess that I have
no hope that this proposal will be accepted by either
party, and still less by the Greeks than by the Divan.
The attempt, nevertheless, appears to us so justifiable
that you must declare in its favour.

And now I come to the point when the Powers,
after having surmounted the first difficulties, will be
able to enter on the subject with the Porte, and to discuss
the means of pacifying Greece. Foreseeing that this
will be one of the subjects which will particularly occupy
the Conference, we flatter ourselves that the following
observations will be favourably received.

Any project for pacification grounded on a basis between the ancient order of things and the real independence of the Greeks will have necessarily to struggle
against two equally formidable obstacles—the objections
of the Porte, and the refusal of the Greeks to return
under its sway on any condition whatever. The objections of the Porte do not all arise from mere pride, tenacity, or blind repugnance. Some of them are founded
on more solid arguments. The Porte will have great
difficulty in removing the religious scruples which are
opposed to any arrangement tending to submit to the
Christian authorities Mussulman subjects inhabiting the
countries administered by the Greeks. To remove this
great obstacle—unknown in the provinces where, as in
Wallachia and in Moldavia, the Turks have never been
domiciled—it would be necessary either to expel entirely

the Mussulmans from the parts placed under the new
régime, or to create two heterogeneous administrations
on the same territory, which would cause grave complications. The Porte would be very unwilling to subscribe to concessions which would be of no avail in the
other provinces of its Empire, where a great number, if
not the majority, of the population is composed of
Christians. It would moreover be afraid that these
concessions would be but a feeble barrier and an insecure guarantee against a renewal of attempts on the
part of its Greek subjects in favour of their political independence.

On the other hand, the Greeks, although enfeebled
by divisions, and little capable of long maintaining a
struggle disproportioned to their means, perhaps still
less capable of forming an independent State, are nevertheless too much excited against the Turks by four
years' successful resistance, and by a natural enthusiasm
supported and nourished by the feeling, real or fictitious,
that Europe is in favour of their cause, to submit to
any plan of pacification which has not their absolute independence for its basis.

To oppose to the objections of the Turks, and especially to those connected with religion, the threat of imminent war, would be to place that Government between
two kinds of death, of which the fanaticism of despair
would perhaps choose the longest and the least dishonour-
able. On the other hand, the conclusion which the
Powers propose to themselves; which has been the basis
of their concert for more than four years; which has
been connected with their political and moral conduct
since the foundation of their glorious alliance—this conclusion which they have so often proclaimed, and never
lost sight of in the most critical times, will it allow them

to drift into war, when they seek only for the preservation and security of peace? Assuredly not.

Is it to be supposed that, in the present state of things, any Cabinet would feel disposed to take up arms against the Greeks? We think not.

What, then, remains to the Cabinets, if the blindness or obstinacy of the Porte puts it out of their power to labour seriously for the pacification of Greece, and paralyses the only means of action adapted to the success of the enterprise?

Here is our opinion on this subject. In considering every possible means of negotiation that could be used under this painful supposition, we can only find one which seems to us to unite chances of success with the security which the Emperor our august master regards as compatible with the character of his policy. This means would be the eventual admission of the independence of the Greeks, not as the recognition of a right, but as a measure of fact and necessity, directed as a threat against an opposition otherwise insurmountable. To establish this distinction it is sufficient for us to show the allied Cabinets that in our thoughts we separate the means and the end, and that, while admitting that even in the event of a defeat in the way of persuasion and conciliation we should not be deprived of all resources, we at the same time point out the limits of that to which we should have recourse. . . .

In fact, the thing to be done is to announce to the Porte that, in case of a peremptory refusal of concessions considered indispensable, the Powers, decided at all costs to end the present troubles, see the necessity of admitting the independence of the Morea and the islands, if the Porte itself does not make this resolution unnecessary by wise and efficacious measures, fitted to

put an end to a state of things incompatible with the
peace and well-being of Europe.

The Cabinets will perhaps be surprised, Sir, at the
idea which I have just imparted to you. But we
sincerely desire the pacification of European Turkey ;
we wish it above everything, and therefore will reject
no means which will bring it about, however little it
corresponds with our wishes and general feelings.
You know enough of the mind of the Emperor our
august master to know that when it is necessary to
take up and advance an affair, his Majesty yields to no
difficulty, at the same time circumscribing his action
within the exact limits which he will neither conceal
nor exceed.

To resume, it will suffice to reduce the instructions
to the smallest possible compass.

1st. You are authorised, Sir, to take part in the
conferences to be opened by the Russian Cabinet, conjointly with the representatives of Austria, France and
Prussia. You will join in the conferences with all the
freedom inspired by the confidence placed in you by
the Emperor our august master, and under the restriction solely of your instructions.

2nd. We recognise as the aim of the Conferences of
St. Petersburg—

In the first place, to take into consideration the
means of putting an end to the insurrection in the
Morea and the isles of the Archipelago ; to re-establish
peace in those parts of the Ottoman Empire on the
basis of the sovereignty of the Porte, and the maintenance of public tranquillity ;

In the second place, to consider the most useful
advances for this object, as well towards the Ottoman
Porte as towards the insurgents—advances the execu-

tion of which shall be committed to the representatives
of the four Powers at Constantinople;

In the third place, to agree on a moral guarantee
providing that, whatever may be the issue of these
steps, the political peace of Europe shall not be disturbed.

3rd. The demand of an armistice between the two
contending parties being regarded by us as having the
character of a pacific intervention, you will admit this
demand, while considering the best means of carrying
it out.

4th. As to the forms to be observed and the means
to be employed in the explanations with the Porte, the
present despatch contains all necessary instructions for
the time being.

A grave and, from every point of view, deplorable
circumstance has just complicated this affair afresh.
You will understand that I speak of the unexpected
resolution which the British Government has just
taken. . . .

It seems to us indispensable that the Powers
should immediately enter into an explanation with the
British Cabinet on its evident change of position.

It ought not to be difficult for the Cabinets, united
and with one object clearly defined and loudly declared,
to announce to the British Government, by a simple and
frank declaration, that they persist in the benevolent
intentions which the Cabinet of London itself until lately
had recognised as just and salutary for the re-establishment of peace in the East; and that, considering it
for their common interest to be enlightened on the
step England intends to take in the isolated position
it has chosen in this affair, they believe they have a
right to demand from the British Government whether

its retreat from the council of the Powers is not to be followed by some step prejudicial to their design for the pacification of Greece, or whether it will not lead to demonstrations and measures opposed to the object of their efforts.

Such is the line, Sir, which we have marked out for your action. I beg you to keep it before you, and to follow this most important and most difficult of affairs with the zeal which belongs to your character and the uprightness characteristic of your Court.

Receive, &c.

Metternich to Lebzeltern, in St. Petersburg, Vienna, January 15, 1825.

776. . . . You remark that in my despatch (No. 775) I restrict the subject of the negotiation to the pacification of the Peloponnesus and the islands of the Archipelago. It is, in truth, to these countries that we ought to limit the efforts of the Powers.

The Russian Memoir of January 9, 1824, embraces in its provisions all the provinces of the continent, such as Thessaly, Acarnania, &c. How could it be reasonably supposed that an arrangement could be arrived at with the Porte on such a vast scale, and which would bear, with the exception of some parts of Roumelia, on almost all the provinces of European Turkey where Christians are mixed up with Turks! The truth of this observation is so evident that it was M. de Tatistscheff himself who first made the remark to me. I know for certain that he has written to his Court stating the plain truth.

I should have insisted on the distinction in my despatch, but I preferred to leave to the Russian Cabinet the opportunity of taking the initiative in this amend-

ment. I therefore beg you to make it understood at
the Conference, that in speaking of the pacification in
the Levant we mean the deciding of the fate of
the inhabitants of the Morea and the Archipelago,
and of those provinces alone which can be rightly called
Greek. If the proposals of the Russian Cabinet should
extend further, you will not refuse to take them
into consideration, but you will make no attempt to
conceal that we fully realise the enormous difficulties
which prevent any real hope of success. The most
superficial knowledge of the real state of things in the
countries which we exclude from our calculations, the
mixture of Mussulmans and Christians forming the
population, while the Morea has been evacuated by
the first, and the isles have never contained Turkish
inhabitants—these considerations alone are enough to
justify our reasoning. The establishment of a Southern,
Western, and Eastern Greece, cost but the stroke of a
pen to the editor of the Russian Memoir: it would be
quite otherwise with the execution of a measure which
would be nothing less than a transformation of the
pachaliks of Janina, Arta, Prevesa, and others into so
many Christian magistracies. . . .

In my instructions to you I mention a step to be
taken towards the Court of London. I think this
should be done on the day following that when the
Cabinets arrange their points of view, and fix their
plans for the negotiation at Constantinople and the
declarations to be addressed subsequently to the Greeks.
The overtures to be addressed to the British Cabinet
should declare frankly what the Powers wish, and
demand formally an equally frank declaration on the
part of the British Cabinet, especially inquiring if it
intends to oppose, directly or indirectly, the measure

of pacification projected by the allies, or means to adhere to the line of strict neutrality.

I do not consider it prudent or useful to go further, for any invitation to the English Government to stand by the cause and support it would be regarded as a triumph, whether it rejected the offer of the Powers or accepted it. The interest of the day being moreover the sole guide which one can rightly attribute to the policy of Mr. Canning, no human foresight could determine beforehand which of the two sides he would take.

Metternich to Ottenfels, in Constantinople, Vienna, January 29, 1825.

777. I have informed you, by one of my despatches of the 6th of this month (No. 774), of the arrival of Mr. Stratford Canning at Vienna. You know that the project of engaging our Court in a different course from that which we have hitherto followed in concert with our allies—a project which appears to have been the principal object of Mr. Canning's mission—has entirely failed, and that we have expressed ourselves to the Cabinet of Russia in a way which has left no doubt as to the firmness of our intentions.

Before the effect produced by these communications at St. Petersburg could have been known to us, M. de Tatistscheff informed us of some despatches which had been addressed to him, dated December 26. We learnt from them that his Majesty the Emperor Alexander, having been informed by direct reports from London of the difficulties which the British Government made to the conferences on the pacification of the Greeks, and of the line taken by Mr. Canning of not associating England with these conferences, has decided to break off all discussion with the Cabinet of London on this subject.

We had foreseen that the refusal of the British Government to take part in the conferences would be no reason for the Emperor of Russia to renounce them; and as we shared his views on the subject, we were able to reply without delay to the proposal of the Cabinet of St. Petersburg to proceed with the conferences in spite of the declarations of England.

The affair having arrived at this point, we thought it indispensable to send Count Lebzeltern instructions to guide him in the deliberations about to be opened. With this you will receive a copy of the despatch (No. 775) addressed to him, which I send for your own private information.

A few days after this despatch was sent off, Count de La Ferronays arrived at Vienna, from whence he goes to St. Petersburg. We have heard from him that the French Cabinet, persuaded that we regard the affair in its true aspect, is quite disposed to join with us, and follow the line we have indicated as the most useful and prudent.

By the time the present despatch reaches you, the Porte, I have no doubt, will be aware of the attitude taken by the British Government. I know that Mr. Turner has been authorised to communicate the correspondence of Mr. Canning with the Greeks to the Reis-Effendi, in case the Divan should evince a desire to take cognisance of it. If this communication has not taken place, you would do well to induce the Reis-Effendi to demand it. It will not escape you, Sir, what advantages we may gain in our relations with the Porte from the imprudent and irregular conduct of the English Cabinet. The Ottoman ministers will not fail to inquire the motives which have determined England to withdraw from a friendly attempt at pacification which occupies the other Cabinets, and to which the English minister had more than once announced his intention of contributing. If Mr. Canning had covered his refusal with the pretext of not wishing to join in steps which could displease or give umbrage to the Porte, they might, at Constantinople, have been somewhat grateful for his reserve, and have perhaps passed a less favourable judgment on the conduct of the Continental Powers. But since it has been shown, by Mr. Canning's own confession, that his withdrawal was only caused by the declaration of the Greeks against any pacification not grounded on the basis of their independence, there can no longer be any doubt of the spirit which directs the British Government in a question so essential for the interests of the Porte. You will take care, when the occasion offers, to make the most of these observations ; and the part which England has just taken concerning the Spanish colonies in America will furnish you with a sufficiently striking commentary. . . .

I have already informed you that we shall use the proper means to strengthen our squadron in the Archipelago and in the Ionian Sea, and that his Majesty the Emperor has authorised me to concert, conjointly with the Aulic Council of War, on the measures which can guarantee as far as possible our navigation and our commerce in these seas from the additional dangers to which the attempts of the Greek cruisers, tolerated and protected up to a certain point by the British authorities, may expose them.

METTERNICH'S OPINIONS ON CANNING'S POLICY.

Metternich to Esterhazy, in London, Ischl,
August 7, 1825.

778. I do not wish you to leave London without enabling you to express yourself clearly on many subjects of great importance, if you think it would be useful to do so.

You, Sir, who have been so long the enlightened and zealous interpreter of the thoughts and wishes of our Court to a monarch whom the strongest ties attach to Austria, need not to be reminded of the immutability of principle and political system of our august master the Emperor. Nothing is variable in these principles and intentions, for our principles are just, and our proceedings free from all secondary views.

The policy of his Imperial Majesty has all the value of a religion; it is neither influenced by passion (from which the Emperor is exempt), nor restrained by the attitude of the Government. Our calculations are never confined to the passing day or to the needs of the moment. Placed face to face with the future, and giving to temporary embarrassments no other value than that of transient and variable symptoms, our point of view is extended but unchangeable, and our line of action never varies in its direction. You are acquainted with all the questions which, for the last fifteen years, have agitated society; also with those which have furnished matter for more special explanations between us and England. You have been a witness on the very spot of a change of tactics on the part of the British Cabinet which we shall ever regard as deplorable. · I am certain that your personal opinion does not differ from our own, either on the causes or on the effects of this change. It should therefore now be easy for me to express myself freely to you, with the absolute certainty that you will understand every one of my words in its true sense, and that you will know how to make the best use of them.

Two truths have for me all the value of positive axioms.

The first is that there should be no clashing of interests between England and Austria; that, on the contrary, their great political interests are common to both.

The second is that everything in the conduct of the present English administration that differs from that of the preceding administration rests on grave error. This may appear too hard and too plain-spoken. I should, however, belie my conscience if I did not plainly express my thoughts.

On the other hand, I admit that there is a fundamental difference between the situation of the British Government and that of the Governments of the Continent, and that to require from the first all that can and should be expected from the second is a vain enterprise which will prove nothing but the ignorance of those who undertake it. The stress I place on this difference and the needs connected with it, for the direction of affairs, is not slight; it is on the contrary large and justified by strong conviction.

In admitting this truth, I feel that I have less cause to dread being accused of cherishing impractical views.

In England a man has sprung to the head of affairs. He has aimed at founding his power on an appeal to the prejudices popular in his country. Up to this time he has succeeded in his enterprise; but has he served his country and the general cause, which is undoubtedly also that of England? I have no doubt as to the reply, and events will show that my opinion cannot be contradicted. I do not even require to seek its justification in a remote future; the facts of every-day life come already to support it.

Its insular position separates England from the other parts of the civilised world. It has drawn and will draw very decided advantages from this position when its Government does not extend this separation to the moral interests common to all States. The science of the English ministers consists in distinguishing to which of the two classes the subject which for the time claims their attention belongs; and here it has latterly fallen into error, the consequences of which will be very grave, both for the kingdom itself and for the whole world.

The first source of this error—allowing for the influence of personal considerations on the English political administration of recent years—consists in the way in which it has regarded the Alliance.

In touching on this subject, I feel myself called upon to make certain concessions to the British Cabinet. I make allowance for the embarrassments and difficulties which more than one false interpretation, and more than one attempt at direct application, both forced and erroneous, of a spirit which might be allowable to the

Cabinets of the Continent, but which has caused the English Cabinet much uneasiness and perplexity. There is not one of the occurrences to which the reproach would be applicable which I could not easily point out, for there is none which our active solicitude for the preservation of the real benefits of the Alliance and the most intimate and regular relations between England and the Powers has not foreseen, has not combated, and sometimes considerably modified.

In making this concession I feel more especially called upon to distinguish between what is reality in the Alliance and what is only illusion—in fact, to distinguish between the real thing and the abuse of it.

The moral essence of the Alliance rests alone upon the principle of preserving everything that has a legal existence, and of a happy union between the great Powers on this principle. If such is the spirit of the Alliance, in its active application to special cases it should submit to the common law. It is for prudence (and the consideration of possibilities is certainly one of the first conditions of prudence) to weigh, as each case occurs, the nature of the object to which an action should be applied that otherwise might turn against the very object of the Alliance itself. Examined closely, the principle is that of the life of all States : it supports one of the first needs of society, the security of property ; it exists everywhere, and loses nothing of its correctness, or of the necessity of its application, under whatever form a Government may be placed. If the principle has been pronounced too strongly, the fact is due to the attacks which mad fanatics have made on the social body, and which they still continue to make. To attack the principle of the Alliance is to attack society. To protect oneself against the Alliance, or to abandon it, is not to understand the Alliance, or not to understand oneself.

Such is the reproach I cast on Mr. Canning, a reproach which history, always impartial, will also cast on him.

By placing the question as I have just done, one can understand the recent proceedings. The Secretary of State has too much experience in business to think seriously of a system of isolation and concentration in favour of what is more easily called the direct interest of Great Britain than proved to be so; besides, his thoughts have never extended beyond the separation of the conduct of England from that of the Alliance. But it is just here that the error lies. In such an undertaking one would have to separate oneself from the vital principles of society, and in more than one special case it would be found that the action of the Powers on the affairs in point would not have been claimed but for the existence of the Alliance.

I do not hesitate to declare that, according to my firm belief, in the Eastern Question one sees the allies, but not, strictly speaking, the Alliance. Its fundamental principle—that of respect for existing rights and for the value of treaties—assuredly acts as a guide to the Continental Powers in this complication; but could it have been otherwise, or would it have been otherwise, if the Alliance had never existed? It is not from London that I expect a negative reply. And, nevertheless, where do we find the English Power in this grave conflict? The course which its Cabinet has recently followed has tended to make more difficult the solution of a complication which its own interests should have hastened.

Has it not been the same with the affairs of the New World? . . .

I admit that Mr. Canning belongs to those men who seek to open up new ways, or what are called so; that he may attach to certain clamours and to certain suffrages more value than they deserve in reality; in short, that he believes he will obtain more facility and success in what he regards as the support of a national policy! If such is the case, Mr. Canning is but deceiving himself, and this the event will prove.

Europe at present has but one real need, which is political repose; this would sustain the prodigious bound which industry and commerce have taken. England wishes for repose as much as we do. She should therefore not favour that which tends to disturb it, and which but for our firmness would have already produced much evil.

Count Münster addresses to me the question, 'If, in the present state of things [he is speaking of the Eastern Question], it would not be better to strengthen the union of Austria and England rather than to weaken it?'

My reply to this question will be short and precise.

Austria, considering the first conditions of its existence, should never depart from the principles which actually form the true and only basis of that which custom has made us call the Alliance. Anything which, in the present situation of things and the state of public feeling, would tend to cement a special union between us and England, would infallibly ruin us. A political body which rests on unchanging principles cannot alter its course to adopt one which its very authors can only characterise as concession to English popular opinion—a feeling most precarious in its essence, as everything is which owes its existence to the favour of the people. We are convinced that by the firmness of our conduct and the force of our moral attitude we shall continue to render great services to the world and to England herself. We shall not deviate from our line of conduct, and we have to face two alternatives: either the British Cabinet may return to its former ways—considering the natural mobility of popular opinion and the danger of the extremes to which it leads, it may after a long circuit rejoin us where it left us; or perhaps the steep incline on which it is placed will take it to a distance which it is not given to us to comprehend, much less ever to attain. In this case—which our wishes for the cause which we regard as the good one make us unwilling to admit—we shall still be strong from our antecedents and from the very essence of the principles we have invariably maintained. This calculation presents in our opinion not a single weak side, for we are quite convinced that on the whole the sound policy of England does not desire, and never could desire, anything but what is for the true and permanent interest of society. If I am not mistaken, Mr. Canning belongs to a class of men who sometimes join in affairs without ardently wishing their success; these men speculate on the advantages of the moment, and at the same time try to secure their capital apart from the enterprise. Such speculations rarely succeed, and we could not in any case embark in them. It is doubtless unnecessary for me to warn you against imagining for a moment that in these observations we have alluded to the true and valuable support of noble old England, or to the thoughts of the monarch whom the Emperor regards as the most constant, the most prudent, and the most enlightened of his allies and friends.

Metternich to Esterhazy, in London, Ischl, August 7, 1825.

779. I leave the use of the preceding despatch (No. 778) to your discretion. If you think that its contents should be read to the King, the Duke of Wellington, and Count Münster, you are at liberty to do so.

The sketch which I have given of Mr. Canning's policy is in obedience to my conscience. What I advance as the ground of his calculations and of his daily conduct is, without any doubt, strictly true. I have no need to search far for the comparison which I have made between him and those speculators who are at the same time in certain enterprises and out of them. The truth of the comparison is shown by the contrast (evident to those who know the progress of affairs) between the support which Mr. Canning has given to the emancipation of the Irish Catholics and the American and Greek insurrections, and the well-known desire of that minister that these same enterprises may be unsuccessful. Mr. Canning has, on the other hand, furnished us with a proof by the direction which he has given to the arrangement between Brazil and Portugal, that he is in no doubt as to what are sound and correct principles, nor of the importance of not abandoning them whenever he considers it is for his own interest and that of England to maintain them. Mr. Canning uses, as it suits him, two weights and two measures. I believe that by this fact alone he injures the real and permanent interests of his country ; on the other hand, it is certain that we could not act thus without bringing on ourselves immediate ruin.

The turn which affairs in Greece have taken is well calculated to make the British Cabinet thoughtful. We have arrived at the moment for its solution. The Greeks, whose true interests might have been secured by an agreement between the Powers, will succumb entirely, unless, indeed, Russia goes to war with the Porte—an event in my opinion unlikely even now, but which would have been impossible if England had acted in concert with the Powers. It was possible to avoid the true mean between real evil and the imaginary good, and this Mr. Canning did. The good which has been accomplished they owe to us.

The point which it seems to me we should especially dwell upon to the King is the deep regret of the Emperor at having been abandoned by England in the pacification of the Levant. The thing is so inexcusable, so contrary to the undoubted interests of Great Britain, that it presents more than one side on which it may be approached. It is impossible that the whole affair should not cause great embarrassment to Mr. Canning, and that its issue, whatever it may be, should not give as many reasons for reproach for what he has done as well as what he has omitted. It may be allowable to repose when there are many chances of favourable results, but it is never allowable to hesitate when there is no such chance.

THE AUSTRIAN MARITIME TRADE IN THE LEVANT.

Metternich to Lebzeltern, in St. Petersburg, Ischl,
August 13, 1825.

780. One of the last Reports from your Excellency touches a subject on which there is evidently some mistake that I ought to remove.

Count Nesselrode appears to suppose that our maritime commerce in the Levant, far from suffering by the insurrection, will, on the contrary, gain by the state of confusion which reigns in the Morea and Archipelago. The thing is absolutely false, and is contradicted by the extreme inconveniences to which our commerce, and consequently our Government, are a constant prey.

To show the true state of the case, it will be sufficient perhaps to adhere to a general rule. It is a fact—and experience has constantly proved it—that all regular commerce must suffer by disorder. Now, the more regular our maritime commerce with the Levant is, the more it owes its wide extent to the confidence which the merchants have in the strictness of our commercial laws and in the loyalty of the owners of our merchant vessels, the more prejudicial is the present state of things to our commercial interest and the prosperity of the empire. Such is, indeed, the case.

Notwithstanding the keeping up of very costly maritime stations, of which the whole charge falls on the State ; notwithstanding the absolute necessity of augmenting them, in order not to lose the whole of our commerce, it has suffered a sensible diminution, as the statistics testify. This diminution is owing to two causes.

One is the insurrection—a state of things which favours all kinds of disorder, and which, among other inconveniences, furnishes the Greek populations with the opportunity of transforming themselves into pirates.

The other is the competition at present sustained by flags hitherto strangers to the Black Sea with those which up to this time have alone possessed the right of admission.

The first of these causes is altogether intolerable, and the more difficult it is to get rid of it, the more the Emperor our august master desires its speedy disappearance.

The second cause is of quite another nature. It rouses in his Imperial Majesty his innate sentiment of justice, and induces him to the application of a policy as sound as it is vigorous—a policy which does not allow him to hesitate when it is necessary to employ useful means to a desirable end.

The Emperor thinks that the exportations from Southern Russia should not be stopped in consequence of the Greek insurrection and the difficulty of navigation, which he feels may be indefinitely prolonged. There is no sort of representation which has not been made by the departments of the interior against the support we have given to the admission of the Sardinian flag—a support which we give and will give also to the other commercial Powers. These representations are natural on the part of these departments, and are justified by experience. If the very important reports from the port of Genoa alone are consulted at St.

Petersburg, it will be easily seen that the appearance
of the Austrian flag there has diminished more than
two-thirds in the course of the year 1825. This fact
of the admission of a great number of flags in the
Black Sea has caused a positive decline in the industry
and revenues of Austria; but the Emperor consoles
himself with the thought of having done what is useful
and agreeable to his Imperial Majesty of All the Russias,
and having secured still further the maintenance of
political peace in Europe.

This is the whole truth very simply stated. I am
too anxious to enlighten the conscience of Count
Nesselrode, and I know too well how much he desires
to avoid error not to address these few words to
you, to which I will merely add the request that you
will bring them to the knowledge of the Secretary of
State.

THE EVENT AT NAUPLIA.*

Metternich to Gentz, Vienna, September 9, 1825.

781. I candidly admit that I consider the declaration of the Nauplia Government in favour of the English, and all the circumstances accompanying that event, as a true *deus ex machina*—a divinity which is always the faithful companion of those who 'are in the right.' What will Canning do? That may be left to him to decide, but this much is certain, that, do what he may, and how he may, he will always stick in the mud.

How easily we can now bear Russia's reproaches at not having taken up the excellent '*mesures coërcitives contre la Porte*'! How well their application would have matched Hamilton's splendid operations! Do you think that we shall be asked again to force the Porte to subjugate the Greeks? Is not Cochrane's expedition in the most charming harmony with the present course of affairs? To make it quite perfect it only remained for General Roche to instigate Hamilton to pursue his present line of conduct. The whole is a magnificent structure!

Tatistscheff agrees with me, as to the advantage of this event. He no longer thinks that the Russian troops

---

* This event was the resolution of the Greek Council to place themselves, in the name of the clergy and the people, under the protection of England. An act to this effect passed and signed by 2,000 persons was protested against by General Roche in the name of the French Philhellenic Committee. —Ed.

will march upon Moldavia, because he believes that the English would, in this case, take possession of Hydra. Time will show what is to be done, and the greatest proof of wisdom will be seen in skilfully allowing time to ripen matters.

I have based my remarks in the ‘ *Beobachter* ’ of the 8th on the article taken from the ‘ *Spectateur Oriental*,’ and have worded it most carefully.* I only wait for the right moment to speak out more distinctly. There are cases, and this is one of them, where silence is of the greatest moment.

P.S. *September* 11, 1825.—I send you a short summary of a conversation with Tatistscheff on the last despatches he had from St. Petersburg (No. 782). Nesselrode’s last letter is full of lamentations. When a Cabinet like the Russian is in such a mood it must be encouraged, and truthful words are the best encouragement. These I believe I have used in speaking to Tatistscheff. He has remarked on them very well in his Report, in so far as what I said needed commentary :

* The ‘ *Beobachter* ’ (Observer) of September 8 took from the ‘ *Spectateur Oriental* ’ notes on the Nauplia event, on which Metternich remarked as follows :—

‘ A new scene of the Greek insurrection has just opened. What has been long expected has at last taken place : the members of the Philhellenic Committee are in conflict with themselves and the revolutionary Government, and the members of the latter are disputing among themselves and with the various leaders in the Peloponnesus and the islands. Impartiality requires the historian to wait for fuller accounts before entering on a discussion of the elements which produce the present chaotic situation. The question will soon be solved, whether the interference of so many foreign elements, the introduction into Greece of those passions and errors which party spirit has in our agitated times called forth in Christian Europe, has been advantageous to the cause of Greece or tended to its ruin. As soon as we can see sufficiently clearly to obtain trustworthy material for the history of our time, we shall, firmly and without reserve, step forth, as we have from the beginning of these events in the East, without paying any regard to the widespread system of deception.’ Gentz considers these remarks the best and most forcible ever made on the subject.—ED.

according to my judgment it was clear and distinct, and will be everywhere well received.

I thought well to send you this little work, as it contains a summary of my belief. This is exactly how I look upon the present position in Turkey, Greece, and England. If I could myself and alone represent the Continental Powers in Constantinople, as in other places, I should soon bring the whole quarrel to a good and speedy end, for at the present moment everyone is wrong except myself.*

* Gentz in his answer, dated Gastein, September 17, says:
'I should not call your despatches to London "bad work in a smooth form," but a very vigorous and decisive step in a very simple and moderate form. It is no easy matter to answer your last two questions. I am delighted with the plain language your Highness used in your conversation with Tatistscheff. The remark "*que ce que nous rencontrons journellement de difficultés et de répugnances à Madrid, nous devons pour le moins aussi le rencontrer à Constantinople*"' is invaluable.

SKETCH OF A CONVERSATION WITH
TATISTSCHEFF.

(Enclosed in No. 781.)

782. Will recent events alter the moral and material situation of the four Continental Courts in the Eastern affair ?

Let us consider what the Courts have desired up to this time.

They have desired that peace should be universally maintained and treaties respected. The object of their moral action has been the prompt pacification of insurgent provinces; indeed, as a pledge of future tranquillity, they have sought to ameliorate the fate of the people in these same provinces, having at the same time regard to the needs of mankind and the rights of sovereignty.

These views and desires are legitimate and correct, for beyond and apart from them will be found partial or general war; a clashing of great political interests; injury to principles nobly and usefully defended by the Alliance; and trouble of the most serious character—in a word, all that revolutionists desire.

When, three months ago, the intervention of the Powers for the pacification of Greece was offered for the first time to the Divan, the latter refused to allow it. It may be supposed that it was induced to this refusal by a repugnance to foreign interference in what it regards as a domestic affair. Its repugnance may have been strengthened by the conviction that the Ottoman forces would be sufficient to quell the insurrection. There is no need for us to discuss the strength or weakness of the Ottoman Government; it is sufficient that we recognise the Porte as a Power, and we have no right to be astonished that the feeling of independence dominates the Sultan and his council. The difficulties and opposition we have met with at Madrid we must certainly expect to meet with also at Constantinople.

The Greek insurgents, however, have not yet shown by a single step or movement that they are disposed to second the generous views of the four Courts. This is only natural. The leaders of a revolution are never disposed to allow of any capitulation to the sovereign. Any capitulation appears to them equivalent to death, or at least to the ruin of their cause. ' All or nothing ' is their device. In this judgment I separate the real leaders of the insurrection, the men of action from the people. The Courts would not have anything to do with the latter in the first instance, but with the authority so-called, if it were only because in the midst of the general disorder it forms a centre of deliberation, and in it all action is concentrated. What I say of insurgent Greece applies to all countries in revolution ; but further, the strength which the Greek Government would not have had if left to itself has been to a great degree lent to it by foreign aid and influence.

The state of things in Greece is something like that in Spain when the revolution was stopped at Cadiz. But there are, however, some remarkable differences. It will suffice to mention two : the existence of the Greek islands, and the very different action of England in 1825 from what it was in the affairs of Spain in 1823.

In short, if Europe saw with regret that England showed a decided dislike to the salutary interference of the Continental Powers in the affairs of Spain, the British Government did not then expose itself, as it has since, by the support of the revolution in Greece. I myself believe that, having been led farther than it intended, it will recoil before the consequences of its ill-disguised intervention.

The difference between the position of England and that of the Continental Courts is for this reason very great. The latter have never abandoned the principles of equity and reason; they have nothing to retrace. Can and will they go forward in this same way? The reply is easy.

They can go forward, for nothing in their situation is changed, while that of all other parties is altered, and, in my opinion, altered for the worse.

The Porte ought to consider that its arms alone cannot terminate the affair. One of two things: either England will accept the offer of the Greek Government, or she will reject it. If she accepts it, the Sultan will have nothing more to do with its subjects and insurgent countries, but with the British Power. If the British Government refuses to undertake the conquest, it must be regarded as naturally coming forward and intervening in the pacification. Of these two, the offer of intervention by the Continental Powers must bear, even in the eyes of the Divan, quite a different character, both of freedom and real impartiality, from that of England.

The situation of the Greeks is essentially changed. They have, in fact, renounced their political independence. Europe now has the right to decide to what Power they should belong. The question is political and very simple, and unless the triumph of Liberalism has already reached such a point that the Powers recognise in the people or in fractions of States the right of putting themselves according to their good pleasure under other masters or protectors, the statement I make is unanswerable.

England, in short, has received a good lesson on the consequences of her system of isolation. If she has no ideas of conquest it must be plain, to the eyes of every impartial judge, that her conduct, her proceedings, her actions, and her refusals to act, have only given trouble to everybody and injured herself. If Mr. Canning's system conquers, the question changes its aspect, and both Turks and Greeks are driven back on political ground. Then, indeed, many other interests than their individual interests will necessarily be touched, and it is neither to Constantinople nor the Greek Senate that the Powers will turn to seek for counsel.

Will the Powers advance on the same principles which have hitherto served as their guide? I can answer for the determinations of the Emperor my master, and my part goes no further.

THE JESUITS.

*Metternich to the Emperor Francis, Pressburg,
October* 18, 1825.

783. In accordance with your Majesty's gracious commands I have given most serious consideration to the memorial of the College of Jesuits in Galicia,* as well as to the opinions of Abbé Frint and his Royal Highness the Archduke Louis. I consider it my duty to communicate my opinion to your Majesty openly and without reserve, according to my principles on all State affairs, whether great or small.

The matter must be clearly placed in two different points of view, to enable your Majesty to judge rightly and truly.

* The Jesuits, banished from Russia and Poland, were received in the Dominican convent at Tarnopoli, in Galicia. They were urged to moderate the statutes of their order. They were to renounce all communication with Rome, nominating an independent vicar-general for the Austrian province, and not limit their work to missions, but undertake also parish work and education; they should not follow strictly the *ratio studiorum* under the control of the society, and should personally engage, by written promise, never to leave the Austrian monarchy. The negotiations were prolonged without coming to any result, till the Society of Jesus, in the year 1825, received the imperial order to communicate directly with the Emperor as to their wishes and demands. The society, in an address to his Majesty, set forth the incompatibility of the above-mentioned reforms with the spirit and essence of their institutions, summing up all their wishes and requests in the principle *sint ut sunt aut non sint.* The Chancellor had to give his opinion on this address (a masterpiece of dialectic), and it was in itself and in its results favourable to the Jesuits— that is to say, to the ' old Jesuits.' An imperial decree, issued November 17, 1827, gave full permission to the Jesuits in Galicia to live according to their statutes and their vows.—ED.

The one is determined by the general circumstances of our time.

The other is Austrian, and administrative.

With respect to the first I propose the following questions :—

Who are the Jesuits ?

It seems to me that this is the first point to be examined in the most frank and unprejudiced manner. At the time of the so-called Reformation — a time when spiritual life had been roused and quickened by many abuses contrary to the spirit of the Church—it happened, as it always does when the idea of reform takes possession of the masses of a nation, that the building which was meant to be restored was almost entirely destroyed!

In the midst of the dangerous contest, so bravely taken up by your Majesty's glorious ancestors, a man arose who stemmed the evil by the most powerful barriers.

This man was St. Ignatius. His mind, as truly Christian as it was keen and clear, enabling him to see the weak points of society, he created a body which, with all its various parts, formed one impenetrable whole; and this body he made over to the head of the Church for its defence.

It was inevitable that such a body should become a *status in statu*; that according to its nature it should gather strength by its conflicts. But two other things were also inevitable. The form adopted—namely, that of a secret society—could not but produce abuses in the institution itself, which the reforming party assailed vehemently. It soon came to such a point that even the most clearsighted could scarcely recognise in Jesuitism the original ideas of the Society. Yet the Jesuits, in spite of their degeneracy, would doubtless have forced Governments to a salutary reform—*i.e.* to bring back the Institute to its true principles—if the so-called philosophical spirit of the eighteenth century had not got the mastery, and exterminated the whole society. The difference between the *Society of Jesus* and Jesuitism is very important—and must be so in the eyes of those who think as I do, because I regard the Institute as a defence against the attacks of error, and condemn Jesuitism in all its forms and tendencies. The clearest proof of the soundness of the principles on which the society is based is seen in the fact that even the abuses, however deplorable they may be, have never caused it to deviate from its great aim—support of the Church and the throne, and victory over the enemies of both! Were it possible to doubt on this point, we must be convinced by a consideration of the furious persecution, the excessive irritation, the rage with which all friends of reform, from religious reformers down to the meanest Radicals, have attacked the Jesuits.

It remains a matter of question whether the Holy See has acted wisely in calling the Jesuits into life again; but there can be no doubt whether their existence, according to their original statutes, would prove useful or injurious. I, for my part, can easily decide the question. The means by which victory was gained in a comparatively less evil age cannot be bad when the age has become more evil. Here we may once more appeal to the feelings of all the adversaries of law, belief, and legal right. If these sectaries did believe one of all the stories laid at the Jesuits' door, they could not do better than recall them to life as a means to gain their end. I can therefore say nothing against the old Jesuits. But are the new like the old Jesuits?

The answer to this question depends on the management shown by the Holy See and the Governments which admit Jesuits, and not a little on the rage of their antagonists. A body, dissolved, as to its legal forms, for forty years, can scarcely be expected to be ever the same institution again. It is, however, certain that the same evils beget the same necessities, and that the form which the founder of the society availed himself of may be again adapted to the present time. But it can never be as useful, because, although the battle of to-day may have the same motives as the battle fought by the reformers, affairs in the thirteenth century differ widely from those of the sixteenth.

These reflections, in connection with the proved usefulness of the society in the first period of its existence, are certainly consoling. We cannot expect that the society, if re-established in the pure sense of its statutes, can spread so quickly or so widely as it did at its first foundation, but neither is it probable that its abuses will develop with the same rapidity or reach the same extent. When the last remaining Jesuits were forced to emigrate from Russia, it would have been my humble advice only to permit them to pass through your Majesty's realm. It would not have been more difficult to introduce the newly established society into the kingdom than it would now be to banish it.

I am placed by my position on a very high point in the centre of agitated Europe, from whence I overlook the crowd, and can therefore judge of the effect of great measures. I use the words ' great measures ' deliberately, because no event would be more likely to excite general wonder than the closing of the Jesuit college now existing in Galicia. However this might be done, it could only add to the triumph of hell upon earth, and act

injuriously upon other Governments, particularly upon
the French. And if in peaceful times individual States
are justified in considering their private interests before
all others, the same cannot be said of more agitated
periods.

Referring more directly to the monarchy, the following remarks may be made :—

' The Society of Jesus,' says Abbé Frint, ' is in contradiction with the opinions of modern politicians and the
Imperial control of ecclesiastical matters ' in Austria.
Contemning, as I do unconditionally, the authority of
the so-called modern politicians, the first of these
contradictions is of no value to me. The second
deserves more consideration because it is a very important matter for Government to be placed in contradiction with itself. This is not the place to enter
into the details, nor to follow out the leading idea,
which ought to be grounded on an examination of
the Emperor Joseph's ecclesiastical reforms, showing
whether they truly promoted the welfare of religion
and morality (and therefore also the welfare of the
State), or whether these institutions were only the result
of a theoretic system refuted by practice. This question may be regarded as decided by Abbé Frint in the
picture. only too faithful, which he has given of the
position of convents. All that can be said of members
of ecclesiastical orders in general may, in my opinion,
be applied to the Society of Jesuits. It is generally true
that the whole is better than the half, and this may be
particularly applied to a body like that of the Jesuits,
which so easily gives the opportunity for abuses.

Jesuits are no Jesuits without the fundamental
statutes of their society. Where these are stultified
or abolished, there can be no true Jesuits. Now, it is a

well-known fact that new forms under old names will soon destroy what was once good and useful, while bad and hurtful things will live on under the protection of the old name. I say, therefore, without hesitation, ' No Jesuits, or the old Jesuits '—that is, the strict rules and principles in their first pure conception ; and even then I would say as unhesitatingly ' No Jesuits at all,' if I thought that their institutions were not suited for times of danger, or if I believed them to be in themselves bad.

Moreover, what guarantees would be offered by a mere aggregate of persons who, to form a body, began by violating its laws, and, while refusing obedience, promised obedience anew ?

I do not consider myself called upon to investigate the question, whether the teaching of the Jesuits and their system of education are the best. Their doctrine is entirely and essentially opposite to ours. I confine myself to condemning our doctrine. Whether the Jesuits' doctrine is the best possible, I do not know, but it is certainly better than ours, for it is monarchical in form.

Further, I would respectfully propose as follows :—

That it may please your Majesty to grant a certain time to the Jesuit college in Galicia, to test its efficiency for the work it has undertaken. The precise length of this period it is neither necessary nor desirable to fix ; and the permission should only allude to the request of the members of the college not to be disturbed in obeying the rules of their order.

To enter upon the practical part of the affair and attain the desired end (a period of probation) certain points, decided favourably for the college, must be communicated to the *ordinariate* at Lemberg, and the Jesuits must be informed that your Majesty has granted

their request, with the intention of showing by deeds
the sincerity of your Majesty's feelings.

In this way a certain hold would be attained to induce the Jesuits to act fairly and honestly. If they
will not or cannot do so, it always remains to us to take
such measures as would be most unsuitable at the present time. If this experiment should answer its purpose,
your Majesty could well grant an extension of time.

It appears to me necessary for your Majesty to take
the college, as an institution on trial, under your Majesty's personal protection, deciding upon the form which
will secure the superintendence of the college, and render
harmless the collisions which must be a natural consequence of the jealousy of the Government.

THE OPPOSITION IN THE DIET OF PRESSBURG.

1825.

Metternich to the President of the Lower House: Vienna, December 11, 1825.

784. I have given to your letter of the 10th inst. the full attention demanded by the interesting nature of its contents, and increased by the great weight which I attach to your personal opinions in so critical and important a period as the present. My mind endeavours always to grasp the essential substance of things, to get at the root of the evil; symptoms are only useful in my eyes so far as they are instructive, and I allow them to pass quickly before me, merely following their traces, because, if quietly studied, they may guide us to fundamental truths. Seldom in my public life have I come upon these latter so quickly as with respect to the concerns of the present Diet: for this reason, that in Hungary I encounter all those things on which during my whole public life, especially during the last ten years, I have made war. The Diet has entirely taken my ground. I did not move from my position for so long that I came to know every spot of ground in its whole extent. As I am always anxious to communicate with you, and as your last letter and our last conversation assured me that we understand each other, I ask you to consider the following remarks :—

In Hungary the Government has to struggle with

two Oppositions: one, the natural result of circumstances, is the old Hungarian Opposition; the other represents the spirit of the age. When the Diet was opened these two Oppositions were mingled together; time alone will be able to separate them, and this will and must be done if Government keeps invariably to the right, in a really constitutional sense. The Hungarian Opposition, which sincerely desires to sustain the Constitution, will be paralysed by this line of conduct, and unconsciously take the same position as that on which the King himself has taken his stand. The notions of the Opposition about the Constitution are indeed strange and in many points entirely wrong, but are always based on loyalty and patriotism; and such an Opposition could only be dangerous for a Government whose wishes were the reverse of those honestly entertained by the King. The second Opposition desires disorder, for this is its natural element; and by feigning to support the Constitution it only makes use of it as a kind of weapon to attack Government—that is, authority. Monarchy is the great object of its hatred, and consequently also the Hungarian Monarchical Constitution. With regard to this matter I will send you some not unimportant notes. The firmness shown by yourself and the Archduke in the last session must have separated these two Oppositions.

. . . I will now in the strictest confidence give you some particulars of what occurred between young Count Stephan Széchényi and myself. I know this young man from the beginning of his career, and I have done a great deal for him. He has quick parts, but, like most of our young people, no solid knowledge—a want which he makes up for by a kind of cultivated instinct. His ambition is boundless; he is not frivolous, but a sort of

political spitfire, although he can be deep enough sometimes.

During my stay in Pressburg I observed (without
showing it) that he wished to open his heart to me. I
gave him the opportunity of doing so without directly
touching the point. At last, a week after the Court's
departure, he called on me, expressing his desire for a
confidential conference. I made him understand that I
could both speak and listen.

He now went into the subject, talking a great deal
against absolutism, against the supposed opinions of Government, on the ignorance the Court had shown with
respect to Hungarian affairs, on his anxiety that the
Diet would come to a bad end, &c. It was the day on
which the Royal answer upon the first address of the
Diet had been published. I told him that I was quite
ready to discuss the Royal resolution. Point for point I
brought forward, silencing him so thoroughly that he
left me with the remark that I was entirely right. Then
he went back to his club, to change his opinions again.

The day of my departure from Pressburg I received
the letter (No. 785) I now enclose, and I informed
him that I should be very pleased to enter into real
discussions about its contents. Expecting him every
day—as he had said to my commissioner that he would
call on me immediately—I marked his letter with marginal notes, and you will find them on the copy.

Meanwhile time passed away; the last royal rescript
had been issued, and the face of affairs was entirely
changed. Some days ago Count Széchényi presented
himself to me. His friends here had observed a strange
disturbance in his deportment. The first look I gave
him confirmed this. I received him kindly, telling him
I was still quite willing to make my observations on his

last letter, although affairs had been changed in their most essential points. He expressed his readiness to hear them, and had nothing to object after my reading his own letters and my notes. This done, I told him I was about to speak of his personal position as my conscience and my heart prompted. I acknowledged that I considered him as a man lost through vanity and ambition—one of those who bring unhappiness upon themselves.

The Count, much . affected, interrupted me here, entering into an exposition of his opinions, which are in the main as follows :—He is, he says, a man of active and ambitious mind, who desires to leave to posterity an honoured name. He has undertaken a part which, although difficult to maintain, promises a rich reward. The shallowness and apathy of the Hungarian magnates grieved him deeply, and he had therefore determined to endeavour at least to animate the Hungarian youth. As it was their fate to go astray, they much needed a guide, who ought to be a good and faithful subject and patriot to fill properly a position demanding so much tact and consideration. This position he had attained, and would try to use it to support his Majesty's good designs, &c.

I replied that no doubt he gave a true account of his feelings, but that they only confirmed me in my conviction that he was a 'lost man.' To prove to him that I was not wrong, I would only ask peremptorily whether he would dare to make the same confessions to his friends as he had made to me. He answered unhesitatingly that this would be impossible.

'Then you must be a traitor either to me or to your friends—that is to say, a traitor to yourself: that which never has prospered, never will prosper, and you will pass through the same dismal experience as all who have taken the same line have gone through before you—you will sink into the mire ; or if you turn round you will be branded by the very party that led you astray.'

The conversation that ensued showed me that Count. Széchényi, when quite calm, would think as I do; he complained of the extravagance of his young friends' ideas, and described some of them as mere madmen, who made the American Republic the model after which they strove. These he opposes, and hopes to convert some of them to his views.

After a discussion of three hours, he left me, much moved and dejected ; and as this took place at the time when I usually receive visitors, I should not be much astonished if the fact of so long a conversation between Széchényi and myself would soon be generally known.

I give you all these details, because they throw light on the situation in Pressburg. It appears to be evident that the Széchényi-Karoly Club belongs to the new Opposition, and that one of its leading men is not at all satisfied with it. And thus it will be, if the Government remains firm, and proclaims the truth honestly. This has conquered other things than the excitement in Pressburg.

I have shown you more than once that the party in Opposition looks upon the Circular-Sessions (*Circular-Sitzungen*) as the best means of furthering its bad and foolish plans. As long as this leaven is not removed, order cannot be thought of. The question only remains how and when this beneficial work can be undertaken—a question which no one can answer better than yourself.

The object of the moment will be to point out to the old Opposition that the new Opposition runs counter to all its constitutional labours. If once the two parties are divided, it would be best to spare the latter of the two; but to eradicate the other entirely, for it spreads like a horrible disease.

If your Excellency had yielded at the session of the 8th inst., the affair would have been lost in principle for the Government and the old Opposition. You have therefore by your firm conduct rendered a very important service. I am, with respect, &c. &c.,

METTERNICH.

Letters of Colonel Count Stephan Széchényi to Prince Metternich.

(With marginal notes by Metternich.)

785. *Pressburg, November 16, 1825.*—Most Serene Highness! Some days ago, you were so good as to permit the discussion of a subject which, as it concerns my country, of course interests me deeply.

It cannot be denied that the chief cause of many of the evils of the world is merely misunderstanding, and that sometimes the smallest trifle, even one little word, might turn to advantage an affair lost for want of thorough explanation. Your Highness has not asked my opinions on the affairs of the Diet; and, as I do not possess the deep and intimate knowledge which would enable me to make new disclosures to your Highness, I feel somewhat embarrassed in writing to you. But these considerations must not hinder me from fulfilling my duty, by drawing your attention to some circumstances and some objects which you, in your elevated position, can see less clearly than I who have them close before my eyes.

(*a.*) The idea that matters belonging to the administration are less clearly seen from an elevated position than from a lower one, is not always correct. He sees who has good eyes,

and the larger the space extended before him may be, the surer
he is to see rightly. The first advantage of a high position is
that it enables us to rise above the prejudices of the masses;
and, since it is not given to man to be free from error, higher
positions present at least the possibility of an extended influence
not to be attained in narrower spheres.

Your Highness told me, the other day, that most
people judge of objects wrongly because they do not
examine from all points their own position, the general
circumstances, and their power of influencing it. We
ought, you said, to be provided with everything likely
to throw light on the object to be judged of.

With regard to the Diet, I venture to state my
humble opinion that, although your acquaintance with
the Hungarian Constitution excited my greatest astonishment, your information on some points was not absolutely correct, and your opinions sometimes erroneous.
I am therefore convinced that I do you a service by
drawing your attention to some matters which have
escaped your notice, telling you quite honestly what
others dare not or will not tell you.

Your Highness must permit me to remind you that
we agreed to consider the distrust of the States of the
Government as the chief cause of all the disagreeables
(if I may so call them) which have occurred. Distrust
is want of confidence; and how is it possible, without
changing human nature, that confidence can reign where
promises are seldom kept; where the law is always explained in favour of the King, and to the disadvantage of
the people; and where, to speak plainly, affairs just now
have the appearance as if the Constitution were on the
point of being overturned?

(b.) Trust and distrust are doubtless fruits of experience.
But under certain conditions and in certain times they may be

mere delusions. I know only one period of Hungarian history in which Government threatened the Constitution. This was in the reign of the Emperor Joseph, much praised by the Liberals. In the year 1790–1, the Constitution became nominally and actually stronger than it had been before Joseph II.'s accession to the throne. In the next reign, that of the Emperor Francis I., there were twenty-six years of war. The six Diets, held in the general agitation, show not the smallest trace of want of respect to the Constitution on the part of the King. Now, in a time of peace and security, his Majesty has convoked the 'Reichstag,' and has given expression to those feelings which have been the firm and noble basis of his reign for thirty years.

What reason is there for distrust? It cannot be the principles of the monarch; for why should he exclude Hungary alone from the principle he has so often and so openly proclaimed in Hungary as elsewhere—'the maintenance of all existing rights'? Why should he give the lie to himself before his people and before the whole of Europe? If it was only want of experience which was the cause of the phenomena at the Diet, the Royal speech should have overcome them; for he does not speak as the Emperor spoke who intends to do the reverse of his words.

Is the distrust based upon facts? Why not expose them; why not be ready to have them explained?

Is there not a good deal of calculation in the manifestation of distrust? Is it not possible that Hungary has caught the malady of the time? Is there not in Hungary, as everywhere, a party to whom authority is disgusting, which uses law to cover private interests, and a systematic opposition as a means of gaining popularity? The further course of proceedings will prove if this be true.

I could prove all this by examples, and if you will judge impartially you will find I am right. But I will not detain you except on the essential matter of the Diet. His Majesty has gratified the States by a fatherly address, asking them to discuss the consolidation of the Constitution. The States, keeping firmly to their laws and customs, have been working and discussing for four weeks. At last they present most respectfully their memorial, the merit of which I will neither discuss for or against, being beside the question and not belonging to my subject. But there can be no doubt that the States consider the points mentioned in the above-named memorial as the most important means of supporting their Constitution, and are convinced that in presenting it to his Majesty they fulfilled their duty to their King and their country. Some weeks afterwards his Majesty's decision was made known to the States, the contents of which plainly express the principles of a quite absolute monarchy.

(c.) This representation of facts might be disputed as to its most essential points. It is true that his Majesty has expressed the sincere desire to fortify the Constitution by filling up the deficiencies of legislation, by reforming the administration of law, by establishing certain institutions which secure to a country, richly endowed by nature, the advantage of well-regulated industry, as health and well-regulated strength alone enable our bodies to enjoy life. Again, it is true that the States, after the loss of four weeks as far as public matters are concerned, have expressed their complaint against some facts and asked for some measures, the cause and rights of which I will not discuss here. It cannot be denied that the answer was delayed, but this was the will of Heaven, for the King fell ill. What value the explanations in regard to the principles of absolutism supposed to be expressed in the Royal resolution really possess, the next answer of his Majesty will bring to light. . . . Opposition counselled by passion will rarely hit the mark.

I am not going to examine how far it may be right or wrong to look for the principle of absolutism in the above-named Royal resolution. I will only ask if it is possible that the States, which cannot see any other meaning in it, can have after all much confidence, or if the anxiety be not pardonable which urges them to gain security on certain points of the Constitution.

(*d.*) Where no other sense can be found, further examination is certainly superfluous. The question whether the Prince's words do contain the sense of absolutism appears to me more to the purpose.

Can we ask a man who fears that his house is falling, to discuss the improvement and comfort of the interior?

(*e.*) No! but he would do wisely not to be alarmed till he has quietly examined whether his anxiety is justified, or if it be only a chimera.

Your Highness respects and honours all institutions which custom has sanctioned; the fundamental idea of your principles is legitimacy. You are so logical in your political and private life, that I am convinced of your wish to maintain the Constitution of Hungary in all its cardinal points as pure and sound as it was before the accession of the present dynasty.

(*f.*) The maintenance of the Hungarian Constitution must in every respect be considered so sacred a duty of the ministry, and so plain a command of right and prudence, that I should destroy my whole former political life by lending a willing ear to the contrary. But the more firmly and steadfastly I have taken my stand, the more freely I have a right to pronounce my confession of faith, which is as follows:—

The Constitution will never be threatened by a wise and just King. That which has defied the storms of time for eight centuries has proved its strength.

The dangers which threatened the Constitution come from a very different source. In times of violence, of bold experiments, in times when experience is insulted and displaced by theory, long-tried customs have always to go through hard struggles. Nowhere can such rich material for combat be found as in the whole affairs of Hungary. What in other States would simply be regarded as a change of form, would in Hungary endanger property, existence, and legal rights, and end in destruction. The changes wrought by time therefore bring danger, and what judgment can the calm observer, the true friend of Constitution, form of men who charge the King—and what is more, the present King—with the attacks with which his enemies threaten the general welfare ?

I must be very much mistaken if I interpret the leading idea of the conversation with which your Highness honoured me the other day, in any other sense —when you compared our Hungarian Constitution with a precious jewel which ought to be kept like a relic.

(g.) This remark contains all that I have said above.

When I reflect on this, as I hope, false conception of our situation, and the groundless anxiety of the States as a source of much evil, I cannot but lament that mutual enlightenments and explanations are not insisted on, the more as it would be easy to satisfy the States without violating the least right of his Majesty.

(h.) I believe that I may guarantee the fulfilment of this excellent desire, which is also mine.

To attain this purpose his Majesty should in his next resolution express the sincere constitutional feeling which he affirmed by oath on his accession to the throne. All the remarks which seemed to lean to absolutism would, if not repeated, be forgotten of themselves.

(i.) His Majesty must go further and proclaim, as error, what is error.

His Majesty should permit, without any condition, the legal convocation of the Diet, and this permission ought to be entirely independent of other political events and circumstances, as it touches upon the fundamental element of the Constitution clearly expressed in our laws and binding on the King.

Your Highness must confess that my countrymen, even if they have appeared to disadvantage, are worthy of the confidence of a just monarch. Can a man be a loyal subject of his King who does not cleave vigorously to the laws of his country? I do not believe it, and I shall always doubt the true worth of him who is unable manfully to defend his rights. I am convinced that I shall not offend your Highness by this letter, written with the greatest respect, for truth never offends one who is true himself. I am, &c.,

STEPHEN COUNT SZÉCHÉNYI.

DEATH OF THE EMPEROR ALEXANDER.

Metternich to Ottenfels, Vienna, December 18, 1825.

786. The shocking event which I mentioned in my preceding despatch is both more unexpected and more serious than can well be conceived.

In such an event reason requires that a statesman should face the truth, and to attain this end he must be careful to relinquish every feeling which could make him deviate from the simple search for probable and possible facts which may assist in regulating the approaching future. This search should be founded on his knowledge of individuals.

I abstain here from anything like a panegyric on the Emperor Alexander. His qualities, his virtues, his actions, both public and private, his faults and his weaknesses, have been clearly seen in the course of a reign of more than five-and-twenty years. They belong to the domain of history. I may be allowed to add that the materials for the history of the period in which the Emperor Alexander reigned, are in my opinion nowhere better known than at Vienna. I have no doubt either that this my conviction will be generally shared by all the enlightened men in Europe.

Moreover, we know his successor equally well, and it is on this double knowledge that I found, without fear of mistake, the following opinion on the first actions of his reign.

The Grand Duke Constantine has great parts, his

heart is noble and in the right place, his political principles most correct ; often little agreeing with the sentimental and romantic ideas of his august brother, he nevertheless most faithfully carried out all his wishes. No one knew how to obey better than the Grand Duke.

His youth was darkened by such impetuosity of character that his reputation has suffered considerably. Age has done much to calm this heat, and his wife exercises upon his irascible nature a great and salutary influence.

His policy will be entirely pacific. The bent of his mind has two objects : in politics, the support of the monarchical principle ; and in an administrative point of view, the internal amelioration of the empire. I deceive myself, if the *History* of Russia does not begin where the *Romance* of Russia ends.

I have every reason to believe that he will not interest himself in any way with the fate of the Greeks. He has always declared with contempt against them as a nation and with animadversion as subjects in revolt. He is devoted to Austria and to the union between the two Empires. He detests the English and despises the French. He looks upon Prussia as given up to revolution.

Such is substantially the view presented to our minds by the change of reigns. The future alone can prove if the presage will be confirmed by the actions of a reign which, according to all reports, will have many difficulties to surmount. The first of these will be, that the bonds of discipline have been much relaxed under the mild reign of Alexander, and consequently the acts of the new Emperor, interpreted by the fear he inspires, will gain for him a character for hardness and create a feeling of constraint which the nation has not experienced for more than five-and-twenty years—that is to say, for the lapse of a whole generation.

Is there a chance that the natural heir to the throne will not accept the crown? Many persons think so. A very short time ought to tell us what part the Grand Duke has already taken. If the Grand Duke Nicholas were to succeed (which he could only do after a formal act of renunciation on the part of his eldest brother) it would be impossible to cast any horoscope whatever of the new reign.

However this may be, this unlooked-for event, which the correspondence from Odessa will no doubt have made known at Constantinople before the arrival of the present post, must produce great excitement at the Ottoman Court.*

You will find M. de Minciaky very much embarrassed; you must pay him the greatest attention, and you cannot express too strongly the profound grief experienced by the Emperor our august master at the loss of an ally who was at the same time his life-long friend.

I can say nothing further at present. It is singular and deplorable that I should have to give you instructions on an event which, though apparently authentic, is not absolutely certain, and which, as you will observe, is not yet announced in our public journals.

Metternich to Lebzeltern, in St. Petersburg, Vienna, December 22, 1825.

787. In writing to your Excellency, it would be superfluous to revert to the probable or possible consequences of an event as unexpected as enormous in its inevitable consequences.

I send you some portions of correspondence which

will show you that up to this time we are still ignorant which of the two brothers will occupy the throne of Russia. M. de Tatistscheff has no doubt that the Emperor Constantine's first step is grounded on calculations on the opinion which he thinks predominates in his favour in Russia. M. de Tatistscheff believes that he wishes to be urged to retain the crown. I suspend my judgment on a fact which a few days will bring to light.

A new era is commencing. My spirit is transported by it and it sees. . . .

The choice which the Emperor our august master has made of the Archduke Ferdinand is undoubtedly most suitable, and will be at the same time very useful in a business point of view. This Prince has right and deep feelings, he is placed morally on the same line that we take ourselves; neither his mind nor his principles need give us the least anxiety. He will bring to your Excellency instructions which will be the more easily arranged as His Royal Highness will not leave Vienna until we know which of the two brothers is to occupy the throne of Russia.

PRINCE METTERNICH'S LECTURES TO THE ARCH-DUKES FERDINAND AND FRANZ CARL IN 1825.

Sketch in Metternich's handwriting.

Monday, January 17, 1825. First hour.

1. General idea of politics and diplomacy.
2. The advance of science in consequence of the ever increasing spread of civilisation. Ministry of Cardinal Richelieu.
3. Institution of secret State service. Its functions and objects. Its action on the administration.

Friday, January 21, 1825.

1. The idea of true policy and diplomacy. These are limited to the permanent and real interests of the States. Disadvantages of a policy grounded on mere passions.
2. Comparison between the policy of Louis XIV., Napoleon, and Frederick II.
3. Reflections on Austria's views of aggrandisement.
4. What is Austria's true policy?

Monday, January 24, 1825.

1. The spirit of the age.
2. The French Revolution.
3. *Principes de droit et de fait.*

Monday, January 31, 1825.

1. Effects of the French Revolution in the whole of Europe.

2. Secret Societies.
3. Their general tendency.
4. Their formation.
5. They are but means to an end.

Friday, February 4, 1825.

1. Secret Societies, continued.
2. Freemasons : their first aims not culpable. But they have been divided into so many sects that Freemasonry proper no longer exists. It serves as the ready prepared instrument to spread and increase the intrigues of secret conspiracies against religion and the State.
3. Carbonarism. Adelphism. The Carbonarist institution is remarkable, because by its simplicity of form it makes the sect suit the ideas of the lower classes.

CHARLES ALBERT PRINCE DE CARIGNAN,
AFTERWARDS KING OF SARDINIA.*

A contribution towards the understanding of his character. By Prince
Metternich.

789. After the beginning of the revolution in
Piedmont in 1820–21, King Charles Felix was firmly
resolved to exclude the Prince de Carignan, who had
come forward as one of the leaders of the Revolution,
from the succession, and to name his son heir to the
throne.   In departing from a pragmatic hereditary succession the King wished to secure the sanction of the
Emperor Francis, but the Emperor opposed those
measures.   He was of opinion, and I fully agreed with
him, that exclusions of such a peculiar nature cannot
but be destructive of peace (see No. 557).   When the
Emperor in 1825 visited Lombardy and Venetia, this
question was the subject of an animated correspondence.
King Charles Felix himself proposed to meet the
Emperor at Milan.   The Emperor profited by the
opportunity to influence the King's decision.   He
declared that he could not receive the King till the
question of the non-interruption of the hereditary succession had been settled, in which case the Emperor
would prefer an interview at Genoa to an interview at
Milan.   'The Piedmontese,' wrote the Emperor, 'will
be much gratified if I visit them, and Genoa will be

---

* This sketch was written many years later, but is inserted here as the
events to which it refers occurred in 1825.—ED.

grateful if she is chosen to be the place of rendez-vous.'

The King agreed, and engaged to abandon his inten-tions with regard to Prince de Carignan, on the under-standing that the Prince de Carignan should be intro-duced to the King by the Emperor after the interview of the two sovereigns at Genoa. This plan was strictly followed. On the arrival of the Emperor at Genoa, where the King had arrived some days before, a courier was sent to Turin requesting the Prince to present himself to the Emperor at Genoa. The King, very much dis-pleased with the whole affair, said to me, " *J'ai cédé à la volonté de l'Empereur, autant par suite du respect que je lui porte que par suite de l'hommage que je rends au sen-timent qui l'anime, et qui est celui de l'ordre appuyé sur des principes et sur l'expérience. Ce dont par contre je ne puis me défendre, c'est de la conviction que ce sera l'Autriche qui en particulier aura à se plaindre d'un homme dont les idées sont entièrement perverties !* "

I answered that the Emperor's line of conduct had not been dictated by any feelings of confidence in the Prince; that during the discussion of hereditary succes-sion he had kept strictly to the question itself, without regard to the personality of the heir apparent; and that of two evils he had chosen the least.

Two days later the Prince de Carignan and his wife arrived at Genoa. A private house had been prepared for his reception by the King's order, and he went im-mediately to see the Emperor. After an interview of an hour with his Majesty, he stayed three hours with me, and as it was late in the evening, I could not see the Emperor till the next morning. He received me with the words, 'Well, what impression has the Prince de Carignan made upon you?' Being anxious to know

what impression his Majesty had received during the
long conversation, I asked the Emperor not to alter the
chronological order of events. 'The Prince has not
made a very favourable impression upon me,' answered
the Emperor; 'he is a "talker," and these people I
distrust!' 'I see in your Majesty's words,' said I, 'the
very same impression that I received in our three hours
conversation.' 'For all that,' said the Emperor, 'nothing else can be done in the matter but what we have
done.' The same morning the Emperor presented the
Prince to the King. Charles Albert knelt before the
King and begged forgiveness with tears. 'It is to the
Emperor,' exclaimed the King, 'and not to your birth
or to me that you are indebted. Never forget that,
and never give your protector reason to regret his
generosity.'

The Prince declared he was firmly determined, and
the rest of the monarchs' visit to Genoa passed off
quietly.

The political and personal course taken by King
Charles Albert after his accession to the throne need
not be touched on here. Up to the year of the coronation of the Emperor Ferdinand at Milan (1838), he gave
no cause for complaints on the part of Austria. The
Emperor and the King met at Pavia, where I also met
the King for the first time since 1825.

The King of Sardinia had his quarters in the same
house as the Emperor, who received him on his arrival.
The King passed half-an-hour with the Emperor, and
when returning through the Emperor's anteroom he
called me, and taking my arm led me to his apartment,
when the following remarkable and characteristic conversation ensued. Sitting by my side on a sofa, the
King began :—

'I have waited with much impatience for the happy moment when, after the years which have passed between our first meeting at Genoa and that of to-day, I am able to ask you this question: "Are you content with me, and do you consider that I have fulfilled, or not, the engagements which in 1825 I contracted with the Emperor and his minister?" You will perhaps be surprised at my addressing this question to you, so to speak, point blank. I do so for this reason: I read at Genoa, both in the face of the Emperor Francis and on your own, that you did not place entire confidence in my explanations of an unhappy past, nor in my engagements with regard to the future. I confess to you that I was not surprised; I should have even been astonished if your impressions had been otherwise.'

Myself: 'The Emperor and I did not doubt the intentions which you expressed to us, but the possibility of your ever being able, even in the very interest of your future, after the evils of 1820 and 1821, to repair the faults which an unfortunate enthusiasm had caused you to commit. You have kept your word to the Emperor, and if he were placed before you, Sire, he would confirm this judgment.'

The King: 'I am delighted to see you accept what I regard as a full justification of my conduct as a ruler. But this is not all. The circumstance of our meeting is too precious for me not to take advantage of it in the interest of a cause which is common to us, and at the same time is that of the whole social body.

'Do me the favour to listen, and accept what I say as the greatest proof of confidence. There is a vast conspiracy in the world; it seems to be only directed against thrones, but is really directed against the peace of the whole social body. I need not tell you this; what I wish to prove is that I am not, as many others are, the dupe of a faction; on the other hand, there is no doubt that the position of the King of Sardinia is the most difficult of all positions. This is owing to the faults of the Piedmontese nature, a timid sort of nature, at once daring and fearful, disputatious and cunning; the position of the head of a country animated by such an unhappy spirit is rendered eminently difficult, for it is always hampered, and must therefore be ever open to suspicion on the part of the other Cabinets. The Piedmontese mind is before everything anti-Austrian; the very air that blows from France nourishes this tendency. You know what I think of the policy *du juste milieu,* and you know that you can reckon on me. But there may be occasions when my conduct will not appear clear to you. On these occasions address me directly. Write to me and do not trust your letters to the post, but send them by a safe hand to your ambassador at Turin. He would give them to me himself without speaking of the matter to anyone, and you will receive my explanations in the same way.'

Myself: 'I shall very rarely permit myself to use the privilege which your Majesty gives me, and for this reason. I know the Piedmontese mind; I know how very difficult it is to lead. The only way to deal with it is by perfect openness on the part of those who have nothing to conceal, either of what they wish, or the course they mean to take.'

The King with difficulty agreed to my opinion. But I held to it firmly, and the documents of the secret State-office prove that I remained faithful to it.

1826.

EVENTS OF THE DAY.

Extracts from Metternich's Private Letters to his son Victor, to his Mother, and to Baron Neumann, from January 1 to December 25, 1826.

Metternich to Neumann, Vienna, January 1, 1826.

790. Nothing new yet in the affair of the Emperors. On the 29th, Constantine made several ladies at Warsaw put off the mourning they were wearing for Alexander; he will have it that the Emperor lives. They say the Grand Duke Michael returned to St. Petersburg in consequence of an order from Constantine which he found at Kowno. Meantime all the troops—except those of the Kingdom of Poland—have taken the oath to the Emperor Constantine I.

Tatistscheff has not had mass said in the chapel attached to the embassy, because he does not know for which Emperor to pray. He has orders to receive the oaths of Russian subjects; he delays his decision, for he believes that Constantine will end by accepting the crown. Russia, in the meantime has no master, and Poland finds herself under another *régime.*

The liberal newspapers make the most of this strange situation; they always bracket me with the Emperor Alexander, and they are not far wrong, but they do themselves no good by it. The liberals thus warn his successor against separating from a man who knows how to resist them, for I doubt very much the Emperor of

Russia ever becoming a good republican. If poor Alexander had not committed faults in his youth, and if in mature age he had not '*manqué de quelque chose,*' as Napoleon said, where would the Liberalism of to-day be? If from the heights of Paradise things below can occupy one, Alexander comprehends me now better than he ever did on earth, and his soul ought to come to meet and support mine.

Metternich to his son Victor, Vienna, January 3.

791. The suit between the world and Mr. Canning will not be judged before the tribunal of our embassy in London.

The suit may be gained or lost, but it will be pleaded. Judgment will be pronounced in the first six months of this year. In June I will remind you of what I now tell you.

. . . The affairs of the Diet of Hungary will soon be terminated. We have gained every case, and those who formerly fought against the Court are now fighting among themselves. This is just an example of the fact that when Kings know when to say ' No ' they gain their cause. The Emperor has thanked me in the most touching way for all my trouble, for it was quite by chance that the Hungarian affairs fell latterly on my already overladen shoulders.

Metternich to Neumann, Vienna, January 7.

792. . . . The courier with the news of December 26 has arrived from St. Petersburg. The deplorable struggle is over, and we have an Emperor. I congratulate Russia and Europe. (Nos. 829–831.)

The accession has been marked by a military revolt. I hope that the Emperor, who has behaved well on the occasion, will thoroughly investigate the matter, and not be content with superficial inquiries. Setting aside many private misfortunes, the event has two favourable sides: one is that of preventing the young monarch from believing the honeyed language which will be used towards him by his most determined enemies; the other, that of showing him that material distance is not sufficient to place one beyond moral influences and odious attempts. Russia has *la maladie du temps*, like all other countries. The accession of Nicholas will probably lead to fewer changes than there would have been under Constantine. Nothing remains of the ephemeral and fantastic reign of the latter except several miserable diplomatic despatches on his renunciation. There is nothing to find fault with in the proclamation of the new Emperor, which is very correct; it rests principally on the declaration of the Emperor Alexander in 1823. There is not a single paragraph in it which does not show right principles.

The sea rises, it is very rough, and the wind—of affairs—begins to blow. He is the most skilful who knows how to find its direction, and not always he who goes the fastest.

Metternich to his son Victor, Vienna, January 27.

793. I have received, my dear Victor, your Reports and letters from London. The former are very well done, and the Emperor has read them with interest.

. . . I beg you to fix your attention somewhat more particularly on what the Russians (especially the Princess Bagration) say on the situation of things in Russia. You will see from what I told Vincent in my last despatch what the affair really is. It is neither more nor less than an exact copy of those of Madrid,

Naples, and Turin. The conspiracy has immense ramifications, and the number of individuals already arrested is between twelve and thirteen hundred. Among this number are persons of the highest classes of Russian society. If the Emperor Alexander had lived, the same thing would have happened, and he and the Imperial family would have been massacred. . . . Lebzeltern cannot remain at St. Petersburg. He is too much compromised by his brother-in-law Trubetzkoi.* The public already regard him as a Carbonaro. Ah well! Lebzeltern, with all his good qualities, is one of those who never believe in the existence of sticks until they have been beaten to powder. He believes in conspiracies now his brother-in-law has been arrested as a conspirator. Whenever I expressed my opinion to the Emperor Alexander, Lebzeltern, and oftener still Nesselrode, have taxed me with being a visionary, and with behaving badly to the Emperor of Russia. See what the Russian Carbonari are saying at Paris: every word is an indication to me. It is impossible yet to foresee where the affair will stop. Meantime it somewhat disconcerts our young noblemen.

Another who is almost equally compromised is Felix Schwarzenberg. He has lived on terms of the greatest intimacy with all these young scatterbrains, certainly without knowing anything of the conspiracy which was hatching; but his choice of company is returning on his own head. . . .

Leontine will tell you about our balls. I am in no humour for dancing. I refer you therefore to her accounts.

---

* Prince Trubetzkoi, who was at the head of the conspiracy against the Emperor Nicholas, concealed himself at the house of Lebzeltern, his brother-in-law.—ED.

I yesterday sent to my agents to purchase Plass for me. It is to be sold by auction on the 30th of this month.

794. *February* 14.—I have bought Plass, and it is a great acquisition. I send you a description of the place. These are inferior little engravings, but they shew you the Château de Plass, and I shall be much surprised if you have ever seen anything grander. Besides the *château*—that is, the old abbey—there are three others of less importance. We must decide on the spot which of them can be made habitable without a ruinous expenditure.

795. *February* 18.—The news from Russia are very disquieting for the safety and internal peace of that country. I am writing more at length to Apponyi.

Take a kindly leave of M. de Vincent. He deserves it, for his conduct lately has been admirable. If he had not so many eccentricities he would be perfect in his place, but they spoil everything. Eccentricities are incompatible with business, and as soon as they seize upon a business man he is ruined.

796. *February* 20.—I have not been better in health for many years than I am at present. Ischl has done me a great deal of good. *A propos* of health, you may announce everywhere that the Emperor has been marvellously well since his illness at Pressburg. This will enrage the journalists, who would like to see us both very far from this lower world.

797. *March* 2.—I have suffered for the last fortnight from a cold in the head; it has passed away now, and I am perfectly well. Everybody in the town has either measles or cold. Your sisters as yet have escaped the first of these maladies, and, as the weather has changed suddenly, I suppose the epidemic is over.

Continue to observe the Russians, and tell me all
you know. You have no idea how we are abused by
the Russian knaves. They are only singing in their
natural voice, and this voice they have in common with
all the Radical newspapers in the world. It is a storm
which must be allowed to pass over, and which will not
even wet us; but those who go out in it will be
drenched—that is, the bawlers themselves.

798. *March* 16.—The Emperor's serious illness has
passed away; he has been for six days between life and
death; to-day he is convalescent, but he will need the
greatest care during his return to health. There is, however, every probability of his living a long time, for he
has no organic disease, and his lungs are in a normal state.
I need not tell you that these last six days have been
full of terrible anxieties for me. . Besides the uneasiness
which I had felt from the beginning of his Majesty's
illness, I had to think of the future—or rather to
arrange it.

I have never left the Palace or my desk, and God
has sustained me, as in so many other trials which I
have been called upon to bear in my long and painful
career. God has placed me in this world to labour,
and with this thought I yield to His will. The different
effects produced by the events we have escaped will be
curious to observe. I almost allow myself to hope that
the *Journal des Débats* will give us lessons on what we
should have to do after the Emperor's death. But
petit bonhomme lives still, and that is what friends
and relations did not expect.

Tell me all you hear about this affair. Your *résumé*
of the last despatches from London is perfectly correct,
and I am quite satisfied with your work.

Metternich to Neumann, Vienna, March 18.

799. We have just passed through a very painful crisis. The Emperor has been at death's door; he is saved, and nothing remains of his malady but the certainty that his constitution is, contrary to all appearances, really strong. Good comes out of evil. The probability of his death will have brought many feelings to light. With us there is but one, that of the love which children bear to their father.

It is known by this time that difficult circumstances act upon me only in the sense of an appeal to means of opposing them. On the second day I admitted the possibility of the Emperor's death, and I then passed, so to speak, three entire days under the new reign. Except myself no one knew it, and I believe I may say no one suspected it. But I have obtained much and useful experience; I have learnt what I am, and what the mass of the public believes me to be. I had no need to seek for anyone; all came pressing round me: friends, enemies, and the indifferent—everybody. A great empire, whose movements are regulated by immemorial custom, is a grand and beautiful thing. Its resources never having been disturbed, everything is ready to hand when required.

The trouble is over, let us talk no more of it. God has not taken to Himself in the short space of three months two men so different in their nature and yet united by the strongest and most indissoluble bonds.

800. *March* 20.—I do not know a more difficult post to occupy than that of the Emperor Nicholas. I will give you a sketch of Russia.

Peter the Great changed her frontiers. In Asia he

moved them westward—in a word, he said to Russia, 'Thou shalt henceforth be part of Europe.' He was right in this, but he was wrong to destroy so many of the ancient institutions of the State and not replace them.

Catherine II., entirely European, thought only of glory. She was a thorough woman, and she had the misfortune to live in the era of encyclopædists.

Paul I., if he had not been insane, would have rendered great services to his country. His sentiments were thoroughly monarchical. His characteristics are sufficiently shown in the act by which he regulated the succession to the throne.

Alexander, who was fortunate in taking the crown after his father, was unhappily the child of the age. Always going from one religion to another, from one taste to another, he moved everything and built nothing. Everything in him was superficial and exaggerated, and he ever inclined to prefer bad means to good: at the end of five-and-twenty years he left his empire at the point to which the Emperor Joseph II. had conducted his in nine years. Joseph II. however, was an administrator, and the Russian monarch was not.

The population of Russia is divided into two classes; in this respect it resembles the States of the middle ages; the difference, however, is in the quality of the classes. The aristocracy forms everywhere else the superior class, but in Russia it is only the principal persons—or, we may say, the Court and its suite—who form the superior class.

In an empire thus organised, full of peculiar positions, of necessities which exist nowhere else, the Emperor Alexander wished to introduce the refinements and the abuses of what in my opinion is very improperly described by the epithet of modern civilisation—a monster without a body and all ideas!

His successor will have to search for the body, and he will have much trouble in finding it. Russia is not unlike a banqueting-hall the day after the feast. What in the evening before produced all the effect of solid and brilliant substances is seen on the morrow to be not more valuable than the cloth, false diamonds, embroidery and trimmings of which it is composed.

Old Russia exists no longer. Nicholas has been called upon to create a new one, and my heartiest wishes accompany him in this grand and noble enterprise.

Metternich to his son Victor, Vienna, March 22.

801. We seem to have entered on a time of peace and calm. The Emperor is quite well; not only do we no longer feel any anxiety about him, but we see daily how excellent is his constitution, and how free he is from any bad tendencies. Yesterday, the twelfth day after the beginning of the illness, I passed more than an hour working with him, and his only annoyance was his having still to take care of himself.

. . . Gentz is enchanted with you. If you wish to make him foolishly fond, send him some bonbon or new perfume.

802. *March* 27.—I am surprised that on March 17 you had received no news of the trouble which, since the 10th, had fallen upon Vienna. You would have been much moved, and the arrival of the news of two monarchs dead (for they would not fail to regard the Emperor as such) must have caused great consternation to the good people. I expect the *Journal des Débats* will have given me some very sage counsel in my difficult position. Be that as it may, the dead

Emperor is remarkably well. He got up yesterday for the first time, and it would be impossible for his convalescence to be more complete, more speedy, and more thorough than it is.

I return thanks to God, who has brought me individually out of great tribulation. The idea of being chained more than I already am to my desk ; of not being able to stir from Vienna ; of seeing my business increase tenfold—all these thoughts made me very unhappy, setting aside the fact of my tender affection for the Emperor, a man who has overwhelmed me with kindnesses, who regards me as his greatest friend, and who loves me as I love him.

The popular feeling has been shown in these grave circumstances throughout all Germany. All the accounts show what immense moral power has been acquired, far beyond the frontiers of his Empire, by the simple and modest man who bears the name of Francis I.

The King of Portugal has given me great pleasure by continuing to live.

Thank Pierre d'Arenberg for his care of my flowers ; I will write to him when I have time.

The children are charmingly well. You would not know Leontine. She is very tall and very pretty. She will soon be the belle of society, into which, however, I am far from wishing to thrust her yet. She is, besides, the best little maid in the world. All her masters, among others, adore her. Mademoiselle Tardivau, her governess, has already become quite a Viennese.

803. *April* 4.—We are just in the crisis of the change from winter to spring, and the labour is a difficult one. I hope for your satisfaction that you are more advanced than we are here. Among other things,

we have had a hurricane for the last three days, which
has knocked down everything. Yesterday, for instance,
the balustrade of the " Bellaria " fell in the square, and
it would have struck me if I had come out two or three
minutes sooner to go to the Emperor. To-day, three
grenadiers have been killed by the fall of a chimney.
You see that our upper regions are not very secure.

Metternich to Neumann, Vienna, April 8.

804. . . . The real position of the poor Emperor
Alexander was difficult to understand. He himself did
not understand it, for those who lead things to the
verge of ruin do not see clearly. I was the confidant
of more than one secret thought of the Emperor, and I
have guessed more still. I have been witness of his
fears, and have often even been called to be the judge
of his remorse; but the exact knowledge of Russia was
wanting to me, so that I could not foresee everything.
I saw that a great evil existed, without being able to
fix its limits. I am able to state with perfect confidence that latterly Alexander was occupied with but
one thing, and that was the desire of saving himself and
his country from the ruin which he felt to be certain.

In the lives of men and in the course of great affairs
opportunities sometimes occur which if they can be
seized decide the whole future. One of these moments
was in the spring of the year 1825. If in the month of
March I had been near the Emperor, many things would
have turned out differently for him, and consequently
for his empire.

805. *April* 14.—The Emperor Nicholas has just
taken a grand step in the burning question of the
moment.

If Alexander had done five years ago what his successor had just done, the detestable Eastern Question would have ceased to exist, and we might have helped the Greeks with some reason.

Metternich to his son Victor, Vienna, April 20.

806. I find that M. d'Arlincourt is a type of the period. It is only in times of folly and bad taste that men of his stamp find anyone to applaud them. Your quotations from his tragedy are charming, and they have not failed to produce on all who have heard them the same effect as on the boxes of the *Théâtre Français*.

My plans for the summer can be arranged after the first, or at any rate after the second, news from Constantinople. I say after the second, for I admit the chance that the Divan may resist until the very eve of the peremptory term of six weeks which the Emperor Nicholas has given it. If the negotiation goes on then, I shall gain six or eight weeks, which is what I hope for.

. . . . Your sisters and your grandmamma will be very happy to see you. The former seem to grow as one looks at them, and are very pretty. Leontine danced at my party yesterday. It is the fashion now to dance in the evenings, and I pleased the child by conforming to the fashion. These small dances, which last two or three hours, do no harm to anyone.

Tell Pelissier to make me a subscriber to *L'histoire générale des voyages*, by Walckenaër.

I also wish him to send me Geoffroy's *feuilletons*, six numbers, and the works of Rabaut Saint-Etienne, two volumes.

Metternich to Neumann, Vienna, April 21.

807. If I can (the mud will decide it), I should like to spend the months of July and August away from my desk. I shall go and see a great acquisition I have made in Bohemia, for it is foolish to spend nearly four million francs on a place I do not know. I have contracted a marriage by proxy; they say my wife is very beautiful, but I wish at least to know it for myself.

808. *April* 28.—They have done, in my opinion, very miserable work at St. Petersburg; everything is changed as if by the stroke of a wand. The Emperor from being strong has become weak; his correct political attitude has changed. I shall be able to boast of having co-operated in the March business : I should not like to be responsible for that of April.* If Russia were a country *à la mode,* I should say that the ministers had spoilt the Prince's ideas.

What will happen in Europe? I know not. My most sincere wishes are for the success of an enterprise which, unfortunately, everything tells me will not succeed, or rather that evil will be so bound up in it that it will not be possible to recognise the good.

809. *May* 12.—. . . I am perfectly satisfied with the first conception of the Emperor Nicholas and the way he has put it into execution. It is what his predecessor ought to have done, and what if he had done he would have spared the world from six years of torments, and the Cabinets from being seriously compromised. The Porte would have done then what it will do now : it would have yielded; the Greeks would have been saved, which they will not be now; a civilised existence could have been procured for them with ease : which is what the Emperor Alexander desired, and what we desired with him.

* In March Russia confined her action to her own affairs with the Porte; in April she extended it to Greece.—ED.

We wished for nothing better than to see a free and independent Greek Empire! We proposed it; we were exclaimed against, and I understand why.

Nous ne marchons pas, et nous ne marcherons jamais, dans les eaux troublés ni vers les demibuts.

We wish for the preservation of political peace; but not because we have taken up the utopias of the Abbé de St.-Pierre. In a word, we wish always, and once for all, the contrary of what our enemies wish. The day when they wish for peace, we shall be asking ourselves if the time has not arrived for war.

We wish that these skirmishings between two neighbouring Powers would cease, or at least be suspended, were it only that skirmishings never do any good.

Never, no never, should we advise others to do what we are determined not to do ourselves. Thus we shall never protect a system of conquest. Is it desired to chase the Turks from Europe? Well, let them be chased, and let a great empire be established in their place. But where are the elements of this empire—where is even its population? Where are its institutions, its prince, its people? We do not wish for a republic of bandits, or a monarchy composed and organised by the scum of the revolutionists of Europe. I will answer for it that the Emperor of Russia will never wish in this respect what the Emperor of Austria will not allow. I believe even that in Russia they are still more interested than in Austria that the revolution should not triumph.

We have approved frankly and unreservedly the first determination of the Emperor Nicholas, because it is right, clear, precise, and vigorous, and consequently will attain its end.

We deplore the second affair, seeing that it is of an entirely opposite character. It will lead to no good; the work of April 4 is an abortion which in a few weeks will be disowned by the very people who formed it.*

810. *May* 21.—I am making my preparations to leave on July 1. The world thinks it a great movement; I am sure of profound peace, and I shall be a nobody for two months away from here. I have no urgent need for my health, which is very good, and really much better than it has been for years; but I need repose from the usual burdens of existence. I hope that my stay at Plass will make less noise than that at Paris. The latter, however, had the same political value, in spite of all that more than one simpleton tried to discover of importance in it!

811. *May* 24.—The Porte will yield to the demands of Russia, while it falls with all its weight on Mr. Stratford Canning. One of these facts is as natural as the other.

As Canning always does the contrary of what I should do, it is just to allow that he also thinks exactly opposite to what I think. Perhaps he will find that the part which England plays in these affairs is convenient and useful. All I know is that Mr. Stratford Canning does not know what to do, and that, instead of saving the Greeks, the English policy will cause them

---

* According to the transaction signed in the name of the English Government by Wellington, and in the name of the Russian Government by Nesselrode and Lieven, Greece was to remain dependent on Turkey, paying the Turks a yearly fixed tribute, but governed by authorities of its own choice and enjoying a perfect freedom of conscience and commerce. The Courts of Vienna, Paris, and Berlin were invited to join in the convention. Austria and Prussia, however, declined any direct interference in the affairs of Greece. (No. 832.)—ED.

to be massacred by degrees, and, in fact, ruin them. Is that what it wished?

Fine weather at last. We have made our leap from winter to summer. I pass several hours every day among my flowers, and am quite happy. They are worth more than politics.

812. *May* 30.—The peace of Europe will be preserved; this is the principal thing, and the wishes of all good men will be fulfilled.

The alliance, which has been regarded as dead for the last year, lives and will live. It is I who say so: not the alliance such as its enemies have tried to misrepresent it, but such as it really is, simple, pure, and strong, as everything is which is true—such as, for my own part, I have always conceived and applied it.

They are altogether deceived in London, but that is endemic with them. Wellington has received orders to prevent a war which it is believed he was longing for, but did not wish to take the initiative if it could be avoided! They would have sworn at London that the Porte would never agree to such an arrangement; it has agreed. I may deceive myself, but I think I know better how to estimate men, their needs, and consequently their desires, than Canning.

Metternich to his son Victor, Vienna, May 31.

813. I shall only wait for the arrival of the first courier from Russia—who will bring us news of the effects of the benign decision of the Porte—to fix the date of my journey. Nothing shall prevent it; I shall go straight from here to Plass, where I shall arrive on the 3rd or 4th of August. I shall be there twelve or fifteen days, then eight or ten at Königswart, then, if the skies favour me, about the same time at Johannisberg. I shall end my travels by going in the latter part of August to join the children at Ischl.

You will have heard of the deplorable end of young Lord Ingestre. He was drowned at the Prater, in a pond of water about as large as a medium-sized ball-room. He was mounted on a restive horse; the pond is to the right of the bridge on the road to the *Lusthaus*; the horse not liking to go over the bridge, he took the path by the side of the pond, and there he was thrown backwards into the water. His body was found after much dragging, which proved that the pond was twenty feet deep. To-day they have very properly surrounded it with a fence. In the course of twenty years seven or eight people have been drowned there, and once a waggon and horses. . . .

We have newspapers from Paris up to the 23rd. I expect to-morrow to hear of the effect produced by the news of the Porte's submission. The Liberals have a peculiar talent for deceiving themselves; the reason is that their cause rests on error, and knows not how to produce anything else! To defeat these men one has only to wait. To reach them one has but to stand still. But herein lies the difficulty of the work, and if God has given me one quality, it is that of being able to support the State firm and upright in the midst of tumult. This is what I have known how to do ever since I have been at the head of affairs, and certainly I shall not discontinue what I have found so valuable a specific. When I look round me and find only myself standing on a field strewn with dead and wounded, I must say decidedly that I have chosen a good place! They shall never make me move, and the Liberals, with their whole following of fools and doctrinaries, shall not win the day as long as God gives me strength.

Metternich to Neumann, Vienna, June 5.

814. We are now plunged into a new grief. What a touching fate is that of the Empress Elizabeth! The history of the latter period of the life of the Imperial couple is moral feeling exemplied. How small are the grandeurs of this world! Taganrog and Beleff, two places abandoned by nature and man, and whose very existence was unknown till lately, find themselves surrounded with glory and homage!

We shall not send an Ambassador Extraordinary to the coronation. France and England have sent such a reinforcement that the Emperor does not wish to enter into rivalry with them. The Prince of Hesse will take a simple letter of congratulation to Moscow.

Metternich to his son Victor, Vienna, June 7.

815. I am charmed, my dear Victor, that you have gained your pacific wager, and you know now why the Sultan has yielded, and why the Emperor Nicholas has declared himself satisfied. The greatest events often have the most trifling causes. Your 500 francs have saved the social body and defeated the sanguinary projects of the Liberals. It is fortunate they knew nothing of the fact, or they would have counterbalanced your bet by some national subscription.

Read my despatches for London (No. 832), they will enable you to see into affairs, and the opinion I have of them.

Herminie is forming herself after the model of M. Giroux. I give you two of her speeches this week.

During her arithmetic lesson she was asked what was produced by the division of a unit? She answered: 'Two.' To prove it, she tore a sheet of paper in half.

In her geography lesson Mademoiselle Tardivau asked her who discovered America?

She replied: 'A Mr. Pigeon!' Mademoiselle Tardivau, startled, and not comprehending her, asked her if she were dreaming! 'Not at all,' replied Herminie; 'you told me he was called Colombe. Now, *colombe* and *pigeon* are the same thing!' Odry* would make something of these sayings.

Metternich to Neumann, Vienna, June 12.

816. I am now leading a very idle life. I do nothing of any consequence, except some stupid home affairs, some tiresome protocols of the Hungarian Parliament. I might as well be at Madrid or at Madras as Vienna. For a long time there has been no diplomatic affair in Europe; that which occupies men's minds never had any real value; nothing is worse than to dabble in business without understanding it. The Emperor Nicholas has had the good sense to make himself master of his affairs, and from that moment he knew how to regulate them.

How much time and how many words have been wasted in these unhappy dissensions! The late Emperor made the mistake of wishing for seven-eighths, and of not wishing for the last eighth. Hence all his affairs were guesswork, and nothing is worse or leads one farther astray.

My feeling about the difference of the two affairs— the decision of March 17 and the protocol of April 4— is it not beginning to be, or rather is it not already, amply justified? The idea of Nicholas was good; that of Wellington was miserable. The first will lead to

* A comic actor in Paris at the Théâtre des Variétés.

everything; the second will lead to nothing. The difference is great.

The world, in the meantime, is delivered up to a great and deplorable phantasmagoria. I mean the Philhellenic affair.

If I use this word plainly, it will be said that I have become a Mohammedan. Now, this is what I protest against, and I will justify my protestation.

I commence by asserting that I am a better Christian than Benjamin Constant, Hobhouse, Chateaubriand, the Abbé de Pradt, and all the rest of the set. Then, I am convinced that I am more human than Lord Cochrane and Colonel Fabvier, and further, that I have a hundred times more mind, understanding and sense than M. Eynard—who, by the by, is a man who has annoyed me more than anyone in the world.

Besides all this, I confess that I very much prefer the Greeks to the Turks; for, both being barbarians, there is more hope of Christians than of Mussulmans.

This said, I inveigh against the villany of making religion and humanity a pretext to overthrow the regular course of things; against the folly of Governments which cannot escape from one or other of these charges—either of tolerating what they do not wish to support, or of proving that what they cannot do, these wretched committees can quite well do for them. In the latter case, I should prefer to abdicate, descend from the height of an illusory power, and give up the reins of government to the Philhellenic committees.

This folly, like all others, will pass away, and the poor Greeks alone will have been the victims. If, instead of fighting with phantoms for the last five years, they had done what I was most anxious for them to do, the Greeks —as far as it was possible—would have been saved.

Many things will become clear very shortly!

817. *June* 19.—*A propos* of fashion, here is a new one I find coming in. Mr. Canning is beginning to be called in the French newspapers the accomplice of that abominable Head of the Holy Alliance. I had not expected this, but we always get what we least expect. I shall soon be accused of having drawn up Mr. Stratford Canning's instructions; of having cooked the protocol of April 4; of having commanded Lord Hamilton's expeditions. We live in an age when intellect goes begging. Really it is not worth the trouble of having; it is much too common. Therefore it gives me great pleasure when they describe me as a species of wild beast. Not long ago I saw this in print, and the author of the article was certainly not aware how much he gratified my vanity. Nowadays it is with mind very much as it is with decorations—the way to be distinguished is not to have any.

818. *June* 22.—There are in this world two kinds of minds: one skims over everything and gets to the bottom of nothing; the other grasps things and gets to know them. Canning possesses a great deal of mind of the first species; I have certainly less mind than he, and the little I have is in the second category. Canning flies, I walk; he rises to a region where men dwell not, while I remain on the level of all things human. Hence he will have the Romanticists on his side, while I shall be reduced to simple prosaic souls. His career is as brilliant as a flash of lightning, but as transient; mine does not dazzle, but it preserves what the other consumes!

This is the simple but undoubted truth. It is always discovered by the historian, but it often escapes contemporaries. Men like Canning fall twenty times and rise twenty times: men like myself have not the trouble of getting up, for they are not so subject to fall. The first always amuse and occupy the public; the second often bore it. I must be a very tiresome object to watch to the immense majority of those who regard me; but they must put up with that, for I shall not change.

819. *July* 2.—The West has taken a new flight in its revolutionary career. Don Pedro is praised as the most liberal of princes, and consequently as the model of monarchs, by those who not eight days ago abused him as a tiger thirsting for Republican blood. Extremes meet in the Liberal faction; they know no happy medium.

Those who like disturbances will have them. They believe at Paris that England is an accomplice: they are mistaken, or at least are only half right. The present British Cabinet is the natural accomplice of all the extravagances of the time; it is not, however, the author of them on this occasion, but, the things being done, it supports them and their consequences.

I am so accustomed to see kings look upon themselves as an abuse, that I should not be surprised if I saw one of them begging to be made the churchwarden of a parish. Far from being surprised, I quite expect it. Moreover, I am not put out in any of my calculations, and the Head of the Holy Alliance is without any doubt less surprised than any other statesman at this moment.

A few days ago I was present at a very painful scene. I was in Hungary on business connected with our tiresome Diet. The Chancellor of Hungary (Count Kohary), with whom I had been working and walking all day, and with whom I had dined, was struck with apoplexy while talking to me and old Zichy. He died in the middle of a sentence; I did all I could to help him, but one cannot help the dead.

820. *July* 3.—I have come to the end of my stay. I intend to leave on the 16th for Bohemia ; I shall be by August 10 or 12 on the banks of the Rhine. Politicians are speaking of a Congress at Johannisberg. I know nothing about it, and yet I ought to know. But the world loves fairy-tales, and the human mind has returned to the golden age—that is to say, the age which preceded history. The world is peopled again with demigods; nectar and ambrosia flow everywhere, and Lethe seems to wash the thresholds of the clubs and of more than one Cabinet. It is sad to possess so little poetic spirit that what gives general satisfaction does not affect one. This is the piteous case in which I find myself; I see things as they are, and so many flowers seem to me briars that I feel quite sorry for myself.

A time perhaps may come when things will mend ; people will then have to come down from their stilts to my level, for I am determined never to raise myself to the region in which they are moving.

Metternich to his Mother.

821. *Königswart, August* 2.—I write to you, my dear mother, from a place we all love, and which still bears traces of your beneficence and good taste.

I have found many changes at Königswart, and I think they would all meet with your approbation. There is still much to be done, however.

The court of the *château* is removed entirely. It was necessary to lower the earth about two feet, and to make a slope on the open side. In front of the *château*— that is to say, on the site of the horrible public-house— there will be a beautiful building next year, comprising a coach-house, stables, and a lodge for one of the servants. Beyond this building in prospective, there is a beautiful little farm. I do not think one could find anywhere a place so charming and at the same time so well arranged. It is much improved by the picturesque Swiss cattle. The brewery side has quite a new aspect. The lake near the *château* will be drained this autumn and converted into meadow-land.

Three farms—the Haselhof, the Kieselhof, and the Lehnhof—are either reconstructed or restored, and stocked with fine merino sheep.

The park is lovely, and a great avenue crosses it in the direction of Marienbad. The visitors at the baths love this place, and the part nearest to Marienbad resembles the valley of St. Hélène,* it is so crowded with people and carriages.

. . . I have already had here M. de Tatistscheff, the Princes of Arenberg, Louis de Rohan, Windischgrätz, and twenty other guests. Happily, the right wing of the *château* is quite finished inside, so I have been able to entertain everybody.

Yesterday we all made an excursion to Marienbad : to-day they left me. I expect, however, to-day M. de Pralormo and Count Gaspard de Sternberg. Marienbad is not troublesome, for its inhabitants are contented with a dinner. It has destroyed the solitude of Königs-wart, which has thus perhaps lost one of its charms in the good old times.

. . . I intend, before leaving, to spend with Victor one sad morning in the parish church of Königswart, as I shall not be here till next year, when the sacred remains it contains will have been removed. The new vault at Plass will be finished by next year.

822. *Johannisberg, August* 21.—We arrived at Johannisberg on the 12th. I was obliged to go and see

* Helenenthal, near Baden.

the King of Bavaria at Aschaffenburg; so I slept at
Frankfurt on the 11th.

I find this place very much improved. A great deal
has been done in the course of the last two years, and
the aspect is altogether changed. Really I do not believe that there is any place to surpass this. With all
that has been taken down and removed, the view is not
only enlarged, but it has gained a look of culture and
perfection which nothing can approach. It will take me
four years yet to finish everything; then neither the
castle nor its surroundings will leave anything to be
desired.

The perfection of the climate and especially of the site
is shown triumphantly. I have under my windows a
bed in which there is not a single plant which would
live out of a hot-house during the winter at Vienna or
in any part of Germany.

Here all kinds of magnolias, azaleas, rhododendrons,
laurels, &c., grow in the open air. I have even attempted camellias: all grow and flourish. My planta-
tions have weathered two winters, one of which was that
of 1825–1826; they have therefore stood the strongest
of proofs, and, far from having succumbed in that
rigorous winter, the magnolias have shot up four feet
and a half. All the neighbourhood comes to see my
garden, which is the wonder of travellers. I am going
to-morrow to Coblentz with a party, by water. The
Marquis of Hertford, an old friend of mine, and the
most decided Tory in England, has come here to see me.*
I enjoy his society for more reasons than one: his society
is congenial and our politics are the same. I shall return here the day after to-morrow. Victor and several
gentlemen who are staying here will be of the party.

* See 'Lord Hertford on Canning,' No. 833.

The only drawback to my visit is the number of people who overwhelm me. Every day I have from thirty to forty people to dinner. All Frankfurt and the neighbouring towns inflict themselves upon me. One thing is certain, and that is that if Austria and, I may be allowed to add, her Minister are not loved and respected in Germany, according to the *Débats* and the *Constitutionnel*, the Germans know very well how to hide their feelings. I am distressed at not having Chateaubriand and Benjamin Constant near me.

What a summer, my dear mother! I hope it will do you a great deal of good, and that I shall find you in a most flourishing state on my return, which will not be till after September 15. I must wait for some replies, which cannot arrive before September 7 or 8. My journey will not have been without some good fruit.

Metternich to his son Victor, Vienna, October 21.

823. The Paris newspapers are very badly advised. They wish to kill me, and they cherish me as if they wished to preserve me. The hatred of antagonists such as those good editors would make the fortune of an unknown ambitious man. I, who am neither one nor the other, am surprised at the trouble taken by the scribes who are not feared by him whom they would like to draw into their arena; I have but one regret—not to be able to translate and insert in our own newspapers the absurdities daily published about me by my good friends in Paris and other places. I shall gain, in fact, all that they wish me to lose. For some time I have derived great amusement from the pain which no doubt they intend to give me. Poor men!

824. *October 24.*—Marshal Marmont, who has returned from Russia, has arrived at Vienna. I had a

very long conversation with him to-day on what has passed at St. Petersburg and Moscow.   He has the same opinion of the Emperor Nicholas that I have.   I have no doubt that Nicholas will be a prince such as I think sovereigns ought to be.

825. Your last letter, December 11, interested me very much.   Your judgment on the change of *rôle* between Pozzo and Granville quite agrees with mine, and I do not give up the idea that at Paris they are mistaken with regard to the Emperor of Russia.

It requires great force of character and much coolness to know how to separate what is reality from what is mere tinsel.   I have maintained for four years against the whole world, that the Emperor Alexander did not wish for war.   I was right and the secret of my obstinacy arose from this consideration, that if he had wished it, he would have had no trouble in making it.   When I hear a capitalist talking of a speculation while he does not go into it himself, I know he is speaking of something he does not wish to do.

. . . I am overwhelmed with business.   My situation is like that of one crucified : one arm is nailed to Constantinople, and the other to Lisbon; home affairs occupy the trunk; Mr. Canning is my crucifier, and the Hungarian Diet the sponge steeped in vinegar.   I hope to see the latter come to a good conclusion.

Be civil to the Woronzows, to whom I entrust my letter.   They deserve it; I like them very much, and have known them for a long time.   He is a very right-minded Russian.   If the Emperor of Russia thought of making war, General Woronzow would not go to London to spend eighteen months with his old father.

826. *December* 25.— . . . You will read my despatches of to-day, and you will see that I have had more courage than M. de Damas.   The two ambassadors

declare themselves quite contented. I am, therefore, fifty per cent. more advanced than the French Cabinet.

I am curious to know what Pozzo will find to say about what I have done. Unless he requires a blind obedience on the part of Austria to all the whims which, according to the humour of the moment, seem to suit his taste, he will have some difficulty in discovering why we have not made use of our independence to threaten that of others. Read carefully my secret despatch to Bombelles; you will find there a rather sharp analysis, which is, however, quite justified by the pitiable London affair. (See No. 839.)

. . . I hope you will soon send me the hangings for the drawing-room; it will be finished in about a fortnight, and it is extremely beautiful. I shall open it with a ball; I have ordered benches and white draperies for the occasion; the hangings will be reserved for grand reception days. The decorations of the drawing-room are of a very peculiar kind, and will make a great sensation. Four openings in the ceiling, of which two are for the introduction of fresh air, and two act as siphons to expel the heated air, are quite a new invention, of which I am very proud. When these hatches, if we may call them so, are closed, they are imperceptible, and when they are open, they add to the appearance of the ceiling. This is uniting the useful with the agreeable.

. . . As I am writing to you after all my packets are closed, I beg you to tell Count Apponyi that I have this moment received a report from Alexandria, dated November 25, which informs me that the Pacha of Egypt's fleet—eighty-seven vessels, men of war and transports laden with provisions and ammunition for Ibrahim Pacha—has set sail. Another report from Zante tells me that the fleet has arrived safe and sound at Navarino and Modon. So Ibrahim is re-provisioned.

STATE OF THE EASTERN QUESTION UP TO THE TIME OF THE DEATH OF THE EMPEROR ALEXANDER.

Metternich to Vincent, in Paris, Vienna, January 5, 1826.

827. I have the honour to send herewith to your Excellency a despatch on the Eastern Question. It has no other object but to serve as an instruction to the Archduke Ferdinand in the very probable event of the new sovereign of Russia speaking to him on this important subject.

As the Memoir traces succinctly and correctly the attitude of our Court and the opinion we have always pronounced on the dispute, I have thought it advisable to deposit a copy of it in the archives of our principal embassies.

The Eastern Question historically considered.

828. The insurrection of the Greeks has been condemned from its origin by the principal Christian Powers—explicitly and publicly by some, tacitly and virtually by others—as a revolutionary attempt which the most determined oppression (even if the authors of the revolt had proved the fact) could never justify, and as an event tending to add new embarrassments and dangers to the already critical position of Europe. In any other circumstances the sovereigns, to be faithful to the principles which they have solemnly proclaimed and applied to more than one of the revolutions of our time, would, in the cause of peace, good order, and justice, have given their assistance to the outraged Government, and helped it to stifle as soon as possible a conflagration which threatened the repose of three parts of the world. What prevented them from fulfilling a duty which at the very beginning of the insurrection they would have done in any other country, was not at first, as is now believed, the ascendancy of public opinion; for at the time of that outbreak this opinion was not nearly so general, so pronounced and so powerful as unhappily it has since become, in consequence of the indefatigable labour of factions and the ignorance and credulity of the public.

One consideration only arrested the sovereigns at the very beginning: it was repugnant to them to furnish arms to a Power professing dogmas contrary to Christianity, against subjects guilty, but Christians and unfortunate. It was this which threw them into the painful dilemma of being able neither to aid the Greeks without violating the principles of public right, nor of fighting against them without wounding religious feelings. A passive attitude (very different from a neutrality properly so called) was the only means of conciliating these two great interests. From that time the *rôle* of the Powers was limited to employing all that an enlightened, kind and skilful diplomacy could suggest, and all the means which their united influence gave them, to put an end to a struggle in which they were prevented from interposing with their material forces. In departing from this *rôle* they would have run the risk of rendering useless the only resources which remained to them, or of precipitating themselves into one of those extremities which it was equally important they should avoid.

It must be confessed, since it is the truth and history cannot ignore it—it was Russia who, in the first place, deprived herself and her allies of the advantages of a position in itself very difficult and delicate.

Led, not by views of ambition or cupidity, always foreign to the soul of the monarch who directed her destinies, but by feeble or equivocal counsels, she fell into two faults, the consequences of which could not fail to extend far and wide. The first was that of allowing herself to be led to believe that it was an urgent necessity for Russia to interfere, and to interfere at any price, in the affair of the insurrection, and consequently, as she neither could nor would act on the Greeks, to act strongly on the Porte in any way and by any means she could.

Imbued with this opinion, the Russian Cabinet soon gave to its proceedings at Constantinople a character all the more alarming and the less adapted to the circumstances, since the Porte—amazed at a catastrophe so terrible and unexpected—was absolutely not in a state to judge of its own position, to consult its own interests, or to maintain any political discussions. Russia, believing herself repulsed and offended, and listening only to the irritation of the moment, then committed a second fault, more grave in its consequences than the first—that of recalling her embassy, thus depriving herself of the only means of accomplishing what she desired so ardently—that of acting directly on the Porte.

By this unfortunate resolution, Russia necessarily placed herself in the alternative, either of losing little by little her influence and even a part of her consideration at Constantinople, or of making war on the Porte ; a part abhorrent to the Emperor for many weighty reasons both generous and worthy. His Cabinet, having gratuitously closed all direct avenues, saw itself obliged to confide to the ministers of its allies the grievances and protests which it had against the Porte, and which, indeed, it could not renounce without isolating itself in a question in which it must have such a lively interest.

The allied Cabinets undertook this commission, one of the most painful which could fall to the lot of diplomacy. Their cares and their efforts were paralysed by the retreat of Russia, a retreat which, in the eyes of the Porte, rendered ineffectual or suspected the best combined steps they could attempt. These steps, moreover, formed part of two different negotiations, each of which especially claimed their attention.

The departure of the Russian embassy produced a state of exasperation and fear at Constantinople, which the declarations of the Cabinet of St. Petersburg were little calculated to allay, but were indeed much more likely to strengthen. Each day saw new grievances, new claims, new recriminations, arise on one side or the other; and the efforts of the ministers of the allies were soon restricted to calming the storm ever ready to break out.

In the midst of these disquietudes, they could not lose sight of the great object of the pacification of Greece. The absence of Russia made itself felt in everything relating to that question, and reduced the allies to representations easily repulsed by the Porte. They nevertheless continued to advise moderation and clemency, and tried to familiarise the Ottoman ministers with the best means of arriving at a pacification, which the results of the military operations were beginning to render problematical, and to prepare the way for more effectual negotiations, which the gradual exhaustion of the insurgents seemed to make possible, but which the return of a Russian mission could alone crown with success.

The time will come when justice will be done to the manner in which the allied Cabinets, especially that of Vienna—the central point of impulsion—have acquitted themselves of this double task ; to the inexhaustible patience with which they have braved the difficulties ; to the often-renewed activity with which they have approached so many complications ; to the merit, in short, of having supported for four years the structure of peace and the Alliance against the numerous dangers with which it was assailed, and of having averted from Europe the new troubles with which it was threatened.

The Congress of Verona and the meeting of the two Emperors at Czernowitz in the month of October 1823 had quite reassured the Cabinets as to the personal disposition of the Emperor Alexander. His constant attachment to the Alliance, his moderate and pacific sentiments were again manifested in such a way as to silence all apprehensions. The Cabinet of Vienna worked with redoubled zeal and diligence towards so desirable an end. It had long since recognised the inconveniences and delays to which they were exposed by treating simultaneously, by confounding in one negotiation, two kinds of questions absolutely distinct : those which regarded the demand of Russia as to her principal treaties with the Porte, and those which had for their object the re-establishment of peace in the Ottoman Empire. The first were the most urgent, and at the same time the easier to arrange ; the latter, although of far greater importance, had not yet acquired that degree of maturity which could render their solution near or even probable.

The Court of Vienna formally renewed a proposition

which it had many times advised, that of separating the questions—of settling first the direct interests of Russia sanctioned by the treaties, and of reserving the affair of the pacification to the time when the Powers should have arranged the means of approaching it with most hope of success. This proposition, accepted by Russia, had all the effect which was expected. While simplifying the discussions, it accelerated the re-establishment of the diplomatic relations between the two empires. The sending M. de Minciaky to Constantinople showed the sincere wish of his Imperial Majesty of All the Russias to terminate amicably his discussions with the Porte.

The evacuation of the Principalities, commenced in the year 1823, was concluded ; regulations were made, remedying the annoyances and checks to Russian navigation and commerce exercised in former years; the Porte consented—with some modifications dictated in the interest of her finances—to the principle of granting to all the Powers which desired it the freedom of the passage of the Black Sea. And, lastly, the departure of Lord Strangford from Constantinople, and the delivery of M. de Minciaky's credentials (in October 1824), terminated, we may be allowed to hope, the first act of these long and painful discussions. Thanks to the activity and perseverance of the ministers of the allied Courts, the Porte had met all the grievances and satisfied all the demands of Russia, with the exception of one article, which was not even mentioned in the treaties— the restitution of the former connection between the Hospodars and the heads of militia in the Principalities, an article which has been recently settled by the special intervention of Austria.

The Court of Russia evinced its satisfaction by several measures which seemed to put a seal to these transactions. The Emperor thanked Lord Strangford in the most honourable terms, and begged the King of England to confer some favour upon him. He nominated M. de Ribeaupierre minister to Constantinople, and published the ukase of his nomination. For a short time we were full of hope.

But that most thorny of problems, the pacification of Greece, remained to be solved. In proportion as the difficulties of that affair increased, and the means of action became weaker, the interest of Russia in it seemed to increase. From the beginning of 1824, she proposed to the allied Courts to hold ministerial conferences at St. Petersburg for the purpose of taking into consideration a plan of pacification drawn up by her Cabinet, and to arrange measures likely to be agreeable to the Porte. These conferences, the first of which took place in the presence of the English ambassador, were suspended by the departure of the Emperor Alexander for his eastern provinces; they were to have been resumed on his return, when a fatal and unforeseen incident suddenly changed the whole aspect of things. The English Government, which during the first years of the Greek revolution had constantly acted in concert with the Continental Courts; which even after the change of ministry in 1822 had neither withdrawn nor essentially modified the instructions to its ambassador at Constantinople; which, in short, had actually promised its countenance to the conferences at St. Petersburg—declared to the allied Cabinets that considerations founded partly on its own connection with the countries in the Levant, partly on the difficulty of effecting under the circumstances a reconciliation between the Porte and the insurgents, prevented it from taking part in these conferences. The consequences of this resolution were

easy to foresee. The absence of England would in the
conferences themselves make itself felt by uncertainties
and embarrassments of every kind ; and, whatever might
be the result, any attempt at intervention would lose a
great part of its weight at Constantinople, by confirming the Porte in its long-cherished suspicion that the
principal Powers of Europe were no longer united in
their views and system.

The Cabinet of Vienna was quite aware of these new
obstacles ; but, always ready to second anything in the
least tending to the re-establishment of peace, convinced
of the necessity and animated with the sincere desire of
finding a remedy for the calamities and disorders of the
Levant, it was none the less willing to contribute by its
goodwill and knowledge to the deliberations at St. Petersburg. The result of the conferences answered our expectations. The aim of the four Courts continued to be
the same, but the divergence of opinions was manifested in more ways than one, not only in the choice
of means, but in the possibility of employing these
means. It was soon seen that the most indispensable
elements for forming an effective and feasible plan of
operation were lacking, and that problematical questions
were not ripe enough to admit a positive decision.
That the fruit of their labour might not be entirely
lost, and to prepare the way for better considered and
better arranged measures, the Conference adopted the
plan of charging the ministers of the four Courts at
Constantinople with a verbal and confidential message,
for the purpose of representing to the Porte the necessity of a pacific intervention of the Powers in the
affairs of Greece. This step, executed in haste and at
the most inopportune moment, had the fate which might
have been foreseen.

The Russian Cabinet, having itself no doubt of the use-
lessness of this feeble attempt, determined to push the
question in other directions. Even before it was informed of the refusal of the Porte, it addressed directly
to the three allied Courts an urgent appeal on the necessity of arranging without delay the course they would
follow in the event of the Turkish Government persist-
ing in not accepting their intervention. Unhappily,
this communication from the Russian Cabinet contained
a proposal which the Austrian monarch had always
regarded as incompatible, not only with political interests, but with respect for the rights of others and
the validity of treaties, and, consequently, opposed by
his own conscience—the proposal for a recourse to coercive measures against the Porte, if persuasion proved
ineffectual. The Cabinet of Vienna believed itself obliged, even at the risk of displeasing Russia, to express
its opinion on this subject with the sincerity and frankness which had always characterised its correspondence.
In announcing the grave reasons which prevented it
from acceding to the proposal of the Cabinet of St.
Petersburg, it added considerations which appeared of
sufficient weight to convince that Cabinet that the path
it pointed out was directly opposed to the end it wished
to attain, and that by following it the Powers would
simply provoke fresh and more extended complications
than those they wished to overcome.

The Emperor Alexander, dissatisfied with this reply,
dissatisfied perhaps with the position in which, with the
purest and most loyal intentions, he found himself
placed, maintained a strict silence, disquieting no doubt
for the Cabinets, but which did not shake the confidence
of the Cabinet of Vienna in the greatness of his character. The result, however, was an absolute stagnation

between the Russian and Continental Cabinets as to the Eastern Question—a stagnation which continued until the deplorable event which has plunged Russia and Europe into mourning.

As this state of things could not be indefinitely prolonged, it would have probably ceased with the return of the Emperor to his capital, and in whatever part he had then taken he would have found we agreed with him. For nothing has changed, either in our principles or in our views or in the judgment we pronounced on the Eastern Question from the very beginning; but of course the stability of our principles could not prevent us from following the march of events and adapting our ideas to their progressive development.

Lord Strangford's project brought us back to the ground we never wished to leave. We have always regarded as feeble and barren any plan of pacification which did not include the suffrage and active co-operation of England. But if that Power will agree with the Powers on one of the greatest questions which the progress of the century has submitted to the solicitude of the Governments—if the five Powers, in short, will and can agree on measures practicable and well arranged, Austria will not fail them; and without indulging in chimerical hopes, without answering for a success which human wisdom cannot guarantee, we will take our task upon us and loyally fulfil it.

We are ignorant how far Lord Strangford has been authorised to draw up and communicate his project. If he has acted according to the instructions of his Court, or if the British Government receives favourably the ideas with which the gravity of the circumstances and the prospect of imminent danger for Europe have inspired this minister, we must congratulate ourselves on such a happy augury for the consolidation of the general peace and for the re-establishment of a perfect harmony in the system of the great Powers.

We have but little to say on the motives which we think should determine Russia to fix her attention on the proposed plan. Unless that Power—which nothing will allow us to suppose—prefers to abandon to the chances of war an affair in which the employment of that force would be without a definite object, without known end, impossible to justify, and, as things are, almost impossible to conceive, it is certain that the step proposed by Lord Strangford offers to her an honourable means, either of obtaining what she desires or of withdrawing from a complication which can only lead to the most disastrous results. The public voice in Russia complains especially that the Government has lost its influence, not only in Greece (which would be the fault of events and not its own), but also at the Porte. The arrival of a Russian minister at Constantinople, which is one of the fundamental conditions of the project in question, would soon contradict these complaints. It is impossible that this minister should not be treated with all the respect and listened to with all the deference dictated, if not by the good sense of the ministers of the Sultan, at least by the fear of a second rupture. Even if he should not succeed in all the steps he might take in common with the ministers of the allied Courts to hasten the pacification of Greece, the honour of Russia would be in no wise compromised ; it would only be false friends and perfidious counsellors who would maintain the contrary. Russia, after all, would preserve her present attitude. If she wished, if she could wish for war, war she could have. She would lose nothing and gain much by an attempt in which the risk would be divided with her allies.

We are persuaded, and those who knew the Emperor Alexander well will agree with us, that that monarch would not have refused to entertain a project fulfilling at least what he himself regarded as the first conditions of success in a negotiation with the Porte. This persuasion makes us hope that his august successor will not disdain to entertain it.

ON THE ACCESSION OF THE EMPEROR NICHOLAS.

Metternich to Esterhazy, in London, Vienna,
January 8, 1826.

829. . . . The prolonged uncertainty regarding the accession of the new sovereign of Russia obliged us to delay our explanations on the great political interests in question until we knew which of the two Grand Dukes, Constantine or Nicholas, would bear the burden of the Crown. It was only the day before yesterday, January 6, that we were informed of the accession of the Emperor Nicholas I., and of his proclamation at St. Petersburg and Warsaw.

History contains no episode so singular in its causes as that which has kept a great empire without a head for nearly a month ; one is glad to arrive at the end of such a strange situation. I need not enter into any particulars to your Highness on the circumstances which have accompanied the accession of Nicholas I. The correspondence between St. Petersburg and London is so direct that it would be impossible to tell you anything that was not known in England long before the arrival of our news.

The revolt of a part of the troops, the nature and the tendency of that event, seem to contain a warning to the new monarch not to deceive himself as to the work of innovators—a salutary warning for a young prince surrounded by men given up to the false spirit of the age.

The Circular which M. de Nesselrode addressed to the diplomatic body at St. Petersburg on the day of the accession is set forth in terms which are amply confirmed, in a sense most favourable to us and to our wishes, by the direct overtures which the new Emperor has made to the Emperor our august master. . . .

We have no doubt that the Emperor Nicholas will follow in the steps of the late Emperor in the affair of the pacification of the Levant. The last measure of the representatives of England and France will be regarded by his Imperial Majesty as the first addressed to him by the two Courts. It is therefore very important to draw up correctly, and on fixed and unimpeachable principles, the first advances made by the Powers to the new monarch.

I beg that you will express yourself to Mr. Canning in similar terms to this despatch, and inform us as soon as possible, of any directions which may be received by Lord Strangford.

One painful circumstance, however, will for the present, at least, render any military operation of Russia against the Porte physically impossible. The plague has just invaded the two Danubian Principalities with awful intensity. . . .

The Emperor has given the necessary orders for forming a cordon of the greatest severity. Five or six thousand men must be employed in this service, and I am persuaded that the Liberal newspapers of Europe will tax us with arming in favour of the Turks and against Russia, while they will give to the measures taken by the Court of St. Petersburg an entirely different complexion.

Metternich to Lebzeltern, in St. Petersburg, Vienna,
January 10, 1826.

830. The Emperor has heard with great satisfaction that the generous struggle between the two successors to the throne of Russia is concluded.

The Manifesto published on December 26 by the Emperor Nicholas I. is a monument of wisdom and moderation. It proves to us that the new Sovereign would not have been able, without very evident inconveniences, to act otherwise than he has done. The Manifesto explains the reasons of this conduct most satisfactorily, and his Imperial Majesty in taking his position firmly on the Pragmatic Sanction so happily established by the Emperor Paul has rendered an eminent service to his country and to the whole of Europe. The first need in every country being the clear and precise determination of the line of succession to the throne, it would be impossible to deny that his Imperial Majesty has conferred a great benefit on Russia. It is pleasant to see a powerful monarch begin with such calmness and rectitude of principles the painful career assigned to him by Providence.

The same may be said of the manner in which the Emperor conducted himself on the occasion of the deplorable bungle which was made on December 26. Such conduct in such an event is equivalent to many years' reign.

Nothing, on the other hand, could have been more satisfactory to the Emperor our august master than the terms of the first Circular Note which Count Nesselrode addressed on that same December 26 to the diplomatic body at St. Petersburg.

You would do well, Count, to address to Count

Nesselrode a Note, replying to that of December 26, in the terms we have mentioned, which are those dictated to the Emperor by his own conscience.

Your Excellency will receive herewith your new credentials, both original and copies.

Monsignor the Archduke Ferdinand will start on the 11th of this month.

Metternich to Lebzeltern, in St. Petersburg, Vienna, January 10, 1826.

831. The commendation in the preceding despatch (No. 830) of the first Manifesto of the reign of the Emperor Nicholas is not at all exaggerated. . . .

The more correct this act of the new monarch is, the more one is inclined to blame the various documents exchanged between the Emperor Alexander and the Grand Duke Constantine. Those who did not know the mind of the former must find it very difficult to conceive the existence of such an act as that of August 28, 1823.* The event, moreover, proves, also, that one cannot treat lightly or indifferently acts which require the greatest consideration and the most careful arrangement—those, namely, destined to serve as the foundation of the monarchy—without perilling the repose of empires. If Russia pays for a month's interregnum by the loss only of several hundred men, she will have bought her experience cheaply.

You will readily understand that in the present case the spectators placed out of the fray must have very different impressions from those who occupy the

* A manifesto of the Emperor Alexander in favour of the Grand Duke Nicholas in consequence of the voluntary renunciation by the Grand Duke Constantine of the succession to the throne; in four sealed copies left in the care of trustworthy persons and not opened till after Alexander's death.—ED.

very arena of the conflict. We are also able to judge of the extraordinary effect which the events of the month of December have produced on minds beyond the frontiers of Russia. The two brothers, if they did not know how to advise themselves, would have done well to seek counsel from men capable of regulating a great and important affair in the way indicated by the most simple reasons of State.

The revolt of December 26 will have had the advantage of allowing the character of the young monarch to be seen by the public, and of showing him that Russia is, unhappily, as easy to agitate as all other countries are in our time. I hope a thorough inquiry will be made as to those who seduced the soldiery, for they were certainly in this case only tools in wicked hands. It is just possible that *les hommes en frac*, of whom Count Nesselrode made mention in his Circular to the Russian ministers abroad, will be able to put the Government in the way of discovering how far revolutionary influences have been at work. Russia has, so to speak, been breathing for years the Liberalism of Europe; hundreds of travellers from that nation are steeped in its atmosphere, and have been for a long time waiting for an opportunity to return to their country and the Imperial Court. Facts like these must necessarily leave some traces.

M. de Tatistscheff speaks of having received from Count Nesselrode an order—more explicit even than the text of the Circular from that minister to the diplomatic body at St. Petersburg—to give us the strongest assurances that the new Emperor desires nothing so much as to strengthen the happy and intimate connection between the two Courts. I use the same expressions which M. de Tatistscheff uses, because he has not actually shown me the order ; and if, on the one hand, I am a little surprised at his reticence on so satisfactory a subject, on the other hand it is very natural that Count Nesselrode should not enter into details in the very first days of an accession to the throne which has been marked by so much embarrassment. M. de Tatistscheff added, however, that the new Emperor would take up the Eastern Question immediately, seeking its solution on the ground of the alliance. . . .

I am waiting for your news, Count, with eagerness ; you will have much to tell, and I impatiently expect many details with which your zeal and your knowledge of the places and the men will enable you to furnish us.

THE AUSTRIAN POLICY IN THE EAST AFTER THE TRANSACTION BETWEEN ENGLAND AND RUSSIA, APRIL 4, 1826.

(See No. 809.)

Metternich to Esterhazy, in London, Vienna, June 8, 1826.

832. The terms used by the Chief Secretary to you confirm what I have long observed, that the British Cabinet starts, concerning the most important points of the misunderstanding between Russia and the Porte, from two suppositions absolutely different from those which have guided our calculations. He has admitted, on the one hand, the positive desire of the Emperor Nicholas for a rupture with the Porte, and, on the other, the invincible repugnance of the Porte to yield to any demand addressed to it by Russia. But facts have now placed the truth in the light in which sooner or later it is always seen. The Porte has conceded all the demands of Russia, and this concession has been received with undoubted satisfaction by the Emperor Nicholas.

For a long time, and perhaps always, there has been a total difference of opinion between our Cabinet and that of London on the possibility of a reconciliation between Russia and the Porte. The case has been tried, and the event has proved that we were not deceived in our presentiments.

We have never had any doubt on the following fundamental points—namely :—

That the Russian monarchs (the last like the present), far from desiring the rupture with the Porte, have ever since the beginning of the revolution regarded the war as a very disastrous event.

That the arrangement of the differences between Russia and the Porte, and an interpretation of the Treaty of Bucharest which would tend to remove the awkwardness concerning the retrocession (desired by this Treaty) of some point in Asia, have constantly occupied the first place in their thoughts.

That the arrangements concerning the fate of the Morea and the isles have had but a secondary value for them, and that,

1st. Seeing the absolute impossibility that Russia can ever wish for the political independence of the Greeks ;

2nd. Seeing the impossibility of that Power ever regaining her former influence over them ;

3rd. Seeing, in short, that some sort of dependence on the Porte must necessarily be imposed on the Greeks, instead of that political independence for which they have made so many sacrifices ; the active part which Russia will take in this return to dependence, far from satisfying public opinion, and thus corresponding to the strong considerations which attach that Power to the cause of the Greeks, will be laid to the charge of the Russian monarch.

That any other conclusion of the pacification of Greece than that brought about by the natural course of things can only be attained by the united moral efforts of the principal Powers of Europe, and especially by those of Russia, Austria and England.

These are undoubted truths and I leave them

wholly to your discretion. Do what you think best to enlighten the conscience of the British Cabinet with respect to us; I am not afraid of committing myself, for what I have just written is a matter of history.

The separate negotiation between Great Britain and Russia, and the assent of the Sultan to the first proposals of the Emperor Nicholas, have drawn a definite line between the past and the future ; the claims of the historian begin with the separation between the periods.

The Eastern Question has arrived at the end of one of these periods. It is clear to me that the Porte and Russia will come to an understanding.

What will become of the other part of the affair ?

To reply to this question, I must recal to you the points of view from which we have always regarded the Greek affair.

It is difficult to say exactly what is to be understood by Greece. Is one understood to speak of the Peloponnesus and the isles, or of all the parts of European Turkey which contain a majority of Christian population ? If the Peloponnesus, either alone or with the isles, offers—which we do not admit—the indispensable elements for forming a politically independent State, the existence of such a State would suffice to render that of an Ottoman Power in Europe problematical ; the union of all the countries principally inhabited by Greeks would render it impossible. Thus, in either of these hypotheses, the establishment of an independent Greece would be synonymous with the expulsion of the Turks from Europe.

If—setting aside all considerations of right and justice—the means necessary for the expulsion of the Turks from Europe, and the conditions for the re-establishment in their place of a great Christian State, could be regarded as existing, of all the Powers Austria would lose the least by such a change.

The proved fidelity with which the Porte has regularly fulfilled its engagements, and the scrupulous respect with which it has observed its treaties, make, it is true, its vicinity useful and even commodious to us. European Turkey really affords to Austria all the negative advantages of a sea frontier.

Nevertheless, whenever a great independent Christian State shall replace the Ottoman, that State will become our natural and active ally. Placed between two great and powerful neighbours, it will not be the encroachments of one that aims at no extension, and which in consequence of the physical and moral conditions of her existence never will aim at any—in a word, it will not be Austria that will be feared by the new Greek Empire; her tendency must necessarily be to seek and cultivate its friendship.

To represent us as the irreconcilable enemies of Greece, and to seek motives for our hatred in the fears for our political interests which their independence would inspire, would be as erroneous as to re-echo the many contemptible libels which we consider it beneath our dignity to contradict.

But does the question ever arise among the Cabinets of the expulsion of the Turks from Europe, and the establishment of a free and independent Greece? Certainly not. Nevertheless, the general excitement in Europe is founded on this supposition; the most atrocious calumnies are in this sense directed against the Governments; Austria especially is the daily mark of the factious, who aim at objects exactly opposite to those which could ever be pursued by a sound policy or even the simple calculation of possibilities. Up to this time, instead of seeing the Government oppose this torrent, we have unfortunately been the witnesses of a system of toleration and even of action in a contrary direction.

What has our Court desired, and what ought it to desire? Its desire has been, and always will be that the first causes of so much excitement, of so detestable and dangerous a game, should cease with as little delay as possible. It sees no remedy for the evil except in the pacification of the insurgent countries.

This pacification can only be accomplished in one or other of the three following ways : the voluntary submission of the Greeks to the Ottoman Power; the re-conquest of all the insurgent countries by the force of Turkish arms; or an amicable arrangement, under the influence of the Powers, between the Sultan and his rebellious subjects.

It is this last plan which for five years has occupied the attention of our Court. . . .

Now that, in consequence of the transaction of April 4, we have acquired the feeling of perfect liberty of action, we think proper, for the interest of the general cause, and perhaps even for our honour, to draw a line between the past and the future. No one runs less after affairs than the Emperor our august master ; no one is less jealous than he of seeing them arranged without his concurrence. Let good be done and let evil be avoided, is the sum total of his Majesty's desires.

How can this end be attained in the present position of things? Happily it is not our business either to arrange or propose the means. We have only to wait and hear, with all the interest this question has for us, what will be proposed by the two Courts who are engaged in its solution. . . .

I hope, Prince, that you will thoroughly enter into the spirit of this despatch; it expresses in a few words all our thoughts on the Eastern Question; it is agreeable to historical truth, and to the positions in which the Powers and the two contending parties are placed. You will express yourself in this same spirit, and, as far as possible, in our very words, to the Secretary of State. We leave you to make the necessary explanations so that the British Cabinet may comprehend—

1st. What we have always seen and desired in the Eastern Question;

2nd. What we see in it at the present moment;

3rd. That we are troubled by no views of ambition or of uneasy activity; and that far from desiring to put ourselves forward, either by giving advice, or by taking direct steps, we are in a state of tranquil expectation, prepared to learn what England believes, thinks, and wishes, in an affair which she has suddenly taken in hand, and concerning which it is reasonable to suppose she has some fixed and clearly arranged plan : a plan that should not be difficult to communicate to the Power which ought naturally to be made acquainted with it.

LORD HERTFORD ON MR. CANNING.

Rough copy of a letter written by Metternich, dated August 23, 1826, without address (probably to Gentz).

833. In my present position I am sure to fall in with people unexpectedly who are able to enlighten me on some point or other. Thus, the Marquis of Hertford (formerly Lord Yarmouth) has fallen into my hands. You have, I am sure, heard of this man. As Lord Yarmouth he for some years took part in politics. He was cousin to the late Lord Castlereagh, and son of the king's old friend. I made his acquaintance in Paris, where he was much with Talleyrand. Since his father's death he has thrown himself into Parliamentary work. He is one of the most distinguished and wealthiest Tories, controls ten votes in the House of Commons, and in general plays the part which the high nobility of England grants to those who know how to profit by their own position and general circumstances. Neumann met him at Spa, and, as he intended to visit the Rhine, he encouraged him to pay me a visit at Johannisberg. Hearing this from Neumann, I formally invited him. I passed some days with him which opened a new world before my eyes. I had not for many years met with so independent, thoughtful, and clever an Englishman. His words were like echoes of the past. We talked together quite frankly and unreservedly, and I feel sure that he was as pleased with me as I with him. The difference between our final impressions could only be that whereas he could teach me much, it was not in my power to tell him anything new.

He is of my opinion with regard to Canning; the picture I had made of this scourge of the world corresponds with his; and if in our conversation I pronounced judgment upon Canning's individuality with diplomatic moderation, the truth of it was always confirmed by his own plain words. He calls him and his actions by the right names, strengthening my own feelings with regard to both. Sometimes, too, he overstepped the limits of mere polemics, and the following is the substantial point of view from which he judges of Canning.

Hertford maintains that things have attained their height, and that the next session of Parliament will show this. He and all Tories, he says, have exhausted their patience, and are firmly resolved to begin the fight. This feeling was one motive for their resolution; the other was the death of the Duke of York, the brother of King George IV. The Duke, said Lord Hertford, had for years been regarded as the firm support of the Tories, a fact which had done much to bring about the present miserable state of affairs, first, because in his future the victory of the party seemed secured; secondly, because with the Duke two feelings had equal weight, the cause of the throne and the respect due to the King. Whenever the leading men of the party came forward he endeavoured to hold them back and prevent them from making an attack. This proceeding alone would account for Canning's majority, composed of all the Whigs and a certain number of Tories. This amalgamation would now come to an end, for nothing was left to Canning but to form a ministry with Lord Lansdowne and Lord Holland in the House of Lords. His ambition, however, which was boundless, led him to desire himself to be at the head of the administration.

You will remember that I had heard privat
this arrangement with Lord Lansdowne. On my
him what would happen to Lord Liverpool is
changes took place, Hertford answered 'tha
would descend from the stage without leaving a
behind him. He had displeased the Tories wi
doing enough for the Whigs, and this arose fro
indolence, which prevented him from looking into
thing whatever beyond the next sitting of Parliam
(How true a description this is I need not tell you
'Observe what I say,' continued Lord Hert
'you will soon see the battle begin; at the head c
combatants will be the Duke of Wellington, the
Chancellor, and Robert Peel.'

On my remark that the Duke of Wellington app
to me to be too weak to ensure the success of su
affair, he replied : 'Your remark is just; but W
ton's name is necessary, and with the support c
whole aristocracy and the country gentlemen, w
think their property is endangered, it may be succ
Canning stands quite alone, and although by gr
favours he has contrived to get some clients, th
nothing against the majority of the squires and t
commercial and manufacturing classes, the two
being already ruined by the measures of Cann
his friend Huskisson, and the very existenc
country gentlemen endangered. The only re
Canning had been spared till now (namely,
tainty that the Whigs would be strengthened l
drawal) had entirely lost its weight from th
he, as a member of the ministry, made adv
Whigs.'

On my asking him what view the Ki
of the struggle, Hertford replied that he

of apathy. The calm which reigned around the throne was, in his eyes, Canning's greatest merit. This calm once troubled, the King would wish for, certainly not hinder, the victory of the right party.'

En résumé, I received the impression that Lord Hertford considers a change of affairs inevitable, and the calmness with which he spoke seems to me particularly remarkable. He used expressly the word *Umschwung* (change), and pointed out 'Reform' as the reverse of a success of those plans which he announced as quite decided. His last words on this subject were: 'A middle course is no longer to be thought of, and with Reform the throne disappears.'

To illustrate Canning's line of conduct he told me several anecdotes, some of them very amusing.

He thinks of the history of the Portuguese Constitution as I do. He supposes that Don Pedro's resolutions are unknown to Canning, and that only two reasons could have induced Charles Stewart to take part in them, either to play Canning a trick, being his sworn enemy, or that he had turned out to be himself a fool—a supposition proved, so it seemed to me, by Lord Hertford, on almost indisputable grounds. Some months ago, the ship in which Charles Stewart sailed to Brazil was wanted for a more important service and exchanged for another. Hearing this, Stewart wrote to Lord Melville that he refused to sail in the new ship, which had been sent on purpose to drown him. Lord Melville showed the letter to Lord Hertford, asking him if such a fancy and such a letter, addressed to the First Lord of the Admiralty, was not a proof of madness. It would be the strangest fate which could be imagined if the English Ambassador became a madman in order to present the world with the Portuguese Constitution!

ON THE MOST IMPORTANT AFFAIRS OF THE DAY.

Metternich to Count Bombelles, in St. Petersburg, Johannisberg, September 7, 1826.

834. I do not wish to leave my present abode without addressing a despatch to you, giving you my impressions on the most important affairs of the moment.

Your despatches of the 22nd to the 26th of July, and of the 15th of August, as well as the first letter which the Prince of Hesse has addressed to me from Moscow, permit me to hope that the confidence I allowed myself to found on the moral position of the Emperor Nicholas will not be deceived.

If that monarch knows what is for his own welfare, he must necessarily attach great value to being on good terms with Austria.

The attempts made by men who wished to disturb the good understanding between the two Empires have failed at Vienna; they will also fail at St. Petersburg, and I do not for an instant doubt that the best means at our disposal for attaining this end is what we have already made use of—namely, the reserve we have imposed upon ourselves.

M. de Tatistscheff, whose personal conduct continues to deserve our commendation, remained a fortnight here. He has now returned to Vienna, where I expect to arrive about the 20th of this month.

The result of the negotiations at Ackermann will be known to you as soon and probably sooner than to us. When the dice are thrown, it is of no use calculating what the number will be. The questions seem to me to have been long since placed on a very simple basis. Russia and the Porte have an interest in common, which is the preservation of peace; it is therefore reasonable that the contending parties should come to an amicable understanding; if they do not they are wrong; and voluntary wrongs, like follies, baffle the foresight of observers.

If the affair is arranged between Russia and the Porte, English mediation would find it very difficult to make room for itself.

According to the most recent news from the East, neither Mr. Stratford Canning nor the numerous English agents employed in the affair have to this day arrived at making themselves heard, even by the Greeks. Disunited among themselves, much more excited against each other than disposed to contribute to one common end, the different chiefs of the insurrection agree on one point, and that is exactly the one which neither England nor Russia aim at: political independence! The people, on the other hand, are sighing for the end of these troubles, and there is no doubt they are ready to submit, if the chance presented itself of capitulating to the Turks.

One great moral struggle, which still continues to make itself felt in the Levant as in many other places, is the intense jealousy and rivalry between England and France. The two parties exhaust themselves in opposing and baffling each other, and it is certainly not the Greeks who will gain by this singular struggle.

The ambassadors of Russia and England at Paris

have received orders to communicate the protocol of
April 4 conjointly to the French Government. I have
just received from M. de Tatistscheff and from Sir
Henry Wellesley two letters, dated September 1, in
which they tell me that they are charged with the same
commission, but that they thought well to await my
return to the capital to discharge it. My reply to the
communication will be in every way in agreement with
that of the French Cabinet. Portugal every day approaches nearer to an open revolution. It is in truth
not a Constitution, but a system of anarchy which the
Emperor Don Pedro has introduced into that country,
and the common ground to be taken by the Courts
seems to me to be found in the following points:—
1. Uniformity of opinion on the nature of things.
2. Efforts to keep the revolution within its own frontiers. 3. Wise counsels to be given to Spain. I will
only add a few remarks demanded by the peculiar
situation of the Emperor our august master, in respect
of his natural relations with the Emperor of Brazil, and
the presence of the Infant Don Miguel at Vienna.

You thought, sir, that Count Nesselrode's first replies to our communications of July 4 last * were unsatisfactory and feeble. My opinion is the same, but
I do not hesitate to say that this was partly owing

---

* Metternich's despatch of the 4th of July concerned a decree issued by
Don Pedro on the occasion of his renunciation of the throne of Portugal,
with regard to the succession of Maria da Gloria, the regency of Isabella,
the marriage of the first with Don Miguel, and the bestowal of a Constitution
for that kingdom. In his despatches to St. Petersburg, Paris, and Berlin,
the Chancellor expressed his doubts and hesitations with regard to the
charter and the alteration of the laws. In writing to London (September 2)
Metternich confined himself to asking Canning (through Esterhazy) the
following question—Who is now sovereign in Portugal, where all the acts of
the Regent (Isabella) are issued in the name of Don Pedro, King of Portugal? Is not the Regency of Isabella in direct contradiction to the fundamental laws?

to the Russian Cabinet's want of more complete information, and to certain special considerations with regard to the Court of London, towards which Court this Cabinet has always had a leaning, even at a time when we were falsely accused of managing England, the only Power with which Russia never wishes to compromise herself.

Since your despatches at the end of July, affairs have progressed, and Mr. Canning himself has furnished us with more than one proof of the difficulties of his situation. This situation is easy to describe. He denies all participation in the drawing up of the Portuguese Charter, while declaring himself in favour of it. But what is easy to describe often presents many difficulties in its development, and this is the case with the affairs of Portugal. Nothing is more problematical than the application of the deplorable work of Don Pedro. It would be difficult to tell how Portugal is governed now, for each day presents singular anomalies. Mr. Canning has evinced a desire to come to an understanding with us on the conduct to be observed by our two Courts in the affairs of Portugal; I thought it right, first of all, to address some questions to him which seem to me fundamental, and which the British minister will have some difficulty in answering satisfactorily.

It is clear to us that there is a happy identity of opinion between us and the French Cabinet, and it seems to be shared by General Pozzo. I have no doubt that the Emperor of Russia, when he is rightly informed, will agree with us; but the more convinced I feel on this point, the less advisable I think it to display any great activity in the matter. Russia should be left to herself at present, and especially by us. The less eagerness, or anything that resembles insisting, we use with the object of influencing the political conduct of the young Emperor, the more chance we shall have, in my opinion, of seeing him take the same road as ourselves. I wish you, therefore, Count, to make your present despatches entirely passive in character. I am away from the Emperor, and do not therefore give you orders, but communications for your own information. If you feel yourself obliged to make some more particular explanation to Count Nesselrode, do it on your own account, as a proof of your personal confidence, and from a feeling that you must trust him as you see he trusts you.

In any case, do not present the questions we have just addressed to London too decidedly, but simply bring them forward as doubts which we have conceived of the regularity of the conduct of the Portuguese Government.

If the Infant continues to show himself well disposed (the Emperor of Brazil has himself begged his august brother-in-law not to spare his counsels to his brother, and made it a duty for his Royal Highness to listen to them), we shall feel ourselves as much at ease in our relations with that Prince as it is possible to be in a position surrounded with difficulties, and involving risk to ourselves and the Prince, in whom the Emperor takes well-merited interest.

I shall leave Johannisberg to-morrow, and take the route by Darmstadt, Carlsruhe, and consequently Upper Suabia and Tyrol, to return to Austria. I have fixed, as I told you above, the time of my arrival in the capital about the 20th September. The Emperor will not return till that time.

THE ATTITUDE TO BE TAKEN IN CASE OF ANY FRESH RUSSO-ENGLISH STEP IN GREEK AFFAIRS.

Metternich to Apponyi, Vienna, November 8, 1826.

835. . . . I foresee the probability of Russia and England taking a simultaneous step with regard to the allies.

. . . Our best-founded hopes depend for the moment on the fact that the French Cabinet, in its answer, avoids going too far. I beg you, my dear Count, to express yourself in this sense, but in the most confidential manner, to M. de Villèle. That enlightened minister must admit how important it is for us not to be accused of wishing to prevent, what a false interpretation would perhaps not be slow to represent, as a project in harmony with the spirit of the Alliance. We shall always be ready to participate in what is really agreeable to the principles and rules of right, but we shall never support what is wrong. Because we wish the former, we cannot be too decided against the latter.

It is clear to me, however, that the fate of Europe will be decided in about six weeks. The present political life or death of Europe will depend on the triumph of England over the religion of the young Russian monarch, or the defeat of her enterprises. The balance is still in the hands of the Continental Powers; with ..... and enlightened benevolence, they ..... the evil; if they are precipitate

in their explanations, they may sanction the very evil
they wish to avoid, and the first error sanctioned by
them will be equivalent to ruin.

Metternich to Apponyi, Vienna, November 8, 1826.

836. The Greek question approaches its conclusion.
According to the text of the Russian despatch, two
possibilities only present themselves : one is, that Mr.
Canning accepts the amendments which Russia has
made to the first propositions of England ; the other
is that Mr. Canning will reject them.

In the first of these cases, no doubt we shall immediately have a new Russo-English communication to the
three Courts.

In the second case, there will be more *pourparlers*
between London and St. Petersburg, and according to
all appearances, the protocol of April 4 will be abandoned.

It is only with the first of these chances that we need
trouble ourselves at present, and to that my letter
applies (No. 835).

If there is to be a new Russo-English communication,
I am anxious the French Cabinet should not reply before
consulting Prussia and ourselves, or rather that in replying it should not prejudice its attitude, principles, or
future.

Mr. Canning's remark, in which he seems to make
no difficulty in admitting the Quintuple Alliance, is
remarkable for two reasons.

First, because the thing is presented by the Emperor
Nicholas as a definite clause of his own agreement with
England ; next, because the crafty and unscrupulous
mind of Mr. Canning may lead him to accede to the
wishes of the Emperor of Russia with the certainty of

being able to arrange the interpretations and applications of what he would regard as a concession made to a mere word.

Indeed, one has only to refer to his letter to Mr. Temple to see that if Mr. Canning crushes the Alliance as he is pleased to define it, he would re-establish it with equal facility on bases suited to his own ends.

Now, if the French Cabinet allows itself to be misled by a phrase, without considering the nature and value attached to it by the Secretary of State, it may bring the greatest evil on itself. I should regard as such the fact, that from that time France would find herself placed in a different position from that which we have maintained in the Greek question. Never shall we violate a principle, and never shall we refuse to accede to a pacification in agreement with these principles. The proposal addressed to the Sultan to renounce his sovereignty and modify it to a suzerainty is a manifest violation of principle.

Mr. Canning's game is to throw dust in the eyes of the Emperor of Russia.

Has that Prince any suspicion of this?

Possibly not; it is probable, however, that he will soon perceive it; and the question is, will he wake up to it in time, or will his delusion last till it is too late?

If the Continental Courts fall into the snare in their turn, the cause will be lost. . . .

I commit to you the matter treated of in my two letters. I have only to beg you to be very cautious, to avoid as far as possible being accused of wishing to stir up the world against so desirable a unity of thought and action.

THE EMPEROR NICHOLAS AND METTERNICH.

Confidential letter of Metternich to the Prince of Hesse-Homburg at St. Petersburg.

837. *Vienna, November* 13, 1826.—To judge from the combinations we were able to make with regard to the Russian affairs, it appears to be obvious: 1. That the Emperor Nicholas has much character, pure principles, clear insight, and great personal confidence in our Emperor. 2. That he feels a certain dislike for myself. 3. And that till now he stands alone, not having yet found the man whom he could regard as a powerful instrument to perform his will, or the useful support as necessary to the monarch as to the man of business. In this description the good far outweighs the evil, and I will frankly confess that I think so little of the evil compared with the good, that I look forward to the future with courage. What is most to be regretted is the hopelessness that, in the surroundings of the Emperor, even one man could be found fit to fulfil the high mission of a trustworthy counsellor. The dislike the Emperor has for me is, I think, of secondary importance, being the natural consequence of long efforts, and it would be surprising if the young monarch, a stranger in the world of politics, had resisted endeavours of so very active a nature. It is evident that the Emperor could not turn in any direction whatever without being more or less actively instigated against me. The whole crew of weak-minded and wicked people, all the fanatics, the doctrinaires and schemers of our days, are against me. What struggles I have daily to encounter, and how thick the clouds in which I see the good people walking about me—these and many other experiences I have enough of. The more firmly I keep to my standpoint the greater the number of my enemies, who are also enemies of all common right and its representative, sound manly common sense.

One unfortunate circumstance has done much to spoil the relations between the young Emperor and myself. When he came into the inheritance of the Eastern affair, which had for five years been so miserably conducted by the Russian Cabinet, the principal statesmen could only excuse themselves by laying the blame on a foreign and hostile power. This has been done, and in similar positions this power will continue to be hostile, having been in the right from the commencement of the affair. I was this power, and the proof is plainly evident. As soon as the Emperor followed the line of conduct I had pointed out as necessary, results were gained which none of the former advisers of the Emperor Alexander desired. But when the firm determination of the new Emperor was seen, the wretched party were obliged to seek some new means for their assistance, and this was presently offered by England. This is the true history of the time.

As a sure means of influencing the late monarch (who died of grief and remorse) against me, the Pozzos and their friends invented the miserable fable that I had proposed to France an alliance against Russia. This story is as true as the other, that in 1791 and 1792 the French Royalists burned their own houses. The more

senseless such tales are the more credible they appear—
a fact well known to novel-writers and scandalmongers.
My desire must therefore be to prove to the Emperor
Nicholas that all these tales are nothing more than lies—
a desire not easy to fulfill, because I have no reason to
believe that the Emperor or his Cabinet will give up the
sources from whence these inventions have been taken.
I venture to believe, too, that the only denunciations
against me are those of General Pozzo, which are entirely imaginary ; and that the whole accusation is only
a pretext to save the monarch from falling under my
influence. If this is the case, all efforts to prove the lie
would be in vain, for it is impossible to teach those who
will not be taught.

However, I have seriously taken into consideration
whether it would be useful to force the Emperor Nicholas
to speak out plainly what he has in his mind. On mature
reflection I do not feel inclined to make the attempt, and
for these reasons :—

The evil in question is so deeply rooted in the
general situation and the peculiar position of the Emperor that, as in most cases of this kind, time and
experience will prove to be the best remedies. The
Liberals honour me by their sneers. This is not their
intention : they wish to make the world believe that the
good cause of legal right is only to the prejudice of one
man. If this were true, my power ought to surpass
that of all monarchs in the world, and what is more, I
must be stronger than my age, or this age very weak.
As things now stand, the truth of the situation, the
strength of the different positions, can only be proved
by the victory one affair, one party, one man (call
it as you like), gains over the other. All between these
extremes must be weak and useless. I am therefore

firmly resolved to try nothing of this kind, but to keep all my strength for action.

At this moment a decision of the greatest possible importance has to be made: namely, whether Russia will unite with England to lay their weight in the balance against revolution or not. According to the decision of this question my relations with the Russian Cabinet will be regulated. I await the decision with calmness. If your Highness can find, quite naturally, an opportunity to tell the Emperor plain truth about the liberty people take with my name, please to do so ; but take care, I beg you, to avoid all controversy on the matter.

AUSTRIA'S ANSWER TO THE RUSSIAN AND ENGLISH INVITATION TO COMMON ACTION AGAINST THE PORTE.

Metternich to Tatistscheff and Wellesley, Vienna, December 22, 1826.

838. The undersigned Chancellor of State, &c. &c., immediately on receiving the communications from his Excellency M. de Tatistscheff and the Ambassador of his Britannic Majesty, concerning the steps to be taken towards the Ottoman Empire for the pacification of the insurgent provinces, hastened to lay them before the Emperor, and he has just received his Majesty's commands to reply as follows :—

His Imperial Majesty observes with satisfaction the interest of these two august Courts in the object to which the Emperor has for two years devoted all his care ; and knows how to appreciate the confidence placed in him by these Courts.

With the same satisfaction his Majesty observes the happy agreement with his wishes expressed by his august allies : and that the measures and plans they propose agree with the proposals made by his Cabinet at the time of the Conferences at St. Petersburg in 1825.

But his Majesty, accustomed as he is to reply to such confidential overtures with absolute sincerity, cannot abstain from drawing attention to some points which do not agree with his feelings, and on which he will proceed to explain himself with the good faith and candour inseparable from his policy.

These points concern the employment of coercive measures intended to force the *Grand-Seigneur*—

To renounce his sovereignty over the Greek subjects of his Empire and to substitute a state of suzerainty;

To admit the mediation of the Powers between him and his subjects in revolt.

The Emperor, in fact, does not know how he can claim the right in either of these cases to employ such measures, or even to threaten the Porte.

In this position his Majesty, animated by the most sincere desire to concur with his august allies by all the means in his power, and considering the pursuit of these means as the fitting object of his constant and serious meditations, does not hesitate to declare—

1st. That he considers it one of his first duties, and one of his first interests, to smooth over as quickly and satisfactorily as possible the hostile relations between the Porte and its insurgent subjects.

2nd. That his Majesty, feeling most deeply the innumerable embarrassments, vexations and dangers of an indefinite prolongation of this state of things in such troublous times as ours, considers himself fully justified in using the most efficacious means both towards the Porte and the insurgents, to put an end as quickly as possible to this deplorable conflict.

3rd. That according to his Majesty's firm conviction the true means to this end is to be found in the similarity of views in the allied Courts, and their perfect agreement in the measures concerted by them.

Influenced by these considerations, his Imperial Majesty commands the undersigned to reply—

1. That his Majesty is ready to join the four allied

Courts in the manner and within the limits that are considered most suitable, and desires that they may be made known to him more fully, provided that the objections concerning the questions of right before-mentioned can be removed;

2. That in case the concert so earnestly desired cannot be established on this basis, his Majesty, while taking an independent line, will none the less concur to the utmost of his power in the aims of his august allies, and will consider it a sacred obligation to co-operate zealously and indefatigably for the success of the proposals they will address to the Porte.

The undersigned desires, &c. &c.

Metternich to Bombelles, in St. Petersburg, Vienna, December 24, 1826.

839. When the last communication was simultaneously made by M. de Tatistscheff and Mr. Henry Wellesley, I thought it well to present to the Emperor in a compressed form the reflections excited by these remarkable diplomatic performances; and this paper you will find enclosed herewith. You will remark that it only relates to the text of the Anglo-Russian acts, and, although I have abstained from there mentioning the communication, it will be impossible for me not to speak of it to you.

I do not believe that so undigested a work could ever be the subject of serious consideration by respectable Cabinets. Here we have the long-expected result of a political combination which shows to three Courts that a discovery to which long deliberation had not been able to lead them had only been the amusement of a few hours for two Courts which till now had been divided by the (apparently) most bitter feelings.

The correspondence between Mr. Canning and M. de Lieven—for the communication is nothing more than that—is confined to proposing two coercive measures, of which one had been formerly considered quite inefficacious, and the other had caused so much irritation to the late Emperor Alexander that, if the rupture of the Conferences of St. Petersburg was not to be explained by more general causes, we might attribute this rupture to the proposal of the second of these measures.

These proposals are :—

1st. The interruption of the diplomatic relations of the five Courts with the Porte ;

2nd. The recognition of the independence of the Greeks.

These proposals, made by Mr. Canning on the 4th of September last, and accepted by M. de Lieven on November 19, are withdrawn, or at least so contracted by the reply of Mr. Canning on November 20 that they are really annulled; for how can the first condition be admitted when England reserves to herself

(a) The unanimous agreement of the Courts ;

(b) The adjournment of the departure of the English and French embassies till the arrival of new orders from these two Courts to their representatives at Constantinople.

What are the arrangements, with respect to this, mentioned in the Secretary of State's letter? They cannot be regarded as legislation, for the recall of the diplomatic agents does not come from the Chambers. It is the same with the diplomatic considerations, for they ought to have preceded the proposal made to the Courts. Then there remain the considerations connected with commerce. What guarantee does Mr. Canning offer to the Courts to which he proposes the simultaneous recall of their embassies that English commerce, first terrified and then consulted, will not demand the withdrawal of this measure?

If Count Nesselrode seems surprised that we have not touched on the question of the interruption of the diplomatic relations, please to deduce the causes of our silence from these considerations, as well as the evident inutility of the measure and the probable effect on the Divan. The second measure is treated by Mr. Canning like the first.

Indeed, what are the limits of the territories to which the recognition of independence extends? Russia, so far as we know has never described them.

The English Cabinet talks sometimes of the Morea and the isles, and sometimes of the territories already set free. At the present moment these territories are reduced to the town of Nauplia and its suburbs; to some roads occupied by the wretched remains of the insurgent bodies; to the Acropolis of besieged Athens; to the castles at Corinth and Argos; perhaps to a strong castle or one or two fortified houses. But Mr. Canning, by the end of his communication of November 25 limited the recognition to territories under regular authority, and capable of maintaining their independence.

To add to the confusion, Mr. Canning's letter dated November 20—to judge by the instructions to the ambassadors accredited to the allied Courts—seems not to be taken into account. It is the first letter, of September 4, which ought to form the instructions for the negotiators at Constantinople. I feel instinctively that it is impossible that the last communication from London to the Courts of Vienna, Paris, and Berlin can satisfy the enlightened and beneficent views of the Emperor Nicholas. In such a strange state of things, we have done what we could ; we have explained our views frankly, and certainly with good will, as to the pacification, which is the Emperor's only object in view in the midst of this deplorable complication !

You will find enclosed a short statement concerning the letter of the Greeks to Mr. Stratford Canning. We have not thought fit to touch on this point in our official despatches, for the two following reasons—because all the caution which we thought necessary to preserve the fundamental principles of the alliance (that is to say, our own principles) is contained in our declaration against the right of intervention in the internal affairs of a third State. By refusing to join in mediation, by not recognising the right, we destroy the basis on which it ought to rest.

Considering the caution on which we insisted with regard to the text of the protocol of April 4, which rests directly on the invitation of the Greeks addressed to England, an invitation which, when closely analysed, presents some points of resemblance with a certain address presented—at a time that surely no one would wish to recall—at the bar of the Convention, in the name *du genre humain.*

If, however, M. de Nesselrode should speak to you of this, you will have recourse to the statement referred to above.

I believe, Sir, that I have now exhausted the subject. Nothing is more painful than to have to reply to questions which in reality are not worthy of a reply. If the two Courts were placed in an upright, open attitude towards the allies who have given so many proofs of their disinterestedness to the world, the affairs would be quickly and easily arranged. Every effect has a cause, and we find the cause of the present perturbation in the character (*faux esprit*) of Mr. Canning, and in the secret views by which he is actuated, and which continually urge him towards inextricable complications. Russian errors form a period of trouble and confusion ; our most sincere desire is to repair them, and we doubt not that in the end we shall do so.

1827.

EVENTS OF THE DAY.

840. *Vienna, January 26,* 1827.—Things in this lower world are in very great confusion. They will come to a solution, for all things have an end; but it is difficult to foresee with any certainty what is the end reserved for us. The worst kind of affairs are those which are difficult to understand; long observation has led me to discover that when this is the case the mischief is in taking for business what is not so. It is with affairs as with writings: obscure passages may always be erased, for in reality they say nothing of any value.

In twice twenty-four hours I shall send you one courier and then a second, in order that the ambassador may have one at his disposal. I begin to run short of couriers—not that I have sent off more than were necessary, but because they have not returned. They are monopolised by some of the embassies.

We have had eighteen days of excessive cold, and the country is covered with more snow than I ever remember to have seen. It has snowed in great flakes for four whole days. The snow is nearly four feet deep, and five hundred carts are at work night and day to clear the city.

Prince de Hatzfeld was last night attacked by severe inflammation of the lungs. I trust he will recover, for his loss would be a great misfortune. He is rather better this evening, after having been bled three times. He was to give a ball next Sunday, which must now be put off, and this will grieve our young ladies as much as the cause does me. I shall open the new room by a grand ball on February 12. It is really a very fine room.

841. *January* 29. — I recommend to you my despatch sent this day. I have disclosed my sentiments a little, and lifted the veil which covers many of the positions. (No. 853.)

842. *February* 27.—Your last despatch, my dear Victor, was very interesting. Your opinions on the affair of the titles agree with mine, as you may see by my despatch of the 11th inst.

The affair cannot stop here; it is repugnant to the nature of things and to human nature. I frankly confess that I have already experienced moments of extreme uneasiness when thinking of you in Paris in the midst of the squabble. I should be sorry that you were mixed up in some bad sort of affairs, which easily happen and are difficult to avoid for one who unites your qualifications as man of the world, an Austrian, and your father's son. I am glad that the young men have taken the thing properly: they rightly attach little value to the *souvenirs de l'Empire*, for the whole matter is, in fact, only a question of these *souvenirs*: the rest is only a pretence.

The Carnival is just over, and glad I am! My balls were very fine, and the concert that I gave on Friday

was still better, and was, in fact, more perfect than can
be imagined.

843. *March* 18.—Since I was mixed up in affairs—
and that is, alas! a very long time—I have never seen
such a silly affair as this of the titles! It will come to
an end, as all affairs must; but it will not die a natural
death, as they flatter themselves in Paris. At any rate,
you take the thing too hotly: there is nothing in it so
extremely pressing.

I hope Count Apponyi will see what I mean by the
instruction that I send to-day. We must have an
answer to the questions we address to the French
Cabinet. Apponyi must not negotiate, but he must
exact a clear and distinct answer for or against. . . .

I have been so much occupied and I am still so
busy with the new turn that we are trying to give to the
Eastern Question that I have no head for anything
else. I shall send everything to Paris in three or four
days, but only for the information of the ambassador;
for, as to the Government, it is not worth even the
trouble of talking to. It will meet us again in London.
(Nos. 855-857.)

844. *May* 21.—I shall not go to Johannisberg, for
I cannot do so, on account of the business, and on
account of the changes being made there. The first of
necessaries in a *château* is the roof, and they are just about
to alter that at Johannisberg. My plan is to settle
myself for July and August at Königswart. I shall
take the children there, and from this point make excursions to Plass and probably some other places.
When I can decide the day of my arrival at Königswart I will let you know and fix the time for you to
come and meet me.

For the rest, I foresee nothing to hinder me from

passing six weeks or two months in the country. I can attend to my business as well there as here, and my health, though good enough, will still be the better for the fine air. The season promises to be fine, and therefore we may hope to enjoy the pastoral life that I propose to lead.

As to affairs, every thing is going wrong, as it always will as long as weak men try to be very clever, without finding out that they only serve as the bad sport of some factions and the chief of factious people (Canning), whom I consider in a very uncomfortable position, although he has become Prime Minister. At Paris, they are quite silly, and we shall soon see in what class of character the young *autocrate du Nord* is to be placed.

Neumann has only made ' *des bêtises* ' at Rio. Do not tell him so : that must be left to me. There is a sort of independence about his character which does not go well with affairs. Everyone who undertakes a mission should begin by submitting himself to the yoke of the thought that serves as the ground of his instruction. Neumann, instead of imbuing himself in our decision never to allow the Infant to go to Brazil, has acted as if the contrary were the object of our wishes. He has dreamed and perspired ; it was hardly worth while to go eight thousand leagues to do nothing more than that. Felix Schwarzenberg has returned fine and fresh from his trip.

845. *May* 31.—Neumann arrived here yesterday, looking like a sinner ; I scolded him, and then comforted him. He has acted like a child where he ought to have acted in a manner more worthy of his usual weight and influence. Neumann's great fault was a want of obedience in circumstances where no latitude had been left to the negotiator. He was ordered to take *ad referendum* the expression of Don Pedro's wish that his brother should come to Brazil. Instead of confining himself to this, he said 'Yes,' when we said nothing; which brought about that the speaker found himself contradicted, which is neither desirable for a Court, nor agreeable for the person who undergoes the contradiction. Neumann feels this, and I think his indiscreet 'Yes' will long weigh upon him.

846. *June* 11.—Read my remarks, my dear Victor, on the plan of the treaty (No. 861). This is a work which will as little escape the remarks of Pufendorf as those of Colnet, and if I have only filled eight or ten pages with my benevolent sayings, it is because I was obliged to restrain my imagination for want of time, but not for want of material. '*Das Salz der Welt ist dumm geworden*,' said the Apostle Paul; he spoke of his own times and most certainly also of ours. I do not think it will please at St. Petersburg.

Vienna is now absolutely empty, and the only thing alive is the opera, which has just become perfect when there is no longer anyone to criticise it. It is a resource for me, and beside that I have only the garden, which has been in a great state of perfection ever since it was put into the care of the new gardener, who seems to be a sort of genius. He has already gained a great reputation among the botanical big-wigs, and I cannot get over my astonishment whenever I trace back his immense store of knowledge to its source. Who would ever have thought that the little *Hausmeister* would become the father of a great man! But you, on the other hand, serve me very badly: since the first batch of camellias you have sent nothing, and if there were no one but you as a purveyor of plants, the garden would be a desert. If ever Mr. Canning plants a garden, I shall recommend you to take care of it. That will be the most crushing defeat that I could possibly prepare for him.

METTERNICH'S MARRIAGE WITH ANTONIA LEY-KAM, COUNTESS VON BEILSTEIN.

Extracts from Metternich's private Letters to his son Victor and to Countess Molly Zichy-Ferraris, from October 7 to December 9.

Metternich to his son Victor, Vienna, October 7, 1827.

847. I told you shortly the other day that here the affair is settled. To-morrow the Emperor will sign the decree which will make Mademoiselle de Leykam a Countess of Beilstein, and after to-morrow I shall announce my approaching marriage.

I do not like to hear that you have not been well for a fortnight and that you do not yet know what is the matter. Your constitution requires care, and I entreat you not to spare it. Ask Gall what he recommends, and follow exactly what he prescribes. Winter is now beginning, and if by chance he recommends your passing some months in a warmer climate than that of Paris, do not hesitate to go—let nothing stop you. You like Maurice Dietrichstein : I will ask him to accompany you. Hyères, Nice, or some place near Genoa—perhaps Genoa itself—would no doubt suit you better than Paris. I hope I shall soon learn that my provisions are needless ; but Gall, not you, must decide. Think of me and the anxieties you will cause me if you do not follow the advice of your physician. Nothing is ever risked by being obedient ; what you will not do for yourself, do for me.

I beg you, my dear Victor, to let me know how you are, and, above all, let Gall write to me. I am waiting anxiously to hear one of two things—either that Gall has no directions to give you, or that you are careful to do what he tells you. Either of these pieces of intelligence will do me good, and I am sure you wish to gratify me.

I have fixed the day for my marriage—on the 29th of this month. It will take place at Hetzendorf, and the Duke of Wurtemburg will remain there expressly for it. Neumann, who is leaving this, will be able to tell you that everything is arranged satisfactorily.

Metternich to the Countess Molly Zichy-Ferraris, Vienna, October 20.*

848. Instead of troubling you with a long history of my affairs, I enclose an extract of a letter which I recently addressed to the only person to whom I have written on the subject. These are my words :—

'I have no need to tell you what you have heard from a hundred people. What I do, I decide with the reason and calmness which are in my heart. In great decisions I ask counsel from no one. All that my friends tell me I know, for I have already said it to myself; what those tell me who are not my friends has no value at all in my eyes. I consult my conscience on these occasions and try to obey it. At the age of twenty-five I should have doubted my ability to judge of the situation of others clearly, or of my own with impartiality. At my age, I am less modest, and have not the same doubts. I know what I ought to do, and I do it. The conduct of men may be influenced by the circumstances which form the setting in which they are placed. That in which I find myself is in an

---

* The mother of Melanie, afterwards wife of the State Chancellor.—ED.

elevated sphere. I am the object of much attention, and the public occupies itself by preference with those who are daily before its eyes. Tittle-tattle is the peculiar characteristic of Vienna society, and this society does not always dream to what independent men may be driven. It is happy for my future life that these unworthy tales should have shown me the path I had to follow; it opposes neither the affections of my heart, nor the first necessity of my private life—a home. That home I am about to find, and it will be a special guarantee of repose, from the fact that it is restricted to one person: I am not going to marry the relations.

' This is my story. It is very simple, for it is very straightforward.

' I complete, moreover, two great and very happy experiences. The truest friends of my life are my family and my master. The Emperor has been my only confidant on this occasion, and he has proved—as he always has—the surest guide and the most tender of fathers. My own relations—all who are first in my affection and regards—have shown themselves as they always have been, my truest friends. What is laid at my door may remain there. I shall know how to defend it.'

849. *October* 25.—My life, my dear friends—for I speak to you all—is a very singular thing, and very unlike that of most people. This life is composed of two parts, which my nature enables me to lead in two parallel lines which never become entangled. One of these parts belongs to the world, and God knows it cannot, without great injustice, accuse me of sparing myself in its service. The other is my own especial domain, and great sufferings have fallen to my lot. I

A A

have lost all which constitutes the happiness of man; I have lived through it all, for trouble does not kill. I need perfect rest; this is the secret of my heart, and is known only to my friends. My heart is not blind; it is not under the influence of passion; it is calm and warm, serene and severe, and—unless I deceive myself— in the right proportion. What I desire is that those who love me should understand me, and I feel that among you I am better understood than anywhere else.

Metternich to his son Victor, Vienna, November 3.

850. My marriage will take place the day after to-morrow. The ceremony has been delayed eight days as your aunt had a cold; and, as the marriage is to be at Hetzendorf, it would not have done for my sister to be absent.

851. *November 13.*—It was with very great satisfaction that I saw by your letter, and by a line which Neumann wrote to me, that your health is restored. I love you too much not to be uneasy when I know you are ill; and I have spent many anxious days. I do not like undecided maladies, and when the fifteenth day arrived and no solution, I had sad fears, which Heaven has seen fit to contradict. I wish Heaven had treated the triple Alliance as it has you—that is to say, that it had cured it.

. . . . As for you, follow Gall's advice. His Philhellenism and his craniology do not frighten me; he is a very good doctor, and he understands the German constitution. If he advises a journey to the South, I should be either for Nice or Genoa. If he advises nothing, do nothing. I shall not recommend you to be careful; I flatter myself you are so. A little care will often prevent a severe illness; and health is not an affair of fancy.

I have made my home as I always desired it should be, simple and without fuss. I have found what I sought, and the poor children are happy, which is so necessary to my happiness. You have written a perfect letter to Leontine, just what my heart would have dictated.

852. *December* 9.— . . . I beg you to tell Count Apponyi that the only news I have had from Constantinople since the 11th are in a despatch brought by the courier; it is dated the 24th, and contains two facts. One is, that at the urgent demand of the Internuncio the Porte has raised the embargo on merchant vessels. The second, that the representatives of the three Courts had a conference with the Reis-Effendi on the 24th.

THE POLITICAL SITUATION IN EUROPE AT THE BEGINNING OF 1827.

Metternich to Apponyi, in Paris, Vienna, January 29, 1827.

853. We regard the present moment as the most critical that has occurred for several years. This critical moment is the natural consequence and, to a certain extent, a necessary condition of the general position of things in Europe, of the various faults committed by the Governments : in short, of two fortuitous circumstances—namely, the appointment of Mr. Canning to the department of Foreign Affairs in England, and the change of reign in Russia.

The revolution, after brooding in men's minds, burst forth in France in 1789. Its violence limited its outward existence to a very short period ; a man endowed with extraordinary faculties was raised up in the midst of the French people ; strong from the cast of his mind and character, and not less strong from the weakness of his rivals and adversaries, he needed but a short time and good fortune to change the anarchy into a military despotism unexampled in modern times. But the same qualities and the same defects which brought about his ascension, produced his fall as soon as he had attained his apogee. Desiring to mount still higher, he fell, and the restoration of the principle of legitimacy, having only been acted on in an abstract sense, has turned in consequence of enormous errors into a new era of the revolution. The latter is, so to speak, ennobled, and Radicalism has hoisted the banner of Liberalism.

The conduct of public affairs between the years 1814 and 1820 has enabled the factions to measure the moral forces of the different Governments. New revolutions have broken out. Mr. Canning has been called to the helm of affairs in his own country, and the bent of his mind, his strong and his weak sides, his incapacity in so many essential points, and his great adroitness in others, lastly his exalted ambition, have allowed him to choose his part; he chose one which was open to him: he put himself at the head of Monarchical Liberalism. From that time the world had to take a new colour.

The moral death of the Emperor Alexander had preceded his physical death. Deceived in everything, weighed down with regret, wanting that force of mind which if he had but possessed would have prevented him from preparing so many troubles for himself, that unfortunate Prince has left the throne to a young successor, who seems to possess many of the qualities which his predecessor lacked. But, unhappily for Europe and for himself, his first steps on the field of politics have been stultified by the grave errors committed by some weak-minded men.

The fate of a whole future depends on the struggle between the qualities which we are glad to regard as belonging personally to the monarch, and the need which must be felt by his feeble counsellers of justifying what cannot be justified either before the tribunal of reason or even before that of a certain wretched diplomacy which ought to be banished from the Cabinet of every great Power.

Mr. Canning has made use of the Emperor Nicholas as we often see adroit speculators make use of heirs who inherit a great fortune while still young and inexperienced.

The question of the day, as of the future, depends entirely on the part that will be taken by the Emperor Nicholas, or, to express myself more correctly, on that which he must have already taken, and which we shall hear of immediately.

But whatever steps Russia may take, the time of ease for Mr. Canning is past. Difficulties of every kind have commenced. Whatever determinations the Court of Russia may take, nothing can alter this fact. If these determinations are according to our wishes, what the English Cabinet has made and undertaken and encouraged since the accession of its chief will be restrained in its development. If they should not bear this character, Mr. Canning will be smothered under the weight of his deplorable success. The master of a vessel carrying a regular flag may enter into speculations and hazardous enterprises disapproved by the laws of prudence and even by those of justice; but he cannot, without the consent and agreement of the whole crew, take up the line of a freebooter. . . .

Unhappily, two Governments directly contribute to aggravate the dangers. One is that of France, the other that of Spain; and both lack wisdom, strength and foresight. Of the two the latter is the stronger, for it is the attacking party.

I do not know if many judges of public affairs will judge as I do; but this opinion agrees so thoroughly with my inner feelings that I have no hesitation in pronouncing it.

The two Governments are under the influence of fear; but there are many shades of this feeling: there is a fear which leads to capitulations without end; there is another which hardens men. The French ministers have the first; the second belongs to Spain.

In this position of things, our attitude is expectant without being impassive. Whenever we can see clearly we shall know how to act.

THE APPROACHES MADE BY RUSSIA TO AUSTRIA.

Metternich to Esterhazy, Vienna, February 14, 1827.

854. The Court of Russia is inclined to make approaches to us. You will have proof of this in the instructions which M. de Lieven must have received. Alliance, uniformity of views and conduct in the affairs of Portugal, Spain, Italy, &c., is the order of the day. They wish us to join in the treaty which, according to the proposal of France, must replace the protocol of April 4; if this wish of the Emperor Nicholas cannot be attained, he desires at least that we should support it. Our decision will not differ from the spirit of our reply of December 22 to the last Anglo-Russian communication (No. 838). We will never violate what we feel to be principles. It is thought at St. Petersburg that England did not wish for the form of a treaty. Consequently, they would regard her as released from the protocol. We see risks in this move, and we will not sacrifice our position, which is strong because it is correct. . . .

The last word of the relations between Russia and England is found in the fear with which the two parties inspire each other.

Continue to maintain an amicable footing with Mr. Canning, and cultivate also your relations with M. de Lieven.

I shall take care to furnish you with all the support

necessary in the negotiation on the Greek question. You shall immediately have proof of this. In the meantime seem to be ignorant of everything, and make good use of your time by finding out what effect the communications from St. Petersburg have on Mr. Canning.

INSTRUCTION FOR THE LONDON CONFERENCES.

Metternich to Esterhazy, Vienna, March 26, 1827.

855. The Court of Russia has invited us to send you the necessary instructions and faculties, so that your Highness may contribute to the establishment of an agreement between the five Courts on the subject of the pacification of the still insurgent countries of European Turkey. The Emperor, far from objecting to this desire, finds it agree so well with his own intentions and wishes, that his Imperial Majesty thinks he can hardly show enough eagerness in granting it.

In consequence of this determination you will find enclosed (No. 856) the instructions which by the Emperor's orders I have the honour to address to you.

Their contents are clear, and embrace all aspects of the affair. . . .

You will take care to inform Mr. Canning and the representatives of Russia, France and Prussia of the directions we have addressed to you. Your Highness is moreover authorised to make them confidentially cognisant of the very text of your instructions. . . .

From the moment that the agreement we desire is established between the representatives of the Courts, your Highness may consider yourself authorised to take part in the deliberations to be arranged in common, in order by your signature to shew the agreement of your Court in the act which is the object of all our efforts.

Your Highness is aware that we have always been persuaded that it could only be by a clearly-stated uniformity of views and action in the five Courts that thére would be any chance of success for this plan. You will therefore not be surprised at the eagerness of his Imperial Majesty to agree to means likely to bring about the desired result.*

Instructions to Esterhazy, Vienna, March 25, 1827.

856. The Court of Russia having invited us to contribute to the establishment of a centre of agreement between the five Powers, and to send instructions to London to this effect, the Emperor our august master, always disposed to associate himself with his august allies in the search of means to put an end to the troubles and calamities which still weigh heavily on European Turkey, has ordered us to furnish you, without loss of time, with the instructions necessary to enable you to take part in the deliberations about to take place in the capital of the country in which you are residing.

Our directions are similar to those which you have received at different times during the last six years. You are acquainted with the negotiations and *pourparlers* which have taken place between the Cabinets on the subject of the pacification of the Levant. You know especially the replies which we addressed to the last

---

* Gentz writes (March 11, 1827) to Metternich: ' The Russian Cabinet has produced a project for a convention; the French, a second; England (as representing the Greeks), a third. Perhaps it would be a clever thing for Austria to come forward with a fourth. Have we not as much right to do so as the others? It is true that this would only increase the perplexity; but it is really not our interest to make so very bad a thing clear. The thicker the darkness, the sooner will the meddlers in it break their heads.'—Ed.

simultaneous communications from England and Russia, and the instructions to the Internuncio last December. Our task is thus limited to informing you of the determinations of our august master, incited by the new demand which the Cabinet of Russia has addressed to us.

The affair in its new phase must be considered with two points in view:

1. An agreement between the five Courts;

2. The most natural and therefore the most likely means of arriving, not only at an agreement between the five Courts, but also at rendering this agreement useful and effectual in the interest of the pacification.

We readily admit, with regard to the first point, that the wishes and fundamental views of the five Courts present no essential difference.

As to the Emperor's feelings relative to the object of the agreement, I have nothing fresh to tell you. You know that the real pacification of the Levant has at all times been one of the chief objects of his solicitude. I need not, therefore, enter into the reasons which influence the wishes and calculations of our august master. Independently of considerations relative to the administrative or commercial interests of his own Empire, nothing of what concerns the general interest, nothing which tends to the good of humanity, can be indifferent to his Imperial Majesty. On the other hand, how can he conceal from himself the numerous grave inconveniences and positive dangers attached to the continuance of troubles which form a stumblingblock between the Great Powers?

As a proof of the desire of our august master that an end should be put to this complication, it will be sufficient for us to send you the text of our above-mentioned instructions to the Internuncio, and of the explanations on the same subject which that minister has been charged to make, in case of necessity, to the Divan itself. We may therefore regard this subject as exhausted both towards the allied Courts and our own agents.

In approaching the second point, it seems to us most important to consider the difficulties which up to this time have been raised against the establishment of an agreement between the five Courts.

If during the first period of the affair England did not entirely remove herself from all participation in the *pourparlers* which took place between the allied Cabinets, she retired at the very moment of the opening of the Conferences at St. Petersburg, and from that time refused her concurrence as much to the Conferences as to the steps agreed upon at them.

At the beginning of last year, the relative positions of the Powers experienced a complete change. The Courts of Russia and England entered into a separate negotiation. The protocol of March 23 (April 4) was the result.

In the deliberations between the years 1822 and 1825, the four intervening Courts at the Conferences were maintained on one common basis of principles.

The protocol of April 4 established different bases.

At the conclusion of the communication which the two signatory Courts of the protocol made of this act to the three other Continental Courts, France declared herself in accord with the terms of the Anglo-Russian transaction.

Prussia declared herself ready to subscribe to these same terms, provided the five Courts were unanimous.

Austria declared she could not for her part admit any departure from the protocol. But we engaged to support by all the means in our power the necessity of the pacification.

Quite recently, the French Cabinet proposed the transformation of the protocol into a treaty between the five Courts. The Russian Cabinet accepted this proposition.

Without knowing officially, we have every reason to believe that a similar declaration has emanated from the British Cabinet.

The Cabinet of Berlin remains true to its former declaration.

Our declaration concerning the first Anglo-Russian act has of course been a sufficient reply to the new proposal.

According to rumours which have reached us from St. Petersburg, the French Cabinet has communicated to that of Russia a project about the treaty in question which the latter has declared it cannot admit.

Your Reports of March 1, however, inform us that the Court of London would have not only accepted the proposal of converting the protocol of April 4 into a treaty, but that it would be equally ready with France and Russia to sign the project proposed at Paris.

We do not know what the French project is; it is thus placed beyond the sphere of our judgment, and, as far as we know, the Court of Prussia is not better informed than we are.

In the meantime, the English ambassador at Constantinople sent to the Reis-Effendi a few days before the arrival of M. de Ribeaupierre, and seconded by M. de

Minciaky, a formal note expressly founded on the basis
of the protocol. . . .

This is the history of the affair, and at this moment
it is not an easy task to furnish you with instructions.

To give them a basis founded on antecedents, we
have but to take for guide the invariable principles of
the Emperor and the facts of the case.

The former have been explained with so much precision in the despatches which have emanated from our
Cabinet for the last six years, and especially in those
which since the beginning of the present year have
been brought to your knowledge, that we can only
repeat ourselves while insisting on the divergence between the terms of the protocol of April 4 and our
points of departure.

Reduced to the most simple terms, this divergence
may be stated as follows :—

To prove to the Sultan the necessity that he should
pacify his insurgent provinces ; or

To prove to the Sultan the necessity of allowing
these same provinces to be pacified, and of contributing
what means he can towards that pacification.

According to the first formula, the weight of the
Powers would be brought to bear on one object—
namely, the admission on the part of the Sultan of
the necessity of the pacification.

According to the second, their action would bear
equally on two objects : in the first place, on the admission of this necessity by the Sultan ; and, in the
second place, on the recognition by him of the right
and necessity of foreign mediation.

A very simple question arises in our minds. Would
the weight which would suffice for the first of these

concessions suffice equally for the second? We do not
think so ; and for these reasons :—

The Courts will be powerful so long as they rest on
the evident necessity of a pacification aided also by
calculations of their own interests, and those of the
Ottoman Power ; so long as they do not attack in any
way the sovereign authority of the Sultan, and, far from
injuring him, make the most of those acts of condescension which, though in fact imposed upon him, have the
appearance of benefits conferred by the sovereign authority on an unhappy people—pledges of the repose and
stability of the empire. Driven to his last retrenchments,
how could the Sultan withstand an urgency grounded on
such bases? Would it be a blind repugnance? But the
firm determination on the part of the five Courts not
to retrace their steps after a first demand—a demand
justified by powerful considerations and by the undoubted necessity—should certainly suffice to overcome
this repugnance ; as in the case (which we do not admit)
of a refusal, it would be evident to the monarchs, and
to all right-minded men in Europe, on which side reason
and wisdom lay. On the other hand, the Courts will
be weak as often as their weight, instead of bearing by
preference on the main question, is used in favour of
particular forms. The Emperor has a firm conviction
that this would uselessly endanger the success which
might be hoped for under the latter system, and consequently his Imperial Majesty, while desiring the same
object as the allies, has reserved to himself, by his
last replies to the signatory Courts of the protocol of
April 4, the liberty of using the means he considers
most efficacious.

We will now inform you of our point of view on
some questions which we think must have a decided

influence on the success of the double enterprise of establishing an agreement between the allied Powers, and of using it in favour of the common cause.

Supposing that it were possible to remove the essential difficulty of our acceding to such an agreement, you would have to bring forward the following observations :—

The general idea of the pacification comprises the past, the present, and the future.

The remedy applicable to the past is oblivion. The recognized form is that of an amnesty pronounced by the sovereign authority.

The measure applicable to the present is a truce, in the technical or military acceptation of the term—that is to say, a suspension of warlike operations properly so called. This measure, indispensable in itself, would nevertheless only be proposed to the Porte in consequence of its previous assent to the principle and fact of the pacification.

Lastly, the future can only be secured by the establishment of such a state of things as will secure to the contending parties the hope of a lasting peace, and the preservation of the reciprocal advantages derived from the present pacification.

The means of arriving at such a state of things will be found, we think, in the two following articles :—

I. Separation of the Christian and Mussulman population ;

II. Guarantee of the Powers in favour of the two contending parties, which guarantee must be confined to the execution and maintenance of the agreement which has been made use of to establish the pacification.

Ad I. This basis seems to us the only one which

need occupy the attention of the Conference at London, being that which, in reality, embraces the whole question.

Its application necessitates so many important ideas, and the taking into consideration so many local circumstances, that the arrangement of the means of execution and of the limits within which they should be confined cannot come under the domain of a Conference in London. Meantime we feel convinced that the basis can only be practically applicable to some of the isles and to the Peloponnesus.

. In the former, the two populations have never been mixed ;

In the latter, the Turkish population has been destroyed or expelled, and the troops of Ibrahim Pacha must not be mistaken for a permanent population. The fortresses must remain in the power of the Porte for the maintenance of its sovereignty, and in the interest of the Greek race, as well as in that of a real pacification. The system on which this pacification will rest, as we understand it, not having for its object a political emancipation of the Greeks, one of the first pledges of the solidity of this system, and of the security which it will give to the Greek tribes of enjoying a durable tranquillity under a *régime* of political dependence, can never be found except in a measure which would prevent the latter from becoming daily the sport of guilty ambitions within and intrigues without.

The civil liberty of the countries under the new *régime* cannot be better established and guaranteed than by a stipulation giving up to them the power of administering their own laws, and retaining their own usages and customs. What are these laws and usages ? It is not for the Powers to define them. The Porte,

contenting itself with an annual tribute, which would
be brought to Constantinople or deposited in some place
of security, would have no motive for interfering in
what could not interest it directly.

Ad II. A definite guarantee of the kind alluded to
would be of great utility ; we should consider it advantageous for both parties.

The sovereign authority would find in it a pledge of
the future tranquillity of the pacified countries, and
consequently the guarantee of its own peace, both
internal and political.

The people of the Morea and of the isles would, on
their side, find in this guarantee the inestimable advantage of the peaceable enjoyment of those good things
which nature has lavished upon them, and be able to
develop the elements of prosperity offered to them by
their soil, their industry and their commerce.

We have now to approach a subject of the highest
importance : which is that of the comminatory and
coercive measures to be employed against the Porte in
case it should persist in its refusal to entertain the
overtures made by the allies concerning the pacification and the measures proper to bring it about.

We will explain this with the frankness and straightforwardness characteristic of our august master.

Two comminatory measures have been arranged
between the two signatory Powers of the protocol of
April 4 : the interruption of the diplomatic relations
with the Porte, and the threat of establishing direct
relations with the insurgents.

A third measure having been brought forward—
namely, that of employing the fleets to intercept communication between the army of Ibrahim and Egypt,
together with an amicable attitude of these same mari-

time forces towards the Greeks—seems to have since formed the subject of an understanding between the Courts of London, St. Petersburg, and France. In its last communications the Court of Russia made some allusion to a fourth measure. It was merely hinted at, but not with sufficient clearness to enable us to describe it as rupture with the Porte.

As to the three measures distinctly announced by Russia and England and accepted by France, we find but one gradation. Moreover, it is clear to us from the last communications that neither the Cabinet of London nor that of St. Petersburg attributes any sensible effect to the recall of the embassy from Constantinople, and we share that feeling.

On the other hand, open contact with the Greeks might, naturally enough, be regarded by the Porte as an act of positive hostility; if such should not be the case (and we are inclined to think that the Sultan will not be anxious to regard it in this sense), this measure certainly would not lead to the political emancipation of the Greeks—a result which the Powers seem to lose sight of.

As for the employment of the fleets, how could the Powers have recourse to that step without putting themselves into an openly hostile attitude?

There still remains the fourth measure indicated by Russia. This measure, employed as a comminatory means by the five Courts, and directed towards a clear and precise end—the only one which could effectually answer the expectation of the Courts—seems to us the most certain to bring about the consent of the Sultan to the pacification; and, consequently, it is the only one which appears to us of a nature to be seriously discussed between the five Courts.

The Emperor is, from conviction and feeling, unwilling to admit the chances of a war with the Porte. He would regard it, not only as the greatest misfortune which could happen to Europe, but as leading the Powers to results in every way opposed to those which they propose. But his Imperial Majesty is invited to give his opinion and pronounce a judgment on the most effectual means for attaining the pacification without endangering the general peace; far from refusing this request, he expresses his views with perfect candour.

You have here, Prince, all the thoughts and feelings of our august master, and by them you will be able to regulate your language and conduct.

Your instructions may be summed up as follows:—

1st. You will announce to the Secretary of State and to your colleagues that, in consequence of the expression of a wish of his Imperial Majesty of All the Russias, you are authorised to take part in any common deliberation of the five Courts on the means of bringing peace to the Levant; the deliberations taking place either in the form of regular conferences or in that of confidential *pourparlers*.

In either case, you will take care to bring forward the different points of view above-mentioned— namely, those relating to the clear and precise definition—

(*a*) Of the end or aim of the agreement to be established;

(*b*) Of the moral attitude of the Powers in the establishment of so desirable an agreement among themselves;

(*c*) Of the choice and employment of the best means for attaining a real pacification.

Two things, however, may occur, for either of which we ought to be prepared.

One would be an agreement between the five Courts on the basis of our principles, and especially of those which were set forth in our reply of December 22 (No. 838). On that, your Highness must declare yourself ready to corroborate the act by your signature recording the result of the common agreement. We have, however, one remark to make concerning the form to be given to such an act.

The denomination ' treaty ' seems to us little adapted to the circumstances, and we much prefer the not less binding but more suitable form of a ' convention ' or a ' protocol.' Your Highness will take care to make this distinction.

In the other case, the signatory Courts of the protocol of April 4 may strictly maintain the terms and points of departure from that act, and the other Courts may agree. You would then, Prince, have to declare that your Court will maintain the terms of its Note in reply to the last simultaneous communications from England and Russia, continuing, however, to regulate its action at Constantinople on the line and within the limits of the instruction to the Internuncio on December 30, 1826.*

* This instruction culminated in the notification that the Internuncio was to take no step till he was informed of the commencement of the negotiation by the representatives of England and Russia ; but in that case he should counsel the Porte to compliance—that is, that he should say that the Porte might decline mediation and do of its own accord what the mediating Powers desired.—ED.

ADDITIONAL INSTRUCTIONS.

While the Emperor authorises you to express yourself frankly on the only feasible comminatory measure which he thinks calculated to make the Sultan decide on the pacification of Greece—namely, the threat of a rupture with the five Powers simultaneously—our august master would not satisfy his conscience if he did not beforehand draw a precise limit between the threat of a rupture to induce the Sultan to grant peace to his insurgent countries and the realisation of that threat by an actual European war against the Porte.

Consequently, the Emperor now declares that whenever he consents to join the four other Courts and proceed conjointly with them to the comminatory measure, his Imperial Majesty, trusting in the wisdom and moderation of his allies, has no doubt that, in case of a peremptory refusal on the part of the Sultan, they will consider it indispensable that a deliberation on future contingencies should take place; and he reserves to himself to take part in it, each of the intervening Powers possessing the most entire moral independence.

Metternich to Esterhazy, in London, Vienna,
March 26, 1827.

857. The present despatch arises from a combination of circumstances so peculiar that your Highness must absolutely be informed of our moral attitude to enable you to render to his Majesty and the general cause the services which we expect from your well-known zeal. I will therefore give you a rapid sketch of our observations and intentions, and I beg you to give your best attention to this *résumé*.

You have followed for so many years the progress of affairs, both as an observer and an actor, that you must certainly share our conviction that the politics of Europe have undergone a radical change, in consequence of the change of ministry in England after the death of the Marquis of Londonderry, and also in consequence of the death of the Emperor Alexander and the accession of the present monarch in Russia. I should undertake a useless task if I made a profound examination of the causes which have most influenced the changes we mention. It is sufficient to say that the order of things established between the years 1813 and 1815 has succumbed because it was worn out and inapplicable to the new conditions under which the Powers are placed—conditions partly owing to faults committed by themselves, and partly produced by a number of causes which in the course of time arise and develop of themselves. We cannot conceal from ourselves that the union known under the name of the Alliance has for some time been little more than a pretence, a sort of formula, recently conjured up and employed according to individual needs, and sometimes distorted or inverted in its application in consequence of other sentiments or other needs, real or supposed.

Indeed, how would it be possible to find in the conduct of England, since Mr. Canning's accession to power, one single trace of the Alliance?

Who would not admit that the act passed between England and Russia on April 4, 1826, has done manifest injury to the principles of this same Alliance?

France has never comprehended the Alliance, and in reality has never taken part in it.

Austria and Prussia alone have remained faithful to the principles of the Alliance, and we in particular have never deviated at any time, or under any circumstances, from its salutary rules. We have acted thus because the principles of the Alliance are those of public right, and consequently ours, and because of the importance which we attach to preserving a name even when the thing itself has ceased to exist. While admitting in theory that the Alliance long has been nothing more than a mere abstraction, we are nevertheless not surprised to see the Emperor of Russia make an appeal to the Alliance—or at any rate to its forms. It seems to us perfectly natural. A work so undigested as the protocol of April 4—a protocol from the first stultified by the interpretations, explanations, and reserves which the Court of London applied to it in November last—not being able to bear any other fruits for the two contracting parties than those of disorder, the time has come for the scales to fall from the eyes of the least clearsighted. This moment had long ago been foreseen by us when the work engendered by the distrust of two contracting parties, and by the jealousy which these same parties entertain for each other, is put in practice.

The Russian ambassador arrived at Constantinople, and from that moment the protocol of April 4 was doomed.

Experience seems to have convinced the Russian Cabinet that without our concurrence the re-establishment of order in the Levant would be impossible. It therefore reconsidered its conduct towards us; but it was anxious to obtain the concurrence of England as well as ours. This is doubtless the origin of the Emperor Nicholas' idea of trying to establish in London a centre of agreement between the five Courts. . . .

You have, on the other hand, remarked for some

time signs of approach made by the British Cabinet. The last explanations of Mr. Stratford Canning with the Internuncio have given a new complexion to symptoms which I am very much inclined to describe rather as those of great embarrassment than as those of confidence in us.

But let us keep to matters of fact. Of these one of the most curious is the last despatch from Constantinople. . . .

Has Mr. Stratford Canning, in throwing himself, so to speak, into the arms of our minister, acted in virtue of positive orders from his Government? I can hardly go so far as that. But it is a certain fact that the protocol of April 4 no longer exists in any possible application.

We are thus working on new ground; we are called upon to explain ourselves, and although the formal instructions which you will receive to-day had been drawn up previous to the arrival of the last news from Constantinople, far from having thought it necessary to change them, we have been confirmed in the pursuit of the plan which we had traced for ourselves.

How do Russia and England really wish the Greek affair to end? It would be very difficult to say, and I do not trouble myself to find out, as I have a feeling, which I may admit without much fear of being contradicted, that the two Courts themselves are not very clear on the subject. Were I compelled to occupy myself with the solution of occult questions, it would seem to me less difficult to decide what these same Courts do not wish, and what they do not know how to wish. . . .

We admit as certain that the Emperor of Russia wishes to have done with the Greek question. The public is ready to believe that his aim is war. You see by the Reports from the Internuncio, that the diplomatic body at Constantinople may be considered as having adopted that belief. Our opinion is that they are mistaken. We believe that the Emperor Nicholas would not refuse to make war, but we do not believe that he desires it. I will go further. I do not believe in the possibility of the Emperor of Russia making war on the Turks without its leading to consequences diametrically opposed to what he desires to attain. He desires the end of the present troubles, and war would be the beginning of new troubles likely to be even more grave in their consequences.

I have read to Tatistscheff and De Severin the instructions to your Highness and the reservations concerning the comminatory measures. They declared themselves perfectly satisfied.

What will Mr. Canning think of our work? I cannot say.

You will make it your business to place this *résumé* before him, and to explain our thoughts with perfect candour.

We, too, desire the conclusion of an odious complication; it is, indeed, the object of all our wishes. In fact, we regard the continuance of such a position as the one in which we have for many years been placed, as one of the greatest inconveniences we can imagine.

If England wishes what we do, and wishes nothing that we do not, we ought to come to an understanding.

We desire the return of the insurgent populations under the sovereign authority of the Sultan, but we do not desire to lead them back to be massacred.

We see the gain to the Porte, and at the same time to the people, in certain concessions which the sovereign authority might make, and in certain precautions which would secure to the Sultan for the present and for the future the submission of his rebellious subjects ; and to the latter the pledge of present and future tranquillity.

We desire such an agreement between the allies as will attain this double object, for we believe it can only be attained by this means.

We do not desire any encroachment of Russia on the rights of the Sultan, but we desire the re-establishment of the public peace, so urgently demanded in the interests of commerce.

Why should England not desire the same? Does she wish to sacrifice the main question for a vain shadow? Does she wish to maintain the plan of mediation at the expense of the possibility of pacification? Will she, in short, object to everything that can be done and obtained by the agreement of the Powers, because this agreement may recall to Mr. Canning what, on the faith of a few factious journals, he is accustomed to designate by the name of the Holy Alliance? If this is the case, we will not depart from the attitude we assumed at the end of the year 1826.

Place these questions before the English minister, and endeavour to prove to him that, if truth loves simplicity, we ought certainly to find ourselves on the line we have adopted.

For the rest, in your explanations with Mr. Canning and your colleagues preserve the calmest attitude. You will be there as judge. . . .

Accustomed to be understood by you, Prince, we are confident that we shall be so now, on an occasion so eminently important. We consider it so, not because we attach any real hope of success to the attempt to establish an active agreement between the five Courts, but because it is impossible that this singular state of things should not lead to the truth being made known in many peculiar situations. The disorder which has reigned for six years in the Eastern Question will not yield easily to a preconceived idea of the Emperor Nicholas, which, moreover, is not perfectly clear to anyone; but we run no risk in supporting it, and we obtain a knowledge of the different positions, and are able to prove to our allies that the disorder which has seized on so many minds has left ours intact.

THE DECLARATION OF RUSSIA REPUDIATING
ESTERHAZY'S INSTRUCTION.

Metternich to Esterhazy, in London, Vienna,
May 26, 1827.

858. A courier who arrived here from St. Petersburg on May 21, brought to M. de Tatistscheff the first reply to the communication which we made to the Court of Russia of the instructions addressed to your Highness on March 25 (No. 856).

This reply agrees with the Reports which Count de Bombelles transmitted to us of the reception which had been given to the communication of our despatch. Your Highness will find enclosed (No. 859) the textual copy of a declaration made by the Russian ambassador to me. I laid it before the Emperor, and his Imperial Majesty has commanded me to reply to the ambassador in the terms of the enclosed (No. 860).

He considers it necessary that you should be furnished, without loss of time, with orders which your position in London requires in consequence of our directions of March 25, and I acquit myself of this duty.

We replied on December 22, 1826, to the simultaneous communications of England and Russia (No. 838). Since then, the Court of Russia has invited us to transmit to you instructions and full powers, with the object of establishing in London an agreement between the five allied Courts. This task has been fulfilled by my despatch of March 26 (Nos. 855–857). His Imperial Majesty of All the Russias has declared that he would be understood to maintain, without any deviation, the basis and the terms of the protocol of April 4. Your attitude must therefore be also founded on our first directions of December 26, and remain within the limits therein marked out.*

You will, therefore, not take any further steps in consequence of our instructions of March 25, our action being no longer directed towards London.

Declaration of the Russian Ambassador.

859. . . . The undersigned declares—

That the Emperor sees with the most lively regret the Court of Austria bringing forward proposals on the Eastern Question which differ from those of his Imperial Majesty, and not adhering to the project of a treaty and to the measures which he had communicated to that Court;

That his Imperial Majesty cannot adopt the course which the Court of Austria invites him to follow;

That his present situation obliges him to carry out the enterprise which has for its object the pacification of Greece on the basis of the protocol of March 23 (April 4);

But that if there exists some difference between the opinions of the two Cabinets as to the ways which should lead to this end, it appears to the Emperor that there can exist no difference as to the end itself; and his Majesty hopes that, faithful to her declaration, Austria will second

---

* The limitation consisted in this, that the Austrian Cabinet declared itself ready to meet any agreement of the five Powers, provided the language to be addressed in common to the Porte did not overstep the limits of friendly advice.—ED.

Russia in this grave juncture, by not departing from the forms which His Majesty considers most essential.

Metternich's Reply to the Russian Ambassador.

860. The undersigned declares :—

1st. That his Imperial and Royal Apostolic Majesty is much grieved that the views he has brought forward in the instructions to his ambassador at London have not met with the approval of his Imperial Majesty of All the Russias ;

The more the Emperor is convinced of the perfect identity of his wishes concerning the pacification of Greece with those of his august friend and ally, the more he regrets that the Courts cannot agree on a step which, in his opinion, brings the strongest force to bear against the weakest part of the resistance opposed to them by the Porte ;

2nd. That as the reply of the Court of Russia to the last simultaneous communication of England and Russia replaces his Imperial and Royal Apostolic Majesty on the position which he took on December 22, 1826 (No. 838), and as his Imperial Majesty never departs from an engagement he has once made, he will return to the course indicated in the reply of December 22, 1826, of which the official Note which the Internuncio addressed on March 12 last to the Porte has already furnished the most precise application.

METTERNICH'S SUGGESTIONS AS TO THE CONDUCT OF THE PORTE WITH RESPECT TO THE TRIPLE TREATY.

Metternich to Apponyi, in Paris, Vienna, June 11, 1827.

861. I have had the honour to inform you, in the despatch which we have entrusted to the French courier on the 6th of this month, that I would not lose an instant in laying before the Emperor the communication of which the Marquis of Caraman was the bearer.

His Imperial Majesty is deeply sensible of the new proof of confidence which his Most Christian Majesty has given by informing him of the project of the Triple Treaty. The Marquis of Caraman, in making this communication according to orders he had received from his Government, expressed a wish that Austria would be able to join in the transaction.

The French Cabinet grounds this wish on the motive which would doubtless have the greatest value in the eyes of our august master if he could be sure that by his agreement to the act in question the Alliance would once more appear in its true light, and if the Power which has unhappily separated itself from its protective bases would return to its guardianship.

The few words which I had the honour to address to you by the courier of June 6, joined to the numerous explanations on which our Court has entered with her allies since the end of last year, must have convinced

C C

you how very far we are from believing that the
Alliance—a moral power of so pure and so grand a
nature—could be served by a transaction founded on
the bases of the protocol of April 4, 1826. The more
we understand the value which his Most Christian
Majesty and his Cabinet attach to the Alliance, to its
existence and its preservation, the more frankly can
the Emperor express himself to the French Court his
thoughts, his fears, and his hopes. That Court was the
first to whom we communicated the results of our labours
of March 25 (No. 856), and they should have sufficed
to prove the eagerness with which we seized the first
occasion when we could explain the grave considerations which prevented the agreement of Austria to
the bases and to some terms of the Anglo-Russian
protocol, and the changes which would have permitted
his Imperial Majesty to unite himself formally to his
august allies in the pursuit of an affair which, besides
its great general interest, is so intimately connected
with the peculiar interests of his Empire. The last
declaration of the Court of Russia, which I had the
honour to transmit to you by my courier of May 31
(No. 859), has shown you that our hope has unhappily
not been realised.

The objections we made to the stipulations of
April 4, 1826, apply equally to the project of the
treaty; it is sufficient to study the text to be convinced
that these objections have lost none of their weight.
The project contains the same dispositions and phrases
which seem to have been placed there only to increase
the anomalies which struck us in the protocol.

Mediation is extended to three Powers.

The change of the sovereignty of the Sultan into a
simple suzerainty is expressly stated.

The interposition of the maritime forces of the Powers between Egypt and Greece—consequently between two parts of the same empire—is not only maintained as to the forces of the Viceroy of Egypt, but is extended to the direct forces of the Sultan.

To these hindrances to our agreement are joined others of much greater consideration.

We see in no part of the projected treaty any clearly defined aim, but on the contrary we see, and particularly in paragraph V. of the additional and secret article, certain anticipations which, far from producing the pacification which is so desirable, open a vast field for new and indefinite complications.

The reservations so often repeated in this project, particularly in paragraphs III. and IV. of the secret article, relating to the maintenance of peace with the Porte, seem to us so impracticable that, setting aside the nature of the measures themselves, their existence is by no means reassuring.

Lastly, there is one thing which seems to us to stand out with so much clearness and force in the project that we feel obliged to mention it: which is, that the whole of the stipulations point to no other definite result than the political emancipation of the Greeks—a result which will consummate a new revolution in Europe—a triumph the reaction of which on the whole of Europe is far beyond our calculations; which would give birth to a new era of war and disorder in European Turkey, and an enormous extension of the English preponderance in all parts of the Levant, and consequently in Italy and other States washed by the Mediterranean.

Penetrated with this idea, his Imperial Majesty considers that it is impossible for him to accede to the terms of a treaty which, in his eyes, contains the first elements of a future so injurious to the general repose, and which, moreover, seems to him unfeasible. His Majesty will never fail to assist the cause of peace, with all the means in his power—an aim which inspires every action of his Imperial and Apostolic Majesty, and is also shared by his Most Christian Majesty.

These considerations and the frank and confiding manner in which they are laid before a Court which cherishes the same desires with ourselves, should suffice to justify to that Court a moral resistance resting on considerations so serious.

But even if his Imperial Majesty were not prevented by these important considerations, he would still be inclined to ask himself whether in the painful and dangerous position of the affair he is not stronger, and therefore more useful to the cause of peace, by maintaining himself firmly on his principles than by sacrificing them with the desire of saving by his agreement the appearances of an Alliance which one of its principal members constantly disowns. There is indeed no doubt that, faithful to a course which has acquired all the consistence of a political system, he would not fail to disown this Alliance either formally or by his silence if ever he were supposed to co-operate in its work. Indeed, we do not believe that the British Ministry, as it is composed at present, will ever allow itself to be accused of the least tolerance for a union it holds in horror ; and the terms in which, even before the last change, the Cabinet of London expressed itself on the Eastern Question leave us in no doubt that, since the concurrence of the five Powers would recall this union, it would assert the independence of its principles, and separate its cause from that of the allies.

I beg you to lay the present despatch before the French Cabinet. In it will be found the feelings of the Emperor our august master frankly expressed, as well as thanks for the recent loyal and kindly action of his Most Christian Majesty towards his august friend and ally.*

Metternich to the Emperor Francis, Vienna, July 7, 1827.

862. To-day's Berlin post has brought me Reports which I respectfully enclose. The desire expressed at St. Petersburg seems to be this—to go on fearlessly. Russia is in a position to do this herself, but to wish to drag England into this Northern complication is an undertaking which, once for all, cannot succeed. This matter needs no profound calculation, no great knowledge of affairs, but only sound common sense, to which even the autocratic will must finally yield. We, on our side, need nothing more than to go forward in the path we have so prudently chosen. Your Majesty may here see a very singular spectacle which may lead to great evils, but will never answer the purpose of the very badly advised Russian Emperor.

* The Triple Treaty in question was signed in London, July 6, 1827, between England, France, and Russia.—ED.

THE FRENCH MEASURES CONCERNING
THE PRESS.

Metternich to Apponyi, in Paris, Vienna, July 2, 1827.

863. I desire, more than I hope, that the measures which the French Government propose to take with regard to the press will answer the purpose. All legislation concerning the press, having in view the repression of its excesses, will fail in its object; and if a preventive censorship, in the true sense of the word, can alone attain it, the durability of the measure is an essential condition of its success. A temporary censorship is nonsense.

I am not in a position to form an opinion as to the chances of a majority for the Government in the newly-elected Chamber; but it is clear to me, on the other hand, that the preservation of the Chamber of Deputies in its present form will lead to the fall of the monarchy. It is, unhappily, but too true that experience never teaches those who do not know by instinct how to find the paths of safety. It was faults committed by the supreme authority which caused the downfall of the throne in France. The anarchy which was the inevitable consequence of this downfall, ended in military despotism—in that heroic remedy which, after having re-established public order, is always liable to exhaust itself by its excesses or to sink under its own weight. The Restoration—due to Napoleon's spirit of conquest—instead of deriving its strength from historical ele-

ments and the institutions of the Empire favourable
to authority, entangled itself with a stupid *doctrinairism.*
In this short sketch I truly describe the present situation.   I have been called to play a part in the great
changes of our miserable times ;   the Liberal Princes
did not understand me, and their Radical counsellors
detested me.   The first were wrong ; the others were
right.

Napoleon, who could not have been wanting in the
feeling of power, said to me : ' You see me master of
France ; well, I would not undertake to govern her for
three months with liberty of the press.'   Louis XVIII.,
apparently thinking himself stronger than Napoleon, is
not contented with allowing the press its freedom, but
has embodied its liberty in the Charta.

CANNING'S DEATH.

Metternich to Esterhazy, Königswart, August 19, 1827.

864. I am sending a courier to Paris, and I wish him to go on to London, although it is impossible for me to give him anything of the nature of instructions for your Highness in the extremely critical position in which England is placed in consequence of the decease of Mr. Canning. I will not even enter on a consideration of the consequences of this unexpected event; I shall trust to you for information on the probable consequences which such a change will entail on England and consequently on politics generally.

I do not think it necessary to repeat to you the opinion we have from the first entertained of the merits of the man whom Providence hurled upon England and Europe like a malevolent meteor. As for me, you have heard me long ago pronounce the judgment which his contemporaries have already formed of him. The task which the impartial historian will have to fulfil concerning the public life of this man will be easy. He has shaken everything and destroyed a great deal, but he has built up nothing—a sad but common thing with men of his stamp. England is delivered from a great scourge. Will the world seek for compensation for the evil which has been done to it by him to an extent which cannot be estimated? This important question can only be answered in ways and by means so far beyond our powers that all we can do is to wait and hope.

We have great confidence in the Duke of Wellington. His social position and character give him a position and impose duties upon him peculiar to himself. Our sincerest good wishes will attend his steps; and if the Duke seeks for some place as *point d'appui*, where the support of the good cause is free from individual views, prejudices, and errors, he will go, I flatter myself, to seek it at Vienna.

I beg you, Prince, to express yourself in this sense to his Grace, and receive yourself, &c.

Metternich to Esterhazy, Königswart, August 19, 1827.

865. It would be difficult for me, without falling into numerous repetitions, to enter into details with respect to the great event which, with astonishing celerity, has come to my knowledge.

Mr. Canning's career has been that of a meteor; he rose rapidly to be extinguished in an instant, and your last Reports contain proofs that, as always happens with meteors of this nature, profound darkness succeeds his disappearance. His public life belongs henceforth to history; the immediate and indirect consequences of his actions are what we have to do with, and the field is so vast that it can only be explored in a corresponding manner. Neither shall I stop to tell you my suppositions on the composition of the new Ministry. In consequence of the inheritance of disorder which Mr. Canning has left to his colleagues and to his country, calculations at this distance are impossible. I do not hesitate to say, however, that the next Administration will have great difficulty in assuming a definite form. Order succeeds disorder only by degrees, and I do not

know a man in England strong enough to rule the
numerous parties who are continually struggling openly
against each other. What seems to me certain is, that
the Parliamentary set of whom the deceased was a
member, will not be the party to form the new Administration.

METTERNICH'S INTERVIEW WITH
KING FREDERICK WILLIAM III. AT TEPLITZ.

Metternich to the Emperor Francis, Teplitz,
August 28, 1827.

866. I arrived here on the 21st, and yesterday and to-day I prepared matters for my discussions with the King. I cannot give your Majesty a better account of the results of our interview than by assuring you that the King's opinions on the really important questions of the day do not differ from those of your Majesty. He desires what your Majesty desires, and his knowledge is great and extensive. He is particularly well informed on the circumstances of the Russian Emperor; he has no prejudices on this point, and I could tell him nothing he did not already know. He is very anxious that the disagreement between ourselves and Russia should be forgotten; and he goes so far in this wish that I was obliged to ask him not to trouble himself so much about an affair in which the course of events is beyond all anticipation. When right and truth are plain, time and experience are the best allies. But it is not the less pleasant to see a Prince who forms his judgment impartially before God and the world, in such a state of mind, and the influence which the Prussian Court naturally exercises on the Russian cannot be without advantages for us.

I drew the King's attention to the impression Canning's death must produce in Russia, and I made it clear to him that, where one Power is ready to act for the good cause, its influence can only be weakened by the appearance of a second Power. The King's opinion on Canning's merits or demerits agrees entirely with that of your Majesty. He looks upon his fate as upon one of those revelations of Providence which are quite unaccountable. The affair of Hesse Cassel I have brought to a happy conclusion. Prussia is quite willing to arrange matters amicably.*

The message which the King gave me bears the impress of his heart and of the deep feeling he entertains for your Majesty. The King is, as your Majesty knows, extremely laconic, and his words, therefore, have the greater weight. The King said that the importance of his present position in the world had been clearly felt by him only from the moment that he had become convinced that his views and opinions are in perfect agreement with those of your Majesty. Never before, certainly, has the King used such expressions to a foreign Power. . . .

To-morrow I shall go to Dresden, stay there two days, and then return to Königswart. I think I shall arrive there about the 28th.

METTERNICH.

I received your news with pleasure, and I hope you will express my gratitude to the King of Prussia in an appropriate manner. I wish you good health and fair weather; here it is cold and wet.

FRANCIS.

Persenberg, August 28, 1827.

---

* This refers to a disagreement between the Courts of Berlin and Hesse Cassel on some domestic matters.—ED.

METTERNICH'S CONVERSATION WITH COUNT DE LA FERRONAYS ON ORIENTAL POLITICS.

Metternich to the Emperor Francis, Teplitz, August 23, 1827.

867. I perfectly agreed with Count de la Ferronays*
as to the language he is to use in Paris and St. Petersburg. He goes for some days to Paris, returning very
soon to St. Petersburg. His opinions on the monarch's
moral point of view, and upon his whole Court, are
ours. It is a great pity that the Count, who in both
places is highly esteemed, had not always held his
present opinions. He is a convert, and therefore
has much to reproach himself with. To give an
example, he told me that it is only now that he has
recognised the superiority of the definitions which we
proposed from the first, above all the other means of
treating the Oriental question. His opinion is that the
present difficulty between St. Petersburg and Vienna
has been created by the Russian Cabinet as a kind of
game to endeavour to force us to submit—a game which
will soon come to an end if we remain firm. Having
the same impression myself, I persuaded the Count, as
the first result of our interview, to defend firmly and
vigorously to the Emperor and Count Nesselrode, the
opinion that we shall never cede one point of our right.
The Count de la Ferronays is convinced that Canning's

* French Ambassador at St. Petersburg, for the time staying at Teplitz.—ED.

death has produced an impression in St. Petersburg the consequences of which are incalculable, because the Emperor (who always understood Canning better than Nesselrode did), after having founded the whole of his Oriental structure on the English minister's existence, sees it suddenly without any firm basis. The Count de la Ferronays is convinced that the Emperor will only make war in case of extreme necessity.

Metternich to the Emperor Francis, Königswart, September 2, 1827.

868. Yesterday Count de la Ferronays left Teplitz for Paris, passing through Königswart. We arrived at such a good understanding that his sojourn in France must be advantageous. The Count is one of those men who (although of clear intellect) out of mere ignorance easily take the wrong course, which they honestly abandon on more serious consideration. He now knows Russia's ground as it really is, and he ascribes all the unpleasant complications in the Eastern affair to a kind of game in which the young Emperor has been, against his will, entangled. He also attributes some of the evils to the French Court, which took far more notice of Count Pozzo's opinion than of the despatches and accounts of its own ambassador in St. Petersburg. The Emperor Nicholas has now committed himself so far that he greatly fears that he will be forced into war against his will. This agrees with my account of the Emperor's former and present position. In this unpleasant situation, Count de la Ferronays expressed his wish to be charged with a message from me to the Cabinet. I seized on the idea, and carried it out as follows. ' My advice,' said I, ' is that of common sense. Three Powers have joined together for very

vague purposes with very confused words ; one of the
three Powers has just been paralysed, and I doubt if
the feeble English Government will be able to move as
boldly on its dangerous path as Canning would have
done. Here, therefore, nothing need be done hastily.
The absurd Triple Alliance is only in its first stage : try
to prevent the French Government from helping on its
further progress ; take in your sails and make sure of
your position in a sea so full of rocks.

'What I desire to know is how the following questions are to be answered :—Supposing that the Porte
rejects all the proposals of the three Powers ; supposing
that the coercive measures of the Powers prove to be
ridiculously insufficient ; supposing, too, that the Russian
Emperor finds himself so committed that he cannot avoid
war : what would be the attitude and the line of conduct
adopted by the French Court?'

Count de la Ferronays could not, of course, give
me an answer ; but he is of opinion that France, in such
an extreme case, would turn to Austria, begging her to
place her weight and power in the scale of peace.

I answered that this was a quite natural idea, and
that I could reply with the greatest candour, 'Tell your
Cabinet that France will find us prepared to do our
best for the maintenance of peace on the following principles :—

'1. That the Powers acknowledge the re-establishment of peace in Greece to be the basis of the treaty in
place of the former basis.

'2. That the Sultan himself must carry out the pacification.

'3. That the Powers show themselves as friends of
the Porte and enemies of the revolution.

'4. That there is to be no question of the abdication

of the Sultan, or of a Greek Government, a Greek flag, Greek fortresses, &c.'

' Under these conditions, and these only, can our assistance be given.'

Count de la Ferronays shares these views, and will endeavour to support them. Events alone can show what the result will be, and in looking forward allowance must be made for the frivolity of the French Ministers.

METTERNICH.

Received and noticed. God grant that your interview with Count de la Ferronays may have the desired effect upon his Court.

FRANCIS.

Weinzierl, September 6, 1827.

METTERNICH'S PROPOSALS TO THE PORTE WITH RESPECT TO THE TRIPLE TREATY.

Metternich to Ottenfels, in Constantinople, Vienna, October 3, 1827.

869. I find myself in a position to entrust you with an important and delicate mission, the value of which you will understand when you have read the present despatch.

In order to arrive at a possible solution of the immense problem before us, it is necessary that we should plainly state the real position of things. To this end I must divide the subjects as follows :—

I. The situation of the Eastern Question at the present moment, and the respective position of the three Powers in coalition with regard to the Porte, and of the latter with regard to the Powers ; the relative position of the three Courts in the Triple Treaty ; lastly, the position of our Court in the whole affair ;

II. Probabilities relative to future contingencies ;

III. Opportunities of arrangement which the different situations of the Courts and the probabilities in the march of events may give us.

Ad I. The examination of the situation of the three Courts with regard to the Porte, and of the latter with regard to the Powers, not being here a question of rights, must be made a question of facts.

The affair at present in contestation has arrived at one of those decisive periods when neither one party

nor the other can draw back without compromising a
strict point of honour.   This affair in its present phase
is no longer the Greek question ; the Turks have scarcely
pronounced this name in their recent discussions ; it is
a question of mediation peremptorily demanded by three
foreign Powers, and peremptorily rejected by the Porte.
The difference between the two questions is great ; it is
precisely that difference which has determined us to
separate our course from that of the Courts that signed
the Treaty of London.   The debates of the day turn
much less on the pacification of Greece than on the
means adopted by the Courts to force the Ottoman
Government to bring it about.

The reality is thus effaced by the form ; and experience of all times teaches us that, in politics as between individuals, quarrels of this nature are the most
difficult to arrange.

To judge of the situation of the three contracting
Courts between themselves, it is sufficient to know
their respective interests.   If these interests coincide on
one principal point, the maintenance of political peace,
they clash on a number of secondary questions, and
on more than one they are entirely opposed.   This
divergence of interests has necessarily enfeebled their
action.   The ministers of the Porte have not failed to
discover this ; they see in the union of the three Courts
merely a fictitious and fragile bond, and flatter themselves with the prospect of profiting by a division
which they consider inevitable between political bodies
so little homogeneous.

Lastly, as to the position of Austria in the whole affair,
I need not explain it to you—you know as well as I do
how we have invariably regarded this question.   That
the pacification should take place ; that it should be

brought about by the wisdom and consolidated by the moderation and clemency of the Sultan—such were, such are still our wishes, and any means we have thought would contribute to realise them have always been seized upon with eagerness by us. Our isolation in the affair arises solely from the invincible repugnance of our august master to violate what he regards as a principle of incontestable right, and from his conviction that any enterprise which departs from this rule cannot prosper. Certainly the beginning of this enterprise, so much and so long debated, is not likely to alter the opinion of his Imperial Majesty.

In short, the three Powers and the Porte are placed in a position which exercises the most disastrous effect on the liberty of their movements, and which renders it as difficult, if not impossible, to advance as to retreat. That of Austria, on the other hand, is perfectly free, and our mobility is complete.

Ad II. The examination of the probability of future contingencies is founded more or less on the questions I have just treated.

We should be quite contented, for our part, if the Porte decided to abate its resistance, and if, instead of meeting the allies with an absolute refusal, it would prove to them that it is the method and not the ground of their proposals to which it objects ; if it declares, in a word, that it wishes for pacification, and that, provided they do not pretend to extort it by orders and threats, it will find means of coming to an understanding with them. But may we yet reckon on this chance? Unhappily, everything makes us think that we must renounce it.

Ad III. The really most important object of all is that of seeking means by which we can hope to bring the affair to a more happy *dénouement* than it promises at present.

I frankly confess that we should not have had courage to enter into such an examination but for the invitation which has recently been addressed to us by the British Cabinet. For of what avail would have been the best wishes on our part if there had been no basis on which we could found a hope? We have had six years' experience of the Eastern Question, and the sad results of this experience were not likely to induce us to renew the fruitless efforts we made during that long time with all the frankness, impartiality, and solicitude of which the Emperor has given so many proofs to his allies and the world in general throughout the numerous crises of the last five-and-thirty years. But an appeal having been made to us, we should have failed in our duty if we had not replied to it. . . .

The real difficulty of the moment is found, in our opinion, in two apparently irreconcilable facts, of which the reality must also be recognised if we are not to fall into grave mistakes. One, that there is a revolutionary movement, threatening directly or indirectly the tranquillity and the existence of a great part of the Ottoman Empire, and which must be stopped at any price; the other that the Porte has no longer the moral power (supposing even it has the material power) to combat the movement by its single efforts. I know what the ministers of the Sultan will reply to this observation. They will say what they have so often said: 'Let them leave us alone, and we will soon settle our own affairs.' I admit—and how can any one dispute it?—that if the first Courts of Europe had not been for so many years occupied with an event which no doubt the Porte would have been very glad if they had left alone, and if the agitation produced by this event on the public mind of all countries had not made them feel obliged to occupy themselves with it, the insurrection of the Ottoman provinces would sooner or later have come to nothing. But can we efface the past? By yielding to useless regrets, can we change the results? The Triple Treaty exists; the ultimatum of the three Courts has gone forth,* and the Porte cries out in vain against these transactions — it must submit to the consequences, unless it can find means of disarming them.

It is first of all necessary to put a stop to the evils which must inevitably arise from the conflict between the demands of the intervening Courts and the peremptory refusals of the Porte. We are not called upon at present to give our advice on the means or terms of the pacification of the Greeks. It is a question apart, the importance of which we do not forget. But what claims our attention in the first place is the political struggle between the Powers who propose and the Government that rejects a forced mediation, which the former regard as necessary to bring about the pacification, and the latter believes absolutely derogatory to its rights. To this question all the embarrassments and dangers which we wish to remove are attached. The separation of the subjects in litigation appears to us once for all the first condition of success. We thus return to a distinction analogous to that on which we previously insisted so strongly when, unhappily without being attended to, we never ceased to protest

* An ultimatum was sent to the Porte on August 16, 1827, by the Ambassadors of England, France, and Russia, to which no answer was given.—Ed.

against the system of confounding the affair of the insurrection with that of the Russo-Turkish differences.

That we may be able to find a way of salvation, the Porte must be made to comprehend that it cannot escape from these dilemmas by mere refusals and a passive attitude; that, even when it has decided not to shrink from any danger, the three Courts will none the less be placed under the necessity of a positive decision; that the honour of the party who, in such a violent crisis, runs the most risk, is not compromised if it is the first to attempt to bring about a solution of the complication; that, in short, statements addressed to a Power which is both its friend and that of the Courts which the Porte must necessarily at present regard as enemies can never humiliate those who have the good sense to make them. You see what I wish to arrive at. The Porte should address us confidentially; it should express to us its desire to put an end to the embarrassments which even its vanity must regard as more or less shared with the three Courts; it should choose, for its first step, the form of asking our advice, or any other form it may consider convenient; in a word, it should address us with the object of enabling us to address our allies. This step can have no inconveniences; it is applicable to the state of things such as it was at the time of your last Reports, as well as to that when the conflicting parties are already engaged in material action. The effect of an attempt to which the Emperor might agree in consequence of an initiative taken by the Sultan towards his Imperial Majesty is without doubt placed beyond the sphere of our foresight. But if this consideration does not stop the Emperor, why should it stop the Sultan, who would lose nothing, even if it did not succeed?

I authorise you then to make, under the seal of
secresy, the following overtures to the Reis-Effendi.
You will say to him from me :

'That we see with great vexation the embarrassing
and eminently dangerous situation in which our friend
the Porte is placed ;

'That the very fact of this situation must convince
the Porte that, not being deceived as to the march of
events, we have constantly acted towards it with that
loyal frankness which characterises the well-known
policy of the Emperor our august master, and belongs
to an enlightened friendship which does not allow him
to conceal from his friends the evils with which he believes they are threatened ;

'That, in our opinion, the Porte is not only running the deplorable risk of an open rupture with the
three Powers, but it is also exposed to the danger of a
direct war with Russia; a war which under present
circumstances that Power would undertake without any
views of conquest (of which we are far from suspecting
the Emperor Nicholas) but solely with a view to overcoming the opposition his proposals have met with at
Constantinople ;

'That, according to our firm conviction, the safety
of the Ottoman Empire requires its Government to do
everything in its power to put an end to a crisis which
can only lead to the most disastrous extremities ;

'That to this end we consider we are giving the
Porte a new proof of our interest in its preservation
and prosperity, by suggesting that it should express to
us confidentially the regrets it feels for the state of
tension (or of open war) produced by a fatal discussion
with the Powers friendly to Austria, and claiming our
good offices to assist it out of this complication and

replace it in a position corresponding with its desire of maintaining political peace and re-establishing tranquillity in its own States.'

If the Porte should agree to this step, you can assure it in return that we shall regard it as a sacred duty to devote all our efforts to the attainment of so desirable an object, and that we shall neglect no opportunity of making known to our allies its conciliatory disposition.

However, as it is easy to foresee that the steps which our Court may take in consequence of such an overture would be received by the allied Powers with much more confidence and favour if they were accompanied by some tangible evidence of the moderate and pacific intentions of the Ottoman Government, we do not wish to conceal from the Porte that our means of action would be greatly strengthened by its consent to a temporary suspension of hostilities. We are quite convinced that this measure, which would much facilitate the employment of our good offices, and essentially contribute to render them efficacious, would impose no real sacrifice on the Porte, while this suspension of hostilities, carried out in a way compatible with the dignity of the Sultan, would neither prejudice his rights nor his interests. If nevertheless, seeing the extreme repugnance with which the proposal of an armistice seems to have inspired the Porte, it should be impossible for you to induce him to take this last step, you must not regard his refusal as a reason for discontinuing your efforts, and you must persist in doing everything that is possible to give weight to your representations.

In any case you will take care to make the Reis-Effendi comprehend that the overtures you make to him are dictated solely by our solicitude, the knowledge we have recently acquired of the position at Constantinople, and the serious apprehensions we entertain on the matter. You must not allow the slightest suspicion that we have founded hopes of a better future on secret communications from another Cabinet. The knowledge of this fact would not fail to influence the resolutions of the Divan in a sense contrary to our benevolent intentions, and to confirm its expectation of an approaching disunion between the three Courts—an expectation which has already not a little contributed to its determinations.

You must yourself feel how important it is to lose no time in an affair which may any day be irreparably embroiled. Knowing your zeal and devotion to the service, I need not beg you to use all the promptitude of which the forms of Ottoman diplomacy admit. As soon as you can announce the result you must send me a courier extraordinary.*

Metternich to Ottenfels, in Constantinople, October 17, 1827.

870. In the peculiar and dangerous position of affairs between the friendly Powers and the Porte in consequence of the Triple Treaty, I am not able to-day to send you a regular despatch. Events move on, and

---

* In consequence of this despatch, which arrived at Constantinople on October 20, all the members of the Divan met at the house of the Grand Vizier, when the sketch of a letter addressed to Prince Metternich, requesting the interposition of Austria, was drawn up. The Sultan himself wrote on it these words: 'The Emperor of Austria is our old friend, and is worthy of all our confidence, for he has given us constant proofs of his good feeling. I have also long been aware of the remarkable qualities of Prince Metternich. With the confidential communications and assurances of the Internuncio before me, I consider the Grand Vizier's letter thoroughly good.' The letter here alluded to (No. 875) was sent to Prince Metternich, but it was too late, for an unexpected event had entirely changed the political situation, and frustrated the hopes attached by the Porte to this step. Five days before the letter was despatched, unknown to those at Constantinople, the battle of Navarino had been fought.—ED.

we are, no doubt, the only Cabinet which is not experiencing one surprise after another.   At St. Petersburg, Paris and London, it was not doubted that the Porte would yield to a strong collective step of the three Powers ; Count Nesselrode made bets on this illusion, up to the very day when the last negative reply from the Divan arrived.   Placed in closer correspondence with us, the French ministers, disappointed in the hope they had so long cherished, and convinced by facts of their error, assured us that the interposition of the squadrons—if only as a matter of time—would surely prevent the disembarkation of the Turco-Egyptian fleet in the Morea.   Both calculations are shown to have been mistaken, and there has happened also what always quickly happens after moral defeats.   The Cabinets are all in a great state of irritation, and the Tuileries in a perfect fury, and inclined to attribute to us the ill-success of a cleverly-conceived plan.   They refer to your refusal to join your colleagues at the time of the last triple arrangement, and the five Austrian merchant ships which were employed as transports in the Egyptian fleet complete our misdeeds.   I informed you of my opinion on the negative attitude you have recently assumed.   I am convinced that you were bound to follow the particular line of conduct I pointed out—the thing is past, and is no longer a question of the moment.   Recriminations run high.   At Berlin, they dread the moral effect ; at London, they are full of regrets ; at St. Petersburg, they have said so little that we are in need of explanations : while at Paris they are venting their rage against us, and our perfidy has become a sort of proverb.

Through it all you see I am very tranquil on our account.   I do not fear words, and those dictated by a consciousness of wrong are always poor words. What I do fear are the extremes in the positions of the opposite parties; the vanity of two sensitive Powers such as Russia and France, and the embarrassments in which the new British Government will find itself; I fear on the other hand the extreme rashness of the Turks in an affair where their feelings are wounded, and where the weakness of their opponents' attitude may contribute to blind the Divan to the reality and undoubted imminence of the greatest dangers. We pointed out in our last despatch the way in which alone the situation of affairs can be altered.

Has the Porte comprehended us? Has it seized our meaning and does it understand the risks to which it will certainly be exposed if it shows itself incapable of comprehending us? Experience alone will prove, and reasoning is useless, for all I can say I have said, and what the Divan can comprehend it will have comprehended already, or it will be too late, both for itself and for the success of our good intentions.

If the Porte is disposed to accept our suggestion, you will have only to maintain it in its good disposition. If it has only admitted the first part of our proposal, you must insist on an armistice also: if it has refused, you must warn it that we foresee war, with all its possible consequences.

Do not fail to let us know the results of our overtures of the 3rd inst.

CODRINGTON'S LETTER.

Metternich to Werner, in Berlin, Vienna, October 29,
1827.

871. . . . The false rumour that Austrian men-of-war had formed part of the last Turco-Egyptian expedition induced Admiral Codrington to take a step towards the unknown head of this supposed expedition so contrary to the common rules of war and sound policy that the Emperor would think it derogatory to his dignity to let the question drop. His Imperial Majesty has therefore commanded me to write to London on the matter, and you will find enclosed (No. 872) the despatch which I have addressed on this subject to Prince Esterhazy.

Metternich to Esterhazy, in London, Vienna, October 29,
1827.

872. We have received from Constantinople the enclosed despatch (No. 873) sent, without being addressed to him, to Rear-Admiral Dandolo, chief of our squadron in the Archipelago. It contains the complaints of Vice-Admiral Sir E. Codrington with regard to the pretended services rendered by our vessels to the Turco-Egyptian fleet surrounded by the English and French Admirals in the port of Navarino, and warnings, in very strong language, of the dangers to which our ships would be exposed if they interfered with the operations of the squadrons of the three Powers, who, by the treaty of London had united to aid the Greeks.

Rear-Admiral Dandolo has himself replied to the declaration of Sir E. Codrington, and the British Government will soon be informed of his reply. The affair is, however, of a nature to claim the attention of the Courts which it concerns; and, persuaded as we are that the British ministry sincerely desires to maintain the most amicable relations with us, we do not hesitate to give our opinion on the English Vice-Admiral's letter with all the frankness inspired by the rectitude of our own cause and our knowledge of the just and benevolent feelings of England.

With this object we communicate to your Highness the following observations, suggested by the perusal of the above-mentioned document:—

1. The instructions given to the commandant of our squadron in the Levant expressly forbid any Austrian vessel—either of war or commerce—to enter a port regularly and effectively blockaded by either of the parties engaged in the actual struggle; but,

2. The blockade of the port of Navarino has not been regularly announced, and it was not likely to be suspected, inasmuch as not one of the Powers which could proceed thither had declared the fact of a state of war between itself and the Ottoman Empire;

3. Notwithstanding the absence of the indispensable formality of this declaration, it is certain that no Imperial vessel of war has entered or attempted to enter that port since the English fleet appeared before Navarino on September 19, the date of Vice-Admiral Codrington's letter; that the Austrian schooner 'La Vigilante' was at Navarino previous to the arrival of the Egyptian fleet, for the purpose of demanding the

restitution of the property of an Austrian vessel which was wrecked on the coast and pillaged and the crew inhumanely treated by a band of thieves; that this schooner had left the above-mentioned port before September 12, the day of the arrival of the British squadron at Navarino; and that, moreover, no Imperial vessel of war 'has made part of the Egyptian fleet' either before or after its arrival;

4. Therefore, the complaint of Vice-Admiral Codrington has no real foundation, while the form of his declaration is contrary to the usages observed between friendly and allied Powers; for this document—even admitting that the English Vice-Admiral believed himself authorised to take such a step—instead of being addressed to an officer anonymously, should have been addressed to the head of the Imperial squadron, who was alone in a position to judge what reply to make to the demands of the English Vice-Admiral;

5. Without entering here into delicate and intricate discussions, it appears to us incontestable that the question of knowing whether the squadrons of the Powers allied by the Treaty of London have the right to exclude from all communication with the places and coasts of Greece the ships of every other European Power, making 'no distinction between their ships and those of the Turks,' and to prevent them with threats 'from acting in opposition to the signatory Powers of the treaty,' cannot be decided between naval officers. This question should have been discussed and arranged by the Courts: in short, in order to regulate the relations between the different squadrons, in so new and undefined a position as that which has arisen from the recent proceedings of the three Powers, a previous arrangement should have been made, agreed to, and

recognised by all the Powers whose vessels frequent the seas of Turkey and Greece.

I wish you to repeat these observations to Lord Dudley, begging that minister to give them the attention they seem to me to deserve, and to arrange things between yourselves in such a way as to prevent disagreements and misunderstandings, unjust accusations and embarrassing claims, between the naval officers of the two States. The Secretary of State is too wise not to see the justice and importance of our desire, and to appreciate its motives.

The grievances proclaimed by Vice-Admiral Codrington, to which we have replied, seem to bear principally on the material assistance which our vessels may have furnished to the Ottoman fleet. But, judging from some of his expressions, he complains of the mere presence of some Imperial vessels of war in the neighbourhood of Navarino. Now, although we have every reason to believe that on September 19 no vessel of war was to be found in the port of Navarino, it is nevertheless possible and even probable that one of these vessels may have arrived afterwards, not in the port, but in the neighbourhood of that place. But under what pretext could a neutral vessel be prevented from being—either as a spectator or in consequence of orders it may have received from its chiefs—near a place where events are taking place with which it has nothing to do? The officers of the Imperial vessels could certainly not be accused of having fanned the flame of discord at any period of this deplorable struggle; wherever they have appeared they have spoken words of conciliation and peace. . . .

As for the new circumstances to which the proceedings of the three intervening Courts may have given rise, we invariably keep to the line prescribed by loyalty and friendship. It is not for us to judge of the measures these Courts have determined upon, and we scrupulously abstain from obstructing the operations which may ensue from them, as we sincerely desire that they may lead to the pacification of the Levant. But at the same time we flatter ourselves that the Government of his Britannic Majesty would desire us to be rightly informed of its ulterior views in the present state of things so that we may give clear and positive orders to those charged with our interests in those countries and seas which, some day or other, may become the theatre of the most important events.

Vice-Admiral Codrington's Letter of the 19*th September,* 1827.

873. Vice-Admiral Sir Edward Codrington, Commander-in-Chief of the British naval forces in the Mediterranean and the Archipelago, learning that some vessels belonging to the Emperor of Austria form part of the Turkish fleet, and are actually in the Port of Navarino for the purpose of carrying on hostilities against the Greeks, has the honour to inform the officer commanding the above-mentioned vessels that, by a treaty signed between Great Britain, France, and Russia, he is charged to prevent the arrival of assistance in the way of men, arms, vessels and naval munitions to Greece and the islands of the Archipelago, and that, consequently, it will not be in his power to make any distinction between Austrian and Turkish vessels. Respect for the Imperial flag and for the nation with which England is in alliance induces the Vice-Admiral to choose this means of preventing a collision which it will be very easy to avoid; and if the Austrian commander does not show the same desire to preserve the vessels of his Imperial Majesty from the inconveniences they will experience by continuing to act in opposition to the allied Powers, that officer will be responsible for the consequences.

His Britannic Majesty's ship 'Asia,'
    September 19, 1827.

NAVARINO.

Metternich to Apponyi, Vienna, November 13, 1827.

874. A few days after the departure of the last courier from Paris news arrived there of the terrible catastrophe of Navarino.

It did not surprise us in the least. We always said that the Triple Alliance could have but two possible results—either complete inaction or war.

The event of October 20 begins a new era for Europe. What are the consequences to be expected? We are quite unable to determine, much less to foresee them. One thing is certain — namely, that the total destruction of the Ottoman navy must be most fruitful in consequences. In this respect everything is changed.

The Ottoman empire has ceased, for the moment, to belong to itself. Constantinople is defenceless against a combined invasion of land forces, supported by reinforcements echelonned along the Black Sea, and provisioned by a fleet. The chain of the Balkan is no longer an insurmountable obstacle, and an army crossing the Pruth could now calculate its success, and fix the moment when Constantinople should be blockaded by land and sea. . . .

What effect will be produced in the capital of the Ottoman empire and in the provinces by the event of Navarino? What we know of these countries enables us to foresee many sad possibilities and not one happy one.

We may infer that the Sultan will decide, in consequence of the sanguinary affront he has just received, to resist everything.

We may also suppose that in an extremity so disastrous the will of the Sultan may yield to the impetuosity of an entire population driven to exasperation. The Ottoman fleet is, so to speak, the patrimony of the capital; immense efforts have been made quite recently for its equipment, and now not a single remnant of so many sacrifices will reappear in the port of Constantinople. Thousands of Turkish sailors have fallen victims of an event, which the immense population of Constantinople will have some difficulty in understanding, seeing that the representatives of the Courts to whom the victorious squadrons belong stay on quietly. How far will the fury of the population extend, and to what sacrifices of reason and prudence will the Porte find itself reduced, so as not to succumb under the reproach of having been either the accomplice or the dupe of circumstances?

Lastly, we consider it possible that the popular movement may result in a state of complete anarchy; that the reigning family may become the immediate victims; that the reforms which the Sultan has lately undertaken may be turned against him as attempts contrary to law; and that the destruction of the fleet may be regarded by a superstitious people as a punishment from Heaven. Constantinople will, indeed, then be like a hell in which the wildest passions are at war.

If Providence should turn the feeling of public misfortune among the Turks into apathy we might have some hope; but with the Turks this does not seem at all probable.

The considerations I have just laid before you

have lately formed the subject of the gravest and most
sombre meditations of the Emperor.   You know the
activity of his mind, the rectitude of his thoughts,
and the warmth of his feelings.   The event of Navarino, its causes, and its more than probable consequences, all place his Imperial Majesty in the most
painful moral situation.   I confess to you that, in the
long course of more than eighteen years in which I
have occupied a position bringing me daily in contact
with his person, I have never seen our august master
more painfully affected or uneasy.

At the very time when such grave cares were
occupying his Majesty, the post from Constantinople
of the 25th of this month arrived.   It brought me the
letter from the Grand Vizier, a copy of which is enclosed (No. 875).   I made it my duty to lay it before
the Emperor without delay.   .

His first impulse was to dictate a reply in which I
was to inform the Porte that, as all the thoughts and
anticipations of his Imperial Majesty had been mistaken, he knew not how to venture on new ground,
having no basis whatever for his calculations.   Feeling,
however, that this would show a want of confidence,
he afterwards decided to order me to communicate the
Turkish official note to the representatives of the three
Courts.   I have myself carried out this order to-
day.* . . .

---

* In this letter to the representatives of the three allied Courts, of November 12, Prince Metternich says: ' In laying this despatch before you, I
must inform you, by the express order of his Imperial Majesty, that in
charging his Cabinet with this communication, the Emperor fulfils a duty
which neither his relations towards the Porte, nor those towards the allied
Powers, allow him to avoid; nevertheless his Imperial Majesty limits himself to this step, wishing it to be understood that he does not, and never will,
act as mediator in the differences which are raised between the three Powers
and the Ottoman Porte.'—ED.

I have no orders to give you concerning this step. The Emperor regards it as a relief to his conscience, without attaching to it any practical value. However, I feel the necessity of urging you to assure Baron de Damas that, although the Emperor felt bound to undertake to make the words known, he strongly protests against acting in any way as a mediator in a situation which defies calculations. The Emperor desires that you will not allow the least doubt to spring up in the minds of the Cabinet of his Most Christian Majesty; the representatives of his Majesty at London and St. Petersburg have received the same command. If the three Courts desire to make us the medium of a reply to the Porte, his Imperial Majesty will forward it to Constantinople, whatever may be its tenor. If they desire no reply to be made, the Porte must also be informed of that fact.

. . . I beg you to communicate the present despatch to Baron de Damas. It accurately describes the Emperor's feelings concerning an event new in the records of history, and in a position of affairs which, since it baffles all calculation, should prevent statesmen from undertaking the useless and thankless task of attempting it.

Mehemet Selim Pacha, Grand Vizier, to Prince Metternich, Constantinople, October 24, 1827.

875. It cannot have escaped the wisdom and experience of your Highness that, agreeably to the decrees of Divine Providence, the maintenance of order and peace in the world can have no solid foundation save in the recognition of the rights of sovereigns over their subjects, without which, indeed, the social state cannot subsist. This is an undoubted truth. Nevertheless, your Highness cannot be ignorant of the nature of the extraordinary circumstances that have recently arisen between the Sublime Porte and certain friendly Powers, and have led to a state of things which is neither peace nor war. The proposals made by the Powers and the measures resulting from them, while they seem to aim only at promoting the general tranquillity, in reality tend to disturb the peace of the whole world. This state of things has assumed a character which must strike with astonishment every wise and just statesman. Notwithstanding this, the Sovereign Porte takes now, as in the past, the straight path of justice, and, maintaining the principles of moderation and peace, has up to this time omitted nothing to preserve the bonds of friendship, and displayed both generosity and humanity in its sentiments. Nevertheless, neither the calm and moderate conduct of the Ottoman Government, nor their reasonable and just replies, have been able to overcome the tenacity still manifested by these Powers, who seem to have forgotten all respect due to the Sovereign Porte and the Mussulman people in general. This state of things naturally afflicts the Ottoman minister, and profoundly grieves the heart of the Sultan. Although it is beyond doubt that the Almighty will lend His divine assistance to those who depart not from the straight path and the cause of justice, and that, notwithstanding his troubles, the confidence of the Sovereign Porte in this Divine protection is not shaken, yet he would prefer before everything the preservation of peace and the re-establishment of public tranquillity. This end, however, can only be attained when all that concerns his internal affairs is left to his will and pleasure, and when the re-establishment of the repose and tranquillity of his

States is entrusted to his own means—which he does not cease and never will cease to use with the moderation necessary to sound legislation. Then the peace and tranquillity which form the principal object of the wishes and cares of the Powers will be re-established in the most perfect manner; then the discussions which have been raised, without any provocation on .our part, between the Sovereign Porte and the Powers in question, will cease; all cause for misunderstanding will disappear, and the Sovereign Porte is ready to place himself again on the best relations of friendship and sincerity towards these Powers.

The sentiments of the Sovereign Porte in all that regards this excellent object thoroughly agree with those of the Imperial Court of Austria, his friend and most valued neighbour, and in consideration of the bonds of intimacy and special confidence which exist between his Majesty the Emperor and his Highness the Sultan, and the sincere and friendly relations which have long reigned between the two Governments, without even a shadow of dissatisfaction, his Excellency the Reis-Effendi has already had several conversations on this subject with Baron d'Ottenfels, the Internuncio of Austria residing at Constantinople. Nevertheless, the Ottoman ministry have judged it convenient to address the present amicable and confidential letter to your Highness, with the object of showing you for the first and last time their manner of seeing and judging events, flattering themselves with the hope that, as Austria is a great Power, the sincere and true friend of all the other Courts, she will employ her good offices and beneficent endeavours to overcome a crisis that has arisen, without provocation on the part of the Sovereign Porte, between it and its friends, from their

unjust interference in its internal affairs; to the end
that all unsuitable proceedings and measures may be
avoided, all that has taken place forgotten, and the ties
of friendship between the Porte and the Courts re-established. This is what we have pleasure in hoping from
the friendly and beneficent sentiments of your Serene
Highness.

Metternich to Apponyi, Vienna, November 13, 1827.

876. I must remind you that you cannot too much
insist on the fact that the Emperor, by not refusing to
forward the Grand Vizier's letter to its destination, has
no intention by doing so of placing himself as mediator
between the three Powers and the Porte, and still less
between the Porte and the Greeks. It is certain that
if either of the parties had requested the mediation of
his Imperial Majesty, a decided refusal would have been
immediately given to the request. And the Grand
Vizier's letter does not contain a word that even in a
forced sense could give the supposition that the Porte
would go so far as to ask for the mediation of Austria.
The Sultan must dislike all idea of mediation, just as
we recoil at a word which has acquired a terrible
celebrity from the cruel abuse which has been made
of it. . . .

What effect will the arbitrary exploit of the English
admiral produce on the English public? I shall be very
much surprised, if the feeling be of a kind to please
those who have to clear themselves from very great
faults. One of the greatest a Government can be
guilty of is to have failed in foresight. Now, if history
does not pass over such faults in silence, the authors of
the transactions between the three Courts in the years

1826 and 1827 will have to encounter the bitterest reproaches.

No one can foresee what will be the consequences of the affair of October 20. One of the most probable will be horrible massacres in those places where the Christian population is mixed with the Mussulman. Another which must be expected is the enormous loss likely to be sustained by commerce. The description which in my last despatch (No. 874) I gave of the state to which the Ottoman Empire is reduced in a military point of view, is, most unhappily, a true one. Admitting that the Emperor of Russia may take a part which, I cannot but acknowledge, is a natural consequence of the advantageous position which the two other Courts have made for him, what means have the two Powers themselves of preventing the total ruin of an empire with whose existence they have so many direct interests? The fleet at Sebastopol is ready to set sail. An army of a hundred thousand men is echelonned from the Ukraine to the banks of the Pruth. The Turks have neither army nor fleet to oppose to these forces, and the maritime resources of the allies, which have destroyed the last defence of the Turks, are themselves disabled. . . .

I send you the copy of an official Report addressed by Admiral Codrington to his Government. Never before has a Report of this kind come from the pen of an English admiral. All that Machiavellism put in action, and injustice applied to politics and war, can invent in the way of rashness is to be found crammed into this remarkable performance.

Please to take the greatest care to keep us informed of the impressions produced by the development of events both on the Government and on the different

parties in France. The time approaches when we shall
have to make great decisions, and hence we ought not
to be left in any doubt as to facts. Therefore, do not
spare the couriers. For the rest, assume an attitude of
perfect impassibility. Our watchword now is, that we
no longer understand at all what the three Courts have
wished or do wish ; and therefore that we have no
longer to answer to them for anything that we wish or
may wish.

Your duty is to make yourself acquainted with
everything in order to inform us; nothing more. I beg
you to read the preceding despatch to M. de Damas and
M. de Villèle, as a proof of our personal confidence.
Whenever there is any question as to the Emperor's
impression, you cannot be too decided in your expressions. I cannot well use the word ' indignation' in diplomatic correspondence; it is, however, the only word which
really represents the feeling of his Imperial Majesty.

*Metternich to the Emperor Francis, with His Majesty's
remark, Vienna, November 26, 1827.*

877. . . . From Constantinople we are without
news beyond the 10th. It must, however, arrive almost
immediately. From Jassy we hear that the war may
be considered as begun. The details your Majesty will
find in the Reports. On the 13th inst. people in St.
Petersburg were still in good hopes of the compliance
of the Porte, and full of delight at the taking of Eriwan,
which event will certainly make a contrary impression
in London.

At Paris everything is in commotion. The elections
in twelve departments were known, and were entirely
Liberal, and in consequence they seem in the capital to
have come to blows. Everywhere it is like a real earth-

quake; and all this is the result of Liberal politics. To judge from the English newspapers of the 14th inst., it appears that the public voice is lifted more and more against the Navarino affair. I have had an article from the 'Times' (the ministerial journal) inserted in the *Beobachter*, which, by the shallowness of its arguments and the number of its reservations, shows how gently the Government is feeling its way. The Opposition journals are so strong that we cannot give one extract from them.

METTERNICH.

The enclosures are herewith returned. According to them it really seems that war is impending. God grant that this is not a contrivance of the Liberals to occupy the Powers while they use the opportunity (as, for instance, in France) to break out and advance their own views. I await with great impatience the news from London and Constantinople.

FRANCIS.

Vienna, Nov. 27, 1827.

Metternich to Werner, in Berlin, Vienna, November 29, 1827.

878. I have this morning received a despatch from London, dated November 20, which is hardly intelligible, because the Reports of the embassy are full of references to a despatch of two days before, which, having been directed to Paris, has not yet arrived here. However, from the despatch of November 20 it is clear—

That the public voice is less and less in favour of the Navarino affair;

That the British Government is not well satisfied with the Grand Vizier's letter.

Far from being surprised at these two facts, I think them quite natural. The loyal feeling which is one of the happy features of the English national character must be shocked by an act which all the sophistries in the world can never represent as lawful. Commerce must be alarmed; the City merchants can hardly take in good part what disturbs it. Liberalism has not yet succeeded in introducing itself into the figures of the counting-houses.

The Grand Vizier's step is an ineffectual step, and if we consider it so, others besides ourselves will, for the best reasons, think so too. I am not, however, sorry that they are annoyed about it in London, for it may be inferred that they were there in favour of the right course; therefore, they do not desire a rupture, and this fact is nothing new to me.

The contest is now taking place where enterprises dictated by Liberalism always end. The things disappear, and the formulas remain; the English Cabinet will certainly be ready to bargain for the pacification, provided it can escape the mediation. Thus we have seen the hottest French republicans, not only not perish for the Republic, but not make so easy a bargain for the interests of the revolution; just as we have seen latterly Imperialists contented with everything except Legitimacy. But it is precisely in this undoubted rule that lies the great difficulty of bringing the affair to a peaceful conclusion. The Sultan will be, in fact, as disposed for peace as he will be immovable in his determination never to recognise the right of foreign mediation. The genius of revolution is disorder; and to attain a state of disorder it creates difficulties in every affair which are not in the affairs themselves. How is the course of two far-seeing Powers like Austria and

Prussia embarrassed by the considerations I have here indicated!

I send you the first proof of an article which will appear in the *Beobachter* of to-morrow. We have felt the absolute necessity of giving a short account of what has passed at Constantinople since the arrival of the news of Navarino. Our public takes the most natural interest in what occurs in a State with which we have every kind of contact; therefore we must speak, and this is certainly not easy at a moment when it is often as impossible to say all as to say nothing. I hope M. de Bernstorff will not think that what we have said lays us open to blame.

Metternich to the Emperor Francis, Vienna, November 30, 1827.

879. Your Majesty will find enclosed Reports from London of the 19th and 20th inst., and from Paris of the 20th inst.

The Reports from Paris show only the greatest confusion in both ideas and things. I beg your Majesty to cast your eye over my son's letter,* for, in my opinion, it contains very just views of the circumstances of the moment. I very much doubt myself whether the ministry can hold together: and if it falls, it has only deserved its fall too well. On the other hand it can, however, only be replaced by a worse.

Prince Esterhazy's news of the 19th inst. is in the highest degree interesting. It is plainly to be seen that the public voice is more and more against the position of things in the East; and our credit increases in pro-

* Prince Victor was then an attaché at the embassy in Paris. The letter is not forthcoming.—ED.

portion. The Report of the 20th inst. contains the opinion of the English Cabinet on the letter of the Grand Vizier to me. This opinion could only be what it is, and is therefore not in the least surprising. Mine on these Reports your Majesty will please to find in the despatch which I yesterday sent to Berlin (No. 878).

At the same time your Majesty will see from Werner's Report from Berlin how clear and even strong are the views of the Cabinet there.

METTERNICH.

The enclosures are herewith returned. Their contents are not very consolatory, except for the satisfaction which my maxims receive on the part of England, and the hope that England will put a stop to the pirates. We must endeavour to make use of the present situation and, so far as we safely can, manage that England and France put a stop to Russia, if there is still time; moreover, we must endeavour that the Turks go on quietly, and thereby gain time to bring them nearer to the other Powers as much as possible without offending their principles.

FRANCIS.

Vienna, December 1, 1827.

Metternich to the Emperor Francis, Vienna, December 9,
1827.

880. A despatch received to-day from Constantinople brought me the enclosed Report of the Internuncio. It consists of two parts, the practical and the moral. The first is confined to two facts. On the 25th the embargo on merchantmen at Constantinople was taken off; and at the conference between the representatives of the three allied Courts and the Reis-Effendi on the 24th the word Mediation was not uttered by the first; words of pacification seem to have fallen from the latter. From the Report of the Internuncio of November 24 we have hopes of further approaches. The same hope, however, cannot be derived from the despatches of General Guilleminot just received, which the French agent read to me. Concerning the moral part of the despatch, I can only lament that an importance is attached to the Grand Vizier's letter which its contents in no way justify. From my last despatch to Baron Ottenfels, which I had yesterday the honour of laying before your Majesty, you will have seen what I think of the matter.* The Internuncio was also under another delusion—namely, that we were anxious for mediation. On this point he is already corrected. Since there is a possibility of a truce at Constantinople, I thought it necessary to send an extraordinary despatch to the Internuncio, in which my definite overtures were stated. If by the touch of a magic wand I could get to Constantinople, I would take a wager that I would soon put an end to the business; but where the distance is so great, the simplest things are difficult to attain.

The whole affair turns on the words Mediation and Pacification: it did so at its very beginning, and now it is plainer still. The first word represents the revolutionary principle; the second, everlasting right. But the fight is angry, for, unhappily, Canning has placed the three Courts on the basis of the first. I yesterday experienced an unhappy proof of this truth. It seems from the official despatches, which Herr von

* On Dec. 6, Metternich wrote to the Internuncio that he might set before the Reis-Effendi the insufficiency of the step, and tell him that the Grand Vizier's letter had made in Paris and in London the same impression as it had made on people in Vienna—namely, that they lamented its inadequacy, since it did not contain a word as to the suspension of hostilities.—ED.

Tatistscheff received to-day, that there is great rejoicing and triumph at St. Petersburg over the 'grand and noble' victory of Navarino. Of this I think nothing, for this is the only language suited to the Emperor's position. But it is otherwise with a private letter of Count Nesselrode to Herr von Tatistscheff, which the latter allowed me to read. In this letter Count Nesselrode raves and rants. In it was the following sentence: —' What will our friend Metternich say of this grand triumph? he will repeat his old tiresome principles; he will talk of right—*vive la force!* It is might which rules the world nowadays, and I am very glad to find that I and my comrades can leave the regulating of affairs to the admirals. These are the men to cut the matter short! Never has there been glory comparable to that of this moment!'

This is how Carnot and Danton, and afterwards their imitators, thought and spoke. They were signally overthrown, however, by the same old and tiresome principles, and that will be the end of the ranting Count Nesselrode. The only question is what will go to the bottom before him and his feeble comrades.

METTERNICH.

The despatches of the Internuncio are enclosed herewith. You are quite right in saying that everything turns on the words Mediation and Pacification; and if you were on the spot, and the distances were not so great, you would, with the help of God, make an end of these unhappy affairs in the East, without setting aside sacred principles and rights, as Count Nesselrode is weak enough to desire, and which might have the most frightful consequences.

FRANCIS.

Vienna, December 10, 1827.

1828.

THE EVENTS OF THE DAY.

Extracts from Metternich's private Letters to his Son Victor, from January 1 to May 15, 1828.

881. *Vienna, January* 1, 1828.—I shall begin this year, my dear Victor, by telling you of my desire for your happiness. Mine is much bound up in this desire, for you know how great a part you occupy in my existence! How earnestly do I hope that we may soon be together again!

As to the other aspects of my life, they look very sombre for the year 1828. On no side does anything smile on me, and, alone in the midst of a crazy world, I should at least have the right to grow tired of my solitude, if the feeling of *ennui* was compatible with that of anger and contempt. If ever the want of all right feeling in what is styled Liberalism was shown in all its nakedness, it is in the proceedings of the year which has just passed. Incapable of constructing anything, · even of making a mere screen for themselves, the Courts, under the influence of that sect, are now in a position like that of the savage in the midst of civilisation. Everything is in disorder in Paris and in London, and all would be disorder in St. Petersburg if the victorious autocracy was not there to swallow the scraps thrown to them by the Liberal Alliance for that purpose.

I cannot properly make any travelling plans for the year 1828. Shall I be able to leave my office, which

will probably soon be changed into headquarters again?
I cannot tell; what I do know is that I shall have you
come to me somewhere or other.

. . . . The works at Königswart go on very well.
The last account that I have received leaves me no
doubt that if we have the happiness of going there this
summer we shall hardly know the place. But God
knows, however, if I shall find means of leaving my
desk! I should like to be able to go to Johannisberg,
and to pass through Königswart either in going or
returning. I should stay all June at Johannisberg, and
it would be a very great pleasure to me to see it again.

882. *January* 24.—I believe all you tell me in your
letter of the 15th on the sudden ministerial change in
France (No. 891). That country is lost, and my calculations with respect to it are no longer of an active
character; they are simply defensive. I have observed
affairs too closely, and Heaven has given me too sure
an instinct, that I should not have some foresight. This
is what M. de Villèle lacked. He was a man of business, not a statesman. Nations do not vanish, they
are transformed; and this is what most certainly awaits
France. The institutions she possesses do not suit her,
and they will fall to pieces. But many things, even the
throne, may yet fall before they do. For France there
is nothing but the Republic or the Empire; that is to
say, confusion or the excess of power. The Republic
is a dream; the Empire is a reality. It is possible
that France may have yet once again to pass through
confusion to arrive at order. Neither this confusion
nor this order will be in all respects like that which
has existed. Never does the same malady invade the
same body and show the same symptoms: but that
does not prevent a new malady from resembling the

old. Since the world began, never has a country shown such an utter want of men fit to conduct public affairs as France at this day. Bonaparte was right when he said—and he said it to me twenty times—'They talk of my generals and my ministers; I have neither, I have only myself!—you have not me, but you have generals and ministers better than I have!' Without boasting, I may say that we have better men than any that France has, or has had since the Restoration; and France has not the Emperor of the French with his good sense.

My attention and my efforts are directed towards England and Turkey. Canning wished to kill me; it is I who have killed him and his feeble acolytes. There are resources in England, for there is a public spirit; and it is this very spirit that is wanting in France. That country is rotten to the core.

I expect M. de Caraman very soon. You can tell me nothing of him that I do not know. He has latterly written letter after letter to all his correspondents to announce that he had escaped wonderfully well! I shall not push the farce so far as to congratulate him.

The months of March, April, and May of this year will decide the future. If the Sultan has as much common sense as he ought to have, he will end the business. In this case I shall be free in the summer months; if not, not.

883. *February* 11.—I should much like you, my dear Victor, to read in passing my despatch to London. Sit by Count Apponyi and read it together. You will see that it is interesting.*

The crisis has arrived, and as I am an old prac-

---

* This referred to the reconstruction of the English ministry under Wellington.—Ed.

titioner in the maladies of the social body, I am not more alarmed than is necessary. What I cannot do is to know or predict how things will go : certain it is that the crisis may turn against the folly of the age which has caused it; and the country that is most seriously ill is France, and France is also the country whose future is the least promising. A country where all the moral elements are extinct cannot help itself, and Providence alone knows what will become of this Babylon.

Ours is really the only vigorous attitude; and if it does not seem to be so in every case, it is because the spot on which to rest our lever is not yet marked out. I have survived Napoleon and Canning ; I hope I shall survive even evils still more flagrant. It will be for you young men to fight its residues. The idea that you in your turn will be called to do this will sustain me in the midst of the troubles of life.

Gentz has given the lamp to Antoinette ; do not tell Count Apponyi. Gentz was distressed at the shape of the lamp : he does not like anything Gothic, because the Goths are dead. I have promised to indemnify him with chocolate. Send me some boxes of *bonbons* of this material wrought in the most artistic fashion. He would give the Cathedral of Strasburg for a good piece of chocolate.

884. *March* 26.—You will read my despatches of this day,* my dear Victor. I will not use the little time I have to spare in speaking of anything but your own future. I have already told you that I reckon on seeing you this summer, and then we will consult about

---

* This referred to the despatch of March 24 concerning the Russian circular despatch by which Russia gave the great Powers to know that her Guards had received orders to march. See No. 894.—ED.

our doings. Meanwhile, consider two things settled :
you will break up your camp and leave your post of
attaché at Paris when you leave that city, and the following winter you will enter on the position of minister.
I placed your name on the list I presented to his
Majesty, and he has agreed to it. I have an idea of
going into Bohemia and to the Rhine, but both these
things depend on circumstances. The great men of our
time have given up guiding events.

In what a state of confusion do things appear! Disorder seems the ruling spirit of the day, and this spirit
will not fail to change daylight into the darkest night.
A new divinity is wanted to say once more, *Fiat lux*;
but I know no country where this divinity reigns.

885. *May* 15.—A long time has elapsed without
my being able to write to you except by the ordinary
post, which I never think of doing. I leave that to
Leontine and the others. The departure of M. de Caraman was so hurried that I could not take advantage of
it, and the courier who ought then to have been sent
was delayed by the frightful amount of news that followed, requiring us to direct our efforts to other places
than Paris.

I write to you to-day, which is the fifty-fifth anniversary of my birth. I have prayed for you more than
for myself, for you are in the spring-time of your life,
while my season is the autumn. I desire to live to
guide your career, to put our domestic affairs on a
footing that will give you the least possible difficulty ;
I wish to live, too, for public matters, since the world
yet has need of me, were it only that I hold a place
which no one else could fill. To be what I am my
antecedents are necessary, and one can as little replace
an old minister as an old tree.

I think your grandmother is failing very much. She now keeps to her bed and sofa, and the physicians consider that she is in a state of atrophy. Her head and her heart are young and full of sense; it is only the machine that goes no longer. She will be seventy-four next December. One of her greatest wishes is to see you once more. She said something the other day which describes her state exactly : ' *Il y a longtemps que je me sens vieillir, mais depuis quelque temps je me sens défaillir.*' She looks as usual, but is excessively thin. She takes strengthening baths.

The die is thrown, and the situation is simplified ; it is, in fact, easier to understand the reason of the enemies' guns than the reason of guns placed with a show of pretended friendship. God knows to what France is coming ! If it were only a question of the direct interests of that country, the foreigner would have nothing to look for there ; it is otherwise when it is a question of the influence which the events in that kingdom exercise on the whole social body.

FROM WALTERSDORF.[*]

Extracts from Metternich's private Letters to Gentz, from June 28 to September 13, 1828.

886. *Waltersdorf, June* 28, 1828.—Prince Esterhazy, as easily happens with people at a distance, is asking too much ; he demands more from the ministry than I do.   As to the Eastern Question, but one way is left for England to show her power—namely, the tearing up of the Treaty of London.   This the Duke of Wellington, who took office with the treaty, cannot do ; and if he could, the decision would be useless if not sustained by the peremptory declaration, addressed to Russia— so far, and no further !   No one in England is prepared for this step ; and if it were otherwise the whole power of England would be used up, not against Russia, but against France. How would this injure Russia ?   Hardly at all ; for while the two Powers are watching each other, Russia would be master of the situation, go its own ways, and reach the goal quite independently.   The whole Triple Alliance may be compared to a poison, paralysing the vitality of its members.

* At the time of the encampment at Traiskerchen, near Vienna, Prince Metternich resided at Schloss Waltersdorf, and Gentz was released from his official duties while the encampment lasted.   It appears that this encampment was regarded with some suspicion on account of the Russo-Turkish war, and moreover that it was really used to hide the design of arming part of the Austrian army.   That Russia looked upon the affair in this light may be seen from Nesselrode's letter to Tatistscheff, saying that the Emperor Nicholas would send some troops to the frontier if Austria did not desist from arming.—ED.

In all points the opinions of the English ministry are ours, particularly with regard to Portuguese affairs. The existence of the Junta in Oporto and the conduct of Palmella has called forth an opinion similar to ours, and the ministry has pronounced its disapproval of Palmella's last steps. In Paris the state of things is most miserable.

887. *September* 11.—I received your despatches almost at the same time as the communications from the Prince of Hesse. As he gives all the military news to the military authorities, I know merely the few facts he writes to me, and from which I draw the following conclusions :—

1. That the operations are badly conducted.

2. That the Prince knows nothing at all of politics; he mentions neither Heytesbury nor any of his colleagues, and even Nesselrode only in connection with Portuguese affairs. The last conferences with Lord Heytesbury are therefore entirely unknown to him.

3. That the Emperor Nicholas must receive news from Constantinople which are the reverse of a true statement of facts : for instance, that the Sultan has lost all presence of mind; that he is without troops and resources; that the Grand Vizier marched out with an army of sixty thousand men, taken from the lowest rabble, who disappeared at the first action, &c., &c.

4. That up to this time only 1,200 men of the reinforcements could reach Varna.

5. That Varna has not been besieged yet, but is on the point of being so.

From Lord Heytesbury's despatches I see that the culminating point of the Triple Alliance has been reached sooner than I expected. In consequence of the English ministry's senseless consent to the French expedition (see No. 899) France and Russia have taken up a hostile position against the Porte; meanwhile England still continues her war of words in a state of peace.

But the hour of decision is near. England cannot say Yes; and if she says No, the Triple Alliance has come to an end. At the first moment she will say neither Yes nor No, but will be forced to act in a negative sense. This is my presentiment, and you may tell this to Lord Cowley. With or without the taking of Varna the campaign of the year 1828 will end in the middle of October. Then the winter begins. If this time is not used for serious negotiations, if the Governments pursue the same miserable course, the year 1829 will bring complications which may lead to the overthrow of all present political relations. We may then expect several years of war, and experience will affirm it *aut aut*.

Tatistscheff's audience was only to introduce to his Majesty four Polish spies, sent by the Grand Duke to the camp here.

I am sorry that your antipathy for these spies prevents your coming here. It is a most important moment —to-morrow Tatistscheff sleeps in your room, because the day after is the great review, which was put off by his Majesty till the arrival of the Prussian princes.

888. *September* 13.—The letters from Odessa are like those from the Prince of Hesse. The latter really say no more, and less they cannot contain, since there is nothing in the world less than nothing. From Semlin we have the confirmation of the news that the Russian batteries before Schumla have been taken. Perhaps more will happen before the Emperor returns to the army, and many a disaster may take place after his arrival. War is a power which cannot be played with unpunished.

I had yesterday a two hours' conference with Prince William of Prussia.* The result of our interview was—

That I saw plainly that the whole complication is the result of the puerile opinions of the monarch and the absurd sophistry of those about him.

That it had been undertaken without consideration of the possible resistance of the Turks.

That ways and means had been offered by the English.

That the Emperor thinks it only natural to ask untold millions from the Turks as compensation, and the destruction of all the fortresses on the Danube and Bosphorus as a kind of guarantee.

That it has never been supposed that England would raise the least objection to such demands.

That the war has taken a quite unexpected turn, and that the Emperor is very anxious to make an end of it.

This *status questionis* does great honour to the Russian Cabinet.

The best picture of the present position was unwittingly given by the Prince of Hesse: ' The Emperor picks lint at the Empress's table ' shows sufficiently the state of affairs. Meanwhile Nesselrode picks political lint; but he has wounded the English Cabinet so deeply that it will be difficult to find the right plaster. I talk quite openly with the English.

Everything goes on here so quietly that I scarcely am aware of the existence of the camp. Sometimes I take a drive to the camp instead of walking in the park.

* His Majesty the reigning Emperor. See No. 901.—ED.

DEATH OF METTERNICH'S MOTHER.

Extract from a Letter to Countess Molly Zichy, December 15, 1828.

889. I have once more experienced a most grievous loss—one for which there is indeed no consolation. If my mother had not been my mother, she would have been my life-long friend, so many points of contact were there between our minds. There is no need for me to tell you of the fine qualities for which she was so eminently distinguished. All the rarest excellences of heart and intellect were united in her. Our intimacy has been a long one, and in its whole course I have never seen a moment which has not been devoted by her to the best feelings. For the last two years I have seen her death approaching, but it has taken place much sooner than was expected by her physicians. She has ceased to be—this is the description of her end, for malady, properly speaking, she had none.

Read the newspapers, observe what has passed and is passing, and you will see that the affairs of the world pay no regard to my faculties, moral or physical; public concerns go on without pause, and my mind has to endure while my heart is full of sorrow. As for the affair and what has come of it, we are not to blame, but that does not prevent the burden which weighs upon one who is in the right from being very heavy to bear. Rich people have the advantage over me in that they can repose by the side of their treasures;

if they had always to carry them on their backs they would very soon throw them away. It is not possible for me to repose by the side of my business, nor can I get rid of it day or night. To be rich as I am is poverty indeed.

AUSTRIA'S POSITION AT THE BEGINNING OF THE YEAR 1828 IN RESPECT TO THE EASTERN DIFFICULTY.

Metternich to Ottenfels, at Constantinople, Vienna, January 6, 1828.

890. Your Excellency's Reports of December 11 reached me on the 25th.

Meantime despatches from London and Paris, as well as news from St. Petersburg, arrived, which enable us to judge of the situation at these different centres. However difficult or even impossible it may be to give you an exact representation of a state of things unexampled in history, I will nevertheless endeavour to sketch in boldly and truly its main features.

France and England may be considered as having no Government. The ministers in these two countries only exist from day to day, and I share the opinion of all calm observers when I assert that neither of these administrations can maintain themselves. Their last and great support is the difficulty found by both monarchs in choosing men in the least degree likely to be able to bear the burden of affairs successfully, and the jealousy of each other felt by the extreme parties, who, although both in England and France they may unite to turn out the present ministers, would each be most unwilling to cede the battlefield to their rivals.

The French Chambers will open on the 22nd of January next; the sitting of Parliament in England will begin on the same day. What is not altered or arranged by that date will be so by the contest in the Chambers.

A calm study of the public journals will have sufficed to show you the causes of the deplorable situation of the two Governments. I need not, therefore, enter into matters lying outside your own sphere of action, but I will confine myself to those connected with the affairs of the Levant.

The situation of the French ministry is in this respect essentially different from that of the English ministry. The two Governments, after having entangled themselves in the most frivolous manner in a dilemma impossible of happy solution, have done all they could to dull the natural consequences of the dangerous attempt ushered in by the protocol of April 4, 1826, and completed by the treaty of July 6, 1827, which only served to bring the moral and physical confusion to its height. The varnish of philanthropy covering these transactions has seduced many weak minds; the coryphæi of the Liberal system supported them because they suited their subversive views. As long as the mere *pourparlers*, conducted in the usual diplomatic modes, concealed the true state of the question from the general public, the two Governments had an easy game to play. The battle of Navarino inaugurated a new era. Facts speak quite otherwise than words.

The effect produced by this unjustifiable event is different in England from what it is in France. In the first of these countries the national feeling has been quickly aroused, and the feeling is that of justice. The ministry will be attacked by an immense majority, and

it must defend what does not admit of serious defence,
nor even of an interpretation in the least degree favourable. The ministry, too, is no less injured by the strange
party divisions among its members, than it is by the more
·or less direct part they have taken in the diplomatic
transactions which have brought on the present crisis
between England and the Ottoman Porte.

In France, on the contrary, the battle of Navarino
was received with almost general favour. The prism of
glory very quickly transforms objects in France, and the
present generation is hardly accustomed to take feats of
arms at their true value. That of Navarino has found
admirers among men of different parties—the Revolutionists, for the sake of past memories; the Bourbon
party, from delight at having a royal military trophy to
vie with those of the Republic and the Empire. Lastly,
the ministers hoped to draw from the event the double
profit of a distraction to the public mind, and the final
success of their political plans. The articles in the
·Governmental journals—that is, the *Moniteur* and
Gazette de France—prove with what inconceivable
frivolity the ministry proclaims the chimerical advantages to result from the events at Navarino. It is only
quite latterly that voices have been heard in France
against the progress of affairs in the East. These
protests emanate from the Royalist party as well as
from that of the Revolution. None are based on principle; they form part of the attacks made against all
the acts of the Government, and they only furnish to
the next session some arguments to add to those that
the united oppositions use against the continuance of the
present ministry.

The only Court that is beyond the embarrassments
under the weight of which the two allies are likely to

be crushed, is that of Russia. Everything up to this time has turned in favour of the views of this Power, although the system it follows is false, and rejected as much by sound reasoning as by right and justice. Mr. Canning's dangerous idea of taking a prominent part in the affairs of the Levant, and at the same time barring from Russia the way to new conquests, has brought its own punishment. The end proposed by the unlucky minister has not been attained; on the contrary, the young Emperor of Russia now finds himself not only launched in a career from which the best policy should have kept him aloof, but an extraordinary coincidence of difficulties at home and abroad places the two Governments that are allied with Russia in a situation where, not knowing how to guide themselves, they are still less capable of guiding the decisions of their formidable ally. Events, therefore, move on according to their natural bent and the good pleasure of the Emperor Nicholas.

The last news from London and Paris do not allow us to doubt that the two Courts have given their consent to the occupation of the two Principalities on the Danube by Russian troops, with the double clause that the entrance and the occupation of these territories should have no other character than that of a coercive measure to force the Sultan to submit to the terms of the Triple Treaty, and that it should be performed in the name of the three Courts, who would continue to regard themselves as bound together by that treaty.

This is the historical position of affairs at the present moment; its aspect is as dark and undefined as the two transactions whence it is derived. No one but the Sultan can cut this inextricable knot, and I must confess that nothing he has done up to the present time enables us to calculate with any certainty as to what he will or will not concede in the last extremity. In proof of this assertion some facts will suffice.

War against the Porte was signed morally on April 4, 1826. It was corroborated and extended on July 6, 1827. Actual war began with the first shot fired at Lepanto by the English Admiral. The battle of Navarino was only the second act. You see that I put aside all the performances of Hamilton and his party during the years preceding the explosion. The course of the Porte for the last six years has been incomprehensible.

During the first four years it did nothing to repress the revolution.

In the course of the fifth year it confided the task of bringing the Morea to submission to the Viceroy of Egypt.

In the sixth year that submission was no nearer.

In the seventh the Porte's fleet was burned, and she hardly raised her voice, except to assure the Powers who made this frightful attack upon her of her sincere desire to maintain the most friendly relations with them. On the other hand she did not vigorously prosecute the war against the insurgents; the revolution, instead of being restrained, was left perfectly free.

The Porte neither negotiated with the Greeks nor with the Powers. At last she addressed herself to us, and what did she say? That she prefers peace to war!

The *pourparlers* are broken off, and she addresses a circular to the Cabinet which again says nothing more.

The three Courts are as ill-informed as we are; if there is a difference between us, it is confined to feelings. We still think that the Sultan at the last will accept war. In Paris and London they do not believe this. At St. Petersburg they do not take the trouble to examine the question ; they have decided to run the risks of war if the Sultan accepts it, though they are inclined to avoid it if he will concede all that they demand of him. The difference in the measures required by the two cases has no doubt been foreseen; if war is accepted they will demand from the Porte what war will procure ; if peaceful councils prevail, they will confine themselves to the stipulations of the Triple Treaty. What are the limits of these stipulations—especially, what is the limit of the chief ground on which it rests—namely, how is the Greece of which it speaks to be defined ? No one knows. What are they driving at ? For the position of two of the allied Governments approaches madness, and the third risks nothing, whatever may be the results of the triple efforts.

In such a dilemma what ought we to do, what can we do ? I will tell you, and I authorise you to conceal nothing from the Porte. You will say to Reis Effendi : ' That we see the loss of the Ottoman Empire made, so to speak, certain by the course taken by its Government, and that we are too much interested in its fate to keep silence during a frightful crisis, the approach and continuance of which is to a great extent the result of its own conduct.'

We will permit ourselves no recrimination ; the principal reproach we might make would be that in the gravest circumstances the Divan has not followed our counsels. It will suffice to mention that during the lifetime of the Emperor Alexander, we advised that the Porte should arrange those matters which directly concerned Russia. By granting half of what a few months later she granted at Ackerman there would have been neither the protocol of St. Petersburg, nor the Treaty of London, nor the Triple Alliance, nor Navarino ! The second piece of advice which the Porte did not follow was to enforce with vigour the submission of the Morea.

I know what a man of the stamp of Pertew Effendi will have to reply to what is on our part merely a sincere expression of regret, but on the part of the Porte ought to cause the severest self-reproach. Pertew Effendi will say that everything shown by events to be good or evil is not always feasible or avoidable in an empire organised like the Ottoman Empire. I admit the truth of the remark, but Reis Effendi must then admit that chance alone can in future regulate the destinies of a State so situated.

My desire is to make this fact plain, and I know no duty more pressing than that of bringing the truth before the Divan. . . .

THE CHANGE OF MINISTRY IN FRANCE AND ENGLAND, AND METTERNICH'S ADVICE TO THE PORTE.

Metternich to Ottenfels, Vienna, January 21, 1828.

891. The short time which has elapsed between my last despatch and the present has been filled by two events which, if they could have been foreseen, would still have been of the greatest importance. There has been a change of ministry in France and in England.[*]

The two Administrations succumbed in a great measure by their own faults. I have not the time, and indeed I know that it is not necessary for me to enter into details as to the causes which have brought about these changes. Similar as the situation in these two kingdoms may appear, their differences are no less striking to those who are acquainted with their internal condition and the exigencies of their external policy. However that may be, it is certain that if the cause of right and justice gains by these changes (a more direct consequence of the fall of the English than of the French ministry), it is no less certain that the Porte would yield to the most dangerous of delusions if it should think that by the disappearance of certain individuals it would be protected from the consequences of the

[*] On January 4 Charles X. dismissed the Villèle ministry, which had become unpopular from the dissolution of the Chamber of Deputies, and the creation of a number of peers. In London, Wellington became Prime Minister January 10.—ED.

Triple Treaty. This conclusion would be absolutely false. The Treaty of London exists; and its existence will acquire greater importance for the Court of Russia by the fact that it has for the Russian Cabinet the merit of a positive bond with its two allies in the Eastern Question, just where so many other connecting links have been broken. I have given you, in my despatch of the 6th of this month (No. 890), an exact sketch of the dispositions of France and England with regard to this same treaty. In France, public opinion is decidedly in favour of the Greeks, and in England the carrying out of a treaty is always regarded as a sacred duty. The Porte will, therefore, remain under the weight of the Triple Treaty after the fall of the two ministries, just as it was before that event; and if anything is changed in the situation, it can only be that a well-considered step taken by the Porte may have more chance of being well received by ministers who can scarcely desire to have their first steps encumbered by so essentially bad a business; whilst, on the other hand, the Porte finds itself more exposed to the sword of Russia since the changes which have taken place in France and England than it was before those events, for the simple reason that the very doubt which the Emperor of Russia might entertain of the ability of new men to walk in the ways of their predecessors would make him all the more determined himself to take vigorous measures. Thus, any hope at Constantinople that might be founded on the disappearance of the dangers with the fall of their authors, would infallibly be injurious to the Sultan.

The Ottoman Government, I repeat, can alone give itself the help which no one else is in a position to offer it.

This assistance, the means by which it can and should be employed, we pointed out on January 6 (No. 890). We have received abundant data since then, and, far from making us change our opinion, everything leads us to hope that the Divan, if it is not a prey to the worst and most deplorable of errors—if, in a word, it has not taken a suicidal decision—will be able to bring its affairs to a better state.

The present time is, however, so important, it bears so strongly the character of one of those passing moments when the good that men fail to do turns into so much evil, which they have no longer the power to overcome, that the Emperor makes it a point of conscience to charge you to employ all the representations reason dictates to us, and will equally suggest to you.

You have received orders by the courier of January 6 to enter into explanations with the Reis Effendi ; you will no doubt have done so before the arrival of the present directions, and you will, therefore, resume the questions at the point to which you had conducted them.

You will say to the Reis Effendi :

'That the object of the present despatch is to bring to the knowledge of the Divan the changes which have taken place in the Administrations in France and England.'

(You will here enter upon the explanations and arguments which form the first part of the present despatch.)

You will add, after having given a sketch of our opinions :

'That we consider things and positions have arrived at the last stage in which good can still be done ; but that we do not assume to ourselves any moral power beyond the counsels which we believe we have a right to address to our friend the Porte, and those which, in case we should be listened to by the Divan, we would gladly, conscientiously, and with perfect frankness give to the three Powers united by the Treaty of London.

'That if, in our despatch of January 6, we laid down some general points of view, the present moment seems to require that we should bring forward these points ; and we should fail in our duty of friendship towards the Porte, and at the same time in our duty towards ourselves and the whole of Europe, if we did not attempt to give a more precise explanation of our views.'

You will add further :

'That in following this determination we have no fear of encroaching on the rights of an independent Power ; that to give advice to a friend is not to aim at governing him, nor even to pretend to govern for him ; it is simply wishing to serve him.

'That in advising the Porte to do of its own accord what in the end it will be obliged to grant to adversaries so powerful that it is impossible to doubt the issue of a struggle between them, we are only recommending what under the circumstances must be eminently useful, and what alone can secure it a more tranquil future.'

We are recommending what is useful to it in the present ; for by seizing the interval between the refusal of the Divan to the demands which have been made to it by the Courts, and the return of new demands which will soon arrive, the Porte is able to give a proof of its independence ; we recommend what will be useful to it in the future ; for the object at which the Porte must aim before everything is the real pacification of the

Morea and the islands; and a pacification which did not carry with it pledges of stability would in reality be only a truce which would have no practical effect except to strengthen the enemy's measures—measures which doubtless they would take care to combine in such a way as to make them quite irresistible when their plans of destruction against the Ottoman Power seem to them more easy of accomplishment than at present.

We, therefore, being a Power friendly to the Ottoman Empire, and directly interested in its preservation and well being, ask that the Sultan will decide without loss of time on the measures contained in our despatch of January 6; and we add the express desire that he will establish and proclaim the future *régime* of the Peloponnesus on the following grand administrative lines :—

1. The Peloponnesus shall be governed by a prince *raya,* or the different territorial subdivisions which are included in the peninsula shall be severally governed by a prince *raya* ; ·

2. This prince, or these princes, according to ancient custom, shall be hereditary, or nominated and confirmed by his Highness as sovereign of the country ;

3. The Morea shall pay an annual tribute, which will be placed in the Imperial coffers ;

4. The strongholds in the Peloponnesus must be garrisoned by Turks ;

5. The islands shall enjoy their ancient liberties, and their annual tribute shall be sent direct to Constantinople ;

6. No tributes in arrear shall be claimed—a privilege which has already been offered by the Sultan.

Such stipulations, emanating from the sovereign

power, with the clause of the previous submission of the insurgents, and accompanied by an act of amnesty and a declaration of suspension of arms by land and sea, can be supported by us at the three Courts. If, on the contrary, the Porte does not enter into our views, there remains to us no other means of pleading its cause, since the concessions which it has hitherto brought forward, however honourable as proofs of the clemency and generosity of the Sultan, infer the re-establishment (with some modifications) of the *régime* subsisting before the insurrection; a re-establishment which we believe irreconcilable with the proposals made by the Courts in coalition, and on which they continue to insist, and which, consequently, can never serve as the basis of an agreement, nor put an end to all the immense risks to which the Empire is exposed at the present moment and in the approaching future.

An objection has been made by the Divan to any arrangement by which concessions would be made to the insurgent Greeks, which could not be extended to those of its subjects which have remained faithful. This objection is no doubt plausible, but we cannot regard it as applicable to all cases, and especially to the present circumstances.

Powers, as individuals, are often forced to bend beneath the weight of grave necessities, but this does not make it their duty to generalise benefits granted in consequence of these very necessities. Another consideration not less worthy of respect arises from the examination of this quéstion. The topographical situation of the Peloponnesus and the islands is entirely different from that of other countries also containing Greek populations. We have never seen that the peculiar *régime* of the Danubian Principalities, of Servia, of

Bosnia, even of Egypt, has been or could be claimed by provinces otherwise situated or differently inhabited.

The Ottoman Empire, in which a nation professing Islamism is uniformly governed by religious law, is very different from others. To avoid all false interpretations, it would perhaps suffice that the Porte, in speaking of the inhabitants of the Peloponnesus and the islands, should never make use of the generic denomination Greeks. It is true that the rebels and their partisans affect for this denomination a predilection easy to explain ; but in our explanations we need not sanction it ; and we are moreover persuaded that not one of the Powers engaged in this dispute can seriously entertain a project so chimerical as that of the fusion of all the Greeks into one national body.

You are charged to make these overtures to the Divan, as a sequel to those which we addressed to it on January 6 last, and consequent on the latest events in the different States of Europe.

These explanations to the Porte are not instigated by any other Cabinet ; what we say proceeds from our own heart, and is the fruit of the perfect independence of our political attitude. We desire your Excellency to make the Reis Effendi thoroughly understand this fact ; we would not mislead anyone, and to allow the Porte to believe that we would be mandatories for the Powers in coalition, or for one or other of them, would be both to mislead it and to put ourselves forward as guarantees that the three Courts would unhesitatingly accept the spontaneous determinations of the Grand Signior.

The Emperor ardently desires the preservation of political peace and the integrity of the Ottoman Empire. He would have no hesitation in stating anywhere—at Constantinople as at London, at Paris, and at St. Petersburg—what he considers necessary to attain this double object. His Imperial Majesty does not yield to illusions of any kind; on the contrary, he combats them wherever they are to be seen. He carefully guards himself from confounding the age and the necessities which it creates; he seeks nothing for himself in the affair known for years as the Eastern or Greek Question; he wishes for a lasting peace, and believes this can only be obtained by the means he has pointed out.

He does not present them to the Porte as likely to be agreeable, or as concessions easy to make; on the contrary, he regards them as necessities and sacrifices which prudence sometimes compels Powers to make in order to avoid still greater sacrifices and misfortunes.

The Porte will in reality lose nothing by the sacrifices which we advise, either in intrinsic strength or in resources; we feel by no means certain that it will not gain. If the object should be attained by the adoption of our plan, the Porte, on the other hand, would have given proof of a force of resistance and vital energy of which perhaps we alone have not regarded it as entirely destitute. If the embarrassments in which the Powers in coalition find themselves make them adhere to our plan; if, in short, a durable peace and the establishment of new bonds between the Ottoman Empire and Powers which, from the errors of some men, are hostile, should crown the enterprise, would not the concessions made by the Sultan seem small in comparison with the advantages resulting from them? In crises when the life of a State is at stake, its Government cannot study its own antipathies, and at the present moment the Porte is passing through such a crisis.

If I make yet another appeal to the Divan, I will

found it on the passage at the end of your despatch
(No. 204 B) of December 31.

You tell us ' that the Porte, placing all its trust in
the friendship of the Imperial Court of Austria, is disposed to listen to and accept all the proposals which
the Cabinet of Vienna may make to it with the object
of the pacification of its revolted provinces and of its
reconciliation with the Powers in coalition, being persuaded that these proposals can never be contrary to
its honour, its dignity, or its interests ; it promises to
wait for the overtures of the Imperial Court, and to
confine itself in the meantime to simple measures of
foresight and precaution, without doing anything that
could be regarded by the Powers as a provocation on
its part.'

We ask that this engagement may be carried out.

THE FORMATION OF STATES IN THE EAST
ACCORDING TO METTERNICH'S PROPOSAL.

Metternich to Esterhazy, Vienna, March 15, 1828.

892. I had the honour to inform you that I would soon send you a despatch containing a statement of our opinions on the needs of the present moment. I now acquit myself of this task.

If my last despatch has left no doubt in the minds of the British Cabinet as to our agreement with it in regard to the gravity of the Eastern Question, it remains for me to place before the English ministers what are, in our opinion, the only measures which can turn away from Europe the dangers with which she is threatened.

Before entering on the subject I should fail in my duty if I did not take account of the moral position of our Court with regard to the problem now occupying it. In not doing so I should run the risk of favouring the supposition—however false and gratuitous it might be—that the Emperor and his Cabinet had yielded their principles. It is not so; our principles are immutable, and we never shall recognise rights with which, according to our decided opinion, they are not compatible. Sound practice, on the other hand, forces us to admit that there are cases in which circumstances beyond our power may create situations so imperious, that the search for means of ameliorating them with the least possible disadvantage, should alone occupy the attention of men called upon by their position to act in the affairs of this world. In the presence of such a necessity we find ourselves placed.

The choice no longer exists between what we qualify as good and evil. The good having been rendered impossible, we have only to deal with the evil, and to do all in our power to lessen its consequences.

The Eastern Question in its present state may be described as follows :—

It is enclosed within two limits, from which it seems to have no power to free itself; one is the Treaty of London and the obligations it contains for the three contracting parties; the other is the persistence shown by the Sultan not to yield to any of the demands made by the allies. Threatening measures were indicated by the treaty of July 6. They have been tried and have failed. If the resistance of the Sultan had not been caused by the nature of the conditions which the triple transaction imposed on the Ottoman Power, it would be easily explained by the publicity which even the most secret transactions between the three Courts have acquired almost from the very time of their conclusion. To pursue the course of measures which have received an absolute check, would be to expose oneself to new and certain misfortunes; to extend measures of the kind already employed, would be simply passing to declared hostilities; in a word, to blockade the Dardanelles and Hellespont, to occupy the Principalities, even without passing to a state of war otherwise declared, would be to do less than has already been done at Navarino, whilst the passage of the Danube and the attack of the strongholds which defend the two straits would be war, with all its inevitable consequences. We are aware that there are no intentions but those absolutely foreign to projects of conquest, or the destruction of the Ottoman power in Europe, and that the Courts animated with these intentions are ready to corroborate them by the most solemn engagements. But do the consequences of war depend entirely on the will of Courts? The fall of the Turkish power, the annihilation of the feeble remains of the reigning dynasty, the immediate establishment of a state of complete anarchy in Constantinople and the European provinces of the empire, the massacre of entire Turkish populations on this side of the Bosphorus, and, *per contra*, of thousands of Christians in Asia and Africa : these more or less certain consequences of a war of which the Sultan has already determined the character, can they remain under the direction of those who, while wishing for some only of these effects, only too easily provoke the others? These united considerations speak too openly against the pursuit of a plan which has already proved to be a mistake, and presents terrible prospects for the future !

From this picture—which, however, is not exaggerated—we now turn to a more cheerful prospect. You will find in the enclosed sketch (No. 893) some ideas which we wish to be considered by the Cabinet to whom they are addressed.

You will recognise in this brief despatch opinions which, about the beginning of the year 1825, we expressed at the Conferences of St. Petersburg, at the time of the discussion on the choice of threatening measures, to induce the Sultan to make certain concessions in favour of his rebellious subjects. They were not received then; the Emperor Alexander expressed great surprise at our taking a line that would have led to the emancipation of the Greeks; a step which that sovereign, dreading the consequences of a revolutionary enterprise being crowned with such brilliant success, declared inadmissible. Shortly afterwards the Conferences of St. Petersburg were broken off.

Although we return to the same idea, the circumstances under which we submit it to the deliberations of the British Cabinet are very different from those in which the affair was then placed.

Little inclined to yield to illusions, and far from giving to words an importance not warranted by facts, we see in the coercive measures hitherto proposed by the three Cabinets nothing but disappointment or open war. The plan which we propose may doubtless also lead to a state of open war; but that war will be at least limited to a clearly defined object, and as I believe to the only object definable. When the day comes that the Sultan has to choose between the limited emancipation of a certain portion of his Greek subjects, and the absolute independence of the whole countries inhabited by them, he will find the choice possible, however painful it may be to him to be reduced to make it by Powers with whom he has not actually broken, notwithstanding many undoubted provocations on their part.

If the allied Courts will take the path we have pointed out, they must feel the necessity of determining beforehand how far they mean to go, both as to territorial extension, and the concessions to be obtained in favour of the countries which these concessions concern. Unless the Courts have previously made arrangements on these points, how can they make them the subject of a formal proposal to be addressed to the Porte? And after the catastrophe of Navarino has proved the result of the coercive measures already at work, can we still remain in doubt whether the one question of territorial limits—the first .of all—will be determined in the tri-lateral council!

After having stated our opinion on the means of terminating the most difficult question which has occupied the Cabinets for a long period, I consider it due to the Emperor's character not to allow the British Cabinet to remain in ignorance of the course which, if the allied Courts share this opinion, his Imperial Majesty intends to take towards the Porte.

There would be two periods: the first would be marked by the peremptory proposal addressed to the Sultan, of the administrative and limited emancipation of certain countries inhabited by the Greeks ; the second, which would follow the definite refusal of the Sultan, would be the recognition of the complete political independence of these same countries by the three Powers.

In the first of these periods, we shall not hesitate to second the demand of the allies by our best offices with the Sultan, pointing out in the most energetic manner the necessity of acceding to the demand addressed to him. We shall also support the threatening measure by declaring to the Porte the determination of our Court to enter without further delay into relations with the new State created in consequence of the refusal of the Sultan to yield to an evident necessity.

I beg you to lay the present despatch before the British Cabinet, as a proof of the confidence we have in the sincerity of its desire to spare its own country and Europe from the evils which would be the inevitable consequence of a political war begun on such insecure foundations as those which would in the first instance serve as a pretext for it.

H H

Metternich's Memorandum.

893. The hope of preventing the bursting of the storm by a pacific *dénouement* in the East diminishes day by day. The steps taken at Constantinople in consequence of the Treaty of London have failed in their effect; the operations of the admirals, although more brilliant than those of the negociators, have not been more efficacious. Neither the united entreaties of the Courts who signed the treaty, nor the threats which accompanied them, nor the first fulfilment of these threats at Navarino, nor the explanations which preceded the departure of the ministers, nor the cares and efforts of the embassies of Austria and Prussia—nothing has been able to make the Sultan yield. Whether afraid of the dangerous abyss that might open before him if he yielded to the proposals of the Powers, or from excess of religious scruples, or incurable blindness, the fact remains that his resistance has become stronger rather than weaker, and that, in spite of the most menacing circumstances, the language of his ministers has not changed.

Nothing is more easy than to accuse of barbarous and stupid obstinacy an unhappy Government in which remembrances of former grandeur and glory unite with a profound feeling of embarrassment, humiliation, and defeat, brought upon it by a concurrence of unfortunate circumstances.

The errors of the Porte, its false calculations, its mistaken pride, its terrified despair, are known to all the world; the most vulgar can see them; and it is natural that many of its contemporaries should load it with invectives. But very different and very serious considerations are presented to the tribunal of a more elevated policy. Must the Ottoman Empire succumb beneath the weight of the errors of its Government? Must Europe punish herself in order to avenge on the Porte the crimes of its rebellious subjects? Would it be worthy of the wisdom, would it be worthy of the magnanimity of the allied Sovereigns to cut the knot of this unhappy complication by a war to the death? Would the advantages they might finally obtain for the insur-gents compensate them for the calamities, the horrors, inseparable from a crusade the results of which would threaten not only the existence of Turkey, but also that of the Greeks themselves, as well as the interests of Christianity, the fate of Europeans in three parts of the world, and the foundations of that peace so gloriously established, so happily maintained for fifteen years? The reply to these questions cannot be doubtful. The Cabinets have spoken with one voice. They desire a pacification. If extraordinary measures are necessary, if sacrifices must be made, let there be at least a just proportion between the end and the means. Every victory is bought at a price. And what would pay for the bloodshed, the catastrophes and ruin which would have to be gone through before conquering an enemy whose very destruction would be but the prelude to a new era of trouble and distress of every kind?

Before an irrevocable decree has closed the last avenues of peace, an examination should be made to see if there are not some more persuasive means of negociation than those which have hitherto been employed, and at the same time nearer to the object which the authors of the Triple Treaty undoubtedly had in view. Measures which might have been considered more than rigorous six months ago may now be salvation for the Porte and expedient for Europe.

First, let us consider the present state of the question:

1. A return to the *régime* which preceded the insurrection of the Greeks has become impossible in those of the insurgent countries which from their geographical position and their maritime resources have successfully resisted, and continue to resist, the re-establishment of that *régime*. That is a certain fact, on which all the Powers must be agreed.

2. A change of *régime*, a new political organisation, is therefore necessary for the pacification of these countries. The Courts connected by the Treaty of London have agreed on the bases of it in their transactions, and have required the Porte to accept them under their mediation. Austria and Prussia, who have not taken part in the treaty, have nevertheless recognised the necessity of this change, and have urged the Porte to accept it as the only means of averting the ruin with which it is threatened.

3. The Porte has been equally deaf to the peremptory assertions, the active demonstrations of the three Courts, and to the urgent representations of Austria and Prussia: the means of pacification proposed by its ministers have been in their turn declared insufficient and inadmissible, because while having an appearance of moderation and clemency, they tended only to the re-establishment of the former *régime*.

4. In looking impartially at these proceedings, one is soon convinced that the real question at issue between the Powers and the Porte concerns the principle of this new organisation, demanded on one side, refused on the other; the Porte believing itself ruined by treating on the bases proposed to it by the Powers, and the Powers not being able, without renouncing their prior engage-

ments, to recognise those which the Porte wishes to substitute for them.

It is evidently impossible to find a clue in the labyrinth of these contradictory claims, without recourse to other combinations than those which have hitherto been vainly attempted.

To justify what we are now about to propose, let us glance rapidly at the situation, past and present.

The object of the Greek insurrection—that which the heads of that insurrection have pursued and proclaimed at all periods of the struggle—was not a change of *régime*, but the achievement of absolute independence. The Sovereigns of Europe saw in this enterprise, and the means used to support it, only a direct attempt against the imprescriptible principles of the social order to which they rendered a solemn homage; and all of them more or less expressly condemned it. Not one European Government has up to this day recognised the legality of the insurrection. Whilst working without intermission for a pacification becoming year by year more difficult, whilst demanding for the insurgents that which humanity and religion, seconded by the voice of the people, have claimed for them, the Cabinets did not wish to go beyond that line; and notwithstanding all that some among them have done or allowed to be done for the independence of the Greeks, it has not been sanctioned by any public act.

There are, however, in the course of human affairs, moments in which the strongest wills, the most legitimate opposition, cannot resist an imperious necessity, to which all must submit. The public man must take things as he finds them, leaving to history to reveal the first mistakes, the fundamental errors which produced these sad necessities. It is a fact that revolutions the most culpable in their origin have sometimes ended triumphantly, and that when this has come to pass the enlightened and correct governments have been obliged to come to terms with the most undoubted usurpation. If, then, the peace of Europe is attached to the pacification of the Levant, and if the independence of part of Greece, with all the inconveniences and dangers it will entail, is the unavoidable condition of this pacification, it is no longer possible to hesitate.

This general observation acquires under the circumstances of the moment a very peculiar force. Three of the first Powers of Europe have decided to prescribe to the Porte the terms of pacification, at the same time announcing in an unequivocal manner the consequences of its refusal. Why do these same Powers hesitate to take a part which, while modifying the object, would make no change in the principle of their action ? Placed as they are at present between the difficulty of retracting declarations perhaps too decided, and the prospect of only being able to realise them by violent measures, why do they hesitate to admit the mere fact of emancipation, either as a means of negociation or as a definite result ?

The project we are going to propose unites two immense advantages : that of acting on the Porte more directly and powerfully than even the imminence of danger against which a Government excited by despair will always flatter itself that some resource will yet be found ; and that of preventing a murderous war, or at least of restraining it within clearly defined limits.

To render this project feasible, the Courts must agree beforehand on an exact definition of the parts of insurgent Greece to which they mean to extend their inter-

vention with the Porte. The mysterious uncertainty
with which this question has been constantly surrounded
—an uncertainty prolonged and even augmented by the
inconceivable silence of the Treaty of London—has not
a little contributed to baffle all the proceedings of the
Powers. To put an end to this, the nature of things,
the localities and antecedents, must be considered. In
our opinion, any plan of emancipation, either limited or
absolute, which is not confined to the Morea and to a
certain number of the islands of the Archipelago, must
infallibly end in new refusals, new disasters, interminable
wars—in short, to an immediate or speedy dissolution of
the Ottoman Empire. This is a truth which we need
not attempt to prove; it must be admitted by all who
have the least notion of the geographical, military,
and statistical relations between the provinces of European Turkey. This first point settled, the intervening
Courts should make a declaration to the Turkish Government in substance as follows :

'That the old order of things having been totally
overthrown in the Morea and in a part of the Archipelago by the insurrections which broke out in 1821,
and the re-establishment of that order of things having
become impossible on account of the events which followed these insurrections, the Courts consider that the
only way of putting an end to the disorders and convulsions which desolate that part of the Ottoman Empire is
to establish in the above-named countries a system of
administration in agreement with the bases communicated to the Porte by the official note of August 16:

'That if the Porte consents to the principle of administrative independence as stipulated in the treaty of
July 6, which does not admit the political independence
of the Greeks in the countries comprised in this new

arrangement, a treaty should be drawn up without delay, securing to the Porte the enjoyment of its rights over the above-named countries, and to the inhabitants of these countries the form of government formerly proposed by the Powers. As soon as the Porte announces its formal acceptance of these bases, hostilities should be suspended by land and sea; and the Powers would undertake that these arrangements should be accepted and carried out, both in the Morea and the islands to which these stipulations would apply;

'That if the Porte refuses to accept the present proposals, the Powers would recognise the separation and real independence of the above-named countries, and act accordingly.'

Respecting the insurgent provinces not comprised in this arrangement, they would continue to treat with the Porte on the best means of re-establishing order and tranquillity on a just and stable footing: it being understood that the arrangements concerning these countries would be the subject of amicable negociation, and arranged according to the wishes of the Porte.

If this step taken by the Powers should only lead to a new refusal from the Porte, the measures concerning the establishment of a separate government in the Morea and the islands should be carried out without further delay; the object of the Treaty of London, the avowed aim of the Powers which signed it, would be effectually obtained in ways the least injurious to the tranquillity and the interests of Europe; and the military operations, if it were necessary to have recourse to them, being confined to the defence and preservation of the newly-created State, the war would be prevented from extending beyond its true limits. It would even be possible to maintain—notwithstanding the execution of these measures—pacific relations with all the other parts of Turkey till the Porte itself provoked war, either by acts of aggression against one or other of the allied Powers, or by new hostilities against the countries placed under the special protection of the Powers.

This project, less dangerous, and in reality much more practicable than those which depend either on the spontaneous concurrence of the Porte or a desperate war, is doubtless not free from objection ; this is the fate of all plans made in times of dire extremity ; but it offers several chances of safety which are not to be despised, for :

1. If the Porte, reduced to choose between two sacrifices, accepts the least painful, and prefers the restriction of its power to the loss of a part of its possessions, the Powers would have the double satisfaction of accomplishing the wishes and engagements they have formed in favour of Greece, and of furthering the interests of a Government which is free from reproach as towards Europe.

2. If the Porte, as is much to be feared, listening only to its own exasperation and resentment, rejects a capitulation which would secure to it an honourable retreat, there would be nothing to prevent the Powers from establishing the independence of the Morea and the Islands. The forces they could employ to carry out this measure are more than sufficient.

Whatever part the Pacha of Egypt and his son may finally take, they can no longer defend the Morea against the united operations of the Powers; and the Islands, virtually emancipated, would offer no resistance. It would be, indeed, much less difficult to withdraw these countries from the authority of the Porte, than to organize in them a government calculated to enable them

to enjoy a liberty which hitherto they have most cruelly
abused, and which, if it were not regulated, would soon
become the scourge of their neighbours. But this question, more important and more problematical than that
of emancipation, does not concern us just now.

3. In detaching from the Ottoman Empire possessions like the Morea and the Isles, the Powers would
have reached the utmost limit to which the most determined advocate of the right of intervention could proceed, except by stating frankly that might is right.
To go beyond this limit, to attack the other possessions
of the Porte, to destroy its last means of defence, to
burn its ports or to surround its capital in order to
force from it a consent which it looks upon as suicide
or sacrilege, would be acts of gratuitous injustice; since,
after all, its consent can be dispensed with, and the object gained, without buying it by useless cruelties.

4. What would be repugnant to every sentiment of
humanity and justice would be still more to be regretted
in the interests of Europe. If the military operations are
confined to the countries which they are intended to free,
it is possible, it is even probable, that the Porte, seeing
its absolute powerlessness to re-establish its authority in
these countries, will submit to an inevitable loss (as the
King of Spain submitted to the loss of his colonies),
rather than rush into a war with the half of Europe,
and stake its existence against a dream of power. It is
quite characteristic of the Turks, and in keeping with
their religious and political principles, to yield to necessity, and to make up their minds to resign a province
irrevocably lost, whilst they will defend to the last a
place still occupied by their arms. It would be the
height of skilful policy to avoid, in spite of the enfran-

chisement of the Morea, a complete suspension of relations
between Turkey and Europe, to save the appearances of
peace, and to labour diligently for its return, by drawing
within the narrowest compass the points of hostile contact with the Porte—of bringing, in short, little by little,
this Power not to consider its allies as implacable enemies
sworn to its destruction. On the other hand, what a
picture is presented to us by the prospect of a general
war; of a war which, whatever be its issue, would
overthrow a great empire and shake the foundations of
Europe and Asia!

5. But if the Porte pronounces its own sentence of
death, if it replies by a declaration of war to the ultimatum of the Powers, or if it opposes the emancipation
of the Morea; in short, if by acts of frenzy and barbarous reprisals, it forces the Powers to attack it in its
last retrenchments, what becomes of the plan we have
just advanced? It may yet be believed that the words
and demonstrations of the Porte which have given
rise to this apprehension have been inspired by excess
of terror; one thing is certain—they have betrayed
only a desire to conceal its weakness, and to cause its
defensive attitude to be respected. But if, sooner or
later, it changes its attitude, the wishes we have expressed will be but barren speculations, and then blind
guesswork will take the place of political reasoning.
Let those who may one day be accused of not having
removed these evils never lose sight of two considerations, one of which addresses itself to their generosity
and their conscience, the other to their reason and interest. Let them remember that the first signal which
we expect does not proceed from the Divan, and that
each blow now given to the Ottoman Empire is one

danger more for Europe, a germ of incalculable complications, and the presage of a disastrous future.*

* These proposals of the Austrian Cabinet were rejected by England on
the following grounds. The Austrian Ambassador, Prince Esterhazy, wrote
to Prince Metternich from London as follows:—

'The principal objection, hitherto the only objection which the Duke of
Wellington has made to the plans brought forward by your Highness, would
have astonished anyone except a man who, like your Highness, has from
the beginning of this deplorable complication until the present crisis, which
begins a new period, remained firm on the same ground.

'The Austrian Cabinet proposed at the Conferences of St. Petersburg in
1825, the same measures as it proposed in the spring of 1828. At first it
was the Emperor Alexander himself who positively rejected them, and now
it is the head of the British Cabinet who declares that he does not see his
way to support absolute political independence of the territory to which
they intended to apply the stipulations of the trilateral treaty. "In the first
place," said he, "it would be overturning one of the essential bases of that
agreement, and if I believed it," added the Duke, "not in agreement with the
precepts of justice or good policy to lay down the principle of an absolute
independence at the time of the protocol, how many more reasons are there
now to make us remain faithful to our first idea! How can the British
Government, without opposing the principles it has professed with regard
to the New American States, and recommencing at their expense experiences
it has already acquired, see in that part of Greece even a shadow of the
elements indispensable for maintaining its independence? It is besides
essential not to forget that one grand object which we have in view is
excluded in the too probable supposition of the continuance of the refusal of
the Porte. This object is to establish relations of amity and good neighbourhood with this new State, and thus to heal the wound which otherwise
would always remain open. If," continued the Duke, "we do not obtain the
Porte's consent, its relations with Russia will always remain precarious, and
we shall be always exposed to the same danger which will constantly be
suspended over our heads."'

Russia too declined, see No. 896.—ED.

THE RUSSIAN GUARDS ORDERED TO MARCH..

Metternich to Esterhazy in London,
Vienna, March 24, 1828.

894. Yesterday evening, just as the present courier was leaving, a despatch arrived here from St. Petersburg for M. de Tatistscheff, and I thought it right to delay the departure of the courier until I heard what the Russian Ambassador might have to communicate.

He came to my room soon after the arrival of his courier, and simply handed to me the Circular which his Court has addressed to its foreign embassies, on the subject of the order given to the Guards to hold themselves in readiness to march on the 13th (April 1). To this despatch, which is endorsed *duplicata*, and dated February 29, was added a Gazette Extraordinary from St. Petersburg, dated February 27 (O.S.).* I do not

---

* The Supplement Extraordinary of the *Petersburger Zeitung* of February 27 contained the Sultan's *Hattischerif* of December 20, 1827. In this Imperial Decree (which was not intended as a manifesto to the Powers, but as necessary information to the governors of the Turkish provinces), Russia was designated the irreconcilable enemy of the Ottoman kingdom and faith; the insurrection of the Greeks and the defection of two friendly Powers, England and France, was imputed to Russia; and finally all Mussulmen were called to arms for the defence of the faith, the throne, and kingdom. To this publication by the official journal, the Russian Government subjoined an explanation which left no doubt as to its purpose. Contemporaneously with this declaration to its own people, Russia gave similar declarations to all the European courts in the Circular Despatch of February 29. In these Russia enumerated all its notorious grievances and complaints against the Porte, especially the *Hattischerif* itself. It did not declare war, but prepared for war, and set its troops in motion. To the allies it left the choice of material or moral help, even proposed to them to

send these despatches, for the Prince de Lieven will
have received them long before the present courier can
reach London.

The motives alleged by the Russian Circular confirm
our apprehensions. If I had not already discovered a
parallel with Bonaparte's system, I should be forced to
do so now, in consequence of the new Russian manifestoes. They are modelled on the manifestoes of the
French Empire; it is not only the fundamental idea
which is identical, but the manner of putting it, of dis-
guising it, of making it fluent—all recalls their style.

May it not be said that the Emperor of the North
has been aroused by a sudden attack of the Sultan, that
the Emperor Nicholas has been wakened from the sleep
of the just, from a sleep which nothing has hitherto disturbed, not even the noise of the cannon at Navarino?

An inoffensive and confiding Power is attacked unawares by an imperious neighbour, ungrateful and for-
getful of the numerous proofs of a faithful friendship.
It is the Sultan apparently, who, taking the tone of
a Turk to please his people, has declared war against
the Russian Empire; it is he also who, by his manifesto,
appeals to the allies of Russia; it is he who disturbs
the commerce of a peaceable neighbour; it is he, in
short, who has already begun the war. . . . . But the
Porte has declared war upon us also: read the enclosed
report from our consul at Scutari, and you will see that
our grievances are not less than those of Russia. Our
army, however, will not prepare to avenge this affront
just yet.

suspend their obligations arising from the Treaty of London, in which case
it would continue the conflict alone which the three had begun. It took a
purely Russian point of view of the war, and declared itself ready to hasten,
by this war, the solution of the other questions emanating from the London
Treaty.—ED.

M. de Tatistscheff came to see me this morning. He showed me the despatch of February 14 (O.S.) addressed by the Russian Cabinet to Prince Lieven. The mere reading of it gave me the key to the recent communication made to us by the French Cabinet.

I have no doubt Your Highness knows of the above despatch of February 14. It fulfils all that for two years we have dreaded and foreseen. Full of animus against the English Government, it is a condemnation of the Triple Alliance. The only thing which appears to us less detestable than the rest of this despatch, is the word Peloponnesus, which is there employed to designate the aim of the allies.

Into what a labyrinth of evils is Europe now thrown! On the one hand is the gratuitous war which Russia is now about to begin, but the end of which no one can foresee. Of what avail are simple phrases of moderation contradicted by all the acts of the invading Power, in comparison with the flagrant dangers which all the more surpass human foresight, since the Porte is at the same time assailed from without and harassed at home? Who will dare for a single instant to contemplate the scenes of anarchy to which European Turkey may, and I will even say to which she must, become a prey? If the Sultan bends under the weight of the misfortunes which overwhelm him, what will not be the consequences? If he resists, what will become of himself and his Empire?

On the other hand there is the terrible Greek complication. The allies of Russia are invited to take part in it; the principal Power wishes to admit them to finish the work recently begun; but do they not wish for more? In this case she saves them the trouble; for she alone can manage the Russian affair and the task common to the allies.

If in so critical a moment we can find any one reason for satisfaction, it is, without doubt, the feeling of our entire independence!

It is not our province to set forth anything which could be considered as a plan, or of a nature corresponding with the gravity of the danger. Before collecting our own thoughts, we shall wait to hear what they have to say to us from London. Tell the Duke of Wellington he can speak to us with perfect frankness; he knows well he risks nothing in being open with us. I cannot, by this courier, enter into any details whatever on the new position of affairs, inasmuch as I have not yet been able to submit to His Imperial Majesty the communications just made to us by the Russian Cabinet.

DOM MIGUEL'S FIRST APPEARANCE AT LISBON.

Metternich to Bombelles, in Lisbon,
Vienna, April 7, 1828.

895. It would be superfluous to tell you that the account you give of the weak and reprehensible conduct of the Infant, ever since his arrival at Lisbon, has profoundly affected His Majesty the Emperor, and unhappily leaves us in no doubt that this young Prince, who had every opportunity of founding the restoration of the Portuguese monarchy on a solid and durable basis, and who had moreover the certainty of being supported in that noble enterprise by all the great Powers of Europe, will ruin himself by yielding to perfidious counsels, which, if he blindly follows, will infallibly lead him to perjure himself, and place him in the attitude of a usurper.

Nothing can, in truth, justify the hesitation and delay of the Infant to take the oath prescribed by the Charter ; the ambiguous manner in which he proceeded to this solemn act ; the way in which it has been brought to the knowledge of the public ; the culpable weakness which has from the first tolerated the seditious cries of a vile populace till, emboldened by impunity, they have even taken possession of the avenues to the palace, and there dictated the law ; lastly, the obstinacy with which the Infant has refused to make a proclamation that, while calming anxiety, would have made known to the public

the line of conduct he intended to follow, and his resolution to restrain all, and treat the ill-disposed with
severity.

Such are, however, the irreparable faults which the
young Prince has committed at his first appearance, and
the consequences of which he will find it very difficult
to remove. It would even seem, according to the
news from Lisbon up to March 16, that these first faults
have been followed by faults graver still, and that an
imminent crisis threatens the existence of the Portuguese Government: the dissolution of the Chambers,
pronounced as it appears by the Infant, must hasten
the moment; and if the Count of Villa-Real has actually
sent in his resignation as Minister of Foreign Affairs, I
see no other person in the ministry who could or would
put any limits to the reactions with which Portugal
is threatened.

In so deplorable a situation, for which we see no
remedy, you can imagine that I have no instructions
to give you, except that you must not in any case
or under any circumstances whatever depart from the
principles consecrated by the Protocols of Vienna; *

---

* The most important document in the Protocols of Vienna is Dom
Miguel's letter to Dom Pedro, because in it expression is given to Dom Pedro's
rights and Dom Miguel's duties with regard to the Charter which had been
given to Portugal. This letter, dated Vienna, October 19, 1827, was as
follows:—'Sire! I have received the decree which your Royal and Imperial
Majesty deigned to address to me on July 3, in which your Majesty
nominated me Lieutenant and Regent of the kingdoms of Portugal, the
Algarves, and their dependencies; and in accordance with the sovereign
determinations of your Majesty, I immediately made the necessary arrangements for enabling me to repair to Lisbon, in order to fulfil the wise and
paternal views of your Majesty, in governing and ruling the above-named
kingdoms, in agreement with the constitutional Charter which your Majesty
has granted to the Portuguese nation. All my efforts tend to the maintenance of existing institutions in Portugal, and to contribute as far as is in
my power to the preservation of public tranquillity in these countries, by

they have received the sanction of all the Powers of
Europe; and if it pleases the Infant—who solemnly
engaged to take them for the basis of his conduct
in Portugal—to violate his engagements, the Emperor
our august master will never consent to be an accomplice in so culpable a proceeding. His Majesty will
never depart from the duties imposed upon him by
his sovereignty, his personal relations with the Emperor Dom Pedro, and his latest transactions, in short,
with the Prince, the British Government, and his august
allies; and the Emperor will never favour the usurpation of the Infant Dom Miguel. You have therefore
anticipated the intentions of his Majesty in neglecting no
means, direct or indirect, of enlightening the young
prince as to the dangers of the evil course into which
he is allowing himself to be led; and I quite approve
of your not hesitating to unite your efforts to those of
the English ambassador for this end. If they have been
foiled by a more powerful influence and by the culpable
weakness of the Infant, the fault is not yours, and the
Emperor does you justice in this respect; but his
Majesty, being quite decided in this painful complication
to follow the same line of conduct adopted by the Court
of London, I beg you to adhere to the rules laid down
in your instructions; to take part, consequently, in any
steps in which the English ambassador desires to associate himself with you, in order to prevent the Infant
from departing from the engagements he has contracted;
and, lastly, to be guided by the directions which Prince
Esterhazy may be in a position to send you, after

opposing myself to factions which shall never have my support, whatever be
their origin.'
 The three Protocols may be found in De Castro, *Collecção*, etc., vol. vi.
p. 20 (Lisbon, 1857).—ED.

having consulted with the Duke of Wellington. I have given authority to that ambassador by the present courier, and I do not hesitate to authorise you personally, in case Mr. Lamb receives orders from his Government to leave Lisbon, to depart at the same time and to follow him to London, where you will await further orders from your Court.*

* This did in fact take place. The Cortes convoked by Dom Miguel declared Dom Pedro to have forfeited his right to the throne of Portugal, and on June 26 they proclaimed Dom Miguel King of Portugal, and the Austrian ambassador, like the representatives of the other Powers, broke off all diplomatic intercourse with the Portuguese Government, on account of the illegal summoning of the Cortes, and left Lisbon as soon as it became evident that Dom Miguel would accept the offered crown. On July 30, a decree appeared, signed ' *El Rey,*' in which Dom Miguel accepted the resolutions of the Cortes, appointing him successor to the late King John VI. See 903.—ED.

CONVERSATION OF ZICHY WITH THE EMPEROR NICHOLAS ON THE AUSTRIAN PROPOSALS.

Zichy to Metternich, St. Petersburg, April 24, 1828.

896. I had the honour to deliver to his Majesty the Emperor, at a private audience, on Monday, April 21 (9), the autograph letter of our august master, which I had been charged to present to that sovereign. I will now give your Highness a faithful and detailed account of the conversation which I had with his Imperial Majesty on the important affairs of the moment.

The interview lasted about two hours. His Majesty deigned to listen to me with perfect calmness and great attention. After I had given him the substance of the voluminous communications which your Highness addressed to me by the courier of the 5th—the mere reading of which was a work of several consecutive days for me—the Emperor replied, and explained to me without a moment's hesitation his whole position, and the point of view from which he regarded the duties which the present circumstances imposed upon him, and from which he declared he could not exempt himself in any way without compromising his honour, as well as the dignity and interests of the Russian Empire.

' It is necessary,' said the Emperor, ' to go to the root of the matter, and, to give you a clear and precise idea of my position and my political transactions, I will narrate the events which have taken place since I found

myself at the head of affairs. After the death of the
Emperor, my brother, I was called upon to settle and
conclude an affair which had occupied him unsuccess-
fully for years, and which he had always vainly hoped
to arrange in concert with his allies—namely, the removal of the existing differences with the Porte, and the
redressing of the just grievances of Russia against the
Ottoman Government. The Emperor, my brother, being
convinced that the course which he had followed never
would effect the object, had decided to make war in
order to attain it, and war would positively have taken
place if death had not removed him, and plunged us
into grief by a new catastrophe which threatened the
existence of the whole family. The Almighty has blessed
my efforts: we have not been the victims of that treason; I have triumphed over the abominable conspiracy
against the Emperor my brother and all my family; I
have succeeded in restoring order and obedience; I have
set myself to follow in the footsteps of my late brother,
and I have laid down clearly what justice and the treaties—which the Porte had never observed towards us—
authorise me to demand from it. After innumerable
difficulties and tergiversations, employed by the Turks
to elude our demands, they at last consented (seeing
that my resolution was immovable) to send to me,
at Ackerman, negotiators to terminate our differences
amicably. Whilst we were occupied with this affair,
the Duke of Wellington arrived at St. Petersburg. He
spoke to me of the insurrection of the Greeks; of the
powerlessness of the Porte to put down the rebels and
to restore order; of the horrible sufferings and objectless
bloodshed; lastly, of the losses which the commerce of
all the nations had sustained for years, and to which it
would still be exposed unless an end was put to this sad

state of things. I replied to the Duke that I was quite
disposed to agree to any measure which he thought
likely to lead to that end ; but that, in truth, I was such
a novice in business and diplomacy that I had not entertained the possibility of attaining it by negotiations ;
that if he would give me his ideas I would willingly
accept any means that would lead to it. The articles
of the protocol signed at St. Petersburg on April 4 were
the result of our interview. I should here observe that
it was by my express request that Article V. of the said
protocol was drawn up and inserted, namely :—" That
neither of the two contracting Powers should seek any
augmentation of territory, exclusive influence, or commercial advantage for its subjects, other than those
which every other nation could equally obtain." After
some days of reflection on the part of the Duke of Wellington, he accepted my proposition, and this article
was inserted in the protocol. I believe,' added his Majesty, ' that it is the first time England has been induced
to take part in an enterprise offering expense and risk
without prospect of acquisition or advantage to her
commerce. As it is far from my thoughts to dream of
any increase of territory, this clause was quite accept-
able to me, and I made the proposal to assure myself
that England had not in view the commercial advantages or predominant influence at which she so often
aims. I recollect,' continued the Emperor, ' saying to
the Duke of Wellington : "But tell me, marshal, how
do you think the Turks will take what we are doing to
prevent them from putting down their rebellious subjects ? Will they patiently endure what we wish to
dictate to them ?" The Duke of Wellington replied :
" Oh, the Turks, when they see our serious determination, will never proceed to extremities; all that

will be necessary on our part will be a few frigates to prevent them from commencing hostilities, to intimidate them, and to make them listen to reason ; besides, there will be no war."' The Emperor assured me he then replied : ' But yet, if our frigates were compelled to fire, would the Turks consider these guns as messengers of peace ? ' The Duke maintained that they would never come to that extremity, nor to a war which no one desired. ' The only condition,' said the Emperor, ' which the Duke of Wellington expressly imposed upon me at the time of the signature of the protocol was that Lord Strangford, who was then ambassador at St. Petersburg, was not to be informed of it. I could not at all comprehend the reason why he wished to observe a mysterious silence towards the representative of the King his master, but I promised him that I would only mention it to my allies, to whom I was obliged to give confidential cognisance of the protocol, in order to induce them to take part in it at their convenience. In the meantime our conferences at Ackerman went on firmly, and we succeeded in overcoming all obstacles and signing the treaty which was to put an end to our just causes of complaint against the Porte. Russia was satisfied, and nothing remained but to see the fulfilment of the conditions which had been stipulated for.' Here the Emperor passed rapidly over the succeeding events. ' The treaty called by you " The Triple Treaty " was signed at London in consequence of the protocol ; you and Prussia did not think fit to accede to it, which I shall always sincerely deplore, for I am convinced that if all the five Cabinets had held the same threatening language at Constantinople, and that if we had been able to agree on the form to be employed in order to obtain the pacification of the insurgent provinces, what has since hap-

pened never could have taken place.   The Divan would
have submitted to our demands; the countries in insurrection would have been pacified; the action of the
Holy Alliance would have once more been grandly
manifested, and its irresistible strength would have been
displayed.   I hold religiously to its conservative principles,' said the Emperor, 'and I shall always be the
warmest partisan of the Holy Alliance, which will find
in me one of its staunchest supporters.   I repeat that
I detest, I abhor the Greeks, although they are my co-
religionists; they have behaved in a shocking, blamable,
even criminal manner; I look upon them as subjects in
open revolt against their legitimate sovereign; I do not
desire their enfranchisement; they do not deserve it,
and it would be a very bad example for all other
countries if they succeeded in establishing it.   I have
not recognised the independence of the Spanish colonies
in America, and I think the proposal you have just
made at London concerning Greece is in contradiction
with the principles you profess, and a departure
from your true character.   I remain, for my part, pure
and faithful to my monarchical principles.   I beg you
to tell the Emperor that he will always find in me a
faithful and powerful ally, ready to give him my hand
on every occasion, and to recognise only legitimate
rights.   If he should need my assistance in any complication, he will find me always ready to help him.   I
give you my word, he has but to command me.   I have
no views of aggrandisement, ambition, or conquest.   I
know all the world thinks otherwise; but events will
prove that I wish only for peace, the internal happiness, the prosperity, and the commerce of my people.
The immense loss sustained by commerce in consequence
of the measures of the Porte, the continual provoca-

tions Russia has to endure, the non-execution of the Treaty of Ackerman, oblige me to draw the sword to support my just claims. From the moment my adversaries do me justice, I shall be ready to listen to any words of peace and reconciliation they may bring forward. I do not hide from myself the inconveniences and even the grave dangers of the enterprise which I am on the eve of commencing, but that shall not make me shrink from my duty. If circumstances beyond all human calculations should lead the Porte to accomplish its own destruction, I should deplore it very sincerely. I prefer to believe that this deplorable catastrophe will not take place. I am going to place myself at the head of my army, holding myself in readiness to receive at any instant the overtures which the Sultan may still wish to make when he sees that my part is irrevocably taken, and with the power of stopping my troops when I think it convenient. I shall not make war in the Turkish manner. If the Porte really intends to admit my claims, I will receive its proposals whenever they are made to me. For the rest, no difficulty shall make me abandon my enterprise, even should it result in the fall of the Ottoman Empire. That would indeed be a new misfortune, a disastrous complication, for I see no means of reconstructing that edifice if it fell to pieces. But even this consideration, grave though it be, shall not stop me. I owe it to the Empire of Russia to procure for it what the treaties promise: I owe to it to establish in a clear and positive manner the rights which it cannot renounce. My course is marked out; I shall follow it with constancy and firmness, and if God helps me and blesses my arms, I will prove to Europe that I have no intention of making conquests, and that I know how to be satisfied with my position, such as it is.'

Having listened with profound attention to the words of the Emperor, I respectfully asked permission to make some observations in reply. His Majesty graciously assented, and I answered him as follows : ' You have deigned, Sire, to express yourself with a frankness and condescension which the Emperor my master will rightly appreciate. But suffer me to speak to your Majesty with the loyalty and straightforwardness which characterise my sovereign, and of which it is my duty to be the faithful interpreter. I beseech you, Sire, to read with attention the letter which I have just had the honour to give you from the Emperor. The heart of the Emperor answers to your Majesty's with all the confidence which the purity of your principles, Sire, and your elevated sentiments inspire my sovereign. The grave complication which threatens the peace of Europe imposes upon him the duty of exhorting you, Sire, at a time when great resolutions may decide the destinies of an empire, and perhaps of social order altogether, not to be precipitate, but calmly to consider the remedy proposed to your Majesty by the Emperor for the frightful evils which he feels convinced we may expect unless we can restore to the councils of the allied sovereigns the harmony and system which has been hitherto followed with so much success. Your Majesty will permit me to retrace the steps you have taken in this affair. Your Cabinet, with that of London, signed the protocol of April 4, which has been since converted into a treaty, signed at London, to which France has acceded. Austria and Prussia had reasons which prevented them from taking part in it. Nevertheless we have not ceased to use every effort at Constantinople to remove the differences between the three Courts and the Ottoman Porte. The Sultan has resisted them all. The

battle of Navarino took place contrary to the wishes of
your Majesty and your allies. This event has done
nothing to alter the determinations of the Porte. The
representatives of the Courts at length thought it necessary to retire from Constantinople, declaring that they
could only continue their residence in that capital on
condition that the Porte accepted the Treaty of London. The Porte did not yield, and the representatives
left Constantinople. Your Majesty was thus deprived
of the advantages of the Treaty of Ackerman, the Porte
having declared, after the departure of the representatives, that all that had passed rendered void the treaties
signed between it and Russia; and the Divan, in its
blind despair, has been led into a course which the
Emperor my master highly disapproves. Your Majesty
does not wish for the enfranchisement of the Greeks;
you have deigned to express your feelings and your way
of looking at that question. And yet the Greeks will
be made free, in spite of your Majesty's wishes and
declarations. The Treaty of Ackerman infringed, you
are now obliged to make war, of which you would
not otherwise have dreamed, having obtained all that
you desired from the Ottoman Porte for the real interests
of Russia. The war will still be made against your
will, but as an imperious necessity which circumstances
have required. You desire the preservation of the
Porte, and yet you decide on a measure which will
perhaps ruin it, or give rise to combinations and events
far beyond all the calculations of human foresight.
See, Sire, the picture which I have dared to place before
you, with the earnest prayer that you will weigh what I
have had the honour to represent to you. The future
will some day justify all our apprehensions. There
may be still time, Sire, to give a more beneficial direc-

tion to our united efforts; but it is for your Majesty
to use moderation towards a feeble, irritated, and sus-
picious Government, no longer conscious what part it
ought to take. If that Government could be inspired
with confidence in a better future, perhaps it might consent to the required concessions.'

The Emperor replied: 'I cannot persuade myself
that we shall succeed in making the Porte yield by mere
threats or by negociations; cannon and the bayonet are
necessary to frighten them, and to conquer the resistance which the Sultan opposes to everything we have
hitherto done to prove our desire reasonable. All my
measures are taken to this effect, and I will not draw
back. The injury which this state of things has
done to the commerce of Odessa amounts already to
about thirty millions of roubles. The reports which I
have recently received from Servia inform me that the
Turks exercise every imaginable vexation and cruelty
in that province, notwithstanding the stipulations of
the Treaty of Ackerman. All my ports are closed; the
produce of our soil cannot be sold, because everything
must pass through that narrow channel of Constantinople, which is closed to my vessels. This is my
present position. I have in my hand proofs that the
Turks wished to prevent the peace I was about to conclude with the Persians. These documents will be
published, that the public may judge of the conduct of
the Porte with regard to me. I have, however, succeeded in making an honourable peace with Persia, and
if God helps me in the present enterprise, I shall also
make peace with the Porte, and they will be convinced
that I wish for nothing but what is necessary for Russian
commerce, and what was, in fact, mine by treaty. I
ask you,' said the Emperor, 'what will Austria do, if by

any unforeseen chance the Turkish Government should fall?'

'That is precisely, Sire,' replied I, 'what the Emperor, in his anxiety, represents to you, with the object of avoiding the commotion and general confusion, which would arise in Europe if that event were brought about by the war which you are on the point of undertaking.'

The Emperor then said: 'I have read attentively the memorandum (No. 893) which your Cabinet presented at the Conference of London, on the means which it proposes to the Porte to escape from its embarrassing position with regard to the three Courts. It was long before I could understand it, for I could not persuade myself that your real meaning was that the Porte should entirely give up its insurgent provinces. Such a proposal to the Porte is ridiculous. Besides, it would, I think, be a very bad example to give to the rebels. The Greeks must remain—I repeat it—under the suzerainty of the Porte, if they are permitted to exist at all. But how can your Court propose such a thing while it disapproves of what we desire to do?'

'It is precisely, Sire,' replied I, 'because we believe that the Porte would sooner resign itself to the total loss of a province than admit the principle of an interference and intervention by foreigners in its internal affairs. The religious principles of the Turks reject this interference, and their consent will never be obtained by that means.'

'If,' said the Emperor, 'my allies at London agree to bring this proposal forward, I will not oppose it; but, I repeat, the Porte will not accept it, and I expect no success from this step. As for the suspension of arms, we learn from Paris that the Greeks do not wish to accept it, unless the three Courts, under whose protec-

-tion they have placed themselves, approve. Admiral de Rigny, moreover, declares that he can see no possibility of this armistice taking place, for the Turks would take the opportunity to provision and strengthen their weak .points, and then after three months their position would be as much better as ours would be worse.'

The Emperor terminated this long and important conversation by saying : ' I have expressed my thoughts freely to you ; give an account of them to the Emperor. I shall keep my word ; I employ no *finesse* and have no reservations. I am but a general of brigade, who understands nothing of policy nor of diplomacy ; but I am attached to the Emperor ; I respect him, and he will always find me in the path of honour and principle. If he and I join hands and understand each other, since, we are still masters at home, we have nothing to fear from disorders on any side. We suffice for all the needs of Europe, because our resources, if we know how to employ and unite them, are powerful, and we know how to make ourselves obeyed. What say you to all that is taking place in Portugal ? Is the Infant behaving wisely ? Do they write to you about this ?' I told the Emperor what your Highness wrote to me in your private letter (see No. 895 on the same subject). His Majesty immediately replied, ' Well, without con- .sulting you, I have sent the same instructions to my ambassador. If the Infant can so far forget himself as to neglect his duty towards his brother and sovereign, my embassy has orders to retire from Lisbon, and to .declare to the Infant that we will never give our approbation to any act which cannot be justified before the tribunal of the King his sovereign, of whom he is but the lieutenant. You see,' continued his Majesty, ' that we agree when monarchical principles are in question.

The Emperor will always find it so with me, for I have been brought up in these principles, and events have confirmed me in them.'

His Imperial Majesty pressed my hand, as if he were relieved at having said all that was in his heart, and dismissed me with assurances of his hearty good will.

THE RUSSO-TURKISH WAR.

Metternich to Apponyi, in Paris, Vienna, May 9,
1828.

897. The Russo-Turkish War—that war which we
have foreseen as the only probable, or perhaps even
possible, result of the course which has been taken for
years—is about to begin, and everything shows that it
will be carried on with great vigour by Russia. All
agree that it must be so. The necessity of striking decisive blows to attain the double advantage of a prompt
pacification in those countries where disorder is making
many more ravages than the enemy's sabre, and of
making a strong impression on Europe at the commencement of the war, dictate this course. We do not
say that the plans of Russia arise from the desire of
conquest, properly so called. That Power does not
need to extend her frontiers to be mistress of the
Ottoman domains which border them; she has conquests of another kind to make in this same Empire,
and they will not fail her. The explanations on the
matter of indemnities, of which M. de Fontenay was
the interpreter, do not seem to us as yet to prejudice
the future. They talk of the loss of thirty millions
which the commerce of Odessa alone has sustained.
That allegation is false; Odessa has not yet lost anything, unless one reckons the loss which the prospect of
the war has caused to speculators. But no matter; it

K K

is not a question of the commerce of one town nor of millions that we have to consider. Nothing inclines us to think that the result of the war will be what they expect; everything, on the contrary, tells us that the result will be different. I state this conviction simply as an acquittal of my political conscience, and not as a recrimination on a situation determined by a Power higher than the wishes of Cabinets.

Our desire is that Count de la Ferronays will not alter his course of vigorous action in order to maintain the Triple Alliance; and he may be assured of our frank co-operation in this respect in all places and on all occasions where our voice can exercise a salutary influence.

The knowledge that we, more than any other Court, are able to obtain as to the internal condition of the Ottoman Empire does not allow us to doubt that the success of the Russian armies will be easily accomplished. There is no security for the existence of the Ottoman Empire; and a question which we think should be regarded as indefinable—seeing that the three allies themselves have not yet been able to define it between them —is not of a nature to be resolved by a Government which has no pretensions to wisdom.

The world is thus in the presence of a very great evil, and I should be concealing the truth as to my feelings if I did not assure you that I regard as still more frightful the chances presented by the moral situation of France. My mind is here arrested, and all our wishes are concentrated in the hope that the evil will finally cause the awakening of good men who have allowed themselves to be led to the brink of a declivity bordering on a fathomless abyss. The question seems to me to be reduced to the alternative, whether this awakening will take place before the loss is consummated or not till after the catastrophe; and assuredly tears shed over ruins are at the best but useless tears.

ATTEMPT TO GAIN OVER THE ENGLISH CABINET TO AUSTRIA.

Metternich to Esterhazy, in London,
Vienna, May 31, 1828.

898. The report you have given us of the verbal communications of the Duke of Wellington is appreciated by us as everything is which comes from him. I think I could not better respond to his Grace's confidence than by enabling you to explain with perfect candour our views with regard to the grave circumstances of the moment.

In addressing myself to the Duke of Wellington I am not hindered by any of those considerations which are so often an obstacle to complete openness between Courts.

No one is more convinced than myself of the great qualities which distinguish this Minister—elevation of thought and energy of character ; neither have I any doubt of the value which he attaches to the closeness of the relations between our two Courts.

The analysis made by the Duke of Wellington of the recent declarations from the Cabinet of St. Petersburg entirely agrees with the opinion which we had from the first formed of these documents. (See note to 894).

The substance of the different Russian despatches may be given in a few words :—

Russia, while affecting the greatest moderation, opens the door to tremendous exactions. She wishes by this means to secure a double benefit, moral and material, in advance. Whatever may be the course of events, she wishes to obtain, by the position she has taken, one or other of these benefits, and it will not be difficult to obtain both.

She charges the allies, and more directly England, with the pretended necessity in which she finds herself placed to act as she has done.   .

Whatever happens, nothing will prevent her from being the Power to liberate the Greeks.

Russia speaks of moderation, and renews her protestation that she aims neither at conquests of territory nor at the destruction of the Ottoman Empire.

We have long ago declared to the Court of London our conviction as to the real plans of the Emperor Nicholas concerning the future existence of that Empire. He does not desire its death, but its ruin ; he does not care to add small portions to his territory in Europe— he would require the whole, or the greater part of the whole, to make the enterprise worth the trouble. We are not, therefore, disposed to believe that, at the present moment, the Emperor can aim at material conquests, which would only be made to the detriment of the Principalities. He takes another direction, which must seem more advantageous. He will impose on the Porte pecuniary charges which will tax its resources to the utmost. It remains to be seen if the Sultan can satisfy these exactions. If he cannot, Russia will keep guarantees, and declare she has made no conquests.

The next peace will increase the demands already agreed to by the stipulations of former treaties, and completed by that of Ackerman, to such a point that, in fact, they will leave nothing to the Sultan but the exercise of a useless and dangerous suzerainty over the two Principalities of the Danube and Servia.

The Emperor Nicholas declares that it is absolutely necessary he should have guarantees to protect his commerce. He declares even that he desires the superiority of his influence to be established for ever at Constantinople. By what material means does his Imperial Majesty expect to arrive at these two ends? He does not say so, but there is no doubt that it is only by a positive and recognised preponderance that his end can be secured, for purely moral means cannot attain such an object.

The operations of the Russian army in Asia have commenced. They will be assisted by the operations of the fleet. The Russian forces are about to take possession of Anapa, Sukum-Kalé, and other places on the coast of Mingrelia and Armenia. These conquests appear so simple, and men's minds are so familiarised with them, that it is hardly to be supposed that any Power will consider this an open violation of the declared engagement not to do it. But, if our information is correct, we shall see the Persians in their turn take the offensive against the Turks, and Prince Abbas-Mirza will seek to indemnify the Shah for the loss of Persian Armenia by conquests in the Pachalik of Bagdad.

What will become of the Ottoman Power, attacked on all sides?

Two alternatives present themselves—its dissolution in consequence of a defence out of proportion with the force of the attack, or its submission to demands the necessary effect of which will be equivalent to speedy ruin. In a word, the Porte has the choice between death and a prolonged agony.

Of what importance, on the other hand, are the chances which Russia has managed with such undoubted skill? In either of the cases I have mentioned she can gain the object she has in view. If she contents herself with the second of the alternatives indicated, the Emperor will have found means to indemnify himself for the expenses he will have so gratuitously incurred, and to surround with an aureole of military glory the opening of a reign which had commenced under very sad auspices ; moreover, he will know how to make the most of a moderation to which the whole of Europe will be eager to render homage.

These are the real facts, and the Duke of Wellington has too much candour and rectitude of judgment to contradict them.

In such a state of things, and in face of a future so fraught with evil omens, the head of the Austrian Cabinet would fail in his duty if he did not express himself with perfect candour to the head of the British Government.

We have lately passed through an epoch all the more difficult for us, as the greatest evil has come from England herself, which long tradition had accustomed us to regard as the surest guardian of the many interests common to the two Powers. The same force of circumstances which would certainly have overthrown—if he had not been removed by death—the public man whose audacious conceptions had no other object but that of turning the world round in a circle of which his personal ambition occupied the centre—that same force of circumstances, let us say it boldly, has placed the Duke of Wellington at the head of affairs in Great Britain. The good which has succeeded the evil has not raised our hopes to a degree that seems impossible of attainment. . . .

The Eastern Question is so confused that even the prompt termination of the war now appears in many respects a morally frightful result. England may still exercise some influence on the *dénouement* of the drama; but we do not see that her Cabinet has taken any decided part, although we do justice to the perfect agreement of the Duke of Wellington's opinion with that which we ourselves have formed on the attitude of the Court of Russia and the value of her manifestoes.

You know that we should have considered it as a great mistake if the two Courts of the Triple Alliance had retired immediately from their engagements to Russia, or, what is much the same thing, if by such a decision they had released the Emperor Nicholas from certain of his engagements to them. But we sincerely regret that, when the Emperor of Russia had already made himself master of the occasion, the two Courts had not, instead of deliberating on points of mere form, taken advantage of the existence of their common treaty to arrest, or at any rate to hinder, what may lead to results which cannot be softened when once they are attained.

The despatch from Count Nesselrode to Prince Lieven, dated April 29 last, struck us more with the confusion of its proposals than for any other reason.*

The allies were right to regard themselves as bound by the Treaty of London, but they have committed a great error in separating the Russo-Turkish War from the same treaty. The truth is that the origin of this

---

* On Lord Aberdeen's answer to the Russian despatch of April 19, Gentz writes to Metternich, July 18, as follows:—'The note is written in a florid style, full of tiresome repetitions and punctilious verbosity; the work of a diplomatist who, between the necessity of telling the truth and the fear of displeasing, is driven hither and thither, neither able to defend his own cause (a bad enough one) nor venturing to attack the weakness of his adversaries with vigour; who trembles before the slightest criticism and covers over his well-founded fears with trivial compliments. It is evident that this document is written more for show than for any practical purpose.'—ED.

war is found in the treaty of July 6 ; the Emperor Nicholas should have consequently been stopped then. But the mistake is made, and there is nothing to do but to palliate it by a firm and decided step in future.

The Duke of Wellington will see in my candid explanation a new proof of the great importance we attach to the prompt conclusion of the dangerous course which Russia is now taking, so to speak, under the shield of her allies. A new era must follow the next arrangements between the Powers at war, and if I regard the present as lost, I must with all the more zeal fix my thoughts on the future ; and, in the anticipation of a better state of things between Austria and England, I believe I cannot avoid entering into some details.

I will begin by explaining to the Duke of Wellington what our position really is.

It is customary nowadays to regulate one's views by those of the journalists and pamphleteers. In representing Austria as crushed beneath the weight of inextricable financial and administrative embarrassments, the faction knew what it was about ; it wished to turn away the attention of Europe from a Power which time and events have not been able to make deviate from its political course, and the number of credulous people is immense. The spirit of sound criticism is extinct, and the fact that calumny attacks a living adversary does not enter into the calculations of these credulous men.

Austria is not dying ; we are full of life and vigour ; our troubles are not internal ; our people do not need to be excited—their just indignation rather needs to be calmed by the wisdom of the Government ; our army is what it has always been ; and if the gravest considerations have forced us to stand quietly aloof, we shall never be prevented by material difficulties from using the necessary strength to secure our own safety and to give assistance to those who need our support. It is not at a time—unexampled in the records of history—when three great Powers are united by one common bond, in spite of the views which divide them on the object of their union, that we should find it useful to increase alarm and distrust by putting ourselves in motion.

Austria is a central Power; she needs, consequently, to cover one or other of her flanks; and when Russia, France, and Great Britain are united, Austria cannot move without imminent risk to herself and to the whole social body.

But this state of things must come to an end, and it is to prepare and consolidate a better future that we should devote all our care. The Duke of Wellington may, therefore, be easy as to our internal state, and particularly as to the condition of our army. Our military system is not inclined to parade and play, for which reason it is all the stronger.

But the more we feel our strength, the great moderation which characterises the Emperor our august master, and the importance of a return to perfect confidence between our Court and that of London, the more we regret the daily hindrances to the establishment of that confidence from the organisation still existing in the department for Foreign Affairs in England. With regard to this, I appeal to the conscience of your Highness. In what relation does the ambassador of the Emperor stand with the Secretary of State? And, on the other hand, to what absolute nonentity does it not condemn the ambassador of his Britannic Majesty at our Court! Certainly the present is a most anxious moment, and under the beneficent administration of the Duke of Wellington, Lord Cowley finds himself without directions, just as he was under the administration of his predecessors, which was hostile towards us.

I beg you to impress upon his Grace how necessary and urgent it is that things should be changed on this important point. I have no secrets from the Prime Minister, and no confidence in him who ought to act as his intermediary with Europe. My mind is too practical not to see that Lord Dudley is connected with a whole order of things which will consequently disappear or triumph with him. But it is just because of this that I may expect with impatience that department which exercises such a direct influence over the relations of Great Britain with Europe will, with as little delay as possible, represent worthily the noble and useful thoughts of the head of the present Administration. . . .

I shall soon have the honour of returning to all these subjects, and I beg your Highness to use the most perfect frankness with the Duke of Wellington.*

* See Nos. 887 and 904.

THE FRENCH EXPEDITION TO THE MOREA.

Metternich to Trauttmansdorff, in Berlin,
Vienna, August 13, 1828.

899. The opinion which M. Ancillon has expressed on the French expedition to the Morea entirely coincides with my own. This enterprise injures the Court which attempts it, those who have authorised it, and, in short, the whole social order. To justify the latter statement, it is sufficient to draw your attention to the use the French newspapers already make of an event which is only in preparation, and to the advantage the disorganising factions seek to obtain from it. I should be inclined to treat the follies of these pamphleteers with a certain amount of contempt, but sad experience forbids us to pass lightly over the lucubrations of the French journalists. The expedition to the Morea will be the complement to the violation of principles of every kind which has distinguished the triple affair from the very beginning; it will perhaps serve as the point of departure for a new political movement.

The Greek Question is not, and never has been, anything in France but a mantle to cover a very different game; Philhellenism in that kingdom has had all the importance of an avowed political club. The Government speaks to us of a strong force pushing it forward; and that force, which it can no longer resist, was created by itself. Will it be better able to resist when, by compliance, it will have given to the factions new pledges of its passive obedience? The thing appears to me as little doubtful as is the tendency of parties in France. All are agreed more or less on one subject: that subject is the extension of frontiers. The aim of France is conquest, and the *Mobiles* who have launched both the Republic and the Empire in so dangerous a career now adopt the prevailing opinions. These *Mobiles* were the desire of the leaders at the time of the Revolution in order to occupy the attention of the masses with outward events, and, under the Empire, with the thirst for glory. They now act with equal force on the opposite parties, and each one thinks itself the most favoured. Our prediction, made long ago, of the evils which would necessarily occur and crush the social body at the sound of the first discharge of the political artillery which will burst over Europe — how has it been verified, and will it not be verified still more?

The attack seems to be directed against Italy. The parties in France—and I do not except a great number of Royalists—desire to replace in the peninsula what they call the influence of Austria by French influence. Certain that, without conquests consolidated by time—and the first ought to be that of a neighbouring kingdom—the material preponderance of France could make no way against our deliberate calmness, and our political conduct, (so conservative, and frankly acknowledged to be so by the Princes of Italy), it is to the people that the ambition of the faction is addressed. They are promised a *régime* to which the great majority in the peninsula object. The game is evident, and it is pushed to indecency. It will not make us alter our line of conduct. If it should ever go beyond its present limits, if it should be followed by facts, we shall know how to resist them, and

I hope that we shall succeed in the future as we have succeeded in the past.

What the French have long been accustomed to consider their natural frontiers the masses now aim at attaining, although the more prudent even among the imprudent try to conceal this.

The great and decisive question, therefore, is still, Will the Russian campaign of 1828 put an end to the war? If such should be the case, and it is assuredly the object of all our wishes, things, at least for a certain time, would be restored to something like order. Many plans would be overthrown, and it would take time to create new ones, to prepare them and to execute them, and to collect again the materials necessary for their execution. If, on the contrary, the war is renewed in the spring of next year, Europe will then see what good she gets from the Russo-Turkish War, and from the example of a French army which is to carry liberty and emancipation to a foreign nation.

In the midst of this political confusion, Austria does not take up arms; what we are doing is to count our disposable forces, and also those which are not so. Besides, the French Government is as indifferent to what we are doing as to what we are not doing. It knows both, and it knows especially that our looks are not turned towards the East. Neither are the factions uneasy, but they make a noise and abuse the Power which annoys them. All this is in the natural order of things, and I confess that I should be more anxious if the parties were silent about us than I am when they affect to treat us with contempt. It is the future of Europe which makes me uneasy; and I am quite overcome by the consideration of the causes which have produced so awful a state of things, and which, while the evil is still so great, prevent an agreement between those Powers whose efforts for the maintenance of peace Providence had so long crowned with success.

I have been led to enter into these explanations by the uniformity of ideas which every day proves to exist so happily between the two great intermediary Courts, and of which the few words spoken recently by you to M. Ancillon furnish us with a new proof.

THE THEATRE OF WAR.

Metternich to Ottenfels, in Constantinople,
Vienna, September 4, 1828.

900. The situation, as indicated by the news from all quarters, is as follows:—The Russian army, which did not exceed forty thousand when the Emperor left it for Odessa, is now before Schumla. It has taken several positions, and has advanced as far as the fortifications on the Ottoman frontier. It has covered its position by redoubts; some corps have been pushed forwards into the defiles of the Balkans, in the direction of the communications of the Turkish camp with Adrianople. In the Russian camp they estimate the force of Hussein Pacha at forty thousand men, of whom the half are cavalry.

The Pacha remains quiet; with the exception of some detachments which he has sent forward, no fighting has taken place. One of these detachments, consisting of two thousand horse, attacked the communications of the Russian army and inflicted some damage.

The Russian Guards have crossed the Danube. They are advancing in the direction of Varna. The third *corps d'armée*, under General Scherbatow, is advancing towards Moldavia. It is said to be destined to relieve that of General Roth, who is going to strengthen the army before Schumla. The public voice estimates the reinforcements now marching to join the army at sixty thousand men.

The *corps d'armée* placed near Widdin must have received a reinforcement of twelve thousand Albanians. They have taken a position in Little Wallachia, where the Russians had only a few troops. Count Langeron, having become the commander-in-chief of the two Principalities, has left Bucharest in haste, gathering round him as many as he could to meet the enemy. On August 22 (the date of our last reports from Bucharest) it was said that the enemy had been surprised at Kalafat.

General Menzikoff, whom the Emperor has entrusted with the siege of Varna, has driven the Turks, who were advancing from all sides, back into that place. Some gunboats have been taken before Varna by the fleet commanded by Admiral Greigh. . . .

The enemy has sustained great loss before Silistria, which is making a vigorous defence. Giurgewo, not being carefully observed, had pushed forward detachments in all directions.

Provisions in Roumelia are scarce; the army consequently is suffering. There is a great scarcity of water. The hospitals are crowded.

The corps scattered throughout the Principalities are also afflicted with sickness. The plague has ceased at Bucharest.

The whole situation may be summed up thus:

The Russian army which commenced the war has been found too weak to obtain a decided success. It is clear that the war was undertaken on the supposition that the Porte would yield to fear. This supposition not being realised, great operations had necessarily to be suspended until the arrival of reinforcements.

The plan of the Russian campaign shows deficiencies which might have already led to the most disastrous results if the attitude of the Turks had not been purely negative. I use this word, for 'defensive' would not be the proper term. The defensive does not exclude the offensive under given circumstances.

The position of the invading army is in contradiction to all military rules. To secure but one passage across a river like the Danube, to choose that point on the most distant part of the line, to take Braïla with great loss of men instead of making sure of Rustchuk and Silistria, to fail to provide Wallachia with imposing forces, and allow the enemy to remain master of all the left bank of the river, to rush with a light heart into a long and dangerous defile—this is not to make war, properly so-called, but to reckon on the enemy's faults, and to seek for no success but what results from these same faults.

There is nothing, however, to prove that the Turks have not already committed all the mistakes which the Russians hoped they would ; it remains to be seen if they will continue those mistakes to the end of the campaign. It is certain that a combined operation between the army of Widdin, the numerous garrisons of the places on the Danube, and Hussein Pacha, would already have driven the Russians beyond the Lower Danube and cleared the Principalities. The propitious moment for such an operation would have been that when the Emperor prudently left the army, when it was in so hazardous a position as that before Schumla. When the reinforcements have arrived, the opportunity will be gone.

This is the state of affairs on one side of the picture. The landing of the French expedition in the Morea, which may be effected at this very moment, completes the other side.

What does or does not the Porte desire? That is what no one can say. If it is time that it desires to gain, it is calculating falsely.

Two great Powers are engaged in a struggle with the Porte. They must either be defeated and their armies pursued, or unpleasant conditions must be submitted to. The Porte would have some reason for desiring to gain time if it could reckon on subsequent assistance in these painful conflicts; but as that aid is not to be found in Europe, she is wrong, a hundred times wrong, in not fighting the enemy when it is in a difficult position, or in not yielding the less, where it will infallibly in the end have to yield the more.

If a great and brilliant action were to change the position of things, the first part of the opinion I have pronounced would be weakened, but the second would remain as strong as ever. Beaten, the Russians will not yield, for they could not yield; thrown back for a time, they would recover themselves more easily than the Divan imagines.

I am thus brought back to what I have constantly pointed out. To this I can add nothing, nor will I take anything away. . . .

INTERVIEW WITH PRINCE WILLIAM OF PRUSSIA.

Metternich to Esterhazy, in London,
Vienna, September 14, 1828.

901. Among the foreigners who have come to the camp of Baden (Traiskirchen) are the Princes William and Augustus of Prussia.

The former (see note to 888) is a prince distinguished in every way. You know that he is a close adherent of the Emperor Nicholas, and that he only left St. Petersburg, after a sojourn of several months, when his Imperial Majesty repaired to the army. Prince William had made great efforts to obtain from the King his father permission to join the Russian army. The King refused it.

Knowing the privileges and opportunities of his Royal Highness, I was naturally anxious to hear his opinion with regard to the position of affairs at the theatre of war.

Here are the results at which I have arrived:

I assume in the first place that Prince William is well informed as to the mind of his Majesty the Emperor of Russia. He was with him for months before the commencement of hostilities, and I know for certain that not only has the Emperor great personal confidence in him, but that there is an active correspondence between them. Therefore I consider that the words of the Prince have all the importance of words from the Emperor Nicholas himself.

The following facts, which are certainly not in contradiction with the ideas I have already formed, are thus demonstrated.

· The frightful complication of the moment owes its source to a spirit of levity—I may even say of actual puerility on the part of the young Monarch and the young courtiers who are about him—excited and fomented by the extreme weakness of the Cabinet, and · the culpable folly of some blunderers.

Serious war was considered impossible. How could these miserable Turks, who at each step betrayed their weakness and their fear by submitting to all sorts of outrages—how could they dare to enter upon a war with Russia! Turkish plenipotentiaries would be sure to present themselves as soon as the first steps were taken by the Russian army.

The Emperor was quite sincere in his objection to making any conquests of territory. He simply wished to commence his reign by a brilliant stroke, and at the same time to secure perfect liberty to the commerce of his Empire.

Sounded by me as to the substantial difficulties which might prevent this end from being attained, Prince William assured me he could not say exactly the means proposed by the Emperor, but he thought they might be found in the two following conditions : Demolition of all the Turkish strongholds on the Danube, as well as the forts of the Bosphorus and Dardanelles.

On my observation that the Ottoman Empire might well feel its very existence threatened by the execution of a plan which, for that reason, would meet with a strong opposition on the part of the Porte, and to the

success of which the Powers trading in the Levant would
also find great difficulty in co-operating, the Prince
replied, without hesitation, ' that he did not agree with
me ; that the Porte deserved to be punished, and must
not be listened to ; that, as for the maritime Powers,
they could not with reason oppose the plan, seeing that
it had never entered into the Emperor's thoughts to
hinder commerce, but that, on the contrary, he desired
to make it as free as possible.'

The Prince confessed that the facts had not, up to
the present time, answered their expectations, but that
they would no doubt be fulfilled in the next campaign.
He admitted, on the other hand, that this state of
things endangered the peace of Europe, and that therefore the Powers should try to prevent the necessity for
renewing the war.

Our reports from St. Petersburg convince us that
the war is unpopular among all classes of society.   It is
the same in the provinces, and, what is more, in the
army.   You will remember that this was our opinion
at a time when all Europe thought that the national
and military movement in Russia seriously threatened
the maintenance of peace.   The war is the work of a
few individuals, among whom the Russian Ambassadors
at London and Paris have played the principal part.
We may be allowed to express our regret that nowhere
has the knowledge that we must have of the public
feeling and resources of the States adjacent to our own
been taken into account.

The Emperor Nicholas left Odessa on the first of this
month, by ship.   The diplomatists are all to follow
his Majesty.   It appears that Lord Heytesbury alone has
decided to prolong his stay.   The Empress also intends

to leave that city in a short time, and, after having made a tour of the Crimea, she reckons on returning to St. Petersburg towards the end of the present month.

There is no doubt that some decisive step is to be taken soon after the Emperor returns to the army. . . .

CONTINUED EFFORTS FOR PEACE.

Metternich to Esterhazy, in London,
Vienna, September 14, 1828.

902. . . . The news from the theatre of war
continues to prove the insufficiency of the means the
Russians had at their disposal at the beginning of the
campaign. The reinforcements, which I can hardly
estimate at more than fifty thousand men, should by
this time have joined the *corps d'armée* which they are
destined to support. These reinforcements are composed of twenty thousand of the Guards and about
thirty thousand troops of the line under General Scherbatow. The former are to repair to Varna ; the latter
to the Principalities and to the blockade of the strongholds on the Danube, as well as for the siege of Silistria.
This is a very small number for so many purposes. . . .

Every day also increases the embarrassments of the
Powers, both those bound by the Treaty of London and
those which are not. A course of affairs so directly
opposed to the expectation of everybody must necessarily lead to the most extraordinary complications. I
do not believe that history offers another example of
such a disappointment as the Court and the public of
Russia have met with from the serious resistance of the
Turks. The Cabinet must change their plan, and it
must be vigorously conceived, for the gravest interests
are at stake.

Many of the recent arrangements have been altered.

The Russian fleet in the Mediterranean will throw off the mask and commence hostilities; it will be the same with everything.

What will France do amid all this tacking about? I have no difficulty in predicting. She will continue to press forward in the direction of an alliance with the three Courts, as long as she has the Egyptians in front of her. She will be very much inclined to become the auxiliary of Russia when the French Cabinet is asked to lend a more active support to those Powers. My prophecy, that at the Russian headquarters the French expedition would be hailed as a favourable diversion to the operations of the war, was not long in being fulfilled. I earnestly desire that my presentiments with regard to the political attitude of France in the Russo-Turkish War may not have the same fate.

There are truths so evident, that they cannot be concealed. I regard as such truths the following dangers— namely:

1. That the calculations of Russia having been false, she will be obliged, in case peace is not signed between her and the Porte at the end of the present campaign, to put forth all the resources of the Empire for the opening of a new campaign. From that time she will also change the principle of action she has hitherto declared;

2. That the same causes which may drive his Imperial Majesty of Russia to such dire extremities will incline the Sultan not to enter into any arrangements the result of which would be his granting to the open enemy what that enemy has not been able to acquire by the sword, and conceding to enemies under the guise of friends what, even at the peril of his existence, he has hitherto refused;

That France, actually engaged in the struggle, will not retire, even when the avowed object of her efforts is obtained.   Having once taken up a position in the Morea, the French Government will yield to the temptation of dictating to the Porte the double duty of the liberation of the Greeks and peace with Russia.

As I feel sure that these possible results have also presented themselves to the foresight of the British Cabinet, it seems to me that I am fulfilling a duty to ourselves and the whole of Europe, in begging you to enter into candid explanations with Lord Aberdeen concerning the necessities created by a position of affairs singularly dangerous for the general repose.

Our most anxious care must be directed towards the only point where our moral action may yet replace the many other influences that have been dispelled. We must neglect no opportunity of urging the Porte to return to a state of peace, which it did not break, but which it alone can re-establish. Our efforts have hitherto been unsuccessful, which is not surprising; the Divan opposes us with the arguments we have employed to induce it to yield to dangers which experience has not yet justified. It does not even reply directly to our exhortations ; but it is impossible for us to conceal that when it does, it will address to us two questions—namely :

'By what right does Russia require the Sultan to make sacrifices to free himself from a war which he has not provoked ? '

And 'What security has he that he would have the support of the Powers, supposing he responds to their wishes concerning the affairs of Greece ? '. . . .

Our influence on the Porte may therefore be regarded as void, so long as the general situation is not essentially changed.   What will be the ultimate decisions of the Court of London? It is very important for us to know.

I repeat that, until events contradict it, we allow that the present campaign will not put an end to the war. The winter, then, should be employed in arriving at an agreement between the principal Courts. If the spring of 1829 sees the renewal of the war, and if the same lack of agreement between the principal Courts should be prolonged until that time, Europe will then have to face an awful prospect of troubles and revolutions.

These questions are of extreme gravity. We do not pretend to solve them, but we wish to discover what the Court of London thinks of them. Seven years of real moral warfare have now run their course; but our views have undergone no change, the line we have taken remains the same. We still take the same standpoint as that from which we started, and what we desired then we desire now. Our fears are realised— war is the inevitable consequence of proceedings which, as we felt sure, contained its germs. This war, which no one really desired, has altered the position: will a means of making peace be found between the end of this campaign and the beginning of the next? That is the question, and its answer will decide neither more nor less than the maintenance of the old political order in Europe or its fall.

The difficulties are great, for of all affairs the worst are those which proceed in a manner contrary to the desires of those who take part in them; and the necessity that these parties should be very careful and correct in what they desire in the future is an undoubted result of this position.

DON PEDRO'S CLAIM TO THE PORTUGUESE THRONE.

Metternich to the Emperor Francis, Vienna, September 22, 1828.

903. Sire! Your Majesty has requested me in your despatches from Weinzierl, dated August 29, to give you an exact and exhaustive statement of the disputed claims of the Emperor Don Pedro and the Infant Don Miguel to the Crown of Portugal, based on the Portuguese national and family laws.

It will be the easier for me to fulfil your Majesty's request, as I had not waited for your Majesty's commands to give this important question the most serious attention. As soon as I saw that the Cabinets of the great Powers, especially those of Vienna and Berlin, disagreed in their views on the question whether the Infant Don Miguel had no claims at all to the Crown of Portugal, I began a memoir, in which I examined this question from different political points of view, and with due regard to the fundamental laws of the country and the hereditary succession established for the reigning dynasty. The purpose of this memoir was to point out, on the clearest evidence, that not the Infant Don Miguel but the Emperor Don Pedro would be the legal successor of his father King John VI. on the throne of Portugal; that therefore Don Pedro had the undoubted right to abdicate in favour of his daughter, the Infanta Donna Maria da Gloria, and that this young

Princess must be regarded as the lawful Queen of Portugal. I have the honour to send your Majesty a copy of this memoir, with the respectful intimation that I have communicated its contents to the different Cabinets of Europe, partly to enlighten them on this intricate question, partly to warn them of the efforts and intrigues of Don Miguel's party and the widowed Queen, his mother, which are intended to exclude your Majesty's grand-daughter from the succession to the throne of Portugal.

The memoir had, besides, the effect of suspending the decisions of the Powers, so that we gained time to prepare a favourable reception for the proposals I had to make, and which were intended to put an end to all these dangerous complications, without violating Queen Mary's rights.

Before I give an account to your Majesty of the negotiations I entered upon with the Cabinets of the Powers, particularly with England, I believe it necessary to enter first upon a strict examination of the statutes of the Cortes of Lamego, the Pragmatic rights of John VI., because the rights of Don Miguel have been founded upon these acts, to the disadvantage of the Emperor Don Pedro and Queen Mary. I flatter myself I have proved the groundlessness of these claims; but if, after reading the memoir, your Majesty still retains any doubt on the subject, I hope to convince your Majesty by further explanation, that your Majesty's grand-daughter alone is lawful Queen of Portugal.

1. Till the House of Braganza was raised to power, the constitution of Portugal was nominally and in some of its chief features monarchical, although it was in reality limited by the participation of the three estates which, under the name of the ' Cortes,' claimed to represent

the sovereignty of the people. This was especially the case with respect to all laws made from time to time to settle the hereditary succession in the different branches of the royal family ; and, as frequent changes of government and throne-revolutions very often brought questions forward which affected these laws, the Cortes exercised more than once the right to settle those questions, sometimes with the King's sanction, sometimes without it, usually according to the will or the interest of the party in power.

2. Of these decisions two are particularly remembered by the Portugese nation and in the works of the historians and legal writers, and are considered by the modern advocates of the old Portuguese political law as the basis of all others. The constitution of Lamego, given under King Alphonso I. (according to some in 1143, according to others in 1181), and the declaration of the Cortes of January 28, 1642, which, after the revolution excluding Spain from the throne of Portugal, acknowledged John IV. Duke of Braganza, King of Portugal. Very serious doubts have always been raised as to the validity of these documents. The constitutions of Lamego are, as is proved by their style, the work of a barbarous age, only curious, even if their genuineness were fully proved, as an historical monument, but certainly not as a source of law, under entirely different circumstances. The declaration of 1642, never sanctioned by the monarch raised to the throne, bears on each line the stamp of its origin, the purpose to which it was consecrated, and the circumstances out of which it originated. The principle, common to both documents, was the exclusion of a foreign prince from the throne. On the separate articles of these so-called fundamental statutes whole volumes of polemics could

be written, although, as has been proved in the enclosed
memoir, there is no connection between them and the
present discussion: a fact also mentioned in the protest
of the Brazilian ambassador, published in London, which
I likewise enclose.

3. No assembly of the Cortes took place after
the revolution of 1642, and during all the following
reigns there is no mention of the Cortes and their
principles. During these periods the kings exercised
the supreme power, undivided and unlimited, they decided the most important matters without the assistance of the Cortes; they made and repealed laws; they
regulated the whole administration of the realm and
its colonies as they chose, assisted only by powerful
ministers and other state officials; they made war with
foreign States and entered into treaties and alliances.
The Cortes is not even mentioned in the most decisive
epochs of modern history; not during the negotiations
before and after the Peace of Utrecht, nor during the
powerful and extensive reforms of Pombal, nor in the
long reign of King John VI. It never raised its voice
at the important moment when the royal family emi-
grated to Brazil, nor took the slightest notice of anything happening there, from the elevation of Brazil to
the rank of a kingdom till the breaking out of the
Brazilian revolution. When, in 1820, the revolution in
Portugal broke out, the name of the Cortes was abused
to gain the semblance of a legal sanction for the overthrow of all old constitutions; but the Cortes of the
Revolution had nothing in common with the old Cortes
but the name; in form, spirit, and system it was a
national assembly after the modern fashion, which, like
that of 1791, forced upon the monarch a form of government hateful to the majority of the nation. When

this assembly was overthrown in the year 1823, different projects to re-establish the old Cortes were conceived but not realised. At last in 1825 the important treaty which settled the independence of Brazil was signed through the mediation of foreign Powers, without the assistance of the Cortes, the political existence of which must therefore be regarded as extinguished.

4. This being the position of things, King John VI. had the undoubted right to regulate the hereditary succession according to his own wishes, and if he thought fit, not to exclude his firstborn son and his descendants from the Portuguese throne, a decision he could have taken after a mutual agreement, according to the treaty of 1825; if he not only silently but expressly named Don Pedro his successor, there could be no legal obstacle to this decision. Not the least objection was therefore raised against these arrangements, either at the time when the treaty was signed, or when John VI., a short time before his death, appointed his daughter Maria Isabella regent, nor during the interval between King John's death and the beginning of his son's reign, and all European Courts acknowledged these arrangements to their fullest extent.

5. If, after the practical extinction of the Cortes, any other tribunal or any other authority could have had the right to attack the decisions of John VI. on the pretext of violation of the Declaration of the year 1642, the first decrees of Don Pedro ought to have sufficed to annihilate these pretexts. The avowed principle (the *ratio legis*) of the statutes of 1642 had been to prevent the crown of Portugal from being given to a foreign prince, or to a Portuguese prince residing in a foreign country, even if he could prove a constitutional claim to the throne. Don Pedro met this objection by re-

nouncing his indisputable birthright, and leaving his
rights to his daughter. He dissipated the fears which
the minority of this princess might excite for the future ;
he chose his brother for her husband and co-regent,
consequently he had fulfilled all the claims of the statutes
of 1624. The future Queen was a Portuguese princess,
after her father's abdication the next in succession ; separated for ever from Brazil, engaged to reside in Portugal, and the future bride of a Portuguese prince.
Donna Maria therefore united in her person all the
qualities and titles prescribed not only by the law of
succession, but also by the mere local Portuguese law ;
and blind party spirit alone could refuse to acknowledge
her incontestable rights.

6. Don Miguel, in accepting the regency, has acknowledged the rights of his imperial brother as well as
those of his future wife. Bad advisers tempted him to
aspire to the throne, but even to them it appeared too
bold a step to attempt to gain it by mere arbitrary
power; they resolved, therefore, to call into being the
phantom of the old Cortes. Even if this step had been
taken with the purest intentions, the Regent being
merely the representative of a higher authority, was not
entitled to take it without the sanction of the nation.
The power he himself did not possess he could not
bestow upon others ; and that the Junta, the mere
assembling of which was high treason, should decide who
was to be King of Portugal, was even offensive to common sense. The execution, too, of the whole enterprise
was in harmony with the spirit in which it had been
proposed and the end to which it tended. The so-called
representatives of the nation were only chosen instru-
ments and notorious accomplices of the usurpation.
The discussions of these two or three tumultuous assem-

blies were only the echo of all that fanatical party spirit
had prepared and arbitrary power was willing to execute.
The decisions of this sham parliament had exactly as
much political value as the decrees of the *Trombetta
Final* (a Portuguese journal).

7. From the above remarks it is evident:

(*a*) That according to the laws of hereditary succession established in all the reigning houses of Europe,
modified in Portugal only in some peculiar cases, Maria
da Gloria has become the only legal heir to the Portuguese throne after her father's renunciation;

(*b*) That even the statutes of 1612 could not be
used as a legal objection against this succession;

(*c*) That the convocation of the Cortes ordered by
Don Miguel without any right or authority must be regarded as an illegal act, powerless to weaken the rights
of Queen Mary, and that, consequently, the decisions of
this assembly were in every respect null and void.

Further, it follows that the Powers which did not
hesitate to withdraw their ambassadors from Lisbon
and to break off all communications with the new Court
of Portugal, from the moment when Don Miguel
usurped the Portuguese throne by accepting the crown
offered to him by the Cortes, have at this moment the
undoubted right to refuse to acknowledge the Infant
Don Miguel as King of Portugal, and to take fitting
measures to secure to the young Queen Mary II., the
only lawful Queen of Portugal, the crown of that
country.

This declaration of the Powers, if it is to answer the
end proposed, must necessarily be supported by some
measures threatening coercion, which would probably
seriously disturb peace; for, in taking such a step, the
Powers would give the revolutionary party in Portugal

new ardour (a fact which certainly could not answer
their interest or their intention), as Queen Mary is too
young to reign herself, and a regency would only com-
plicate the difficult position of Portugal. It has, therefore, been necessary to think of means of adjustment,
which would prevent further mischief without compromising the rights of Queen Mary, or placing the Powers
in contradiction with their former declarations and line
of conduct. The means devised by me will, I believe,
unite the different interests, and consists in blending
Queen Mary's rights (rights acknowledged by the Powers
in the Treaty of Vienna, as well as by the Infant Don
Miguel) with the rights which Portugal grants to this
Prince. Indeed, if the rights of the two hostile parties
were united by a marriage which had been before
planned, if the right be given to Don Miguel to divide
with the young Queen the throne of Portugal, with the
title of King and the power of co-regent, till she has
reached a marriageable age, a legal basis would be prepared for the Powers, whereon to re-establish the peace
of Portugal in a solid and lasting manner. To prove
the advantages thus offered, I have written some short
and concise notes which may serve as a kind of supplement to the memoir, and which I have the honour
to send to your Majesty. I have sent both documents
to your Majesty's Ambassador in London, asking him to
communicate their contents to the English ministry, and
authorising Prince Esterhazy, in case the arrangement
therein proposed is approved by this Cabinet, to demand
that it be taken as the basis of negotiations with Rio
Janeiro to gain over the Emperor Don Pedro to our
views of the matter. The English Cabinet not only
received my proposals very favourably, but has also
resolved that they shall be considered as the basis of the

instruction to Lord Strangford, who has just left for
Rio Janeiro to settle this affair with the Emperor.
Baron Marschall received similar orders, and has been
charged to support the endeavours of Lord Strangford
as heartily as possible. Lastly, your Majesty will permit
me to remind you of your own letter to the Emperor
Don Pedro, in which you advised him to place the
rights of his daughter Mary under the protection of
the European Powers. Nothing has, therefore, been
neglected to ensure the success of this important negotiation, and the spirit of toleration and prudence, as
well as the conciliatory spirit of which Don Pedro has
latterly given numerous proofs, permit us to hope that
the success of this negotiation will correspond with our
desires. We shall probably encounter the greatest difficulty in Lisbon, not only from the Prince but also
from the Queen his mother, who from the first opposed
the Prince's marriage with the young Queen Mary.

But, on the other hand, there is reason to believe
that the Prince must be anxious to be acknowledged
King by the Powers, and that he will seriously consider
the matter before he refuses to accept the offer of conciliation which we proposed in Rio Janeiro, and are
about to propose in Lisbon, as soon as we know the
Emperor's resolution. Neither can it be without effect
if the Prince sees that the Powers are firmly resolved to
keep the position they took in opposition to him from
the moment of his usurpation. In this sense the last
declaration of the English Secretary of State, made to
Don Miguel's unacknowledged agent in London, may
have the greatest effect. All the different Courts agree
so far on this matter. The Cabinets of Paris, Berlin,
St. Petersburg, and Madrid, to which I communicated
my proposal as soon as I was sure of its being favour-

ably accepted by the English ministry, have joined us unanimously.

I therefore hope that this explanation will suffice to allay your Majesty's anxieties with respect to the claims of your granddaughter to the Portuguese throne, and show the care with which I have endeavoured to defend them. It only remains for me to add that I enclose copies of the Edicts of August 29, 1825, and November 15, 1825, with the Memoir and Notes, in case your Majesty may like to see them.

A TEMPORARY AGREEMENT OF POLICY BETWEEN ENGLAND AND AUSTRIA.

Metternich to Esterhazy, in London, Vienna, October 8, 1828.

904. Lord Cowley has allowed me, under promise of secrecy, to see the last despatch from the Cabinet of London to Lord Heytesbury. This despatch does honour to Lord Aberdeen. It is well written and conceived, and expresses frankly the opinion of the Government on the political conduct of Austria. The despatches in question confirm the satisfactory impression you had yourself received from the English ministers. In this important respect we cannot be otherwise than perfectly satisfied.

I wish I could say the same of the general situation of affairs. This is, from whatever point we regard it, the most critical and the most dangerous possible.

The position in which the young Emperor of Russia finds himself is most embarrassing. . . .

Can the Emperor Nicholas allow his own defeats to go unpunished? Will he not be forced to avenge his own mistakes? This much must be admitted, but what is one to expect in the future?

According to its well-known habit, the Porte will not yield, and the successes—as real as unexpected—which the Turks have achieved in the first campaign, are not likely to incline the Sultan to give way.

In this state of things there arises an inevitable

necessity : namely, that the English Government must declare which side it means to take; what the choice will be I cannot yet foretell. Between an explosion of ill-temper and the ease with which it has hitherto lent itself to the fantasies of its allies, there is a middle course which alone can serve the general cause without exposing Europe to terrible commotions. Will the Cabinet take this course? It is impossible to say, and yet everything depends upon it.

I told you in my last despatch of Prince William of Prussia. Since then I have had an opportunity of seeing how the events of the war have astonished him. He has thus furnished me with another proof of the extreme imprudence with which the operations must have been conceived by his Imperial Majesty of Russia. A defeat, or even the possibility of one, was never admitted at St. Petersburg. It was, in a great measure, Count Nesselrode who protested against opening the campaign with more considerable forces, not only from the conviction that the Sultan would yield without hesitation, but principally to avoid the expenses falling too heavily on the Porte, in consequence of the indemnities it would have to pay. The Russian Cabinet thus economised for the Turks, and certainly confusion of ideas could no farther go. I am anxiously awaiting your news, which must necessarily throw light on much that is still dark to us.

PEACEFUL DISPOSITION OF THE PORTE.

Metternich to Esterhazy, in London,
Vienna, December 2, 1828.

905. . . . . A great change has undoubtedly taken place in the moral attitude of the Porte, the reason of which may be found in the two following circumstances —namely, the character and intelligence of the Sultan being particularly striking, and the removal of the Greeks from all participation in the political affairs of the Empire.

The Ottoman character now presents itself in all its simplicity. It is no longer influenced or travestied by the shadows which belong to the Greek mind; and among that nation the Fanariotes have without any doubt for many years furnished a particular class, demoralised by all kinds of vices. It was only through a prism held by this caste that the Porte saw Europe, and that the Cabinets perceived the Ottoman Government.

If the resistance of the Sultan to the concessions which have been required from him for the last few years can be no longer doubtful; and if it seems quite natural that at the end of a campaign which could not have terminated more happily, the Sultan Mahmoud should be no more disposed to comply than he was at the approach, and in the present time of danger, it seems to us that the point of view—thoroughly European —which the Reis-Effendi has developed to our representative relative to the future peace with Russia furnishes material for many new observations.

A few years ago the Divan would have considered it contrary to good Mussulman policy to entertain any idea of a general arrangement or of a peaceful meeting between the Powers and the Turks, of transactions in fact, whose form would be that of a European Congress. Nothing appeared to us more just or wise than the sketch drawn by the Reis Effendi of the consequences of any pacification between the Sultan and the Emperor of Russia, concluded according to the mode hitherto followed between the two Powers.   It is therefore clear to me that there are more dreamers at St. Petersburg than at Constantinople.

The rage against the Courts of London and Paris is great at Constantinople.   It is not so much the expedition to the Morea itself as the taking the fortresses, which excites this feeling in the Divan. . . . Nevertheless, the latter will be wise enough not to quarrel abruptly with the two Courts.   It seems decided on this subject.

While placing these questions in their true light, we cannot conceal from ourselves that there are many other difficulties to hinder the great work of peace.

No warlike enterprise has ever been conducted like that which is to-day costing Russia the most precious of all her blessings, which nothing can either compensate or replace : among these I regard as first that prestige of power, the fruit of a century of efforts and of a finesse and address hitherto possessed by those who guided the political and military affairs of the Empire. The Emperor Nicholas has, most assuredly, spent in one single operation the patrimony of glory and prestige which his predecessors have accumulated since the foundation of the Empire ! That blessing is lost, and it is to a certain extent irreparable. Will the Emperor have that force of character, and that calmness of true wisdom, which enables men to say that what is lost exists no longer, and that under given circumstances the risk of attempting to re-conquer what exists no longer is much greater than ever the happy result of the enterprise could have been, had it even been crowned with the most marked success. Everything is in this question; for in its solution is found the possibility or the impossibility of preventing, by the conclusion of peace, the opening of a new campaign. The latter once begun, everything will be changed in the position of Russia, as well as in that of Europe. In the event of a second disastrous campaign, the Russian Empire would be in a condition which I do not allow myself to think of; and if it were victorious, the Emperor would no longer be able to make a peace in harmony with the engagements which he contracted with Europe and his allies, at the opening of the campaign of 1828.

The Porte on the other hand seems to have established itself on a basis of purpose and determination unassailable by justice and reason. By declaring itself ready to make peace—real peace—and quite determined not to submit to mere capitulations under the name of peace, it is right before God and man. It is so far in the right that, if the parts could be changed between Russia and Austria, the whole of Europe would be very ready to condemn openly that which on our side would be undoubtedly and universally reproved as an abuse of power. Whence comes the difference which, hitherto at least, has been seen in the judgments of Europe on the proceedings of these two Powers? Evidently from the charm which surrounded the Russian Colossus, before the Emperor dissipated it so imprudently. The charm has disappeared, and it has not only disappeared for the Courts and the people of Europe, but also for the Divan and the Mussulman people. What the Emperor of Russia has lost the Sultan has undoubtedly gained in the eyes of the nation, and to a certain extent in those of the European public. The Porte is ready to make peace; but that peace is not, I am very much afraid, one to which the Emperor of Russia will ever consent.

Your last Reports, as well as those which the same courier brought us from Count Apponyi, were at length of a nature to raise our hopes as to the conduct of the trilateral affair. The decision of the two Courts to put an end as soon as possible to their operations, and to consult the interests of peace, in preference to the natural desire of the third Power for the indefinite prolongation of a difference which would continue to weigh down its enemy, seems to us to be the only correct one, and the only one proportioned to the gravity of the circumstances. If I am not much mistaken, the deplorable condition in which the affairs of Russia are at present will tend to rouse a feeling of independence in the French ministry: a feeling which hitherto had scarcely been consulted by the Bourbons since their restoration.

As for ourselves and our political conduct, it cannot afford subject for a doubt in London. We are giving to the world—our friends as well as our rivals—a new proof of the spirit which animates us. Our conscience has not yielded under the weight of a complete isolation; its wishes and its tendency do not change because a catastrophe experienced by a neighbouring Empire might seem to be advantageous.   What we have wished we wish still; we desire the re-establishment of a state of peace, which our constant efforts have not been able to maintain.   The ancient and natural alliance between ourselves and England still exists, it does not need to be strengthenened by words; and if such an important condition of the general safety has seemed to be obscured for a time, the fault has not been with us.   You must be able to recal the time when I expressed the most lively regret that for us and for the rest of Europe England no longer existed.

We must for the moment content ourselves with the return of our two Cabinets to looking at things in the same light.   To go further seems to me impossible.   You have seen us, in times assuredly very difficult, not refuse to take the initiative in many general measures; and even if we could reproach ourselves with having been too ready, we have never yielded to any sentiment but that of strict necessity, or what we considered utility. Now, we can only wait for what will come to us from Powers which, finding themselves in the same difficulties, must feel an equal need of extricating themselves. To go beyond that would be not only to compromise ourselves, but to forget the common interests of Europe.

Metternich to Esterhazy, in London,
Vienna, December 2, 1828.

906. All the news which arrive daily from the Principalities and our frontiers but confirm the deplorable state to which the Russian army is reduced. These news being, however, fragmentary, and there being no authority to collect and put them together, a number of essential particulars are wanting, and can only be understood by induction.

We cannot, therefore, yet decide if the raising of the
siege of Silistria was caused by the inclemency of the
weather, or if an offensive operation of the Turks rendered necessary such a desperate step. It seems, however, probable from the scattered data that both causes
combined. . . .

In the present position of things, it would be impossible for Varna to resist a serious attack, or even a
blockade. The feeble remnant of the army charged to
defend the approaches must succumb to privations, and
Varna itself could not be defended in its present state of
dismantlement.

Such are the results of a campaign which reason
condemned beforehand, and which no wise or vigorous
arrangement has assisted in its execution. . . .

If the campaign of 1812 in Russia showed an error
of calculation which in a man of Napoleon's understanding was inconceivable, at any rate no material means for
the success of his enterprise was neglected by him. In
1828, Russia has made a war which, in proportion, will
have cost her as much in men and materials of war, for,
indeed, one cannot lose more than one has. But in this
campaign the army has never been more than thirty or
forty leagues from her frontiers, and it required a special
effort to create, by the voluntary and deliberate choice
of such a line of action, so many causes of ruin and
death.

A new and great difficulty awaits the Russians in
1829—the exhaustion and total ruin of the two Danubian
Principalities. An administration without example has
there destroyed the greater part of its resources both
present and future. The fields lie uncultivated, and
beasts of burden and those for food are alike ruined and
worn out. It remains to be seen if the winter will pass

without the Ottoman armies invading them, were it only to evacuate them at the opening of the campaign, giving them up again to the enemy in a state of still more hopeless devastation.

According to the most moderate calculations, the Turkish army engaged before Constantinople, comprising the garrisons of the forts, must be upwards of a hundred and fifty thousand fighting men. Asiatic troops cross the Bosphorus daily, and their appearance is said to be very satisfactory.

The present epoch is most grave. An immense reputation is compromised, and must try to reinstate itself. On the other hand, an Empire which we regarded as extinct has retrieved itself. The Powers are obliged to look on at the struggle; we have done what we could to prevent the conflict breaking out; we can now only wait the solution of the deliberations which have been opened between the Cabinets engaged in one act of the drama.

The last post from Constantinople has brought many reports of the situation of affairs in Greece. They bear the impress of the soil from which they spring. Disorder reigns in vacuity—many phantasies and no reality. In the midst of it all the Government has least vitality, and the person the most completely ruined is M. Capo d'Istria.

'

DECLARATION OF THE THREE ALLIED COURTS TO THE PORTE WITH REGARD TO GREECE.

Metternich to Esterhazy, in London,
Vienna, December 12, 1828.

907. In the declaration which the three Courts propose to address to the Divan, the word *provisional* is in truth connected with that of *guarantee*, and in this acceptation it does not present itself to our minds as an insurmountable obstacle ; but if the Divan believes that it can be applied to *delimitation*, it will undoubtedly be an *impedimentum in re*. We have already, and too often, dealt with this question of delimitation for me to be able to avoid returning to it once more. If I touch upon it, it is only to mention the extreme difficulty which I foresee in obtaining from the Porte its consent to a proposal which appears to me incompatible with its well-known principles. The Sultan may confine his action to the Morea and the Cyclades ; he may even renounce their possession ; I will go further : he may, in the event of a disastrous war, be compelled to renounce the possession of countries at a far greater distance, but he will never, now or at any other time, agree to admit in principle a provisional delimitation. . . .

The step now about to be taken by the Ambassador of the Low Countries promises three results—namely :

1. That the Porte will not reply in a satisfactory manner to the triple declaration ;

2. That the course arranged in the Conference at London will produce irritation at St. Petersburg, were it only that irritation which, in Russia more than anywhere else, arises from the feeling of the impossibility of preventing what is unpalatable ;

3. That the medium through which the step will be taken at Constantinople adds to the difficulty which may, in the eyes of the Porte, be found at the root of the matter.

These considerations must necessarily influence us in the part we have to take. But there are others as well, and which, together with the preceding, have made us decide to adopt the course sketched out in my directions to the Internuncio.

These considerations arise from our perfect knowledge of men and things.

Should the Internuncio be invited by M. de Zuylen to join with him in any form whatever in the step he is about to take, he would, by responding to that invitation, cause our Court to depart from the position which, up to this hour, it has maintained in the Eastern Question : a position to which we especially owe the confidence which our counsels still inspire at the Divan.

If the Prussian Ambassador should feel some hesitation, which I admit is very probable, in advancing in the same line as our representative, the Court of Austria would certainly lose its position of benevolent neutrality in the eyes of the Porte.

In short, it must be one of two things : M. de Zuylen will succeed in his step, or he will fail.

In the first case, the Court of Russia will not cease to reproach us with not being able to use our influence with the Divan, except on an occasion when the success of the allies would have the appearance of a Russian defeat ; in the second case, M. de Zuylen will not fail to throw upon our representative a share of the failure.

My ostensible despatch to the Internuncio will show you that the course which we recommend is perfectly in harmony with the system of reserve enforced by the above considerations. But at the same time you will find in the secret instruction* sent to him the plainest proofs of the support which in other ways we can give to the real object of the measures about to be taken. These instructions should satisfy the English Cabinet, to whom alone we entrust the secret.

I beg you, Prince, to make known this despatch and its enclosures to Lord Aberdeen.

* In these secret instructions of December 10 Metternich writes to the Internuncio at Constantinople : ' The two Courts (England and France) have decided to send agents to Constantinople on the very first opportunity. They have announced this decision at the Russian Court. To soften the effect, and with a diplomacy which we are far from disapproving, they propose to the Cabinet of St. Petersburg to leave the representatives of the three united Powers in some port of the Mediterranean, and to send two private agents to treat of the triple affair at Constantinople itself.

' The delimitation of Greece is provisional, but this word has no value in the eyes of the British Cabinet. . . . The idea of the total emancipation of Greece is definitely abandoned by the two Courts. There will thus be no question of those municipal forms which no Government can tolerate less easily than the Porte, and which certainly no people less than those of the Morea know how to enjoy.

' May the Divan rightly estimate the immense advantage of seeing the Triple Alliance broken wherever it is unfavourable to the Porte, and the only clause maintained which is favourable to it—that in which the Emperor of Russia renounces every kind of conquest. . . . The Porte, if it is wise, will make every possible sacrifice of *amour propre* to facilitate the arrival of the English and French agents at Constantinople, and at the same time desire nothing better than to see the two Courts still keep up their apparent state of alliance with Russia.' We know that this step, too, had no success, and the distrust of the Porte in the Cabinets was not less than its confidence in the strength of its own resources.—ED.

PRUSSIA'S POLICY IN THE EASTERN QUESTION.

Metternich to Esterhazy, in London,
Vienna, December 12, 1828.

908. . . . I mean now to speak of the present political attitude of the Court of Prussia.

I have once already approached this question, and I cannot conscientiously change anything in the opinion I then formed.

The moral situation of the Court of Prussia has not changed. But the position of the Emperor of Russia has undergone a complete revolution, and this will always exercise, no doubt, a more or less decisive influence on the Berlin Cabinet.

This fact being beyond dispute, it only remains to examine the following questions :—

What does Prussia really desire?

What can she do and what will she do?

As long as there is no open division between the Courts of Europe, Prussia, I have no doubt, will not remove from the line on which she is placed; but whenever a different order of things is established—a prospect very much opposed to the wishes of his Prussian Majesty and the head of his Cabinet—we shall see Prussia ally herself with Russia.

In naming the King and Count Bernstorff, the wishes of those who at present regulate the politics of the kingdom must not be confounded with those of the great mass of the army and the Prussian *employés* in the different branches of the civil administration. The number of men in the kingdom who think and feel with as much moderation as the Cabinet is restricted. It happily counts among its ranks the successor to the throne, and if there are any political differences they are between the King and the Prince Royal, owing to a leaning (which, however, is only personal affection) that his Majesty has towards the imperial family of Russia. The natural affection which the King feels for his august relative and the imperial family of Russia does not, however, go so far as to make him infatuated with the political system of that Power, of the nature and value of which he is fully aware, and which is directly contrary to the principles of sound policy to which his Majesty is devoted.

It is, in short, to this monarch, and the force—negative certainly, but not less real—which forms the basis of his character, that Europe owes the attitude adopted by Prussia in a most difficult situation. The amount of confidence and true friendship, I might even say of gratitude, which the King bears to the Emperor our august master, for the multiplied proofs of interest and the material help which our Court furnished to Prussia at the time of her frightful disasters, has had its effect. Mr. Canning, whose conduct on all occasions appeared to us to show the reverse of good sense, has, on his side, contributed to decide the attitude of Prussia in the triple affairs. He managed to embroil himself personally with Count Bernstorff at the very moment when a less domineering spirit than that of Mr. Canning would have considered it more suitable to his views to have conciliated the friendship of Prussia.

Never accustomed to live merely for the passing

hour, never satisfied to walk in darkness, but anxious to do everything possible to enlighten the road along which we have to travel, we have never, in the most difficult times, lost any opportunity for making ourselves acquainted with the thoughts of the Prussian Cabinet. To this end we have had recourse to our usual means ; we have established and maintained frank explanations between the two Courts. To furnish a clear demonstration of our manner of proceeding, it will be sufficient to make you acquainted with the last explanations between Vienna and Berlin.

There is no need for me to tell your Highness of the system of calumny indulged in by all parties with respect to Austria. In this the parties are right—they know who troubles them. We present a strong front, compact and difficult to overthrow or even to shake— this fact alone is irritating. From the first day of the French Revolution until now, Austria has always been able to thwart the plans of subversion. In twenty campaigns our Power has been found fighting the Revolution on the very field of battle, and, in the midst of political peace, it was always on our frontiers that the incendiary torches came to be extinguished, unless they were extinguished by the weight of our military forces thrown upon the foreign incendiary. Nothing is more natural than that political factions should be unable to console themselves for our action, so contrary is it to their designs. The conduct of the Russian Cabinet with regard to us might appear less so ; but when the Liberal policy becomes that of the most despotic Power there must necessarily arise a number of contradictions in the conduct of a Power so singularly placed. The effect has not been slow to follow the cause, and the Cabinet of St. Petersburg, with the immense crowd of flatterers of its real or imaginary power, has taken its position among Liberal politicians. From that time Austria has been exposed to Russian animadversion and to the extravagances of an irritation which is all the more violent because it can never find anything to justify it.

Prussia—that is to say, the Cabinet—remains faithful to us. The latter has neither succumbed to Liberal seductions nor to Russian policy ; the storm has passed by it ; it has raged in the kingdom, but neither the King nor his minister has been led away by the more or less general error. I believe that this fact alone is no despicable evidence of the moral strength of the Cabinet of Berlin. For some time this Cabinet has warned us of the intrigues I have just mentioned. Frankness provokes frankness ; therefore, on our side, we have felt it our duty not to conceal our impressions concerning the solidity of Prussia's political course. You will find enclosed the copy of a recent despatch which Count Bernstorff has addressed on this subject to the Prussian Minister at the Imperial Court.* You will see in it the most positive assurances of the non-existence of secret engagements with Russia, and I perfectly believe in their sincerity.

I have already told you our opinion of M. de Bulow. That agent belongs to the faction, and is held there by

* The extract from this despatch is as follows :—' As for the rumours of a double alliance which would be formed on one side between Austria and Sweden, and on the other between Prussia and Russia, we learnt them first in your despatch. The part concerning ourselves gives us no uneasiness. When one has nothing to conceal, one dreads little these false accusations, and I think our movements are too well known for us to be long suspected of being bound by secret engagements. We have not the ambition they ascribe to us, but we have that of maintaining a frank, independent, and open position.'—ED.

a strong tie—his wife. But his own mind inclines to a restless and ambitious policy. It is annoying that he has been chosen to be the representative of his Court at London; for I am convinced that his Cabinet does not always know how to estimate the impressions which M. de Bulow gives of the conduct of the British Cabinet. We find daily proofs of this in the Reports from Count Trauttmansdorff.

The present moment is rich in errors of every kind. All the elements are in motion; things have lost their equilibrium, and are trying to recover themselves. Systems are tottering, and truth is showing itself without disguise.

At such times men's minds cannot easily compose themselves; that takes time, which is precisely what is lacking at a period when everything is done in haste. If anywhere one has the power of employing oneself usefully, it is certainly with us; our country is quiet, and the public feeling is entirely with the Government. In this the difference between our position and that of the Court of Prussia is very great. In that kingdom also public feeling is favourable to the Government; but it follows to a certain extent a different direction from that of the Cabinet. The Russian defeats have materially calmed the exalted hopes of the ultra-Prussian faction; but *per contra* these defeats place the King in a position personally painful. While I acknowledge, moreover, that this is the state of things in Prussia, I must add that the embarrassment is not yet more than embarrassment. The Cabinet is full of uneasiness about the future, and a state of things which may lead to extremes is what it most dreads.

In short, it is afraid of complications increasing to

such an extent that it will be forced to choose which side to take; hitherto it has held aloof.

This is our firm conviction, and I have no hesitation in laying it before the Cabinet of his Britannic Majesty.

RUSSIA'S RELATION TO ENGLAND.

Metternich to Esterhazy, in London,
Vienna, December 18, 1828.

909. I have received by way of Berlin the Reports from our Chargé d'Affaires at St. Petersburg. It is clear to me that it was in consequence of a concert with the Prince of Hesse that M. de Kaisersfeld has drawn up these Reports.

I authorise you to lay them before Lord Aberdeen.

The description sketched in the despatch of November 16 describes I think exactly the position of things and persons at St. Petersburg.

What M. de Kaisersfeld says of the irritation which exists against Austria must be true, for the causes which he mentions are true.

The contents of this same despatch concerning England is what I think most important.

I desire very much—for I think the good of the cause greatly depends on it—that every opportunity should be seized for making it understood at London that, of all the Powers, it is Great Britain which has most influence with Russia. The cause of this influence is so connected with the nature of things that it must be seen at a glance.

Russia is a Power always coveting, and consequently always uneasy. Its nature being diametrically opposed to our own, the relations between the two neighbouring Empires must be affected thereby. On our side there is

no irritation, for we are not in the wrong; it is otherwise at St. Petersburg, where they are rarely exactly
in the right. Our strong and ponderous mass hinders
by its gravitation the approaching march of the Colossus of the North. For want of a better it has lately
fallen upon another neighbour, who was regarded at
St. Petersburg as weaker than experience has happily
proved him to be. Russia does not love us, for no one
loves what is a hindrance; but it dare not make war
upon us openly—the enterprise appears too serious.

Prussia it does not think of.

As for France, it does not trust her, and, in spite of
a great many points of contact and affinity between the
two Cabinets, there will never be a real alliance between
them, unless it is based on a system of conquest and
the destruction of intermediary States.

Then there is England; without contact on *terra
firma* that Power alone can influence Russia, for she is
in a position to do Russia as much harm as Russia
can possibly do to her.

It is sufficient to consider for a moment the conduct
of affairs in the course of the last six or seven years to be
convinced that it was England alone which could have
facilitated, or even rendered it possible for Russia to
undertake, an enterprise which, but for the interference
of Providence, might have been an immense triumph
for Russia. Indeed, during the first and longest period
of the Eastern Question, the Court of Russia never dared
to take a part. As long as England stood aloof, Russia
was contented simply to give an opinion without the
concurrence of the English Power. Russia would not
have dared to undertake anything serious. When in
1825 the first proceedings of the British Ministry of
that period took place, affairs took another direction.

Later on Russia did no more than make use of the latitude which from that time was recognised, and which she regarded as sufficiently secured to her by the other Powers singly or together.

What was true three years ago is not less true to-day, and will not be contradicted to-morrow. What England does not wish Russia will not do. It is, therefore, at London and not at St. Petersburg that we must seek for information concerning the future.

Everything inclines me to think that the British Cabinet will not contradict the opinion we have formed of it, and I will go further and say that it cannot but give its assent to that which contains our full and entire conviction.

SUSPENSION OF WARLIKE OPERATIONS.

Metternich to Esterhazy, in London,
Vienna, December 18, 1828.

910. . . . The operations of war seem to be suspended for the present. The peculiarly rigorous season renders it doubtful whether active operations can be resumed at all. You may be sure that military intelligence from Constantinople is singularly meagre; except two serious affairs, one before Schumla and the other near Bazartschick, in which the Russians sustained great loss, nothing seems to have taken place during the month of November. The Turks, however, continue to speak of a winter campaign.

A new and painful complication has just presented itself to the commercial Powers in consequence of the armed vessels cruising on the part of the Greeks. Several merchant vessels, among which are four Austrians, have already been taken to Egina, and are awaiting judgment. It appears, according to the most recent information, that they will not escape condemnation.

There is in this act an abuse of authority to which we object to submit. But it is more than that. According to the last triple declaration, the Morea and the Islands are under the provisional protection of the Powers. We are not at war with them; by what right can letters of marque be conceded by a country which itself has no real political existence? and what validity is there in the judgments and declarations of brigands? Among the ships captured under our flag and as Austrian property, there is one whose cargo is French property. We hope the Courts of London and Paris will put some restraint on this revival of brigandage and plunder. You are, then, specially desired to claim the support of the British Government in this matter, and we feel sure it will not be refused.

THE YEAR 1829.

Extracts from Metternich's private Letters.

Metternich to his son Victor, Vienna, January 1, 1829.

911. I take this opportunity, my dear Victor, to repeat to you what you know already, that if anyone has ardent wishes for your welfare it is certainly your father.

I received your last letter two days ago; it shows me that you are rather disappointed with Rome. Léontine, who received the same impression from the letter you wrote to her, says it always takes you some time to feel at home in new places.

I am far from sharing your impressions, for our starting-points differ. Rome is the city of recollections, and it offers to the observer a view of three distinct epochs. Full of monuments of ancient times, it retraces the image of what is no more, and yet lives eternally in the records of history. Not less rich in monuments of the middle ages, it again recalls what exists no longer. Lastly, the present has its place there. The present is neither the first nor the second of these epochs—it is now reality; to-morrow it also will be lost in the shades of time.

The two epochs must not be confounded, physically or morally.

Ancient Rome is not Modern Rome—that could not be; nothing in the material world lasts. A little more or a little less stripped of their moss, the monuments remain the same ; restored, they are lost. The late Pope always intended to clean the Forum and drive out the cows and other cattle. That is all that should be done, and it certainly will be done some day. Does this suggest moral reflections? There is only one reflection to make, and that is peremptory—the ancient Romans live no more; the inhabitants of modern Rome are not Romans, and never can be. All the visionaries in the world cannot alter this. Besides, one does not go to Rome for its inhabitants, but to see what those who no longer exist have bequeathed for the meditation of those who think themselves so great and wise because they live in this age of mere words.

In short, it is necessary to know what to look for, and not to seek everything, for nowhere is that to be found. Is it a question of seeing the world of 1829? One must go to Paris, Philadelphia, or Bogota. Is it an object to see industrial life? London, the avenues of the Opera, the boulevards of Paris, Birmingham, or Lyons must be visited. Is it snow that is wanted? This must be sought at the sixty-second degree.

I see you have not yet visited the Museum of the Vatican, and I am glad of it, for, all said and done, it is very disagreeable in the month of January. I am surprised that I had not warned you of the temperature of St. Peter's, and you were quite right to find it out. I am of your opinion about this edifice. The interior of it is much more remarkable than the exterior, and the interior is, I think, much more like a secular building than a church. I do not think that this church inspires devotion. It is a real misfortune for the visitors to

Rome that they know everything from copies bad or good. Except to find the way about the streets, I think one hardly requires a guide in Rome.

912. *January* 8.—I take the opportunity of letting you know by this day's post that you have a brother. Antoinette was confined yesterday at four o'clock in the afternoon with a fine healthy boy. He was baptised to-day, and named Richard Clement Joseph Lothaire. My brother was god-father, as he has been for you all. . . . . Mother and child are perfectly well.

I wished to be the first to announce this event to you, my dear Victor.

I have just heard from Paris that M. de la Ferronays has had a stroke of apoplexy, on New Year's Day, when in the King's room; he seems to be paralysed on one side—this is equivalent to his loss. He had some premonitory symptoms a few days previously; the doctor wished to bleed him, but he refused. See what is the consequence of resistance in certain cases of which the faculty can judge better than the patient. I consider this event as a great misfortune.

913. *January* 16.—Your letter of January 3 arrived by the last courier, and gave me pleasure, because it showed that your health is improved by the influence of the Roman climate.

I am delighted at the respect shown to the ambassador. Count de Lützow is an excellent man; his heart is as good as his head and his temper. I was certain that he would succeed at Rome, and that is why he is there. The more you know him, the more good qualities you will find in him. Big and awkward as he may be, he is one of the best men I know. In 1808, 1809, 1810, and 1811 he was a thorough Spanish Royalist; the services he rendered are innumerable, and they

border on the miraculous, if in the doings of good
people there were any miracle.

I am delighted that you have so wisely gone into
society. The *salons* of Rome are better than the streets;
at any rate, you do not meet wild oxen in them. I recommend you to the studios, which are very different from
the *salons*. Is it in the new *Maison Torlonia* that the
most unhappy of all the Dukes has given you a dinner?
What a grand house that is! If it were mine it would
console me for many things, except being Torlonia himself. You know that he never sleeps in that house, for
fear of dying. A fortune-teller has told him something
of this kind. You will only have a real idea of the
treasures of Rome when you have seen the Vatican.

Antoinette ought now to be recovering, for this is
the tenth day since her confinement, but this is not the
case; she has taken cold, God knows how, and consequently is feverish, but I hope it will soon pass off.

914. *January* 17.—The most terrible catastrophe
has fallen upon me. Antoinette died this morning at
eight o'clock, the tenth day after her confinement.
What the Lord gave the Lord can take away, and man
must bow the head without question. My confidence
is in Him, and I bow to His immutable decrees. My
life is over, and nothing remains to me but my children.
This idea sustains me and gives me courage to live.

I know you will wish to come to me. I absolutely
forbid you to do so. The season is unpropitious, and I
shall be much more easy if I know that you are living
under the influence of a milder climate than ours; so
do not attempt to come on any account.

The cause of my poor Antoinette's death was a
fever—probably suppressed—an inexorable malady. I
trembled for her since the fifth day, when this fever

showed itself. She has not wanted either for care from others or strength in herself, but nothing could conquer the malady. She died as all should die who believe and hope in God.

I have made the greatest possible effort to write these lines. I cannot go on. Good-bye; I wish you all the happiness that is denied to me.

915. *January* 21.—To-day, my dear Victor, I can enter more into details than I could when I sent the last courier. The blow which has desolated my life was then too recent; I was quite stunned; but now my mind, shattered as it is, has regained the necessary strength to tell what has happened.

The poor deceased was safely confined on January 7. Her calculation was wrong; the child was fully developed, so that she had made the mistake of a month. She decided to nurse the child herself if nature permitted, and all seemed to promise well in that respect; but the third day a slight milk-fever appeared. The fourth day passed over, but about ten o'clock at night of that day I found the pulse very much quickened again. In the morning slight traces of miliary fever were visible. After this discovery I knew that danger was imminent. This terrible malady of women in their confinements, of the origin of which I am ignorant, and against which the course of ages has discovered no real remedy, was unhappily too well known to me, and you know that I do not deceive myself readily. But no alarming symptom showed itself after this eruption. Everything went on normally. The ninth day all anxiety seemed to be removed, mother and child seemed doing well, and the eleventh day was talked of for the mother to leave her bed. At ten o'clock in the evening I left Antoinette, who was sleepy. She slept till two o'clock without interruption, when they brought the child to her. She was then quite well, and went to sleep again. At four she awoke suddenly with a shivering fit, which was immediately followed by a burning fever. She sent for me, and I had the doctor summoned. In the course of the day the fever, which resembled those slight fevers which attack women so easily in their confinements after some inadvertence, diminished so much that the physicians thought it would probably be over in the course of twenty-four hours. In the evening there was no increase. The physicians returned at midnight; she was perfectly calm. A little while afterwards she had convulsions; at four o'clock her mind wandered; at eight she was dead, without having regained the use of her senses for a moment. Examination showed that the eruption had invaded all the organs. Such is the deplorable end of a being whom I had thought destined to be, long after I am no more, the friend and mother of my children. No one better than you knows the feeling which led me to contract a second marriage. The necessity not to be alone acted most powerfully upon me. God has decided otherwise, and I submit to His decrees.

In moments of great calamity public feeling is shown. I do not think that for a long time—to my knowledge not since the Emperor's serious illness—any event has caused such a general sensation as that of this sad and sudden death. It was known that on the ninth day she was doing well. On the tenth, at eight in the morning, the news of her death spread through the town. My servants were everywhere stopped; the crowd rushed to our house, and a guard had to be fetched to keep people from being crushed. At the burial, the short distance from the Chancellery to the Church of St.

Michael was so impeded by the crowd that the funeral train could hardly get to its destination. There were several accidents in the church, the altars of which even were invaded. All the crowd wept. This expression of feeling does not console my grief, which will last while I last.

The Emperor, who is certainly my best friend, wishes me to go and stay at the palace. I have refused, however, for the day will come when I must re-enter the house of mourning; therefore it is better not to leave it.

Your sisters have been and are like good angels. At one time I was very anxious about Léontine. She is well now, for grief does not kill. But there have been other catastrophes.

Adam Müller heard of this death from Klinkow-ström, who only wished to prepare him for the news. He looked up to heaven, and said solemnly, 'Now for the first time I know man's fate,' and fell, struck with an attack of apoplexy.

The good and beautiful Countess Taaffe, when she heard the news concerning a friend for whom she had so great a regard, fell into convulsions, after which she was confined five weeks before her time. She is very dangerously ill. May God preserve her! One victim is enough!

After this tale of death and mourning, what more can I say! You are my nearest friend, and you must share my too natural sorrow! May God preserve you and my other children, and thus aid me to drag on my miserable existence so long as He sees fit.

Metternich to Countess Molly Zichy, Vienna, Jan. 23.

916. If I have not written to you before since the frightful misfortune which has thrown me back into

dreary solitude, it is because I have not had the strength
to do so. What can I say to you which the simple fact
has not already told you? I know too well how sincerely you and yours share my feelings to feel obliged
to repeat them to you.

It has been the same for you, dear Molly, as for the
general public; you heard of the death before you heard
anything of the danger. The terrible fever began on the
fifth day. From that day, although there was not one
alarming symptom, a deadly fear possessed me. I knew
the danger of a malady which is never more destructive
than when its aspect is harmless. This disease, this
scourge of the human race, which no one yet knows
how to treat, and consequently cannot cure, makes, in
proportion to the number attacked, more victims than
the plague! The physicians and I were alone in the
secret of the uncertainty so soon resolved into a terrible
reality.

What the Lord gave the Lord can take away; man
must not resist His immutable decrees; therefore I submit, and kiss the hand which has dealt me so heavy a
blow.

But I feel my misfortune most deeply. There are
few individuals who more feel the need of a peaceful
home life, free from agitation and from all cares but
those which here below always interpose between life
and perfect happiness. Nothing was wanting to me;
now I have lost everything for the remainder of my
days.

If anything consoles me, it is the active part that the
public really takes in my sorrow. There is not one
class which does not give proof of this. I do not think
of myself in this, I feel it a homage rendered to the
departed. The other world is daily more and more

'peopled with beings to whom I am united by the closest ties of affection. I, too, shall take my place there, and I shall disengage myself from this life with all the less regret.

You wrote yesterday to Mercy. He spoke to me of your letter; he did not wish to show it to me; it is, I am sure, worthy of you.

Metternich to his son Victor, Vienna, January 30.

917. It is a fortnight to-day since the blow fell. From my feelings I do not know whether this space of time is fourteen minutes or fourteen years. Heaven has given me a strength of resistance to the things of this world that certainly is all I have to enable me to withstand my grief. You know, too, that the double nature which in me moves side by side—the public man and the private individual—never interfere with each other; misfortune acts only on one or on the other side of my existence. I work in order to occupy myself, and I work day and night. Thus I save myself from myself, and it is the only thing I can do.

If I had not before appreciated Léontine, I should have learned to know her during this terrible occurrence. She poured balm into my heart by her whole manner, and by a refinement of attention beyond her years, of which not a shade escaped my attention. God will reward her!

Little Richard is very well; he is strong, robust, and very ugly, which gives me hope that he will not be so when he grows up; he is like no one but himself. The only striking resemblance that he has with his poor mother is in his hands.

I told you above that I take refuge from myself as much as possible in the troubles of Europe. These are great, for the faults which have led to them are immense. God knows what France will come to, and what will become of France! As to the East, I have good hope that it will be pacified. I shall yet have been right for once.

Here there is nothing new, and if there were I should not know it probably. Not that I do not see plenty of people; I even seek to see them, and I have not to take much trouble about it. I cannot be too grateful for the spirit which society shows towards me. My days pass as they always have done. It is not the days that have changed. What has changed is the inward feeling of peace and happiness. I am now once more alone in the world!

918. *February* 4.—Your good letter, my dear Victor, arrived to-day; it is worthy of you, and speaks from your heart to mine.

I should understand your feeling, even if you were not my son, for the case is too striking not to excite a universal feeling of pity. But you, who are the closest friend of my life, and who know its needs—you know better than anyone that I speak truly when I assure you that I have lost half my life. What remains to me is so encumbered with difficulties, troubles, and privations of every kind, that it has little value for me. What value it has still for me arises from my love for my children; the feeling of the great importance of my life for their dear sakes—the feeling, in fact, that I am not a useless piece of furniture in the world!

But it was God's will—therefore complaints must cease and even feeling should keep silence. I have the consciousness of having made happy, so far as it was possible, a being worthy of happiness. Our union, founded on thorough confidence and affection, has never been disturbed for an hour. You have all suffered a serious loss. Antoinette would have continued to be the happiness of my life till my last breath ; after I was gone she would have remained the unchangeable friend of my children. Occupied with them like a real mother, she only thought of their welfare. In her the most upright spirit was joined to the tenderest heart. Calm like myself, reflective, and of tried excellence, I found united in her all that could delight my life. All is over !

To-day I give myself up to a kind of indefinable feeling which always succeeds to great shocks. My health, thanks to my *régime*, has not given way, but I feel physically shattered. My moral powers have always survived the evils of life, and it seems as if my mind would remain firm and uninfluenced by material things till it has the happiness of escaping from their fetters.

I think I have already told you of the many marks of sincere and kind interest which I receive from all sides. You, who know me, will know which among all these have the power of touching me, and which will remain without influence on either mind or heart. To the object of so much attention, of so many cares, trouble of a peculiar kind must ensue. I receive a heap of letters to which I must reply. I receive them from persons who cannot know either me or my misfortunes ; they must be replied to with all the more zeal. In fact, my position is dreadful. I have not yet been able to make up my mind to visit the left wing of the house. I remain in the rooms which are not intended for living in. Sooner or later I shall have again to enter the rooms where I have suffered so much.

Little Richard is very well. He grows and gets fat ; he was a month old yesterday. For the rest, I regret to find that he is no consolation to me. The poor child little knows his loss ; happy age, which does not allow of even a memory !

919. *February* 6.—Our winter continues very severe, and the quantity of snow that covers Austria is remarkable. It is not uncommon for the post to be interrupted for thirty hours and more. I dislike this weather, for it prevents me from taking the air, of which I have great need. I await the spring with impatience. When the winters are severe on this side the Alps, they are generally mild on the other. If it will but be fine at Rome, I will put up willingly with a certain quantity more of snow.

My day is spent in work. I am at my desk by nine o'clock in the morning ; I leave it at five, and return at half-past six. Some friends come to see me from ten till midnight. I began by making a list ; one visitor has brought another, so that some days I have asked myself whether my library—for it is there we live now—would hold all these people. After to-morrow I have announced that the door will be closed. My list includes some ladies and a certain number of men. The Ambassadors are among them, of course, and I cannot sufficiently praise their kind attention. For instance, they have all countermanded their balls during the first week ; an attention which I was certainly far from claiming, but with which I am no less gratified.

I hope that we shall come to an end in the East, but what shall we see in the West? Poor France is in a very, very bad way !

Good-bye, my dear Victor ; take care of your health, and keep your mind easy. God bless you !

920. *February* 10.—I quite understand, my dear Victor, your wish that I could be released for a time from the weight of public affairs—a wish in which no

one joins more heartily than myself. But how can it be possible? I may die any day, and business will go on all the same. Another man will succeed me, and that other I can without difficulty point out. I have even mentioned him in my political testament, just as one appoints an heir in an ordinary will. But this successor, who will be able to replace me without difficulty, could not supply my place for a time, and, above all, not at the moment of a great crisis. This crisis itself might change its character all at once, so that no one can calculate on it; and the most frightful confusion might be added to a disorder already extraordinary. Therefore, I have only to submit to the heaviest yoke a man can have to bear. My nature, however tenacious it may be, can be shattered—I say more, it must be shattered—but my conscience at least will be easy; I shall have done my duty, as the general dies on the battle-field. This battle is important; it is one of those that decide the future, not of one empire alone, but of the whole social order. When armies are called out and the troops engaged at all points, it is not for me to think of yielding my place for a single instant to anyone whatever. The stronger the man who could fill my place, the less he would be able to do my business; for no one can know my arrangements. It is a case when a man must know how to die at the breach, or not present himself there. This is all I can tell you of public affairs. Your wishes are none the less those of a good son and warm friend; I accept them as a good father.

921. *February* 13.—What you say of the detractors of the dear departed one is very true, and is already more than realised. There are none, and I grieve that it is so; for had she lived it would have been otherwise. As to

the past, it is for me as if it had never been. There was something in the poor child's fate so unusual, so striking, both in her elevation and in her loss, that feeling must be excited about her in various ways. Antoinette was not called to her destiny without attracting much attention and disturbing many ideas. Now that all has disappeared, now that there is no present but only the past to study and observe, now history begins, and everyone is agreed. They ask what malice itself could find to say against her? The result is that those who were spiteful yesterday are kindly to-day. Everyone claims to have been one of her friends. The fact is that Antoinette's character prevented her from being anyone's enemy. She was my friend and my children's. Beyond that circle she never sought friends, and her whole life would have been passed in this way. My tears, and those of your sisters—especially those of Léontine, who has lost in her almost as much as I have—are the best eulogy she can have. The woman of whom no one talks is the model of her sex. Napoleon often praised your mother in the same terms, and he was right.

I see that you begin to enjoy Rome as I hoped. There is nothing comparable to that classic soil and the pleasures it provides. They are all of the highest standard and elevate the mind, and that is what many other pleasures cannot do.

922. *February* 16.—The present year is rich in victims. Now it is the unexpected loss of a Pope that comes to disturb my leisure and embarrass me in various ways. The two ideas—death and the Pope—are, however, so much alike, that one's feeling is hardly disturbed. As to the successor, I know many personages who will not be it: but who will be is what I should like to know.

I send you, enclosed, a very curious document for your collection of autographs. It is a letter entirely in the handwriting of Louis XVI. to the late Prince de Lambese, granting him and his brother, Prince de Vaudémont, permission to enter the service of Austria. I found it among my mother's papers—no doubt it had been given to her by the Prince de Lorraine. It is a singular present, for this letter would always have been of great value to the family of him to whom it is addressed. The contents increase the value of the autograph, and the gift is quite historical.

923. *February* 21.—I have finished my despatches for the Conclave, and the courier is setting off.

I received your letter of the 12th inst. by the Florence courier. I am sorry to see that Rome does not escape this terrible winter, which here seems as if it would never be got rid of. No one remembers such a quantity of snow as we have this year. The cold is equally severe; but for some days the sun has been bright, and there are some fine hours for walking. I take as much advantage of them as I can, for I have very great need of them. My machine is much out of order, and it is especially the nerves that are in so bad a state. In reflecting on my life, it seems that so many blows have fallen upon me that many in my place would have succumbed altogether.

I only see, too, around me those who are sad and suffering. Poor Pilat lost his wife this very day. The unhappy husband is left with seven children. Write to him as soon as you can; he will be gratified.

. . . . I send you another autograph. It is a letter of the Archduchess Beatrix; you will see how pleased she was with a portrait of your grandmother I had given her. This Princess is in every way worthy of a place in a collection of autographs, for, beside her personal qualities, she is the last of the house of D'Este, the oldest family in Europe. You know that the house of D'Este Ascania is divided into those of Brunswick and Anhalt. Estes are found as far back as the eighth century.

I shall certainly not tell you who will be Pope; there is little enough to choose between the names; any Pontiff provided with reason will suit me, and there are often cardinals wanting in that rare and useful ingredient to be found under the tiara. I know much more about those who will not be elected. Indeed, this is always the way. I am very glad you are at Rome at the present moment. It is a piece of good fortune.

924. *February 27.*— ... Here we are still in snow. The sun, however, begins to have some power; it thaws in the day, but freezes again at night. I have to-day been for the first time for three months in the garden. One cannot walk a single step except along a little path cut through the snow, which is three feet deep. I went through the hothouses, which are in very good order. The little gardener is really an admirable man. If I could transport this establishment to Mont Palatin, I should ask no more.

925. *March 5.*— .... I see by the last accounts from Count de Lützow that Carbonarism does not disdain to meddle in events. All that will come to an end— so says the 'Courier'—if Cardinal Fesch is elected Pope, in consequence of the protection granted to him by Prince Metternich and the Jesuits! It seems that the 'Courier' has plenty of leisure time to waste for it to occupy itself with such stuff as this; but still there are plenty of idlers in Paris who will believe that Cardinal Fesch is the candidate of our Court!

I see that you are inclined to go to Naples. You

will do well if it is a forward spring; if it is not, do not
hurry too much, for Naples, like all fine countries,
requires verdure. I warn you, also, that Naples will
seem to you quite ugly after Rome. I think even it is
hideously ugly, and it is made worse by its horrible
filth. Of course there is the site, which is admirable.
In your drives about Rome do not forget to see the
stairs at the Palais Braschi. Very likely you have seen
them already, for I think the Cardinal de Milan must live
in that palace if he does not live at the Quirinal.

The last days of the Carnival have given place to
two *fêtes*, one given by the English Ambassador, the other
by the young people. Lord Cowley's fancy ball was,
they say, a great success.

I only know these things by hearsay, and am not
much interested in them. Neither does Lent add or
alter anything in my life. I am not yet able to make
any plan for the summer. I think the probabilities
that I shall not be able to move are, unhappily, greater
than the chances that I may do so.

926. *March* 12.—I write to you at Naples, my
dear Victor, and I send this letter by a special courier.
I suppose you are enchanted with the work of the
Creator under that beautiful sky. Everything there is
lovely—the sky, the earth, the sea. If men had but
seconded the intentions of the Creator, Naples would be
a true paradise, but it is not so. What struck me
especially was the extraordinary want of architectural
monuments in places so near to ancient and modern
Rome. I hope you found a good cicerone. A fortnight
is quite sufficient to exhaust Naples and its environs.
You will have seen the towns of Pompeii and Hercu-
laneum, as well as Baiæ and Sorrente. If you can get
as far as Pæstum, do; in that case you must sleep at

Salerno, and see the Abbaye de la Cava in passing; the next morning go to Pæstum, returning to the same town to sleep, for it is not good to travel by night in the neighbourhood of Naples. You could even see Amalfi the same day.

Do not attempt to climb Vesuvius; at any rate go no further than the Hermitage; you can get so far quite well *à ciuccio*.* To ascend to the summit is extremely fatiguing, and the cold affects one very quickly on the mountain itself.

You will see most admirable things in the studios. Then you must go to see the Catacombs. They are, in my opinion, more curious than those at Rome. One sees there wonderfully well the places of refuge of the first Christians. I hope you have been able to reside in the Chiaja. You must be presented at Court. If you see the King, mention me in the most respectful manner, and also to the Queen.

Ender is now finishing Antoinette's portrait. I called my heart's memory to counsel, and the likeness is perfect. A portrait is a small thing when one has lost all that made the happiness of life; but still it is something.

I send you the programme of the quadrilles at the Duchesse de Berry's. You who know the performers will have more interest in it than I have. You will see that Lady Aldborough figures in them. I am surprised that the Duchesse de Berry takes the character of Marie Stuart. It is rather too near the catastrophe of 1793 and 1794.

927. *March* 26.—I see that Naples pleases you, and I am delighted. The site is perfect, but in my opinion that is all. The country will look still better, for ver-

---

* Neapolitan for *ciuco*, donkey.—ED.

dure is always necessary to a landscape, and that we shall soon have. I was surprised at what you told me of the backwardness of vegetation in Italy; but I have come to the conclusion that the northern plants remain backward in southern countries, while southern plants follow other laws. The trees and shrubs of temperate climates are not more than a fortnight or three weeks in advance of the countries where they are indigenous; so that the oaks, lime trees, and other trees are still budding at Naples when many southern shrubs have already done flowering.

Madame Pasta has just left us; she takes with her the money and the regrets of the Viennese. She has taken, in four weeks and by means of the most wretched representations, forty thousand francs. The Emperor made her *première cantatrice de la chambre*, so that all prospered—her travels, her purse, and her vanity. I still continue to live like a *cénobite*, and I shall make no change till after Easter. The change will not amount to much, for life is nothing but empty forms. Mine is spoiled for ever, and I devote it to God and to my duties as a father and a citizen.

If I could but have an idea what would become of me next summer! There are many probabilities that I shall not be able to stay long away from Vienna, so that I may count the year lost for my tastes and interests. In any case I shall make a tour in Bohemia, for I want to see what is being done at Königswart and at Plass. They are stopped by a number of arrangements which can only be decided on the spot. The manufactories recommence work in July. We shall see whether M. Rippel's prophecies will be realised, and I greatly hope they will.

928. *April* 16.—I send this letter to Rome by a

courier who takes letters to the new Pope. M. de
Lützow will send it on to you.

We have jumped all at once into summer; a fortnight ago everything was covered with snow, and to-day
it is so warm that it was almost impossible to walk out
in the middle of the day. Vegetation does not know
how to keep pace with the temperature, and the year
seems to participate in the folly of the age!

I am sorry you did not stay for Holy Week at Rome,
and that you were not present at the enthronement of
the new Pope. Your loss would have been less if the
weather had been fine at Naples; but I see from a letter
to Léontine that you have a good deal to complain of in
that way. However, by this time you have got over
that difficulty.

Here we have nothing new. I work fifteen hours
out of the twenty-four, and that is nothing extraordinary.
The campaign is about to begin, and if there is not a
negotiation, which I think probable, perhaps I may get
a few weeks' holiday, after which I sigh from the bottom
of my heart. I feel a necessity for getting out of my
prison which I cannot describe. To-morrow it will be
three months since the happiness of my home was destroyed, and I was again left alone with myself and my
responsibilities. During this time I have only seen
those I was obliged to see; after Easter I shall reopen
my *salon*; but it has not much to offer me. For three
months I have not entered the rooms on the other side
of the house, and certainly to return to them will be no
consolation to me.

Imagine my surprise a few days ago at seeing
M. Simon * arrive bag and baggage. He declares that
only at Vienna can his dictionary be appreciated.

* M. Simon had been Metternich's steward.—ED.

He wants me to have it printed, or, what comes to the same thing, he wants me to provide for its author. I have sent them all to Pilat—father, mother, and daughters.

I envy you the happiness of breathing under a southern sky and close to the sea. You will soon have Mr. Robert Gordon at Naples ; he is going to replace Mr. Stratford Canning at Constantinople.

929. *April* 24.—Next Sunday I shall re-open my house. My first return to the world was marked by two great political dinners—one at the Nuncio's, to celebrate the accession of Pius VIII., the other was given by the English Ambassador. I have long promised Dietrichstein that his son should have a holiday. He would have taken it now, if Felix Schwarzenberg had not been called here, to be ready in case the Emperor Nicholas goes to the army and has to be followed by the foreign generals.

930. *May* 8.—I have seen with sorrow, my dear Victor, that you are not satisfied about your health. I attribute this to the bad season, and this is always felt more at Naples than in other parts of Italy—at Rome, for example. The Italian physicians are, in general, ignorant, and only understand their countrymen, who rarely suffer from the maladies which lead travellers from the North to Italy. . . . I hate to know that you are uncomfortable, and Providence has little compassion for me, to judge from the torments it inflicts upon me. I cannot prescribe for you from this distance: your physician at Rome, whom you liked before, will know how to advise you.

. . . The season begins to improve, though it is still very capricious. At the end of two or three fine days we always go back to the horrors of bad weather. This

year is most miserable; nothing is talked of but catastrophes. I do not know which carry off the palm—the
earthquakes or the inundations in Prussia. It is not yet
known how many millions have been lost by these last.

The backward season has also hindered military
operations. The army is still struggling in the mud and
water in the two Principalities near the lower Danube.
This commencement of the new campaign added to the
plague which is spreading in Wallachia, and the disease
which has carried off nearly all the cattle, must have
an effect on the war. This same disease makes great
ravages, too, in our country. With great care, we had
managed to preserve Kojetein; but the disease came at
last, and in less than a fortnight has carried off fifty-four
cows from the farm at Kojetein alone. The malady
is now stayed, and the remainder of the cattle seem to
be saved.

931. *May* 11.—I hope, my dear, that by this time
you are quite well again. Jaeger agrees with me as to
the cause of your illness: it is the coming on of spring
after a very bad winter, which pursued you even into
Italy, where it is much more trying than beyond the
Alps. You would prefer the sirocco to fresh breezes,
and that is because your constitution requires a soft
air. Naples is hard and dry, and not suitable to irri-
table nerves. You will always feel best where the vegetation is rich and succulent, the plants living on air and
water; a volcanic, dry soil will never suit you.

I write only these few lines, for every other subject
is without interest to me.

932. *May* 29.—From what you say, I see that you
have been seriously ill. I was not deceived, for I at
once felt all a father's anxiety at the first hint you gave
me of your indisposition. My uneasiness was increased

from the situation in which you had fallen ill. . . . To-day I had a consultation with Staudenheim and Jaeger about your letter of May 19. They both praised the clearness with which you described your symptoms, and they both think that your malady is the same as that which has already twice attacked you.

As to your journey, they advise that you should stay at least a fortnight at Pisa or Lucca ; and that you should wait for the end of June or beginning of July to pass the Alps. I think they are right on these points. Lead an idle life, and you will soon be restored.

If you want something to read, both interesting and amusing, get the *Mémoires de Bourrienne*. These are the only authentic memoirs of Napoleon which have yet appeared. The style is not brilliant, but that only makes them all the more trustworthy.

933. *June* 5.—I am very glad to see from your last letters that your health has improved. In spite of the horrible weather, Vienna begins to be empty. The younger ladies have this year had a rage for excursions to the country. Whatever the weather may be, they take to the fields, and *fêtes* of this kind, if *fêtes* they are, succeed each other madly. Only a few days ago, in shocking weather, a large party was dragged to Mar-chegg, to the Prince de Palffy's; they got into an omni-bus at seven in the morning, and returned half-an-hour after midnight. In the morning a third of the party had to keep their beds ; another third had lost their voices, and the last third sung the praises of the de-lightful party. You will understand that Léontine does not enter into extravagances of this kind, therefore she is wonderfully well. The Princess de Ligne is at all these parties ; some say it is she who arranges them, others say that they are made in her honour.

I think your second visit to Rome will bring you to my opinion on this city, as compared with Naples. It is with Rome as with all really fine things : they gain by being seen and seen again. God has done all that was possible for Naples, men have spoiled it ; and for it to become what it might have been, the Neapolitans must be sent off to Barbary, and the kingdom be repeopled afresh.

In regard to the people, Tuscany has quite another appearance. The people are a fine race and clean. Nothing is so charming as the drive from Florence to Livourne ; the villages are numerous, and industry is everywhere highly developed.

Good bye ! I hope you will bring your travels to a good termination, and have a pleasant journey over the Alps. It will make me very happy to see you again.

PRINCE VICTOR'S ILLNESS AND DEATH.

Extracts from Metternich's private Letters from July 3 to December 1, 1829.

Metternich to Countess Molly Zichy,
Vienna, July 3, 1829.

934. I have been for some days with my son, who is undergoing very severe treatment; but, happily, is doing well. His health is feeble and his chest delicate. The Italian doctors have treated him for a fever; he is now in good hands, and his condition is improved. Instead of giving him quinine, they have bled him; he was weak and he begins to be strong; he coughed a great deal, now he coughs no more. My life, dear Molly, is a very sad life; every calamity falls upon me. Thus I have become a coward with regard to the health of others, while I have plenty of confidence in my own. You ask about my *soirées*; I can describe them in a word—there are no *soirées*, either with me or anywhere else. Here and there a masculine individual or two comes to me between ten and eleven in the evening; as for ladies, there are none, and I might say, like Stackelberg of the Neapolitan ministers—ladies, we are without. You were present at the sentimental scene Gentz got up for me; well, he has not come one single time to keep me company. Léontine goes to bed at ten, so as to be able to get up early; I work till one, and then go to bed. See my *soirées* and their charms.

935. *July* 9.—I have only good news to tell you of

Victor. He is as well as he can be after three or four months of illness. He has neither cough nor fever nor irritation. Since he was under the rod of my little tyrant he has not taken a grain of medicine; his *régime* is more severe than that of the homœopaths, for it is of water; in three bleedings they have drawn thirteen or fourteen ounces of blood, and each time he has felt eased from a burden. One may now hope that he will recover from what might have been most serious. Next week I shall settle him at Erlaa, a place unanimously recommended by the eight physicians I consulted, as being the mildest and most tiresome. I shall not stay there myself, but have a temporary lodging there; at the end of the month I hope to be able to take my tour in Bohemia. I shall leave Herminie with her brother, and take Léontine with me. This is my plan, and you will easily believe that I have much need of getting away from a place of such sad memories—a place that I leave with pleasure, as a prisoner leaves his dungeon. Each day, dear Molly, shows me more plainly that my life is ended, and that if I am not physically numbered with the dead, I morally belong to them. Do not believe in the effect of solitude on me, for my feeling about realities is never influenced by the *salons*. The *salons*, little or big, do not change what seems to me to be the truth.

936. *July* 24.—Gentz brings you 'Marino Faliero.' It is all I can send you, for I have not the 'Moïse.' I send you the history of Philippe Auguste; it is charming reading, but to be presentable in the *salon* needs some excisions. Among others there are some details about King Philippe's divorce from Ingelburga of Denmark, which are not made for the ears of those who have nothing to do with matrimonial cases of conscience.

Certainly Pope Innocent III. was of all men the least worthy to bear that fine name. One has only to read his letter to the King, to be convinced of that.

I am making preparations for my tour in Bohemia. I hope to start on the first of August, or a day or two later. Victor undergoes a terrible sort of treatment; but it suits him. In really serious cases it does not do to trifle, and the contrary defect is neither to my taste nor the doctor's. Happily, Victor is the most patient of patients and the most tractable of invalids. If I did not know him so well, I should certainly not stir from his side.

937. *Plass, August* 26.—I wished to write to you before I left Vienna, but my departures do not resemble those of other human beings. I have not found a moment to perform the only task which would have been pleasant to me. I remained a fortnight at Königswart. This place is on the way to become beautiful and agreeable. The change made in the last two years is extraordinary, and I see that those who did not know it in its old state can hardly believe it. The country all round, far beyond anything that could be called a garden, is being entirely formed anew. The park will be more than two leagues round, and within that space there is not a point where art is not brought to the assistance of a nature which is here extremely wild. Masses of rock, abundance of water, turf like that in England, and vegetation which I can only compare to that of the Alpine valleys, are, under the hands of M. Riedl and of an excellent gardener, brought to absolute perfection in its way. I think, too, that my own skill does the undertaking no harm; and thus all goes well at a spot which is nowadays one of the most frequented in the civilised world. By means of the creation of

Marienbad, and the new roads making communication
easy and short between Carlsbad, Franzensbad, and
Marienbad, I have only too many people coming to see
my works. Every fine afternoon thirty or forty carriages are collected round the little inn (which will
next year be metamorphosed into a fine *café*), and the
visitors to the baths from all parts of the world visit
those parts of the park that are finished or nearly
so. Among the visitors of 1829 were the Queen of
Hayti and the Princesses Améthyste and Athénaïs, her
august and very black daughters. The book in which
strangers who visit the Museum write their names
(once stolen, but now recovered) already contains more
than a thousand of names, black and white. I have
long seen that there is now no such a thing as distance
in this sublunary world !

The remains of those to whom I owe my being, and
of those who have adorned my life, and whom I have
had the misfortune to survive, are deposited at Plass, in
the chapel which I have consecrated to our future
re-union, and to embellish this locality and make it
worthy of my respect for those who are no more is one
of my chief cares. The chapel is finished, and the
arrangement of the grounds which surround it is now
all that I have to do. This new chapel is frequented
by all the neighbourhood. Three days of plenary in-
dulgence, and the magnificent remains of a Saint Valentine—a martyr of the end of the second century, sent
to me by Pope Leo for it—have attracted five-and-
twenty to thirty thousand pious pilgrims. The place
where stones rise heavenwards in memory of those who
are no more, is not an agreeable residence for those
who remain behind. The mask of the body of Saint
Valentine was made in wax in Canova's studio ; it is

most beautiful, and by a singular chance it is like Antoinette!

We will dismiss these mournful subjects, and, indeed, I ask your pardon for having touched on them in my letter ; but I am too much surrounded by them, and too full of them, not to speak of them. I find that the only letters which have any value to friends are those which depict the moral situation of the writer. It is only thus that they form part of the history of life, and this, and not romance, should count in friendship. Gentz is more innocent in the country than in the town, with an innocence which in a young person would be ingenuousness. He hates Plass, not for what makes it so gloomy to me, but because of the large rooms, the distances of everything, the want of a flower-garden, and the number of dirty sheep, which he would like to see white. Two things console him : one is that he has not to stay there long, and the other that he can see the casting of iron. My new ironworks are in full work, and though he detests black iron, he likes red iron. The only fault he finds with the works is the noise of the hammers, which he would like to have wrapped in cotton-wool, and the howling of the wind through the bellows. He would like a forge without either the one or the other.

I believe that Gentz, the romantic soul, will be with you immediately. He wants to see Henrietta * again, to whom, however, he has not been altogether faithful during the separation. He has increased his list of fifteen by two new beauties, and he looks for more ; in fact, the whole feminine sex will be placed there! Happy Gentz, and poor sex! If he comes to you do

* Afterwards Princess Odescalchi, the daughter of Countess Molly Zichy.—ED.

not forget to get him on the subject of Plass; he will give you a good description. What vexed him most was that during the long space of eight days he did not see one person worthy of his attention, 'not one woman kind, not one cheerful hour; nothing but horrible iron, big rooms, white walls, provincial officials, and miners.' He will never go back there !

I am sorry that Henrietta cannot see the work of a Venetian who is here now, and who makes copies of famous pictures very cleverly. She has invented a quite new manner, which is that of a miniature on wood and varnished. It is like oil-painting, but has all the delicacy of a miniature. The pictures are tolerably large. I have at this moment a copy of the fine ' Virgin,' by Jean Bellin, and the copy is really a *chef-d'œuvre*.

938. *Vienna, Sept.* 11.—Here I am, my dear Molly, back again in my poor prison. It is only pleasant to me from rejoining my children, and I do not complain. I am quite at peace. I find Victor greatly better than when I left. All the symptoms of his malady are much lessened; we must see if this improvement can be maintained. We have nothing, therefore, to build upon, but still there is positive improvement.

Vienna is as empty as a beggar's pocket, so that I see no one except those who have business with me, and there are some among these with whom I should much prefer not to have any business. I shall soon be rid of one of these persons. The Duc de Laval * leaves us almost immediately for the banks of the Thames. I do not know who is to replace him; they talk of M. de la Ferronays, which would delight me. But as your friend Chateaubriand has just resigned his place at Rome, I am rather afraid that M. de la Ferronays, on account of

* French ambassador.—ED.

his health, may prefer Rome to Vienna. This will be decided very soon, and, whoever it may be, any ambassador who replaces Laval will be a comfort. Since the last ministerial revolution in his country, the good man has lost the very little head he had on his shoulders. His absence of mind works so with his anxieties that they become real crises. A few days ago M. de Laval went to one of his colleagues. On going into his room he said to him, ' Well, well, it's all very fine ; but why did you not tell me ? ' The colleague of course replied by the question, ' What is it that I have not told you ? What do you want to know ? Whom do you complain of ? ' M. de Laval, continuing his complaints, his ' Ah well ! ' and his lamentations, obliged the interpellator to repeat twenty times the same series of questions, when at last M. de Laval, rubbing his forehead, said, ' Ah well ! really, I don't know myself what I was going to tell you ! '—and then to have to do business with a diplomatist of this stamp !

I know that if Chateaubriand is sent to us you will be delighted ; but you must remain disconsolate, for we shall not have him !

939. *Dec.* 1.—I am so convinced of the feeling of you and yours, that I do not even thank you. This feeling is natural ; it is that of sincere benevolence and friendship, and certainly, if anyone has need of friends, it is I.

The loss I have just suffered is irreparable, for it concerns one who united in himself the rarest qualities. His long illness and his death are to him the martyr's palm. I have seen many men die in various ways ; I have never seen one depart as my poor son has departed ! Ask all those who were about him during the last period of his life ; they will all tell you the same thing. I do not know what was most conspicuous, the strength of his faith in God, his thorough detachment from everything but high feeling or duty, his perfect calm, or his filial and fraternal affection !

The actual death was for him and for us all a deliverance. He hardly allowed me at last to leave him, and one of the last words he said to me was : 'You, too, will now soon be relieved !' Léontine and her little sister have behaved like angels ; they have been always with him, too ; they were more courageous than I was, or than his attendants, but certainly not more than he was himself.

MISSION EXTRAORDINARY OF COUNT FICQUEL- MONT TO ST. PETERSBURG.

Metternich to Ficquelmont (Instruction),
Vienna, January 17, 1829.

940. The interest of the service requiring that the diplomatic relations between our Court and that of Russia should not be suspended in consequence of the long absence of Count Zichy from his post; and the Emperor's choice having fallen on you, his Majesty desires that you will immediately repair to St. Petersburg.

You will be the bearer of an autograph letter to this effect to the Emperor of Russia, by which our august master accredits you with that monarch as being charged with a mission extraordinary.

In order to enable you to follow the line of our thoughts after we are separated, it seems to me necessary to inform you of our opinion on the three following questions, namely :

1. The general tendency of the policy of the Emperor Nicholas.

2. The attitude of the Court of Russia in the Triple Alliance.

3. Lastly, the relations of the moment between that Court and ours.

I. *General Tendency of the Policy of the Emperor of Russia.*

The Emperor, having ascended the throne in the midst of rebellion, seemed conscious of the necessity of

devoting his first care to the internal administration of
his Empire. The first declarations of his Imperial
Majesty showed this feeling, and it was shared by the
great majority of the nation and by numerous foreign
diplomatists. But some persons, closely acquainted
with the mind and temper of the Emperor, were
of opinion that he would rather recur to the political
errors of the Russian sovereigns of the eighteenth century. To judge by what has happened, these persons
are not entirely mistaken. Indeed, how is it possible
not to perceive that the events which led affairs to
that frightful crisis could have had no other point of
departure but a system thought out by the Emperor
Nicholas? What had up to this time lent a certain
colour of moderation to the proceedings of this Prince
may be explained by his efforts to turn the advantages
his relative moderation had given him in favour of the
real end of his policy. Of two things, one ; either the
Emperor Nicholas followed the course we attribute
to him, or that monarch was a proof of such a facility
for being drawn out of the path of sound policy, that
an absolute want of calculation and reflection could
hardly suffice to explain this phenomenon. But nothing
authorises us to make this admission.

II. The Attitude of the Court of Russia in the Triple Alliance.

Nothing, doubtless, is more difficult than to comprehend the singular course of the Triple Alliance. It is
clearly shown that none of the contracting Courts now
know (if, indeed, they ever have known) which way they
are going, or at what end they may arrive. The approaches between Russia and England, coming after a
very decided estrangement on both sides, were the work

of Mr. Canning. This move was sketched out in the last months of the life of the Emperor Alexander; it was completed under the reign of his successor. The appearance of the Duke of Wellington at the head of the British Cabinet, and the Russo-Turkish War, should have given a deadly blow to a work which had no other foundation than views of personal interest and the development of an unhappy policy.

The course which France has followed in the whole affair agrees with the extreme frivolity and the weakness of the administrations which have succeeded each other in that kingdom. To make great efforts to discover what lies plainly on the surface, is labour thrown away; we shall therefore not attempt to explain the political course of France.

The only one of the three Cabinets which has not varied in conduct since the origin of the Triple Alliance is that of St. Petersburg. The Emperor of Russia—always gentle and smooth in his way of acting, suave and kindly in his relations towards his allies, but vigorous in the pursuit of his own views and interests—knew how to take advantage to the utmost of the protocol of April and the treaty of July 6. He was able to make use of his allies for his own interests, and to give an extension to those interests which they would never have gained with so little difficulty if the policy of England and France had not been chained to the car of the third allied Court.

To analyse the Triple Treaty would be impossible, for it is at once everything and nothing. To define its object and fix its limits is equally impossible; it exists, and it is all that the Russian policy needs from which to take the flight which we have seen. In the interest of the enterprise, said to be a common undertaking, events

such as the disaster of Navarino and the expedition to
the Morea may have been superfluous; but they have
none the less contributed to the advantage of the active
party of the alliance; and it was necessarily in this
alliance so, for Russia alone knew what she required
and what part she could take. Not to have had to
fight the Ottoman naval forces, and to have seen, at
the critical period of the first campaign, a French army
disembark in the Morea, is, on Russia's part, not only to
have been fortunate, but to have known how to improve
upon fortune.

III. Present Relations between Russia and Austria.

It would be impossible to clear up this question
without separating what, in the relations between the
two Courts, forms the antecedents of the present crisis,
and what proceeds from the crisis itself.

In taking into consideration the first of these, I shall
not extend my examination to the causes of the constraint which naturally must exist between two neighbouring empires. This constraint is of the very nature
of things, and it is inevitable when one great political
body, whose well-being rests on the basis of preservation, finds itself in the way of another State which
aims only at progressive encroachments. If sometimes
we have seen the two empires unite, it has only been
with one common aim of aggrandisement, as in the
partition of Poland and the war against the Turks; or
when a common danger has called them to a common
defence—as in the wars of the Revolution and the
French Empire. At the close of the last war, provoked
by the perpetual invasions of Napoleon, there certainly
was established between the two Courts a union resting
on different bases; but this union derived its source

from the personal character of the Emperor Alexander, and the tension at present existing between the two Courts was, doubtless, produced in great measure by a state of things too little in conformity with the Russian nature not to bring about a thorough reaction.

Your Excellency knows the antecedents of the present crisis so well that I have no need to describe the different phases through which our relations with St. Petersburg have passed since the accession of the Emperor Nicholas. You therefore know that at the beginning of his reign, that Prince undertook to assure us that there would be no change in the intimate relations between the two Empires; but his practice has in no way corresponded with his protestations. To be convinced of this, it is sufficient to mention the single fact of the transactions which immediately afterwards took place between the Cabinets of London and St. Petersburg, the substance of which was so opposed to the immutable principles of our august master that it would have been impossible for us ever to have taken any active part in them.

Any such deviation soon leads those who are guilty of it to recriminations and calumny. They began by reproaching us at St. Petersburg for not having entered on the trilateral affair; later on they accused us of preventing the pacification. The reproach was unjust; the accusation is more than that—it is absurd. Any formal denial, however, would be useless and humiliating; the conduct attributed to us is contradicted as much by the evidence of facts as by that of our political interests.

With reference to the position of affairs at the pre-

sent moment, a new difficulty between the two Courts
has presented itself.

The Triple Alliance has had the fate we invariably
predicted; the Russian war, on its side, has not answered the expectations of its authors. Both of these
facts show that we were in the right—an unpardon-
able wrong in the eyes of those whose *amour-propre*
we have wounded by not wishing to follow in their
footsteps.

Three principal causes may thus be assigned to the
state of tension existing between Russia and ourselves :

The permanent constraint which our Power imposes
on our neighbour ;

The reaction of the present reign against the personal system of the late Emperor ;

The check to the triple plans and the Russian
arms.

To these causes must be joined one more, which
cannot be regarded as secondary.

During the glorious years of the reign of the Emperor Alexander, Count Nesselrode was not only the
confidant of the intimate relations between the two
Courts, but in many respects he contributed to strengthen
them. Wanting in energy, and finding his position
insecure, this minister began to yield when he saw the
party opposed to the political system of the late Emperor daily increasing, and preparing for an open attack
upon that same system, and consequently upon those
who had used it. When his own weakness made him
renounce his former principles, he became of necessity
the detractor of the antecedents of his own political
career. From a zealous friend he then became an
adversary, all the more active, since to support his new

part, and save himself from the reproach of manifest contradiction, he had to use every effort to make people believe that it was our arrangements, and not those of his Court, which had undergone a total change. This task must have appeared to him very easy of fulfilment as long as such brilliant hopes were attached to the new moral and political direction taken by the Russian Cabinet ; it cannot appear so now when facilities are changed into difficulties, and definite successes—even supposing them still possible—can only be obtained at the price of efforts and sacrifices of every kind, which are no more popular in Russia than they would be in any other country. The seeming advantages of a bad policy generally disappear with fortune, and fortune so far has not crowned with success an enterprise with which we did not care to associate ourselves.

Having sketched the moral situation as between our Court and that of Russia, it remains for me to pass to the second part of the present instruction. This will include the practical questions most worthy of the active solicitude of the principal Courts, and more particularly of our own.

An enterprise long prepared, and announced to the world with very uncommon emphasis, has failed. This fact alone is important, for, whatever may be the future contingencies in the war which Russia is now making upon the Porte, the stain of the first campaign is ineffaceable. As a great State it may repair losses, however grave; but it has lost that reputation for invulnerability which the Russian monarchs have been able to maintain since the origin of the Empire.

In the present despatch I will content myself with speaking generally ; the chances more or less in favour of rehabilitation, or the risk of new losses, can change nothing of the past, and the future is in the hands of Providence. It is the present moment—that of your Excellency's *début* at St. Petersburg—which alone need occupy my thoughts.

Your attention must be fixed upon two objects—namely :

I. To define accurately the position of your Court in the great conflict of the day ;

II. To ascertain as far as possible the bases on which the ideas of the Emperor Nicholas rest, the direction of his mind, the extent of his projects, and the means which he can or will employ to carry them out.

Ad I. Of the wishes of the Emperor our august master you are well aware. The Emperor will never give up his principles. It was weakness of that kind which, in the transactions of the last three years, was yielded to by the Courts, and obliged us to separate ourselves from their political course. At the time of the rupture of the *pourparlers* at St. Petersburg we were accused more than once of being too firm in the matter of principles.

The experience of those Courts which were not so particular would certainly not induce us to change our ground, if we needed to take lessons anywhere except from our own convictions.

We have always ardently desired that the general peace of Europe should not be disturbed ; though at all times the essence of our policy is pacific, we attach a special value to the preservation of political repose in a combination of circumstances where the consequences of a war cannot possibly be estimated.

What our constant care could not prevent, we fervently hope to see replaced by a state of things more in harmony with the general and common interests of the Powers.

This truth, although verified by the evidence of facts, will not secure you altogether from recrimination on the part of the Russian Cabinet. The position of this same Cabinet is too full of difficulty for it easily to reconcile itself to a Court which, while participating in more than one common danger, is not exposed to any peculiar difficulty.

I do not imagine that either the Emperor or his Vice-Chancellor will dream of re-opening the discussion on the subject of the negotiations which preceded the rupture of the Conferences of St. Petersburg, in the course of the summer of the year 1825.

In any case it would be a very easy ground for you to defend; it lends itself to the defence of opinions which we have always held, for events have justified our predictions.

It is more probable that there will be an attempt at recrimination on our decision not to connect ourselves with the Triple Treaty of the year 1827. But here also the event has spoken in favour of the part we took. The consequences of their rash agreement are certainly not calculated to console those who joined in that treaty for the evil which has resulted for the general cause, and the innumerable difficulties which have arisen for each one of them taken singly.

They will recur, no doubt, to our political conduct at Constantinople. Facts will again reply for us, and these facts are such that no malignant and gratuitous accusations, nor attempts of intriguers, can ever invalidate them.

As often as the Powers aim at open accommodation with the Porte the influence of Austria will be there to support their salutary enterprise, while attempts of a different kind will always be repugnant to the political conscience of the Emperor.

Your Excellency is perfectly informed of our correspondence with the Internuncio. You will, therefore, be able to reply by positive citations to every one of the imputations which may be laid to our charge, or to that of the representative of the Emperor at the Porte.

They will speak to you at St. Petersburg of what they are pleased to call our armaments. No person being better informed than your Excellency is as to our military affairs, I have nothing to tell you on that subject.

Thirteen years of uninterrupted political peace have enabled the Emperor to use for the internal administration of his monarchy a considerable portion of the resources which, according to our former organisation, would have been reserved for military use. During that time candid and well-meant exhortations have been many times made to his Imperial Majesty by the monarchs his allies, and especially by the late Emperor Alexander, on what they did not hesitate to qualify as a dangerous neglect of the principal support of the State.

The epochs of Troppau and Laybach were particularly remarkable in this respect.

During that long pacific era, Russia, of all the empires the least exposed to attacks from without, never ceased to maintain her armies on a footing approaching that of war. Well-organised *corps d'armées* are found echelonned in her western provinces; a new army has been created in Poland. We have remained in a state of perfect tranquillity. The war of 1828 approached, it broke out, and our military attitude underwent no change. But the French Government addressed itself to the Chambers, requiring an addition to the army and numerous subsidies, explaining its demands by the contingencies it declared probable; from that time the Emperor our august master ordered that the reduction which had been made in the military administration should be restored.

This is the history of what they are pleased to call the armaments of Austria. In removing the army from its normal peace-footing the Emperor felt he was but fulfilling a duty towards his own empire and the whole of Europe.

If ever you are attacked on this question, reply and explain yourself as to our proceedings on this point as on all others. Nothing in our conduct requires to be covered with a veil. If ever we have any cause of regret, it is when our usual habit must give way to the respect for some considerations, political or administrative, which deprive us of the power of giving entire publicity to all the acts and measures of the Government.

Ad II. To give you, in the present despatch, a sketch sufficient to guide you to the second object mentioned above, seems to us impossible. We are the more willing to admit our powerlessness, inasmuch as we have every confidence in your powers of observation, and have many reasons for thinking that the ideas of the Emperor of Russia, as to the means by which he would prefer to disengage himself from the grave difficulties in which he is entangled, are not yet arranged. But whatever difficulty he may have in making a choice, he must in the end yield to the hard necessity of making some choice.

I do not think it necessary to explain to you how much our views concerning the needs and resources of the Russian monarch differ from those on which many of the Courts are accustomed to found their calculations. We know what an Emperor of Russia can do, and what he cannot do; we have never written any romance on that empire, and while we have always estimated its resources at their just value, we have never concealed the difficulties which they might find in employing them, on account of many local circumstances and defects in the internal administration. When the public opinion of Europe was led away by more than one deceitful appearance, our judgment continued on that same line of severe equity on which it now stands, when so many blind advisers are ready to change their former part for that of detractors no less blind. The question, too, whether the Emperor of Russia will be able, with chances of assured success, to re-open and carry on the campaign of 1829, is not among those which we consider worthy of examination. The only one that must necessarily occupy us is, to find out the direction which that monarch will give to his policy, for on the solution of that the future will depend.

It is certain that the ground on which Russia finds herself to-day is entirely different from that from which she started in the present war. The Russian and Ottoman armies will no longer be the same at the opening of the next campaign. The Triple Alliance will enter into fresh combinations, which will be the fruit of the present winter. The campaign of 1828 had been calculated at St. Petersburg on the chance of a *coup-de-main*, the success of which had not been regarded as doubtful. An undertaking reputed transient and easy has turned out to be a most serious enterprise. If the hope of being able to bring the war to an end in one single campaign still exists at St. Petersburg, common prudence should nevertheless make the Emperor provide means of war for two campaigns.

In this situation what does that Prince desire? It appears to me that this might easily be found out in a short time.

The rumours which have reached us from different quarters induce us to believe that the Emperor Nicholas is tired of the war, and that his ideas of pacification are limited to the maintenance of the *status quo ante bellum*, or something very like it.

It is said that he has abandoned all pretensions to pecuniary indemnities, and that he will be ready to take as their equivalent the preservation of the fortresses of Anapa, Poti, &c.

It is also said that his pretensions to what in the Russian Manifesto were described as guarantees for the liberty of commerce, are confined to the stipulations already existing between the Porte, Russia, and the other Powers.

Lastly, it is said that the general wishes of the Emperor are restricted to the accomplishment of the stipulations of Ackerman.

According to our view, many difficulties would be removed by arrangements like these. Many, however, would still remain, and those of so grave a nature as to render a peaceful conclusion hard of attainment.

These difficulties are both material and moral.

The Treaty of Ackerman * was the latest result of that preponderance which Russia for so many years maintained at Constantinople. It is easy to see, in the

* By the Treaty of Ackerman, concluded between Russia and Turkey October 7, 1826, the Porte was bound to carry out the Peace of Bucharest (1812), gave up the mouths of the Danube to Russia, and guaranteed to the Russians free trade with Turkey and protection from the pirate ships of the insurgent States.—Ed.

present state of things, that the Sultan will endeavour
to prove that the Treaty of Ackerman shall be the last
act of that character. In stating this theory I have no
doubt that thousands of voices will be ready to reply
with the simple exclamation, that it is necessary to
force the Sultan to renounce a pretension which these
same voices do not hesitate to qualify as ridiculous.
But this is no reply at all. The question is whether the
Emperor of Russia intends to force the Porte to a peace
which would be of a nature to satisfy his Imperial
Majesty in every respect, and in case of the affirmative
there would no longer be any question of peace, but
only that of the continuation of the war.

The Treaty of Ackerman contains more than one
clause to which, we are certain, the Sultan will never
again subscribe.

The wish expressed by the Divan in favour of a
peace under guarantees cannot reasonably signify anything else than a desire for a clear and precise treaty,
in which certain articles—which were simply a blind
to mask new encroachments—should find no place.

Moreover, the real question—the only one which in
my eyes has any practical value—is whether the Emperor of Russia intends to make peace with the Porte,
or if he aims at the renewal of stipulations which, in
reality, have never been anything but capitulations.

In case the intentions of the monarch (for those of
his statesmen will never have that tendency) aim at the
establishment of a state of real peace, we thankfully
admit that the difficulties, even those which at first
sight seem the most grave, can be overcome, were it
only that the Porte itself is enlightened enough to
prefer a state of real peace to the continuation of a
war so fertile in disastrous chances for itself.

If, on the contrary, the intentions of the Emperor should agree with those which we regard as likely to influence his councils, the struggle between these two States will only be terminated at the point of the sword.

I believe I have now reduced the real questions to their most simple form.

The work of conciliation would doubtless be greatly served if the same opinion were everywhere pronounced on the nature and value of the different aspects which the great affair of the moment presents. I dare not hope that such will be the case.

The Court of Russia seems to be applying itself at present to give its political conduct a tone of moderation. Of two things, one—either the Emperor is in reality as moderate in his views as he says he is, or the care which he takes to appear so is a pretence. We cannot form an opinion on what must require so many proofs; we wish we could induce other Cabinets to have the same reserve, and particularly that of France, which espouses with an unhappy facility the one side or the other in questions which at least require a calm examination! You know our opinion of the situation in that kingdom, as far as an opinion can be formed from the most recent data. The situation of France, however, must be grave indeed to be able to distract our attention from the affairs of the East.

For a long time unhappy relations have subsisted between France and Russia. I call these relations unhappy, because they have always depended on fallacious principles, or enterprises menacing the repose of Europe.

What augments the present danger are the grave errors into which a great number of the French

Royalists have fallen. Dupes of their own false theories of national glory, and of the stratagems of the Revolutionists, these men embrace the wildest projects, and their decided tendency towards Russian preponderance has no other foundation than the hope of also serving by that preponderance the interests of the French Power. For many years the Cabinet of St. Petersburg has had an extraordinary fancy for Liberal opinions, even when the Emperor Alexander had become the determined adversary of the revolutionary spirit. This was especially the case when the influence of General Pozzo was all-powerful in the very Liberal council of Louis XVIII., and when the ministers Decazes and Dessoles applied themselves to the realisation of many crude plans, under the feeble administration of the Duke de Richelieu. Thus we have seen M. de Chateaubriand, under the protection of that same ambassador, hoisting Russian and revolutionary colours at the same time. Count de la Ferronays, who is certainly as much Russian as French, belongs also to one of the most Liberal ministries France has yet had.

Nothing in the connection which since the Restoration has more or less actively existed between the two States has changed. What has experienced a notable change is the political situation of the Court of Russia ; and a question the solution of which will be one of the most important in its consequences is, what influence this change of position will exercise on the political connection between the two Powers.

There is sufficient evidence to leave no doubt as to the political and overmastering tendency which the revolutionary faction in France displays every day more and more. A minister so feeble as he who now governs France cannot in any way be counted as a counterpoise in the balance. His tendency is decidedly less monarchical than revolutionary and Russian. Will the Emperor Nicholas support a state of things so dangerous for the repose of Europe, and does he believe he will find by so doing means to diminish the difficulties which weigh heavily on his empire, in consequence of the grievous mistakes which signalised the beginning of his reign? The fate of a whole future is contained in this question.

I can do no more than draw your attention to this subject. To go further, and enter into details, appears to me impossible. Your own observation will be your guide, and I shall consider it my duty to make you aware of every circumstance likely to be of assistance.

It is important for us to know the real thoughts of the Emperor, at a moment full of difficulties for that Prince and of danger for the world. Everything depends upon the direction which, in these grave circumstances, he may give to his policy, and our duty is to do all we can to enlighten his mind on our own account. If we can succeed in opening his eyes to our political conduct a great advantage will have been gained, were it only that he will then be able to choose between two clearly defined parties, a happiness which up to this hour has not fallen to his lot.

First Supplementary Note to the Instructions to Count de Ficquelmont.

Among the causes of the tension between our Court and that of Russia, I ought to mention that of the correspondence of the Russian agents, who are all more or less inclined to flatter the wounded *amour-propre* of their Government rather than to inquire into the truth. National vanity does not allow the Russians to confess

that they may have made mistakes ; and they will end
by themselves believing, from mere repetition, that
their defeats are attributable to the inclemency of the
season, and the manœuvres of the Austrians. I only
mention these difficulties to complete the sketch I have
given you, for time alone can bring the remedy, as time
alone can make the truth known.

I must, however, touch upon one more probable
cause of the species of animosity against the Austrian
Cabinet which seems to characterise opinion in Russia,
at least that of the *salons* and of the officers who surround the Emperor Nicholas. You must study your
ground, and find out how deep this cause has gone :
a study which is, from the gravity of the subject, worthy
of your most earnest attention.

For almost two years before the decease of the
Emperor Alexander, the conspiracy, which in the end
endangered the existence of the throne, as well as of the
monarch himself, had made great strides ; and, so to
speak, tolerated and encouraged by the timidity and
passiveness of the Emperor Alexander, it worked openly.
This conspiracy, however, dared not attack the monarch
in front, surrounded by prestige as he still was, and it
therefore applied itself to discrediting him in the eyes
of the nation.

To represent the Emperor as the servile instrument
of a Cabinet which held him under its tutelage, to
represent him as unceasingly sacrificing the interests of
Russia to European interests, detrimental to the Empire,
was a clever calculation on the part of the conspirators,
for it was founded on absurd national pride, always
unreflecting, always ready to draw from the most im-
pure sources, a lever which is most powerful in Russia.

These conspirators belonged to the nobility, they

filled the *salons* ; there they sowed the seeds which the weakness of the Emperor Alexander had allowed to develop, and the minister, accused and often warned by the public voice, but blinded by an inconceivable security, did not tremble for his position till the day when the explosion took place and he had changed masters. This horrible explosion stripped the throne of its immediate perils, since it exposed a great number of his enemies to the new monarch, but the opinions they had propagated remained. The Government did nothing to rectify them, nothing to vindicate the memory of the late Emperor, nothing to dissipate the accusations which weighed on the ministers whom the Emperor Nicholas had kept ; far otherwise. Without examining the source of these opinions, and only stopping to observe its effects, the Emperor affected to give to his conduct and his language a tone exclusively Russian, and independent of all general interests, hoping thus to escape the reproaches which had attended and saddened the last days of his brother. Firm and courageous at the beginning, he soon yielded to a chimera : he punished the conspirators severely, yet he allowed their works to remain ; he retained the same ministers, but did nothing to re-establish their credit.

I do not think I am mistaken in saying that the conspiracy was not attacked at its roots, and that it still exists ; nor do I think I am mistaken in asserting that the present tension against Austria is in part its work. Circumstances only have modified its language ; then the hatred was against Austria because she influenced the Russian Cabinet and somewhat dimmed its glory ; to-day the hatred is against Austria because she impedes the glory and the interests of Russia.

If we consider the blind resistance opposed by the Russian Government to the reiterated warnings of the existence of the conspiracy, even when it was at the very gates of the Palace of the Czars, we cannot reject the possibility of the same Government obstinately deceiving itself as to the cause of this groundless exasperation. But the remarkable coincidence between the opinions promulgated at St. Petersburg and those put forth in the French Liberal newspapers ought to attract its attention.

Not till you have been some time resident in that capital will you be able to pronounce an opinion on the existence and intensity of an evil which, while seriously menacing Russia, is not less formidable to the whole of Europe.

Second Supplementary Note to the Instructions to Count de Ficquelmont.

I feel it my duty to point out to you two more difficulties which will prevent an early peace between the belligerent Powers: one belongs to the domain of politics; the other to that of *amours-propres*; the latter have played too important a part in the events of the last few years for us to be able to leave them out of our calculations.

The first difficulty is connected with the claim of the Divan, instructed by the experience of a century, to conclude henceforth no treaty with Russia except under a sort of general guarantee from Europe: that is to say, a treaty in which the arrangements on both sides shall be consolidated; which is not left to be revised by subsequent negotiations in which (Turkey has not to fear disputes or fresh encroachments on the part of Russia.

But will the pressure of necessity exercise sufficient power upon the counsels of the Cabinet at St. Petersburg to enable it to deviate from its ancient and unchanging system—a system to which it owes innumerable advantages, and the maintenance of which is possibly the only true aim of the war? Will it consent, in short, to conclude a final peace, to associate the European Governments in interests and transactions with which it has hitherto been too jealous even to make them acquainted? One must know better than we do at present the extent and urgency of these necessities to be able to judge if their voice would predominate over another course—without doubt a vicious and unjust course, but to which the sanction of nearly a century has given, in the eyes of the great majority of Russians, a certain kind of legality, at variance, however, with every feeling of justice.

The second difficulty, which concerns their feeling of self-esteem, would be the initiative which one of the two Powers must take to approach the other. To expect the first advance on the side of the Porte would be a delusion ; to hope for it on the part of Russia would be to look for an impossibility, for this would be a blot that national pride would forgive less easily than the loss of a province, and which it would soon seek to efface. And, besides, up to the present time Russia declares that she wishes for no foreign intervention. If, however, she had seriously decided to repel this intervention, would she discuss, as she has done with France, the conditions of a peace? It follows either that she would not refuse an intervention as a fact provided that it did not bear this name, and even that she wishes for it ; or else that these pacific demonstrations have no other end but to appease the uneasiness of England

and France about a second campaign, till Russia should have gained the six months which she requires to repair her losses, and to maintain at the same time the reputation for generosity which is eminently useful to her in order to conceal her real views.

LATER NEGOTIATIONS BETWEEN RUSSIA AND AUSTRIA.

Metternich to Ficquelmont, at St. Petersburg,
Vienna, Jan. 23, 1829.

941. M. de Tatistscheff received despatches on the 20th of this month.

The next day he came to see me at a very late hour, which he had evidently chosen to prevent any serious conversation taking place between us.

He began by complaining that at St. Petersburg they continued to attach a singular importance to the false rumour of the famous Memoir of our Cabinet. I begged him to say no more about it. He assured me that, quite contrary to his own wishes, he was obliged to do so; that he had received an express order about it, and that to facilitate the painful task he had furnished himself with an abstract from the despatch relative to this subject. . . .*

On reading this, I told the ambassador that to reply to such evidently false assertions would be absurd; that I felt a necessity of a different kind; that, in fact, I should not be satisfied till I had discovered the source which had originated and continued to reproduce such insulting errors.

* This despatch states that in St. Petersburg they had unquestionable evidence that Austria was endeavouring to bring the Courts of Berlin, London, and Paris, into coalition against Russia, with the intention of establishing conditions of peace and imposing them upon Russia.—ED.

R R 2

After this introduction, the Russian Ambassador informed me that he had some other communications to make. Time pressing, he told me that he could give me only a summary of their tenor.

'I have received,' continued he, ' the reply that my Government has just sent to the Cabinets of London and Paris. It is so extremely moderate that it much surpasses my expectation. You know that these two Courts desire that Russia should give full powers to their representatives at the Porte. The Emperor consents under two conditions. He desires that the limitation of Greece should not be restrained, as the allies appear to expect ; he adopts, on the other hand, your proposal of April 5. He wishes that Greece should attain her entire independence ; that she should have a monarchical government, with the exclusion of all revolutionary parties. He formally protests also against the elevation of a Russian prince to the Greek throne.'

I replied to M. de Tatistscheff that the only immediate answer I could make was, that these two proposals would lead to war and not to peace ; that the Courts of London and Paris would never acquiesce in them, and the same might be said of the Porte.

'Do not let us discuss the affair,' replied the ambassador ; ' we will return to it ; only remember that the Emperor believes that with an alliance of three nothing is to be done ; he would like to get five to join. You can seize the ball at its rebound, and re-establish the old relations of intimacy ; the true peace of Europe will thus be found.'

'To move with five,' I interrupted, ' one must in the present affair first get on with three, and the two other Courts will know how to support decisions on which the three Courts shall agree ; but, I repeat, if the agreement of the three cannot be established on your premises, that of five would be equally impossible.'

'Very well,' said M. de Tatistscheff; 'that which neither three nor five can do will have to be accomplished by two. Only Austria and Russia are necessary. At St. Petersburg they are tired of the triple affair. It is clear that it will not work!'

At this moment we were interrupted. M. de Tatistscheff came again to see me in the evening; but as we were not alone, and I avoided giving him any opportunity of speaking to me in private, he yesterday morning addressed the following letter to me (No. 942).

From these facts two things appear to me to be clearly shown—a feeling of great uneasiness in Russia, and a very unfortunate facility on the part of the Russian Cabinet for endeavouring to free itself of all moral restraint. That assuredly is neither good nor sound policy.

I must have some more conversation with M. de Tatistscheff, and above all I must see what he is driving at. It seems clear that the story of the Austrian proposal has been put forward with the hope of intimidating us, a hope as vain as that of seeing us make any sacrifice to rectify a fault which is not ours. Our definite replies are neither doubtful nor difficult to guess. We shall be always ready to help forward the return of peace by the paths of honour and sound policy; but we shall never be found disposed to serve the contrary cause. The different Russian proposals show plainly the desire to drag out the Eastern affair as much as possible. Those which are addressed to the two allied Courts would require several months at least only to be discussed between the three Cabinets; those which have been addressed to us could have no other aim

than to throw disorder into the business, to provoke new
political combinations, and to gain by one means or
another the time necessary for Russia to terminate as
best she can her own differences with the Porte.

M. de Tatistscheff's letter is full of singular *naïvetés*
—I should say inconceivable ones if it were not that
Cabinets, as well as individuals, are betrayed in times
of great embarrassment into very singular schemes.

To present a worthless bribe as a compensation to
us—an invention of which no one knows the childish-
ness better than ourselves ; to flatter our self-esteem
by reproducing our former proposals, without acknow-
ledging that the new situation would give them not only
a different application, but even an application diametrically opposed to our fixed idea ; to speak in the month
of January of the necessity of a previous understanding
between the three allied Courts which we counselled
last summer, and which was then rejected because it
might have led to a conclusion which Russia now
desires quite as much to disappoint—to make such
proposals as these is to prove that they do not know
where they are going, and specially that at St. Petersburg they have lost all power of judging for us. I send
you the present courier, who, I have no doubt, will
join you before your arrival in St. Petersburg. Whether
this be the case or not, it will be expedient to appear
ignorant of the facts of which I inform you. Say that
the courier has followed you according to your orders,
and that he has brought you some documents which
could not be finished before you left.

It is important that you should be informed of all
that has taken place. Instructed in the facts, you will
observe with more ease, and you will be better able to
judge of the explanations into which the Emperor and

Count Nesselrode will enter with you. If either ·of them should unfold himself towards you in a sense conformable to the written or unwritten words of M. de Tatistscheff, your own observation and the contents of the present despatch will enable you to regulate your language.

Tatistscheff to Metternich, Vienna, January 22, 1829.

(Supplement to No. 941.)

942. I must, of course, my dear Prince, give an account of the last explanation that we had with respect to your measures in London, Paris and Berlin, and to the manner in which you have received my friendly representations. It would be well if we could draw up this despatch together ; I will therefore draw up the sketch of it and bring it to you. Meantime I will explain the tendency of the proposals which have been made in London, so that you may be able to determine what support you will give them. We ask that the allies should begin by agreeing between themselves, concerning Greece, on the four points which should fix her future—namely, the boundaries, the form of government, the indemnity, and the tribute. Once agreed on these points, the Emperor consents to give his full powers to the negotiators sent by his allies to treat with the Porte without the intervention of a plenipotentiary of the Greek Government. You already know my opinions as to the boundaries and the form of government. From my sincere and constant desire to be able as soon as possible to re-establish an intimate union between the two countries, I should be delighted if you would seize this opportunity of proving that, far from nourishing hostile intentions and malevolent sentiments against us, you hasten to oblige us. Then, too, the demonstration that I am about to propose to you will certainly impose no engagement which will be disagreeable to you to fulfil.

The necessity intimated by Russia of fixing the final basis of the pacification of Greece before entering on the subject of serious negotiations with the Porte, is too evident to be contested; it is, besides, your own opinion ' that, before making any demands from the Porte, we should define what we wish to obtain for the Greeks.' If, therefore, you will now explain yourself in London and Paris in the sense that ' you recognise the necessity which we have intimated, and, if the bases of the pacification resemble those which you proposed yourself in your Memorandum of April 5, and which did not give too much extension to Greece, you should be disposed to accede to them, and to sustain them by all your influence at Constantinople,' I am persuaded that this measure would give the greatest pleasure to the Emperor, and, at the same time, assure him of the falseness of the report that you had formed a coalition against him. There would be no doubt about the result, and our relations would again become as intimate as they were in better times. For my part I have a presentiment with regard to this, and I should be so happy to assist in bringing it about that I ardently desire that you will not reject the method I propose.

I write to you, my dear Prince, because, having to despatch a courier to Italy, I have not been able to go out this morning, and this evening I shall not be able to see you on account of the ball at the Archduke Charles's. You will also be kind enough not to forget the farewell audience of Strogonoff. I am, &c., &c.

TATISTSCHEFF.

POPE PIUS VIII.

Metternich to Tatistscheff, Vienna, April 6, 1829.

943. The new Pope, who has taken the name of
Pius in order to mark his veneration for the memory of
his benefactor, was Vicar-General in the bishopric of
Imola, and was made Cardinal by Pius VII. in 1816.

During his residence in Rome he always lived out
of the world, and was solely occupied with his ecclesiastical profession. After the death of Pius VII., Consalvi wished to elevate him to the Pontificate, and he
was not elected because he declared he would have no
other Secretary of State than that same Cardinal. The
Zelanti carried it against the moderate party.

He was elected at first by a majority of thirty-six;
a slight error having appeared in the ballot, Cardinal
Castiglione insisted on a fresh one. In this he obtained
forty-seven votes—that is to say, almost unanimity. We
had placed him at the head of those who would be
desirable as Pontiffs. The French Cardinals joined our
Cardinals. M. de Chateaubriand, on the contrary,
patronised Gregorio.

The new Pope has given Gregorio the post of *Grand
Pénitencier*, which he has just left; and nominated
Albani State Secretary. Chateaubriand, in consequence,
will have absolution.

The election was received with general satisfaction
by the Roman public. The choice of the Cardinal is

decidedly good; one must see now whether the Pope will resemble the Cardinal. As it is he who made the replies to the ambassadors, it is clear that he is not wanting in sound political views. He is not, at any rate, a Carbonaro Pope.

THE EMANCIPATION OF THE CATHOLICS IN GREAT BRITAIN.

Metternich to Wellington, Vienna, April 18, 1829.

944. Prince Esterhazy received yesterday, on the part of the Emperor, a command to express to his Britannic Majesty and his Prime Minister the very great satisfaction the signal triumph that you have just obtained has caused his Imperial Majesty.* The enemies of England, of her internal peace and of her power, or the enemies of her present Administration, would alone refuse to join in this sentiment. As we are not among the number of such enemies, we rejoice from the bottom of our heart at this great success. Respect and friendship compel me, my dear Duke, to address these lines to you.

Believe always in the profound respect which I shall ever entertain for you, &c., &c.

Metternich to Esterhazy, in London, Vienna, April 19, 1829.

945. We were informed, two days ago, of the brilliant success which the Government has just gained in the Catholic affair. No news could have been received here with more sincere satisfaction. We see in this event not only the triumph of a cause, but also the consolidation of an Administration on which rests—I

* Catholic Emancipation Bill, April 18, 1829.

do not hesitate to say it—our last hope for the general safety.

The Emperor desires that your Highness should express on his behalf to his Britannic Majesty his sincere congratulations on the issue of an affair which will add a fresh flower to the glory of his reign. He desires that you should also express the same sentiments to the Duke of Wellington.

By a singular accident the triumph of the British Government coincided with a defeat of the French Ministry. The attitude of the two Governments and that of their Parliaments are very exactly pointed out by a comparison of the two positions.

I beg you to forward to the Duke of Wellington the enclosed letter (No. 944) which I think it right to address to him.

OPENING OF THE SECOND RUSSO-TURKISH CAMPAIGN.

Metternich to Esterhazy, in London,
Vienna, April 19, 1829.

946. It would be very difficult for me to give you any information as to what is passing in the theatre of war. Not from want of news ; but the rumours are so contradictory, so disconnected, and so strongly in favour of all kinds of disorder, that the impartial observer must resign himself to wait, and seek only in the results that foundation for his calculations which the preparations do not afford.

General Diebitsch has plenty to do. This we never questioned. The two Principalities are in a state of absolute ruin. It appears that Russia wishes to make war with recruits of sixteen to nineteen years old. I allow that it does not require other soldiers to beat the Turks ; nevertheless, it is certain that it would not take more than three months of a campaign to place two-thirds of the army in hospital. Where grown men cannot escape the hurtful influences of climate and fatigue, children must succumb.

The military service does not present a more favourable aspect than that evinced in the last campaign. In default of beasts of burden, the people—men, women, and children—have been put in requisition for the transport of provisions. It appears that the first serious operation will take place against Silistria. The Turks

have left only combatants in this place; they have
caused all the other inhabitants to evacuate. What will
the Turks do? We know nothing about this; for any
sort of control is impossible when their arrangements
are concerned. This, however, is certain, that they
have collected a great number of men in the Balkans.
Servia and Albania are full of Russian agents, and the
money of this Power is disbursed with open hands.

The fate of the campaign will be again decided in
favour of him who makes the fewest mistakes. This is
the only thing to guide us in looking forward to a
future which depends so much upon chance.

The Emperor of Russia will be at Warsaw on May
15. He will be crowned there *civilement,* for it has just
been discovered that a Greek Prince cannot be consecrated by a Catholic Archbishop; it appears that the
Emperor Alexander had not thought of making the act
of coronation a fundamental article of the Polish constitution. After the coronation, the Emperor and
Empress will see the King of Prussia somewhere on the
frontiers, and then the Empress will pass some weeks
in Berlin. This is what has been decided. Will the
Emperor return to the army? We believe this will
depend greatly on the course of events at first.*

* The following events of the war afford nothing worthy of remark for
our object :—On June 30 Silistria succumbed; from July 17 to 26 Diebitsch
passed over the Balkans, and appeared on August 29 before Adrianople.—
ED.

CANDIDATES FOR THE THRONE OF GREECE.

Metternich to Esterhazy, in London, Vienna,
April 30, 1829.

947. What I foresaw has not failed to happen.
The decision taken by the three allied Powers, that
Greece should be constituted an independent State,
except for some slight formalities which would reserve
to the Sultan certain rights of suzerainty,* has without
doubt caused excitement in more than one reigning
family; and from this cause various political intrigues
may arise. We know that some princes belonging to
Germany begin to covet the Greek throne.† We have
certain ideas—in truth, still very vague—that the King
of Bavaria thinks also of a Prince of his house. The
most probable rumour seems to be that which is connected with Naples.

One remark—and it appears to me fundamental—

---

* The London Conference Protocol of the three Powers concerning
this is dated March 22, 1829; it contains, besides the arrangement for the
boundaries of Greece and the settlement of the yearly tributes, the determination that the new State under the superintendence of the Porte should
obtain a free government, under a Christian hereditary prince, but not
chosen from the families of the three allied sovereigns.—ED.

† Prince Leopold of Coburg, afterwards King of the Belgians, was
among them. At least, Metternich writes some time later to Apponyi, in
Paris, the following: 'I hope that the choice of a regent for Greece will soon
be settled. Prince Leopold must be stung by a tarantula to wish for this
place. To reign over emptiness is a dreary occupation, and yet if Greece
offered nothing but emptiness there would be means of coming to an understanding; but this is not so, for she is, on the contrary, full of all kinds of
disorder.'—ED.

appears up to this time to have escaped the observation of the princes who put themselves in the ranks. This is that the Head of Greece must necessarily belong to the Greek religion. Certainly no Catholic Prince would change his religion, and the King of Naples is greatly deceived if he believes that the Greek people would be contented with a Prince of the United Greek faith. The schismatic Greeks detest still more the Latins, and the United Greeks are as much Catholics as the Latins, and do not hate the Turks. It might be different with Protestant princes, among whom the greater part would make no difficulty about passing into the Eastern Greek Church.

There is no doubt that out of this dilemma a great number of fresh diplomatic intrigues will arise which will all turn in favour of Russia. At the present moment I suppose the Cabinet of St. Petersburg begins to resemble a hall in which the throne of Greece will be put up to auction.

You will doubtless remark that the King of Naples' mind is harassed by the very natural terror that he has had for some time of the possibility of seeing a revolutionary State form itself in Greece, and that he is beset, on the other hand, by certain inclinations of a dynastic ambition. It will not, therefore, be difficult to give an answer to the very friendly proposal of his Sicilian Majesty.

Pray speak with perfect candour to Lord Aberdeen upon the rather strange subject of the present despatch, and invite his Excellency to make us acquainted with the ideas of his Cabinet on a question which cannot fail to present itself immediately to every Cabinet under different forms.

POLIGNAC'S MINISTRY.

Metternich to the Emperor Francis, Königswart, Aug. 13,
1829, *with the Imperial Resolution of Aug.* 18, 1829.

948. When the Report of the Count Apponyi of
the 9th inst. was sent to me, I considered its contents
to be of the greatest importance, and therefore lay them
before your Majesty out of the usual course.

The change of ministry in France is an event of the
highest importance. It gives this impression because
the late ministry, who were utterly wanting in vigour,
were only serviceable for evil. Not less important is the
fact of the entirely Royalist composition of the new
ministry.

Under the new ministry there are well-known
Royalists of every sort. The most distinguished men
among them are :—

Bourdonnaye, Minister of the Interior.

Montbel, formerly Mayor of Toulouse, and an intimate friend of Villèle.

Courvoisier, Commissioner-General of Lyons ; formerly a doctrinaire, latterly an undoubted Royalist.

Rigny, Minister of Naval Affairs, I know but slightly
in relation to his political ideas ; he agrees with us
on the Eastern Question, and his attitude hitherto has
been faultless.

Polignac, Minister of Foreign Affairs, holds our
opinions thoroughly. This appointment will act very
favourably on the English Cabinet and be a thunder-
clap for the Russians.

In theory all this is excellent. But how will it turn out in practice, how will the parties in France arrange themselves, and will the King and the Government have sufficient strength to meet the serious attacks which the new ministry will certainly encounter from the already formed revolutionary party ? *

The whole event has almost the value of a counter-revolution.

METTERNICH.

Approved. The results alone will show to what this change will lead. God grant that it may be according to your wishes.

FRANZ.

Persenberg, August 18, 1829.

* Some weeks later, in anticipation of coming events, Metternich writes to the ambassador, Count Apponyi, in Paris: 'The light that your last despatches have thrown upon the situation of the French ministry have afforded us great interest. Your calm and reflective manner of judging of the position is in conformity with sound practice. There is nothing, I am convinced, to add to or to object to in what you have said. All is true, for all is vague, and it is above all this vagueness which penetrates public affairs in France. I desire from the bottom of my heart, but hardly dare to believe, that M. de Polignac does not deceive himself about the true position of affairs. If his perfect security speaks in favour of his disposition, it is perhaps hardly so favourable to his judgment. This, however, is certain, that the Liberals, too, do not know where they are going, and that everybody in France is weak. You cannot express too warmly our wishes for the duration and success of the present administration.'—ED.

THE PEACE OF ADRIANOPLE.

Metternich to Esterhazy, in London, Linz,
Sept. 21, 1829.

949. We have at last reached the epoch to which
our wishes carried us long ago! We touch the final
dénouement of the Eastern Question; but this *dénoue-*
ment comes before us under an aspect little calculated
to calm the uneasiness of statesmen. At the very
moment when I begin the present despatch the treaty
should be signed at the Russian head-quarters.[*] This
instrument of peace and friendship between the two
empires, although it wears the form of a commonplace treaty, will none the less cause a total change in
their mutual positions and in all their relations with
Europe.

This movement, which terminates one of the most
deplorable crises that have ever occupied the Cabinets, will not be the signal in Europe for that repose
which follows ordinary pacifications. Nothing in this
affair has had any precedent in the history of diplomacy;
everything in its consequences may bring about new
combinations.

On the eve of these combinations we do not believe
ourselves called to criticise the past; the present and,
above all, the future have too much right to command
our exclusive attention; and if I feel the need of ex-

---

[*] The treaty of peace between Russia and Turkey is dated September 14.

pressing myself with regard to things so justly the first objects of our solicitude, my words should naturally first be addressed to the British Cabinet.

I beg you to lay the present despatch before Lord Aberdeen. I flatter myself that he will give it the attention that friends are always disposed to give to the explanations of those with whom in many respects they sympathise.

Above all remember how necessary it is for the heads of Cabinets to divest themselves of all illusion; let them apply themselves freely to the search for truth; and let them not give themselves up to the idea that the present epoch requires only ordinary attention on their part.

The Ottoman Empire is shaken to its foundations. The State condemned to owe its existence to what the mass of the public pleases to call moderation on the part of the conqueror has ceased to be counted amongst the number of independent States. Some great unforeseen revolution, some unexpected war might suddenly raise it from its decadence; but neither the Powers nor the Sultan can found any calculation on such events.

The evil is done; the losses are irreparable; the future existence of the Ottoman Empire has become doubtful, and yet there is no Power more interested than Austria in the preservation of what remains of this empire.

Everything, then, authorises us to raise our voices in ·presence of the new dangers we expect; we think even by proclaiming mournful but salutary truths to fulfil a duty imposed by sound policy. In the name of all that is most sacred, let not the Powers lose in barren regrets for the past, in idle recriminations over foolish errors and abortive plans, the time that should be devoted to the exigencies of the immediate future. In order that it may not come upon us unawares, let the Powers take a strict account of all that lies before us in that future; let them seek the means of preserving what has escaped the wreck of politics; let them draw themselves up on the ground indicated by their common dangers; let them be under no misunderstanding as to the nature and source of these dangers; above all, let them not be ignorant of the part that political Liberalism, and the errors that accompany it at every step, have had in the great work of the last few years! Let them not be deceived as to the necessity under which the Emperor of Russia feels himself to turn his artillery against the herd of innovators! The war which the same factions, who, under the pretence sometimes of policy, sometimes of philanthropy, have declared with real frenzy for the total destruction of the Ottoman Empire, already declare against the moderation of the Russian monarch, will open, it is to be hoped, the most ill-seeing eyes, and will thus serve the cause of reason and right feeling. But the Courts must not limit their endeavours to negative assistance; they must have a clear understanding on their return to a line of conduct which by its firmness and uniformity may yet guarantee the public peace.

Europe is just now in a situation like that of a person after a great debauch. The time of disappointment has come, and then it is that new necessities make themselves felt in all their strength. The time past will not return; other incidents quickly disturb the mind, and what was strongly felt in the evening loses its effect on the morrow.

It concerns us, above all, to know the principles and views that will now be followed by British diplomacy

the information that we ask on this subject we believe
we have a right to expect from the English Government, for we, for our part, do not leave them in ignorance as to our feelings. If the peace that is being
prepared is only to be a political truce, let it be at least
a truce as solid and as complete as possible; let it not
be troubled by alarming agitation, sinister projects, or
by the fancies of this or that Court, so that if the result
of the Russo-Turkish Treaty does not turn to the advantage of the Porte, it may at least leave him the
chance of surviving his defeats. By excluding his European territory from the general guarantee of the European States one great mistake was committed; another,
more important in its consequences, was that of expressly and exclusively subordinating the affairs of
Turkey to the good pleasure of a great and powerful
neighbour. How far will England push this indifference?
Does she—yes or no—consider what remains of the Ottoman Empire as placed under the safeguard of European
policy? Does she desire, as we do, the conservation of
that empire? Austria never aims at self-aggrandise-
ment at the expense of her neighbours. The Emperor
asks nothing from anyone; but he must also desire, as
a matter of reciprocal good faith, that others should not
take advantage of what he can only call the complaisance
of Europe to make gradual encroachments, whether
expressly or tacitly in agreement with disastrous projects. The factions—enemies of peace—will not fail to
advance the idea of a division of the fallen empire.
Will the Cabinets speak out on this project, or will they
by their silence favour a course which has no other end
but general disorder? Will they continue to favour a
system of perfidious calmness? Will they second, or will
they tolerate, the cries against the pretended Austrian

ambition, and the efforts after an alliance wholly directed against the peace of Europe? In short, will the Cabinets persist in the political proceedings by which those years have been signalised that have prepared the present disaster and made a system popular in Europe of which the effects can only end in the indefinite aggrandisement of a victorious Power of that nature, and the enfeebling of all the other Powers; or will they take a position clearly based on the principle of conservation?

These are the questions which ought, more than ever, to occupy us seriously, and on which it is most necessary that there should be no uncertainty. It will not be forgotten that Austria had the courage to go firmly through the tempest without allowing any of her plans to be disturbed, and that, instead of losing time in inaction, she was able to calculate and regulate her resources. To determine on our future course we must, in the first place, be acquainted with the views and intentions of those whom we have already informed of our wishes. I beg you to press the contents of this despatch upon the earnest attention of the English Cabinet. In the past nothing has done us so much mischief as uncertainty. The era now commencing demands certainty.

Metternich to Gentz, Linz, September 21, 1829.

950. As my stay here has been prolonged against my will, and as I do not wish to lose time for important matters, I have prepared the next despatches for England. I send you the rough sketch of my despatch and I beg you to correct it yourself. My aim is, to oblige the English Cabinet to reflect, and to win from them some few results of their zeal. The questions I pro-

pose are natural in our position, and indirectly answer a false and foolish notion which appears in the last private note (it cannot be called a letter) of Lord Cowley to his brother. If the Duke of Wellington now believes that the Powers (and more especially Austria) are going to destroy and divide the Turkish Empire in consequence of late events, the English Minister's frame of mind is much to be pitied. He is wrong, and his mistake will weaken him. I feel it my duty to oppose both these evils with all my might.

Materials for an Article in the ' Beobachter,' by Metternich, September 21, 1829.

951. Peace has been signed between Russia and the Porte ; ratifications on both sides followed ; the cycle of war has been passed through. The event is, in our eyes, an episode in the history of the time.

In looking back into the past, and singling out some movements of the present, we have no intention of entangling ourselves in theories. We wish to point out facts, and these are clearly expressed before the eyes of the world. During the long period of thirteen years Europe had enjoyed political peace. The military events of the years 1821–23 did not belong to the sphere of war. The internal peace of some States was disturbed ; the disturbance menaced Europe with other revolutions, but events were again calmed down.

The first year of war after the Peace of Paris was 1828. With the end of the present year political peace has returned.

Nevertheless, two parties are ready to confront each other. One desires the maintenance of peace by protecting all rights : the Governments and the majority of

citizens of all States belong to its adherents.   The other
party is formed of adventurers of all sorts, of agitated
and excited characters.   The first blesses peace.   The
other is disconcerted at its return.   These parties consequently are in strong opposition to each other.   If it
was formerly difficult to explain the true nature of this
opposition to an unbiassed mind, this is now greatly
facilitated by the open confession of one party.

Latterly the majority of the French journals, and
even some in other States, have, as the organs of this
party, spoken out freely.   The overthrow of all established order under the ensign of the progressive
spirits of the age ; schemes of conquest under the pretence of aiming at so-called natural frontiers, an aim
which each excluded State can expose with equally
rightful claims, so that peaceful agreements are to
make way for the rights of might alone ; the sanguine
hope that in a general struggle of the Governments
men of this party could seize the helm of State ; these
and other more or less openly avowed confessions fill
the public papers of the last few months.   How clearly
those aspirations contrast with the intentions and the
will of the opposite party is evident, and it is as easy to
understand that the re-establishment of political peace
must be in direct opposition to such hopes and such
aims.

It is no less clear that Austria's unvarying position,
calm and peaceful in the midst of the conflict just concluded, her line of conduct ever furthering the maintenance of peace, her remoteness from all projects of
aggrandisement, her toleration of all lawful rights and
established liberties, her conscientious respect for
treaties and the independence of States—such a position,
held by a great central Power, must seem an intolerable

obstacle to those who look for happiness and reward only in changes and revolutions.

We here pronounce once more our profession of faith regarding what is real in the efforts and struggles of the time. It will be attacked by all who profess an opposite political creed. But what will be the result of such attacks? Nothing but a confirmation of the historical truths we have professed.

REACTION OF THE PEACE OF ADRIANOPLE
UPON AUSTRIA.

Metternich to the Emperor Francis,
Vienna, October 9, 1829.

952. The peace between Russia and the Porte forms
an important episode in the history of our times, and
must exercise the greatest influence on the political
situation of Europe, and consequently also on the
Austrian monarchy. Your Majesty is too well acquainted with the position of the States to need that I
should enter here into a minute consideration with
respect to it. I will, therefore, confine myself to the
principal points, and especially those in which our own
interest is affected by the changes already made, or
about to take place.

The European Alliance, founded with the active co-
operation of your Majesty in 1813–14, upon the basis
of sound ideas regarding public rights and regarding
States, and exclusively consecrated to the maintenance
of peace, asserted itself as a fact till the death of the
Emperor Alexander, although subjected to many disturbing influences, and was first formally disavowed in the
year 1823 by England. By the signing of the protocol
of April 4, 1826, it was practically broken. The union
of two Powers, with an aim clearly in opposition to the
fundamental principles of the alliance, denotes the trans-
ition to a new system. France, restlessly aspiring after
political activity, even joined this union, giving it a

regular form by means of the treaty drawn up in Paris, and ratified in London, July 6, 1827. This new confederacy, formed in opposition to the one then existing, became known to the world as the Triple Alliance. Though apparently aiming at the same object, this alliance was from its commencement a wild chaos of incompatible elements—each allied Power being guided by its own peculiar intentions and pursuing its own peculiar line of conduct. England (which must be first mentioned as the first origin of the evil), urged by an exaggerated but not groundless anxiety concerning certain proceedings of the new Emperor of Russia, resolved to avert the danger by sending the Duke of Wellington to St. Petersburg. There can be no doubt that the Duke undertook this business from the purest motives. 'Assure your Government that its safety will be my chief endeavour,' were his words to your Majesty's ambassador when he arrived at St. Petersburg. But praiseworthy as his designs may have been, his errors and blunders were no less than deplorable. The want of judgment and the diplomatic inexperience of this otherwise admirable man were mostly the cause of his unaccountable decisions ; but other circumstances contributed to them. The old alliance had outlived itself in England. The nation, excited by vain demagogues and frivolous journalists, looked upon it with aversion, as upon a bond endangering their independence; and the perverse mind of Canning had strengthened this aversion till it became the most violent opposition. From want of political clear-sightedness, the Duke of Wellington overlooked the circumstance that it was quite otherwise with the Continental Powers. With them, too, the alliance had to struggle with many adversaries, but powerful support was not wanting. By the Liberal

party alone it was everywhere attacked, both secretly
and openly.   The monarchs of Russia and of France
remained faithful.   In Vienna and Berlin it was valued
as much as ever.   The Duke of Wellington believed it
extinguished, and nothing appeared to him more useful
and necessary than to keep in check the Power which,
by its geographical and military position, was most inclined to aim at independence.   He flattered himself
that he could restrain the freedom of Russia's movements by the weight of England's influence, and discovered too late that, to the exclusive advantage of
Russia, he had prepared galling chains for England.

Out of these first unhappy mistakes all those circumstances originated which during the last two years
have brought the Turkish Empire to the brink of ruin.
With the Peace of Adrianople the Triple Alliance comes
to an end.   There is reason to believe that Russia will
not be disinclined to delay its formal dissolution, but
this delay cannot last long.   The creation of a perverted
and anti-national policy could never be popular in England; and after an issue of the war so contrary to the true
interests of this Empire, and so offensive to the British
sense of honour, even the semblance of a union cannot
be maintained any longer.   In Russia, too, where there
never has been a sincere predilection for this alliance,
and where it was only regarded as a temporary means
to gain certain ends, which the Cabinet seems not to
have marked out very clearly, no essential State interest
can speak for it any more.   France at last, so long at
least as the present ministry maintains its principles,
will consider herself happy to abandon an alliance
which gave the most dangerous enemies of the monarchy ·
means for the execution of the most ruinous schemes.
Your Majesty took no part in this perilous alliance,

neither did the King of Prussia. Nevertheless a marked difference existed between the two Governments. We have openly and energetically pronounced against the principle on which the Triple Alliance was based—if that can be called a principle which is contrary to all sound principles. Prussia has, without condemning this principle directly, declared that without the full agreement of the five Powers she would not join in the Treaty of London. Austria alone has been faithful to the old alliance in its full strength. Every Power that is inclined to return to the original principle of this alliance, as well as to the system of which it is the basis, must join with Austria; and that this sooner or later must be done is evident from the nature of things, and from the unmistakable necessities of this age.

The chief principle of the Quintuple Alliance was the maintenance of all legal rights; with this principle alone can general peace be possible; and if in ordinary times no express agreement is needed to secure the sway of this principle, extraordinary means must be resorted to in extraordinary circumstances. The age in which we live is not an ordinary one. Europe is visited by a plague; the maintenance of public health makes it necessary for those charged with the most important of all cares to adopt measures unnecessary in ordinary circumstances.

If such measures are to prove effectual they must be adopted by several States in common; alliances between governments is their first law. The formula for such a union has not been lost for Europe; it has only been hidden from view by violent disturbances. The moment of its regeneration is perhaps not far off. The original elements still exist; the first powerful impulse—it matters little from which side it comes—may vivify them again, and Europe may enjoy their blessings even if in their renovated form they are not proclaimed by all orators.

It is not my purpose in this Report to enter into foreign politics more than was necessary to show their influence upon the home interests of the monarchy, and the connection existing between them and the great European confederacy of States, which in troubled times like ours is felt with double clearness.   With regret we must confess that the Eastern Question would neither have been so seriously discussed, or have had such unfortunate results, if Austria had been in a different position from that in which she finds herself after the reductions of the last thirteen years.   Austria—from its geographical position the true centre of gravity in the European system of States—cannot retire from the place appointed to her without exposing the whole edifice to serious shocks, and the belief in the entire exhaustion of our strength, even if founded less on reality than on general prejudice, has certainly not been without the most useful influence on the course of events within the last eight years.   But though I consider it my duty to proclaim this truth, I am far from considering this state of things to be the only cause of these great evils.   The general agitation of men's minds in a direction far from favourable to external and internal peace has been, and still is, a constant source of the most dangerous disturbances.   Besides this, the complication in the East has been brought about by the natural progress of the Russian powers and the enormous blunders of the allied Courts.   Russia would never have been so easily engaged in an enterprise so difficult to restrain if she had thought it necessary to pay more regard to Austria.

The Peace of Adrianople is to be regarded as a

moment of repose. It destroyed many dangerous and wild schemes of revolutionary politics, and proved the necessity of new political forms. With regard to these we must take our position ; the indisputable power of events will point it out to us : but your Majesty must have the means necessary to maintain it for the welfare of our kingdom as well as the general welfare of Europe. Two points which cannot be separated from each other ought first to be considered—the financial and the military condition of the kingdom. Your Majesty's wisdom, and the noiseless but steady progress of reform in these two most important branches of the administration, have happily brought us during the last few years far nearer to the goal than foreigners, who have only an insufficient knowledge of our state and our institutions, might suppose. But, to fulfil the duties of your Majesty towards your own empire, and, I may frankly add, to satisfy the hopes which all well-disposed persons rest upon Austria, a course must be taken which will secure a firm and solid basis for the great work still reserved for your Majesty's glorious reign—the work of maintaining peace.

May your Majesty graciously accept the following remarks on this question :—

The financial position of the monarchy has doubtless been raised in consequence of the regular progress of the system adopted in 1817. There remain, nevertheless, some measures which have not been thoroughly carried out, and which ought to be improved, and besides, as is always the case with practical enterprises, new experiences have been made, which must be examined and cleverly applied by the Government. The closer examination of the financial question lies so far beyond the limits of the present Report that I confine myself to the following general propositions :—

1. The measures already taken have raised the finances so much that a very advantageous final result may be confidently expected.

2. To gain this definite end, time and peace are necessary.

3. Peace cannot be thought of in the present position of European affairs and the general agitation, if Austria, as the great central Power, is not placed in a condition to command peace.

4. The reduction system followed in the army from the year 1817 to 1828 is therefore not now applicable, even with regard to the financial welfare of the State.

In the course of last year the army underwent important reforms, and as it has been increased on a larger scale than was known to the public, we have, in regard to these matters, less to create than to maintain. Among the real necessities which still require attention I believe I must reckon a practical system of defence. With regard to the moral side of the question, much remains to be desired, and in the perfecting of the moral organisation of the army we must recognise the first conditions of that strength which I regard as the fundamental support of all attainable perfection.

The enterprise is not an easy one; it demands resolution and ability as well as material peace and careful execution; a well-planned line of conduct can alone render it possible, and for the careful execution of this regular and unprejudiced discussions are indispensable.

In regard to administrative necessities, I place the condition of Hungary in the first rank.

The matters here shortly alluded to, and which have all one chief purpose, are those to which your Majesty will grant especial attention. Any mistake in respect to these would remove us further from the goal at which

we ought to aim. Where the first and most important
necessity, self-preservation, is at stake, we cannot be
too careful to discover the best weapons invented by
human skill. Counsel only is of service that is given
at the right moment; if that moment passes, the wisest
counsel has lost its value.

With a deep feeling of my duty I therefore venture
to draw your Majesty's attention to the following points.

When a new political epoch begins, the economical
relations of the State must be arranged with due regard
to the true and well-understood needs of the times, for
which the necessary considerations include financial,
military and administrative questions; and these can only
be properly examined and arranged from one point of
view. From this point all the preparations which will
enable your Majesty to decide the most important
questions must proceed, and it can only be called into
existence by your Majesty's will and direction.

With great respect I therefore propose 'that your
Majesty will authorise me to communicate this Report
to the Minister Count von Kolowrat, charging us both
to draw up a Report and exposition of our views on
these matters, and to lay the same as quickly as possible
before your Majesty.'

METTERNICH.

Placet.

FRANCIS.

Vienna, October 11, 1829.

END OF THE FOURTH VOLUME.

LONDON: PRINTED BY
SPOTTISWOODE AND CO., NEW-STREET SQUARE
AND PARLIAMENT STREET

THE LIFE OF LORD PALMERSTON.

WITH SELECTIONS FROM HIS DIARIES AND CORRESPONDENCE.

In 2 vols. crown 8vo. with Frontispiece to each volume, 12s.

This work, although based upon the previous 'Life of Lord Palmerston,' has been entirely re-edited by Mr. ASHLEY, and contains considerable additional matter and alterations.

'Mr. Evelyn Ashley's volumes could not have been published at a more appropriate moment, for the opinions of Lord Palmerston upon Ireland and upon foreign questions generally have a soundness which recommends them to the perusal of all. Rarely has Mr. Bentley sent out a more fascinating work or one of greater European importance. We have a book with all the attractions of a romance and all the value of a biography of one who was an Englishman first and a statesman afterwards.'—WHITEHALL REVIEW.

London : RICHARD BENTLEY & SON, New Burlington Street,
Publishers in Ordinary to Her Majesty the Queen.

SOME STANDARD WORKS.

The History of Antiquity.
Translated from the German of Professor MAX DUNCKER, by EVELYN ABBOTT, D.C.L., M.A., of Balliol College, Oxford. 4 vols. demy 8vo. each 21s.

Professor Mommsen's History of Rome,
From the Earliest Time to the Period of its Decline. Translated (with Author's sanction. and Additions) by the Rev. W. P. DICKSON. With an Introduction by Dr. SCHMITZ. 4 vols. crown 8vo. £2. 6s. 6d.; or, separately, Vols. I. & II., 21s.; Vol. III., 10s. 6d.; Vol. IV., with Index, 15s.

Also, a LIBRARY EDITION, in 4 vols. demy 8vo. £3. 15s. These Volumes are not sold separately.

Professor Curtius's History of Greece.
Translated by A. W. WARD, M.A. In five volumes. Demy 8vo. with Index, each volume separately, 18s.

'A history known to scholars as one of the profoundest, most original, and instructive of modern times.'—GLOBE.

The Lives of the Archbishops of Canterbury, from St. Augustine to Juxon.
By the late Very Rev. WALTER FARQUHAR HOOK, D.D., Dean of Chichester. 11 vols. demy 8vo. price £8. 15s.; or sold separately, as follows :—Vol. I., 15s ; Vol. II., 15s.; Vols. III. and IV., 30s.; Vol. V., 15s.; Vols. VI. and VII. 30s.; Vol. VIII., 15s.; Vol. IX., 15s.; Vol. X., 14s.; Vol. XI., 15s. The Second Series commenced with Vol. VI.

Sir Edward Creasy's Rise and Progress of the English Constitution.
Post 8vo. 7s. 6d.

Sir Edward Creasy's Fifteen Decisive Battles of the World, from Marathon to Waterloo.
Crown 8vo. with Plans, 6s. Also, a LIBRARY EDITION, 8vo. with Plans, price 10s. 6d.

James's Naval History of Great Britain.
From the Declaration of War by France, in 1793, to the Accession of George IV. With a Continuation of the History down to the Battle of Navarino, by Captain CHAMIER. 6 vols. crown 8vo. with Portraits, 36s.

The Life of Oliver Cromwell.
From the French of M. GUIZOT, by ANDREW SCOBLE. Crown 8vo. with 4 Portraits, 6s.

The Life of Mary, Queen of Scots.
From the French of M. MIGNET, by ANDREW SCOBLE. Crown 8vo. with 2 Portraits, 6s.

The Heavens: an Illustrated Handbook of Popular Astronomy.
By AMÉDÉE GUILLEMIN. Edited by J. NORMAN LOCKYER, F.R.A.S., F.R.S. New and revised Edition, embodying the latest Discoveries in Astronomical Science. Demy 8vo. with over 200 Illustrations, price 12s.

London : RICHARD BENTLEY & SON, New Burlington Street, Publishers in Ordinary to Her Majesty the Queen.